D0886738

Jewish State
or
Israeli Nation?

JEWISH STATE
OR
ISRAELI NATION?

Boas Evron

INDIANA UNIVERSITY PRESS
Bloomington & Indianapolis

© 1995 by Boas Evron

Published in Hebrew as *Haheshbon Haleumi.* © 1988 by DVIR Publishing House, Tel Aviv.

The paper used in this publication meets the minimum requirements of
American National Standard for Information Sciences—Permanence of
Paper for Printed Library Materials, ANSI Z39.48-1984.

Manufactured in the United States of America

Library of Congress Cataloging-in-Publication Data

Evron, Boas.
    [Ḥeshbon ha-le'umi. English]
    Jewish state or Israeli nation? / Boas Evron.
      p. cm.
    Includes bibliographical references and index.
    ISBN 0-253-31963-3
    1. Zionism—Philosophy. 2. Israelis—Identity. 3. Israel—
Politics and government. I. Title.
DS149.E9313 1995
320.5'4'095694—dc20   94-24878

1 2 3 4 5 00 99 98 97 96 95

To my children and grandchildren

CONTENTS

Foreword

James S. Diamond

"A slaughter-house of sacred cows." That is how one critic described this book when it appeared in the Hebrew original in Israel in 1988.[1] At one point it reached the best-seller list there. The publication now of this English version will do nothing to diminish the power of this synoptic work to challenge assumptions that have hitherto been regarded as incontrovertible. A word about this challenge is in order to the American or any other reader whose knowledge of things Israeli has been derived solely from English-language sources and for whom any perspective on Israel that lies outside the normative canons of Zionist ideology is immediately suspect.

This book may certainly be described as non-Zionist, even anti-Zionist, in its arguments. But it would be intellectually and morally irresponsible for any reader to dismiss it on this basis. Anyone familiar with the range and depth of thinking in Israel, especially within the professoriate and related circles, knows that a vision of Israel outside the assumptions of Zionism is not necessarily to be equated with forces inimical to the existence and integrity of the Israeli state or ascribed to Jewish weakness and self-hate.

Boas Evron is a sabra, a native Israeli, whose personal and familial roots in his land go back to the early nineteenth century, before the *aliyot* of the Zionist movement. As a youth he participated in the struggle for his country as a member of the Lehi (Freedom Fighters for Israel). In recent years he has been a presence in Israel's journalistic community as a regular columnist for both the op-ed and theater sections of Israel's most widely read daily, *Yedi'ot Aharonot. Jewish State or Israeli Nation?* is not anchored in the canons of normative Zionism only because it is a trenchant critique from the inside of the ideological foundations on which the state of Israel purportedly rests and a painstaking exposition of what the author regards as the mushiness of these foundations. Evron writes here simply as an Israeli, one who never had to immigrate to his native land and, in spite of the failures of the state that was created there to live up to the expectations he was inculcated to have for it, has never chosen to emigrate. He writes as one deeply concerned about what has happened and is happening to his country. The original Hebrew title of this book is *Haheshbon Haleumi*, which means "a national reckoning." But *heshbon* also means "price." This book is a full accounting of the price exacted by the ideological mushiness that the author sees and explicates.

A related point that I would invite the reader to fix in mind before proceeding has to do with the constructed nature of all historical understanding. Developments in humanistic study of the past few decades have made it clear that history is a locus for human interpretation as much as any more discretely textual entity such as a literary work. That is to say, history, either as the object of the human impulse toward semiosis or the stimulus to it, is an interpreted construct. As such, not only is it susceptible to multiple approaches, but the approaches themselves are also influenced by the degree of legitimacy and authority accorded to—or arrogated by—the various interpreters. In short, history is written by the winners, those who have acquired the power to see to it that their understanding of the past is the one that obtains.

With respect to Israeli history (and, in many circles both in Israel and the Diaspora, Jewish history, too), the regnant construction has been the historiographical hermeneutic of classical Zionism. The essence of this understanding is that: (1) the Jews are first and foremost a polity, not a religion; (2) they have always been a polity, from Biblical times until the present day; and (3) the state of Israel represents the recrudescence of this Jewish polity in modern, secular terms.

But who can say conclusively that this hermeneutic is objectively correct? Who can say that the postulates of Zionism, whether in its humanistic Labor party version or in the amalgam of integralist nationalism and Jewish myth embodied by Likud party ideology or in the rabbinocracy envisioned by ultraorthodoxy, have won? Who can say that they adequately comprehend the Jewish past or, more to the point here, the Jewish and Israeli present?

These are the questions that underlie this book. They are important questions, uncomfortable questions, and are rarely asked in most public discourse about Israel. In formulating his own answers to them, Evron comes to reject the theses of the classical Zionism on which he was raised. He proceeds, instead, from some provocative countertheses derived from the nativist "Canaanism" that he embraced in his youth, countertheses he believes are empirically visible from the historical record: first, if the Jews are a polity, they have always understood themselves as such only in religious terms, as members of a covenant faith community; and second, the state of Israel, as a modern, secular, pluralistic entity, has nothing to do with Jewish polity, which is exclusivist and extraterritorial.

The issue is not which theses are correct. As Evron makes clear, neither the Zionist theses nor the "Canaanite" countertheses can suffice as the exclusive ideational foundation on which Israeli statehood and polity can be predicated. Evron shows that while each has something to contribute, they both misread history in their respective ways and are now passé. Evron supports what he sees as the fundamental realization of the founders of Zionism: that a nation is defined by its territory; its polity is the *result* of the territorial modality of its existence, not the cause of it (i.e., the state creates the nation; the nation does not create the state.) But he also accepts the fundamental insight of the otherwise unrealistic "Canaanite" critique of Zionism: that a Jewish state is an oxymoron. There is a fundamental difference between a Jewish ethnocracy rooted in Jewish particularism and a pluralistic democracy rooted in the secularism of Enlightenment values. He points to a sorely needed fresh stance that I can only describe as post-Zionist and post-"Canaanite."

In developing his arguments Evron marshals a formidable amount of learning and insight, remarkable for someone who is not a professional academician. We may not always agree with his conclusions; I for one think that his perception of North American Jewish life, especially the approaches to Judaism that it has developed, leads him to an assessment of it that is inaccurate. Nevertheless, this bracing book provides an eye-opening picture of America in the mind of Israel or in the mind of a native Israeli, to appropriate and invert the title of Peter Grose's *Israel in the Mind of America* (1983).

Jewish State or Israeli Nation? is a timely reaffirmation of the secular nature of the Israeli national enterprise. Evron's revisionist treatment of anti-Semitism, the Holocaust, and the Arab-Israeli conflict will stretch the mind of the English-reading public as it did of its Israeli readers. It is a valuable induction into the issues that Israel and Diaspora Jewry and anyone concerned about the Middle East will face as the future inexorably becomes the present.

NOTE

1. Uri Sela, *Yedi'ot aharonot*, April 15, 1988.

Introduction to the American Edition

This book appeared originally in Hebrew, in Israel. As it advances an interpretation of Jewish history and of Zionism that is at variance with the one prevailing in Israel and considered there as self-evident, I found it necessary to buttress my arguments with a heavy array of references and quotations, preferably from Zionist and impeccably conservative Jewish sources.

In this American edition, with less of an ideological wall to breach, it is possible to dispense with part of the arguments and the notes in the interest of easier reading. At any rate, many of the latter referred to Hebrew sources not readily accessible to most American readers.

At the time of the original publication, in the spring of 1988, the bipolar structure of world politics still seemed as permanent as the Alps. Part of my analysis of the present and predictions about the future of the Jews in the world rested on the assumption that this structure would endure. The turmoil attending the collapse of the Soviet system, it seems, is still far from settling into stable patterns, and nobody can yet predict what they will be like. Still, one thing can perhaps be stated with a measure of certainty: there cannot be a simple return to the pre–Second World War nationalistic fragmentation of the European system, despite such examples to the contrary as the Balkanization of the former Yugoslavia and the Caucasus. The European Community continues to exist, and the persistence of a Commonwealth of Independent States shows that economic and technological realities impose the necessity for cooperation among the members of the former Soviet Union. The same realities are forcing the creation of the North American Free Trade Area. The absolutely sovereign nation-state, a phenomenon of the post-Renaissance era, has outlasted its usefulness and is, let us hope, slowly being phased out from the advanced areas of the world, despite temporary reversals.

This book links the rise of anti-Semitism in the nineteenth century with the growing tensions within the system of European nation-states. The collapse of the Soviet system and the recrudescence of nationalism have aroused fears that the newly independent states will revert to a 1930s-style anti-Semitism. Indeed, there have been rumblings in Poland, Hungary, Slovakia, and Russia that seemed to confirm such forebodings. But so far these trends have remained marginal. Some observers would ascribe this marginality to the fact that so few Jews remain in Europe to serve as convenient targets. But a far greater number remain in the former Soviet Union, and still no great wave of anti-Semitism has arisen there. Even in Germany the main targets of the neo-Nazis are Turks and other non-Jewish minorities, including such thoroughly "Aryan" minorities as the Poles, in short, rabid chauvinism has taken after other targets and other minorities. Indeed, one significant indication of the changed situation of Jews in the world is that when one speaks of minorities in present-day North America or Britain, one hardly ever means Jews. They have nearly become members of the established white majority. Europe has changed, America has changed, and the Jews have changed.

Another development since this book appeared in Hebrew is the peace process begun between Israel and the Arab countries. Whereas the Israel-Arab conflict was fueled by the Cold War, in which the United States regarded Israel as a reliable ally against the Soviet-backed regimes of some Arab states, the demise of the Soviet

Union left the United States as the single power broker in the region and as such interested in its stability and prosperity. On the Israeli side, even in some pragmatic Likud circles, there has been a growing recognition that another test by arms with the Arab countries could be disastrous and that some sort of accommodation with them must be reached. The former Likud minister of defense, Moshe Arens, stated in early 1992 that there was no way of stopping the Arab world from acquiring a nuclear capability within a few years. Similar observations were made later by Labor Prime Minister Yitzhak Rabin. General Israel Tal, Israel's foremost military thinker and the man who developed the Merkavah tank, stated in early 1993 that the Arabs had already achieved "a strategic parity" with Israel. The purport of all these observations is clear: peace is the only viable alternative for Israel.

As most knowledgeable Israelis share the conviction that, given proper guarantees, the occupied territories are quite superfluous to Israel's security, the conclusions are self-evident. That basically is what fuels the peace process on the Israeli side. These admissions by Israeli spokesmen of the shifting balance of power between Arabs and Israelis confirm in detail the evaluations and predictions made in the last chapter of this book. It seems, though, that I was overly pessimistic about the ability of the Israeli leadership to adapt to circumstances and draw the necessary conclusions from them. As this volume goes to the press, there is perhaps some ground for hope that Israel will become a prosperous member and prime mover in a Middle Eastern family of nations.

I wish to express my gratitude to Professor James Diamond, without whose championing, unfailing generosity of spirit, invaluable suggestions, assistance, and encouragement this book might never have reached the American reader. I owe him more than I can ever hope to repay.

Ramat Gan, Israel

Acknowledgments

I wish to express here my thanks to some of the people who helped me during the several years of my involvement with this work—by reading drafts or parts of drafts of the manuscript, by conversation, and by advice—although a few of them are far removed from my opinions and conclusions. First, I would like to thank the late Professor Uriel Tal of Tel Aviv University, whose warm encouragement strengthened me in my work. Also, to the late esteemed Professor Yeshayahu Leibowitz, of the Hebrew University in Jerusalem, for his comments. Then, in alphabetical order, Mr. Yosef Ben Moshe, for the sources he brought to my attention; Professor Binyamin Cohen of Tel Aviv University, for his comments in the field of classical studies; Professor Dan Diener, of Tel Aviv University, for his comments; my brother, Professor Yair Evron, of Tel Aviv University, for his comments and encouragement; Professor Walter Grab, of Tel Aviv University, for his useful ideas in the field of modern European history; Ms. Yael Lotan, for her comments and encouragement; Dr. Nadav Na'aman, of Tel Aviv University, for his comments and bibliographical guidance in the field of Biblical studies; Professor Yehoshua Porath, of the Hebrew University in Jerusalem, for his comments and encouragement; and Professor Chone Shmeruk, of the Hebrew University of Jerusalem, for his hints in the field of Yiddish culture. I would also like to take this opportunity to thank the Institute for Post-Graduate Hebrew Studies in Oxford and its head, Dr. David Patterson, as well as the employees of the Kressel Library in Yarnton Manor, attached to the Institute, for enabling me to enjoy the quiet and concentration needed to complete my work.

All of them have been generous in devoting time and thought to my work, and as is usual to state on such occasions, the mistakes committed here have been wholly mine.

I also wish to heartily thank my Hebrew editor, Amnon Sasson, for his meticulousness and acuity, which saved me from several gaffes. Finally, my thanks to my wife, Miriam, who has stood by me through the years.

Jewish State
or
Israeli Nation?

Introduction

Not without trepidation and aware of the magnitude of the undertaking, I present this book to the reader. It is not a monograph but rather an attempt to propose an approach to Jewish and Zionist history different from the prevalent Zionist ones. I intend to show that the prevalent conceptions are ideological, that they often distort historical facts, and that their failure to throw light on contemporary Israel and world Jewry is now plain to all.

Despite the depth and perspicacity of some previous attempts in this direction, they have been mostly fragmentary or of a pamphleteering nature, and it has, therefore, been easy to ignore them or to treat them with condescension. It is time for a more comprehensive and systematic endeavor, and it will be for the reader to judge whether I have succeeded in this difficult task.

The problematic situation in which modern Israel finds itself is derived, inter alia, from assumptions and ideologies about the nature of the Jewish people and the Jewish state that have largely been refuted by historical developments. I propose a theory of Jewish and Zionist history that is more in keeping with the facts.

To provide a sound basis for this theory, I must address the somewhat tired question of who or what are the Jews. Although it might, at first glance, seem presumptuous to express an opinion about a question discussed in depth over the centuries by such thinkers as Spinoza, Mendelssohn, Marx, Hess, and Herzl, the Zionist answer to this question did, after all, determine the character of the state of Israel. And the very fact that so many thinkers have felt impelled to return to the subject shows that it is difficult to find a single unequivocal answer to the question. In the course of this work, I attempt to explain the reasons for this difficulty.

It is the common view that the state of Israel was established as a result of the "plight of the Jews" in order to provide a solution to the "Jewish problem," to use Herzl's terminology. The plight of the Jews, it has been claimed, is a result of the fact that throughout their dispersion, the Jews have been not merely a minority; they have been a minority with a set of sociological traits very different from those of the host population—a fact which under certain historical circumstances made them an object of persecution and discrimination.

But minority status, in and of itself, does not necessarily lead to persecution and discrimination. The ruling circles of any society are always a minority, and at times they have also been ethnically different from the majority of the population. Jews have often occupied a higher socioeconomic position than the majority of the population, enjoyed great power and influence, and had the special protection of princes and prelates. Such was their situation during long periods of medieval Spanish history. In most Muslim countries, despite their status as *dhimmis* (people inferior to Mulsims) and despite waves of religious fanaticism (mainly in Shi'ite areas), Jews have never been subjected to persecution of the kind they endured in Christian Europe. In Turkey, Jews have enjoyed a stable, protected position since Constantinople fell into the hands of the Turks. In England, Jews have been a flourishing, protected, and influential group for more than three hundred years. The socioeconomic status of Jews today, in all developed countries with a large Jewish population, is substantially superior to the population average, and their political weight is often disproportionate to their share of the population.

The plight of the Jews, then, is not a necessary and automatic consequence of the condition of being a minority. It arises only with the concatenation of several historical factors, and it may then assume several forms: economic pressure and legal discrimination (as in most of Europe during the Middle Ages and in tsarist Russia within modern times); real persecution, including pogroms (as in Russia from 1881 to 1905); massacre and annihilation (as in Nazi Germany and the countries under its sway and, on a different level of brutality and totality, during the seventeenth-century Cossack revolt in Ukraine and the massacre of the Rhineland Jewish communities during the First Crusade in the eleventh century).

But the plight of the Jews still does not constitute a Jewish problem—another term which cropped up during the nineteenth century. For as long as the Jews constituted a community whose consciousness and organization were determined by religion on one hand and by special privileges and official status granted by the non-Jewish authorities on the other hand, they had problems of existence as Jews—but there was no Jewish problem in the modern sense.

For religious Jews, living in *galut* (exile) does not constitute a problem. It is a situation ordained by the Holy One as a result of their very existence as Jews and will continue until God deems the time ripe to send the Messiah. If this condition sometimes entails persecution, pogroms, and even annihilation, it must be accepted submissively as the will and unfathomable design of the power they identify as lord of all the worlds. Although steps may be taken to ameliorate one's lot by certain arrangements with the authorities, by persuasion or bribery or, if worse comes to worst, by emigration to another country, it is absolutely forbidden to undertake actual measures to achieve salvation, i.e., to try to change the very condition of exile, which basically implies the specific status and form of organization of the Jewish community within the host population. An individual could engage in "calculations of the end" or in fasting and prayer in order to prod the Lord into bringing salvation sooner. But *human* action toward that end is by its very nature reprehensible.

Since by definition a problem is an undesirable situation which calls for human solution, the description of the condition of the Jews in the Dispersion as a problem contains more than a whiff of blasphemy. Any attempt to achieve salvation on the historical, human level carries with it the danger or potential of heresy—a denial of the authority of the creator. An example of this potential is the messianic movement initiated by Shabtai Zvi in the seventeenth century to achieve salvation. It traumatized Judaism and ended in shameful failure, with many conversions to Islam and Christianity, despite Zvi's claim that his movement did not overstep Jewish religious boundaries. Its specter helps explain the reserved, often hostile attitude of the mainstream Jewish establishment toward such attempts.

Gershon Weiler points to the fact that Halachic Judaism took form under foreign rule, either as a national group in its own country (under Persian, then under Seleucid and Roman rule) or as a dispersed religious community, and from the beginning it needed a secular, alien political framework that would enable it to exist according to its particular set of laws.[1] Halachic Jewry was in its ideal state in the medieval sociopolitical structure. This structure, in which various groups of the population maintained their own specialized legal systems, permitted the Jews to keep their laws, too, while absolving them from the obligation of participating in the maintenance of the social-political-military order. Indeed, it was an ideal situation for the imposition of Halachic law on all members of the community, since in medieval society no niche for individuals existed outside their religious affiliation. The rabbinical establishment, therefore, reacted with anxiety and hostility to the emancipation and its resultant equality of all citizens before the law of the state. The law of the state released the members of the Jewish community from the community's juridical authority; to the extent that they still obeyed it, obedience was on a purely voluntary basis.

The "Jewish problem" appeared as a result of the collapse of the religious world view and the emergence of the emancipation. With this development there also appeared the identity crisis that ever since has bedeviled those Jews who left the religious community.

The emancipation was connected with a new form of organization of European society: the secular territorial-national state. This state, by its very definition, was generally neutral in regard to the religious affiliation of its citizens. It did insist, however, that religious affiliation had no political or constitutional implications, these being wholly within the state's domain. It asked Jews to answer this question: does your religion contain any meaning beyond the relationship between man and God, one which calls for a sociopolitical activity distinct from your sociopolitical activity as citizens of the state?

This question was submitted formally for the first time to the "Sanhedrin" of the Jews of France during the reign of Napoleon I. The French national state was prepared to grant the Jews full equality, but only on condition that the Jews declare themselves to be not a separate people but members of the French nation. The Jewish answer, though containing some reservations, was in the affirmative. The Jews declared themselves to be French nationals, and in view of the fact that the bourgeois republic distinguished church from state and made religion the private affair of each citizen, the Jews could indeed view themselves as "Frenchmen of the Mosaic persuasion," as the phrase goes.

According to this approach, later denounced as "assimilationism," the basis of identification becomes national, not religious, and religious affiliations lose the sociopolitical importance they once had. The Jews, according to this school of thought, did indeed begin their historical career as a nation, at least in the ancient sense of the term. But in the course of time, the content of Judaism and the nature of inter-Jewish affinities changed, and Jews are now united by little more than a religious bond. Culturally, French or German Jews are French or German nationals, and their religion differs from that of most French persons or Germans only slightly more than Catholicism differs from Protestantism. According to the ideology of the modern state as embodied in the French revolutionary state, the basis of its organization being territorial-cultural-linguistic, it is indifferent to anything pertaining to religion. It seemed that modern Europe was moving more and more toward this ideal model of the religion-indifferent state, a model that seemed to be necessitated by political logic.

The basic assumption of the assimilationist movement was that humanity, or at least European society, was moving toward ever-growing tolerance, liberalism, and rationalism, and that anti-Jewish phenomena were mere relics of the benighted, medieval past, doomed to disappear sooner or later. But European developments after the mid-nineteenth century—particularly the rise of chauvinistic nationalism, clericalism, then fascism—shook some of these basic assumptions. The integration of European Jews in their countries as "nationals of the Mosaic persuasion" engendered a new kind of Jew hatred, imbibing from the Jew-hating traditions inherent in Christianity but founded on a new basis that corresponded to the new secular structure of the bourgeois state. The several varieties of this hatred are subsumed under the heading "anti-Semitism." The basis of this anti-Semitism is not religious but secular. Jews are considered a "foreign" element in the national body, a difference which religious conversion cannot erase. A nation, it is maintained, must be on guard against the attempts of this element to integrate, since the element is foreign to the national essence and threatens to weaken and disintegrate it.

The thrust of anti-Semitism, then, is the opposite of classical Christian Jew hatred. The Christian Church always strove to convert the Jews, to integrate them into the congregation of the faithful and thereby achieve the ultimate victory of Christianity over its parent, Judaism. (It should be noted, though, that aside from the cases of forced conversions or expulsions, the most outstanding example of which was the expulsion of the Jews from Spain in 1492, the Jews were the only group permitted to maintain their separate faith in Catholic Europe.) The Jews continued to exist because they refused to give up their separate identity. Their Jewishness was not a *problem* for them. It was a problem only for the ruling Christian churches, which claimed to be the true representatives of the true "people of Israel."

The Jewish problem reared its head for the first time when Jews, seeking to become integrated as equal citizens in the bourgeois state, encountered the refusal of society, as distinct from the state, to accept them despite its official ideology. The definition of the Jews as a foreign element by the anti-Semites eventually forced many Jews into introspection and into a positive assertion of their foreignness, then into developing theories to explain why they had not been accepted, what the nature of their "alienness" was, and what they should do to regain their self-assertiveness. For the difference between the subjective consciousness of Jews in previous ages and that of modern secular Jews lies in the fact that religious-traditionalist Jews define themselves. They have no identity problem. They do not care much what the *goyim* think of them; that is only an external problem which one must adjust to in order to manage. Not so for secular Jews, particularly in the West. They lack a national consciousness, a religious backbone and self-awareness, and the non-Jews' opinions of them have a decisive influence in determining their opinion about themselves. Lacking self-determined identifying characteristics, they are left with only the criteria of their non-Jewish environment for self-definition. The basis of their self-definition is then negative, reflexive, nonspontaneous.

It is only natural that the definition of Jewish nationalism was made primarily by secularists, using criteria borrowed from the conceptions and philosophy of the national-secular bourgeois republic. These secularists attempted to build new identities for themselves but were often thwarted by a host society that resisted fully accepting Jews as equal citizens.

I believe, then, that the concept of a "Jewish nation" requires deeper and more careful examination. Clearly, "Jewish nationalism," which the dominant Zionist ideology regards as simple and self-evident, like English or Norwegian nationalism, is in reality quite problematic. The claim voiced by many that the essence of the Jewish people eludes all definition is really an evasion of a serious treatment of the problem, a mystification aimed at avoiding unpalatable facts.

A note on terminology. In this book, the terms "Canaan," "Palestine" and "Eretz Israel" are used interchangeably, according to context. When reference is to archaic times, "Canaan," the ancient name of the country, is generally preferred. "Eretz Israel"(land of Israel) is preferred in Jewish or Zionist contexts, while "Palestine" is preferred in international or Arab contexts. All of these are geographical references to a territory, not political terms. (In religious contexts, the term "the Holy Land" is sometimes used.)

Prologue

The Victory of the Rabbinical Establishment and the Decline of the Nation

The term *people of Israel* is extremely complex, having had several meanings in the Biblical period, a different meaning during the Second Commonwealth period, and yet another meaning during the Middle Ages and in modern times. Its use today creates a misleading illusion of continuity and identity.

The ancient Israelite tribes were a completely different entity from the theocratic aristocracy that established itself during the Babylonian exile and later expanded to Judea when the exiles returned with Ezra and Nehemiah. It was this returning community which, in the name of monotheistic religion, developed an elaborate code of separation from both the non-Jewish "gentiles" and the "people of the land" (*am ha'aretz*), a code that was fundamental in establishing the character of the latter Jewish people. But there is also a world of difference between that small, zealous, introverted, and separatist community and the conquering, expansive, and universalistic religion of the late Second Commonwealth period.

The outline of Israelite and early Jewish history described here is for the most part based on findings of the various schools of Biblical criticism. Of necessity (and because many readers will already be well versed in the subject matter), I deal with only a small portion of the vast literature on the subject.[1] The reader therefore should note that most of the opinions and quotations are disputed. For one thing, the Biblical material itself is often opaque, ambiguous, and replete with mythic material and layer upon layer of editorial redaction. Furthermore, there is hardly another field as susceptible to preconceived notions, to ideologies that serve establishments and their historical conceptions with their attendant apologetics, all quite visible in much of the interpretative literature, even when it claims to be scientific.

The Israelite tribes apparently were descended from the Habiru, or Apiru, mentioned in various Fertile Crescent sources in the second pre-

Christian millennium. These Habiru were bands of nomads who at times were peaceful herdsmen, at times marauding brigands. They often served as mercenaries of the various kingdoms in the region. Biblical scholars today identify them with the Hebrews (according to Biblical genealogies, the Israelites are a *part* of the Hebrew clans). One feature common to the Israelite tribes, or at least to some of them and later adopted by all, is a tradition about their exodus from Egypt. This tradition has no supportive archaeological or contemporary documentary evidence, although it may have a historical kernel.[2]

The penetration of the Israelite tribes into Canaan (ancient Palestine and Phoenicia) was part of a larger upheaval that transformed the world of civilized antiquity in the eastern Mediterranean during the last quarter of the second pre-Christian millennium, the period of the decline of the great powers, Egypt and the Hittite empire. In its wake came the infiltration of the Aramaean tribes and their domination of a part of present-day Syria, the settlement of the Philistine "Sea Peoples" on the Canaan coastal strip south of the Phoenicians' domain, the penetration from the east of the Elamites into Mesopotamia and of the Doric tribes into the region of Mycenean civilization. The penetration of the Israelite tribes—the Book of Joshua notwithstanding—apparently was not accomplished in most cases through war and conquest. (Joshua, written generations later, seems to have been designed to serve later political and ideological interests.) Albrecht Alt established, through textual analysis, that the Israelite settlement took place for the main part peaceably, by gradual infiltration of individual families and clans into the desolate, uninhabited hill country.[3] The Israeli scholar Moshe Kochavi contends that archaeology

> presents a picture which is radically different from the Biblical conquest epic. It shows that the disappearance of the Canaanite culture and the settlement and entrenchment of Israel in its land are not a single historical event, but a complex historical process lasting for more than two hundred years, between the thirteenth and the eleventh centuries B.C.[4]

In other words, the penetration of the Israelite tribes was not a process of conquest and annihilation, but a gradual transformation of the population of Canaan. At times, as in the beginning, there was subordination to the Canaanite city-states. Later there was a process of mutual assimilation, which included bloody struggles and the rise in some cases of the Israelites to dominance as a free ruling class.[5]

The linguistic continuity of Canaan was preserved. Both ancient Canaanite dialects, which belong to the West Semitic family of languages, and Hebrew, which is also part of that group, show no break in continuity. This fact would be plausible only if the settling tribes adopted the local language, and that could occur only through a process of gradual influence. It could not happen without the adoption at the same time of the main part of the local culture, which certainly must have been on a much higher level than that of primitive nomads.

Artifacts unearthed in Ebla, Tel-Mari, and Ugarit (Ras Shamra) all point to cultural and historical continuity of the entire region. Five-thousand-year-old documents found at Ebla contain such names as Abraham, David, Micah, Israel, and Ishmael. Tel-Mari has yielded documents that relate to the structure and institutions of the western Semitic tribes in the second and third millennia B.C. which "throw light on the structure of the Israelite tribal society" and "its gradual settlement in Canaan."[6] The documents of Ugarit, a city destroyed in the thirteenth century B.C., which are written in a dialect akin to Hebrew though different from the Biblical dialect, disclose a complete mythological system that throws light on many expressions and passages in the Hebrew Bible. "Hebrew linguistic and literary tradition continues that of the Canaanites," writes M. D. Cassuto, who argues that only on the basis of this literary foundation can we make sense of the maturity and artistic perfection of the Bible, where tentative and primitive experiments seem absent.[7]

Ze'ev Weissman, in summing up the results of historical and archaeological research, maintains that a reading of the Book of Judges shows that in no description of a war or any other political event does Israel function as a single national entity, except for the war waged by Othniel Ben Knaz against Kushan Rishataim, king of Aram Naharaim—an account which scholars regard as spurious. Nor is there any indication of a national body or a central political institution that determines national policy.

> Critical biblical scholarship now sees the development of Israelite history as the exact opposite of what is presented in the Book of Joshua and in the editorial treatment of Judges. The situation described in Judges is not preceded by any national, religious or military cohesiveness that reached its zenith in the conquest and in the division of the land among the tribes, after which there occurred decline and disintegration. On the contrary: it was only after the various settlements of several different tribes that there began a process of a general coming-together of these tribes. The first national manifestation of this came only with the establishment of the monarchy.[8]

Critical scholarship shows that a similar process took place in the development of the Israelite religion from its primitive beginnings to the elevated level reached by the late prophets. The Bible abounds in glaring contradictions between the text and the central tenets of developed Judaism, despite later Deuteronomic redaction and notwithstanding the hairsplitting efforts of generations of traditionalist exegetes to explain away their obvious meaning. The tenet that God is one, without body or bodily form, is contradicted as early as Genesis 1 with the divine pronouncement in the plural: "Let us make man in our image, after our likeness." And how else, except by willful exegesis and sophistry, could the following verses from

Exodus be explained? "Then Moses and Aaron, Nadab and Abi'hu, and seventy of the elders of Israel went up, and they saw the God of Israel; and there was under his feet as it were a pavement of sapphire stone, like the very heaven for clearness. And he did not lay his hand on the chief men of the people of Israel; they beheld God, and ate and drank" (24: 9). "Thus the Lord used to speak to Moses face to face, as a man speaks to his friend" (33: 11). " 'But,' he said, 'you cannot see my face, for man shall not see me and live.' And the Lord said, 'Behold, there is a place by me where you shall stand upon the rock; and while my glory passes by I will put you in a cleft of the rock, and I will cover you with my hand until I have passed by; then I will take away my hand, and you shall see my back; but my face shall not be seen,'" (33: 20–23).

Even Ezekiel, who prophesied after a lengthy process of refinement and sublimation of Yahwism, renders his vision of the divinity in the following words: "And above the firmament over their heads was the likeness of a throne, in appearance like sapphire; and seated above the likeness of a throne was a likeness as it were of a human form. And upward from what had the appearance of his loins I saw as it were gleaming bronze, like the appearance of fire enclosed round about; and downward from what had the appearance of his loins I saw as it were the appearance of fire, and there was brightness round about him" (Ezek. 1: 26–27).

Since the entire Bible underwent redaction, apparently down to the late Hellenistic period, it would seem that belief in the corporeality of a divinity who occupied a physical location was widely prevalent until a very late date. (Indeed, traces of this concept survive to this very day, as in the supposed connection between God and the city of Jerusalem, his "chosen abode," a connection which by its very nature refutes a purely spiritual conception of the divinity.)

The Bible also contains evidence of human sacrifice to Yahweh, as in the narrative of Jephthah's daughter. The story of the sacrifice of Isaac is clearly a typological narrative that mythologizes the transition from human to animal sacrifice. The rite of the redemption of the first born (*pidyon ha'ben*) may also contain a dim memory of the times when first-born male children were sacrificed to the deity together with the first fruits of both field and flock.[9]

Even when Yahweh was pronounced the single Israelite deity, the existence of other gods was not denied, as is apparent in the phrasing of the commandment "I am Yahweh your God, who brought you out of the land of Egypt, out of the house of bondage. You shall have no other gods before me" (Exod. 20: 2–3). (I have substituted *Yahweh* for *Lord* to bring it to closer agreement with the original Hebrew.) Carefully read, this commandment means simply that in exchange for the liberation of Israel from the yoke of Egypt, Yahweh demands that the people not worship other gods, whose existence is not denied.

The recognition that the Israelite religion was monolatrous at best is apparent in Jephthah of Gilead's address to the King of Ammon: "Will you not possess what Chemosh your god gives you to possess? And all that the Lord [Yahweh] our God has dispossessed before us, we will possess" (Judg. 11: 24). There is a clear demarcation here between the jurisdictions of Yahweh and Chemosh. That Yahweh had never been the ancient Israelites' only god but at most a chief deity is apparent in Gideon's second name, Jerub-Baal, which means "may Baal contend." It may also be seen in that Gideon's father, Joash (whose name [Yo-ash] reveals its connection to Yahweh), erected in his town, Ophrah, under a tree consecrated to the Asherah, an altar to Baal. He obviously saw no contradiction in performing both cults. We also find that King Saul named one of his sons Jonathan (Yo [Yeho=Yo]natan— "Yahweh has given") and the other Eshbaal (Ish-Baal—"man of Baal").

Yahweh, according to one important school, was the war god of the federated tribes of Israel, which constituted an amphyctiony (similar to the Greek federation of that name), an alliance between the tribes and the god for war purposes. This cult in no way contradicted the cults of other gods worshiped at the time by the Israelites. Yahweh became the chief divinity only through the process of monarchic centralization.

Membership in the ancient Israelite tribes was not determined by religious affiliation but by kinship or by a common social framework. It was ethnic or social affiliation that determined participation in tribal rituals. New gods could be added to the pantheon, as when the tribe moved to a new location with its autochthonous deities. We thus find that the Israelite nomads, some of whom undoubtedly worshiped the war god Yahweh, adopted the agricultural Baal and Asherah cults when they settled in the farming areas where the Canaanite pantheon was worshiped, just as the foreign settlers imported by the Assyrians and Babylonians into Israel and Judea after the downfall of the two kingdoms adopted the Yahweh cult.

There are detailed conjectures about the process in which the person of Yahweh was formed and about the development of Israelite protomonotheism in Albrecht Alt's important essay "The God of the Fathers" and in *The Early History of Israel* by Roland de Vaux.[10] De Vaux notes that most modern historians agree that "Israel" as such did not exist until the settlement in Canaan, and only then did its history begin. But the Israelites themselves traced their origins to "Abraham the Patriarch." Abraham was a descendant of Ever, the "Habiru." Each of the various Habiru families and clans worshiped its own gods. Characteristically, in most cases the god is nameless; he is merely the god of the father of the family or tribe ("the God of Abraham"), although we also find mentioned the gods Pahad Yitzhak (Fear of Isaac) and Abir or Adir (the Mighty One, but it may also be translated as "the bull") of Jacob.[11] We may deduce that at least some of the tribes imagined the deity as having the shape of a bull, as is clear from the cult of the "calf" and from the images of bulls placed by Jeroboam, son of Nebat, in the shrines at Beth El and Dan. It appears, then, that there were at least two traditions about Yahweh's form. One tradition, associated with the tribes of the house of Joseph, whose cultic centers were at Beth El and Dan, visualized him as a bull. The other, apparently held by the Jerusalemite priesthood and the tribe of Judah, visualized him in human form, as is evident in the passages quoted from Genesis, Exodus, and Ezekiel.

The cult of the gods of the fathers, as chief deities of the tribes affiliated with them, stood in no contradiction to the cult of the household gods or protective spirits, the Teraphim, represented by statuettes, such as those Rachel stole from her father, Laban, and hid in the saddlebags of her camel (Gen. 31) or which Saul's daughter, Michal, laid on the bed and covered with clothes in order to ward off the pursuers of her husband, David (I Sam. 19: 13). In intertribal treaties, each side would swear in the name of its own god; verses such as "The God of Abraham and the God of Nahor . . . judge between us" (Gen. 31: 53) imply that each side recognizes the reality of the other's god; otherwise it would doubt the binding nature of its vow.

Since the Hebrews were nomads, their gods, unlike the gods of the sedentary Canaanites, had no connection with a particular territory; they guided and protected their people in their wanderings. Sometimes they also gave moving orders, like the command given to Abraham: "Go from your country and your kindred and your father's house to the land that I will show you" (Gen. 12: 1). Prefigured here is a typical trait of the future Israelite god, in contrast to the territorial deities: he is a god involved in time, in motion and change, a god who determines history and can be interpreted through it.

De Vaux writes:

> When the nomadic clans came into contact with the settled people, they used their sanctuaries and worshipped the gods of the country, even though they did not give up the cult of their own god as their patron and protector. The process of becoming settled led to a religious syncretism and to the giving of a personal name to the god of the fathers.[12]

Upon arrival in Canaan, then, the ancient Israelite nomads encounter the chief deity of the western Semites, El. He is worshiped in various places under different names: El Shaddai, El Elyon, El Hai-Ro'i, El Brith, El Olam; in the Ugarit texts he is named Shor El (El the Bull). He is the creator and lord of creation, but he does not intervene in human history. He is a king, and the father of all the gods. (Hence, apparently, the creator who voices a decision in plural terms, in the council of the gods, in Gen. 1; also the god who sits in the company of his sons and converses with Satan in the Book of Job and the god whose sons, as described in Gen. 6: 4, wed the daughters of men, thus fathering the Nephilim, "the mighty men that were of old, the men of renown," similar to the Greek heroes born from the union of gods with mortals.) The adoption of the idea of the omnipotent cosmic god expanded the concept of the divine until it embraced the whole world, not only the family or clan.

In addition to El and the nomadic deity, Yahweh, there is a third element in the fusion that gave birth to the Israelite god—a god from Sinai, a mountain god ("Their gods are the gods of the hills," 1 Kings 20: 23), a desert god. He is associated with Mount Horeb, the legendary site of the Decalogue and the mountain where Yahweh reveals himself to Elijah (1 Kings 19: 8). (Generations would pass before the presence of the god would be associated in the popular Judean mind with Jerusalem and its temple, an association that would never be recognized in the northern kingdom.) Just as the gods of the fathers had a special relationship with the patriarchs, Yahweh had a special relationship with Moses, who, according to tradition, was the leader of one group of Israelite tribes.

That the Israelitic god is a composite divinity, a synthesis of several gods, finds expression, as Alt points out, in the formula "I am the God of your father, the God of Abraham, the God of Isaac and the God of Jacob" (Exod. 3: 6), to which the god in the burning bush adds his name, Yahweh, a name unknown at that time, meaning that he is a god added to the other gods mentioned. The factor most decisive in turning Yahweh into a *national* god probably was that the unified monarchy and the nation were formed while engaged in continuous warfare, mainly against the steady, threatening might of the Philistines. It would be only natural under such circumstances for the war god to become the chief deity.

Although tentative moves to elevate Yahweh to the role of chief deity were made under King Saul, the decisive steps came later. They were the unification of all the tribes under King David, the establishment of Jerusalem as the new capital, the concentration of the Yahweh cult in the temple in Jerusalem parallel to the political power concentration, the immobilization of the Ark of the Covenant, and in later ages the attempts to prohibit Yahweh worship at any place other than the temple in Jerusalem (although the local cults of the Baals and Asherahs continued as ever). The religious reforms of Hezekiah and, particularly, Josiah, which aimed at strengthening the central role of the monarchy in alliance with the Jerusalemite priesthood, always involved the destruction of secondary sanctuaries to Yahweh. These sites competed with the Jerusalem temple and were therefore castigated by the priestly chroniclers of the Jerusalem temple as a sin against God.

The northern kingdom also inherited the Yahwist ideology as a means to a cultic unification of the people. But the looser structure of the northern kingdom and its political instability, manifested in successive coups d'état and the rise and fall of dynasties, compared with the continuous rule of the Davidian dynasty in Judea, forced the northern kings to be more tolerant of the cults of other gods, such as Baal and Asherah, held in reverence by the populace since ancient times. Even Jehu, despite his ruthless "purge" of the Baal priesthood, eventually had to come to terms with the Baal cult. History has shown how a cultic schism immediately attended the political rupture between the two kingdoms. True, the cult of Yahweh remained unique to both monarchies and the prophets constantly urged the kings to impose it by force, which shows that in their minds the cult of Yahweh and the monarchy were interconnected, with the cult constituting in some respects an ideology of the monarchy and an expression of the Israelitic national entity forged by it.

The notion is widespread that the political unity of the kingdom was achieved thanks to a prior unity of religious belief that created a common national consciousness. But this analysis of the material leads one to conclude the opposite—that the unified national consciousness and the religious unity manifested in the Yahweh cult were both imposed by the monarchy. This conclusion is reinforced further by the relative immunity of the Yahweh prophets to royal ire, even when from Elijah on there appear "prophets of protest" who provide Yahweh with a moral dimension and criticize the social and political establishment. Even a prophet of protest such as Jeremiah was merely arrested and confined under comfortable conditions (with a private secretary) that an ordinary prisoner surely did not enjoy (there was only one brief period in which he was in mortal danger). True, there were periods during which the "prophets of protest" were persecuted, as was apparently the case during the reign of Ahab and Jezebel. Even so, Elijah did dare to face down Ahab, and only after he massacred the Baal priests was he forced to flee the wrath of Queen Jezebel, the votary of Baal. The probable explanation is that both sides, the priests and prophets of Yahweh on one hand and the kings on the other, were always cognizant of the fact that in the last resort their interests were interdependent.

The hypothesis that the Yahweh cult was largely imposed on the populace from above and was not the day-to-day, traditional popular religion is confirmed in the people's tendency to continue worshiping the Canaanite gods. In shards discovered in Samaria excavations, names of members of the state bureaucracy contain the combinate *Yah* or *Yo* with greater frequency than the names of the lower orders of society. Ahab, too, despite his "bad press" from a Yahwistic standpoint, named his sons (the sons of Jezebel) Ahaziah and Joram rather than names containing theophoric refrences to Baal. The claims of the Yahwist establishment to exclusivity were not then accepted by the people; they probably belong to a later age, the late monarchic period. One may hazard a guess that even then not all of the Yahwistic priesthood shared these claims. We find that the colony of Israelite mercenaries at Yev (Elephantine) in Upper Egypt during the fifth century B.C.—long after the collapse of both Israelite kingdoms and even longer after Josiah's and Hezekiah's reforms in Judea and Jehu's purge in Israel—maintained a sanctuary dedicated to Yahu (i.e., Yahweh), as well as shrines dedicated to Ashambeitel, Anath Beit El, Haram Beit El, Anath Yahu (the goddess Anath associated with the sanctuary at Beit El, and Anath, the spouse of Yahu). These are not Egyptian deities; they are cults from the land of Israel which the mercenaries, who obviously saw nothing sacrilegious in their worship, imported from home.

Max Weber, on the basis of the theory of the "Amphyctyonic alliance," analyzes the processes of the formation of the self-enclosed communal structure of Judaism and the universalization of the concept of the divinity, i.e., mature monotheism.[13] In his judgment, these processes resulted from the crisis and collapse of the two Israelite kingdoms. He points out that even the ancient Yahweh, the war god, possessed certain extratribal traits. He is the only god we know of who does not have a "natural," "organic" connection with his people but a connection based on a covenant—a covenant on one hand between the tribes and on the other between the federated tribes and the war god. Yahweh is "a god come from afar" (he came from Se'ir, the land of Edom). As a result, we find that even in the Biblical period non-Israelites called on him for help. Weber concludes that from the beginning this god had a universalistic potential, thanks mainly to the possibility of converting the abstract concept of a covenant, a treaty, into a connection independent of ethnic affinity or territorial location.

The rise of the monarchy, urbanization, and the establishment of a professional army resulted in the disarming of the peasants and shepherds and the deterioration of their socioeconomic position. The Yahweh war prophets of the ancient tribal militia (e.g., Samuel) became prophets of protest, fulminating against social injustice, serving as the mouthpiece of the exploited peasantry, and reflecting its nostalgia to the legendary simplicity, without exploitation and class stratification, of the archaic tribal society in the desert. These, traditionally, were the "true prophets," whereas the "false prophets" were the Yahweh prophets who, like Zedekiah son of Kenaanah (2 Kings 20: 11), supported the existing order and represented the monarchy and the urban aristocracy. They were found to be false prophets because of the political defeat of the two kingdoms and the discrediting of their ruling classes.

Yahweh, the god of hosts, reflecting the aspirations of the disarmed peasantry, became a peace-loving god. The miserable condition of his believers was caused by their violation of their covenant with him, a situation which could be remedied by penitence. With the decline of the kingdom this class view was adopted by all classes and became a national view, expressed by Isaiah in his vision of "the Servant of God," scorned and contemned by all nations, bearing their sins, until the time that God shall reward him for his faith and make him a cornerstone of his edifice.

The need to reconcile faith with hopeless reality gave birth to an eschatology, a vision of redemption. The desperate conditions of the present were not a result of Yahweh's weakness in his battle with the gods of other peoples but a part of a grand design of reward and punishment, in which other peoples become a "scourge" in Yahweh's hand. This means that the actions of other nations are conceived as part of a plan designed by the God of Israel, thus leaving no place to their gods. Monolatry, Weber concludes, is thus transformed into monotheism.

But as long as the Israelite kingdoms still existed, this development, whose beginnings are already discernible in the prophecies of Amos, the earliest of the late or "written prophets" (about the middle of the eighth century B.C.), is limited to very small circles. We see this in the fact that almost all kings, in both kingdoms, continue "to do evil in the eyes of the Lord." This does not mean that they suffered from moral defects or were unfit to rule but that they accepted other cults in addition to the Yahweh worship.[14]

From the beginning of the Second Commonwealth period, and even earlier, during the Babylonian exile, there emerges a new group, with characteristics different from those of archaic Israelite society. Nebuchadnezzar's expulsion of the Judeans to Babylonia affected mainly the aristocracy, the priesthood, and the urban artisans. The bulk of the population ("the poorest people of the land"), the Bible tells us, was left at home to mingle with the foreign elements transplanted into Canaan by the conquerors. According to Jer. 52: 28–30, the total number of exiles in the three waves ordered by Nebuchadnezzar did not exceed 4,600 (2 Kings 24: 14 claims a less modest first wave of 10,000 and a second wave of an unspecified number).

As noted, Weber maintains that members of the exiled oligarchy in Babylonia adopted the interpretation (originally prevalent among the oppressed peasantry) of national disaster as God's punishment. They imbued the idea of a covenant with new content, and this morality of reward and punishment administered by God made it possible for them to keep the Yahweh faith even in exile. Since after the collapse their political framework no longer existed, the faith could be preserved only by the development of an intricate system of separation and segregation from the surrounding peoples. Weber stresses that the priesthood had a clear caste interest, since its very status and existence depended on the preservation of Yahweh worship. The fate of the exiles from the kingdom of Israel served as a warning from which to learn. Those exiles had quickly become assimilated among the peoples of the Assyrian and neo-Babylonian empires. If the priests were to preserve their position, they had to establish a "new people" founded on a different basis from the preceding political-national one.

The reform effected by the priesthood and the late prophets in Babylonia (see the prophecies of Second Isaiah, Ezekiel, Zechariah, Haggai, and Malachi, as well as the books of Jonah and Ruth, and the Priestly Code chapters in Deuteronomy) has several basic elements: the presentation of Yahweh as the only God, creator of the world although not embodied in it, whose intentions are revealed through history and lead toward a historical goal; the establishment of a community based on religious worship and deriving its reason for existence from it; and the evolving of elaborate systems of segregation of the members of the community from the rest of mankind. These systems of segregation included marriage (ancient Israelites had no compunctions about marrying outside the group), dietary laws (Genesis relates how Abraham slaughtered a kid in honor of the visiting angels and served it with butter and milk), avoidance of common meals with people outside the community (a practice without a trace in the Bible), laws of purity and impurity, and circumcision (which had never been rigidly enforced). The status of women was reduced to reinforce the cohesion and stability of the family unit (it was apparently at this time that stress was laid on the patriarchal, exclusively male nature of the divinity, a reflection of the ideology which downgraded the position of women). Finally, a most important element of the new religion was the transformation of the Sabbath—probably originally connected with the cult of the moon and celebrated only once a month—into the major religious custom separating members of the community from outsiders.[15] In addition, new religious content was instilled into the ancient nature festivals. The Feast of First Fruits became the Feast of the Giving of the Torah and the spring festival became Passover. The overriding aim of the priesthood, as well as that of the succeeding generations of scribes, Pharisees, sages, Tanna'im, Amora'im, and rabbis, was to imbue every act with a religious meaning.

The new priestly religion began to absorb from the Babylonians and, following the Persian conquest, from the Persians new content unknown to Biblical religious thought, including faith in hierarchical orders of angels and devils. (Angels are mentioned in the Bible, but it seems that in most cases they were introduced by later editors to emphasize the distance between God and man, whereas originally the text meant the appearance of the god himself. With the exception of Zechariah, one of the last prophets, the prophets speak of a direct contact with the deity. Furthermore, the Biblical angels do not constitute a hierarchical order.)

Salo Baron believes that much of this new content was Zoroastrian in origin:

> It seems . . . a reasonable assumption that at least in eschatology, demonology, the doctrine of reward and punishment, and the laws of purity Judaism must have received particularly strong stimuli from the great Aryan religion.[16]

One may hazard a conjecture that this system of angels, devils, and demons was also a consequence of the adoption of the one-god dogma. It parallels both the process that took place in Zoroastrianism a few centuries earlier, when the monotheistic creed of the Persian prophet absorbed earlier pagan beliefs, and the process that occurred several centuries later in Christianity, after it had conquered the pagan world. In both cases the ancient gods were transformed by priests into saints or demons, since belief in their existence persisted and the priesthood had to find a place for them within the framework of its doctrine. The belief in a hierarchy of angels and devils may be seen, then, as a state of implicit polytheism that could at times erupt and become overt. Not only in Catholicism but in Judaism as well there exist, in an inhibited and potential state, all the evolutionary stages that precede monotheism—including polytheism, animism, and magic.

Much more important than this elaboration of a demonology and a heavenly host was the adoption of the Persian belief in the immortality of the soul, of reward and punishment after death, of resurrection—of which there is hardly a trace in the Old Testament. This tenet became so central to Judaism that the sages required only two conditions for admission of Samaritans to Judaism (they had already recognized the Torah): that they confess the sanctity of the temple in Jerusalem instead of the Samaritan temple on Mount Gerizim and that they accept the creed of the resurrection, which the Samaritans had thus far denied, adhering to the older Biblical concept, which does not recognize the existence of another world.

Since the new Jewish community was founded on the Torah and its commandments, not on politics or territory, the priesthood and the institution of religious exegesis naturally became the dominant factors within it. Thus the community fell in line with the innovative, really revolutionary, policy of the Persian Empire. The empire supported and allied itself with the priestly castes of its subject peoples, a policy that tended to neutralize any political and national aspirations on their part. Weber notes that the Persian rulers, by granting the priesthoods special privileges, turned them into natural collaborators with their rule throughout the empire and even beyond.

Hayim Tadmor interprets the verses of Second Isaiah ("Who says of Cyrus, 'He is my shepherd, and he shall fulfill all my purpose'; saying of Jerusalem, 'She shall be built,' and of the temple, 'Your foundation shall be laid.' Thus says the Lord to his anointed, to Cyrus, whose right hand I have grasped, to subdue nations before him and ungird the loins of kings, to open doors before him that gates may not be closed" [44: 28; 45: 1]) as follows:

> In the second prophecy the prophet uses the term "Messiah" [meaning "anointed"] which heretofore was used to denote only the founders of the kingdom of Israel, Saul and, mainly, David. . . . It is difficult for us to understand how a foreign king could be described as a "Messiah," a title not accorded even to the descendants of David by contemporary prophets. . . . Cyrus "the anointed of God" plays an important role in the thinking of the prophet, whereas a "son of David" has no place in it. Thus we see that in contradistinction to the First Temple prophets, for whom the Temple, the Chosen City and the House of David constituted a single indivisible whole, the consoling prophet ignores the royal dynasty and the sublime role accorded in the visions of the preceding prophets to the future "shoot from the stump of Jesse" (Isaiah 11: 1–10). He does not foresee the restoration of the kingdom of the House of David. . . . It is Cyrus, not anyone else, who will rebuild Jerusalem and restore the Babylonian exiles to their land.[17]

What this implies is a renunciation of the national-political dimension, since the expression "the House of David" should be seen as a description of national sovereignty and independence, not necessarily of loyalty to a particular dynasty.

A "return to Zion" to rebuild the temple, rather than to restore national sovereignty, is a uniquely priestly project. The priesthood of Judea, which had now become Jewish—that is, members of the exiled religious community—transferred its loyalty from the house of David to the Persian government, relinquishing any political-national pretension. Priests need a temple. The indifference toward any political aspect of the return to Zion is marked not only by the fact that both Ezra and Nehemiah, who arrived in Judea to reorganize the returned exiles' community life, were Persian officials but also by the fact that their actions were protected by a Persian garrison that was under their command. It is indeed inconceivable that their commands could have been contrary to the wishes of the "King of Kings."[18]

The community that emerged in Babylonia under the guidance of the priesthood and that provided the basis for the return to Zion was very different from the ancient peoples of Israel and Judea. It was an apolitical community based on the principle of ritual purity, the precondition for inclusion. The old covenant of the Israelite tribes with the ancient war god Yahweh was transformed into the "covenant of Father Abraham," an individual pact between each person and Yahweh's ritual community. Contrary to the illusion of continuity which the "Deuteronomic" redaction of the Biblical books creates between the "first" and the "second" temple (a people exiled from its land returning to resettle it after Cyrus's decree), there is no continuity of national identity between ancient and postexilic Israel. They are different entities, although the latter grew out of the former. Only postexilic Israel can be described as "Jewish" in any meaningful sense of the term.

The appearance of the Jewish people, then, is largely a voluntary act—a religious act creating a religious sect. The laws of segregation imported by Ezra and Nehemiah from Babylonia (and heretofore unknown in Judea) were designed to separate the exile community (k'hal ha-golah) from the people of the land (am ha'aretz). Membership in the community was no longer a "natural" ethnic affiliation. The verse "You shall be to me a kingdom of priests and a holy nation" (Exod. 19: 6) takes on special meaning in this connection. The laws of segregation are not the kind that draw ethnic distinctions but rather the kind that in certain early societies distinguish the priestly caste. In this respect, too, these regulations conformed to Persia's imperial policy: unification creates power, which can be translated into political terms and endanger the supreme authority. The more a society is divided into sects and castes, the easier it is to control.

It is also significant that with the establishment of this new ideological basis, prophecy ends. A prophet claiming direct revelation endangers the traditional exegetic framework. From the moment the Torah exegetes were recognized as the exclusive authorities in Judaism, there was no place for prophets. Tadmor notes:

In spite of the broad powers with which he had been entrusted, Ezra's activity was limited to the "community of exiles." He worried mainly . . . not about the political or social conditions of the people in Judea and Jerualem, but about the relations between those returning to Zion and those who had not undergone the spiritual change which took place in the Exile. The community Ezra addresses is called "the Exile," "the members of the Exile" or "the Exile community." . . . Ezra posits the terms "the Exile community" and "the holy seed" (9: 2) in contrast to the rest of the people, the people of Judea, who are defined as "the people of the land" (*amei ha-aratzot*). These apparently included not only Judeans who had not been exiled to Babylonia, but also residents and neighbors of Judea who worshipped Yahweh. . . . A central part in Ezra's world-view was occupied by his desire to single out the community returning to Zion, the returning Judean exiles, and bring them as close as possible to the norms established among the Babylonian Jewish community. This is the basis of his uncompromising insistence on religious segregation. But as against the segregationist position there was also a different school of opinion, which believed that members of other nations would also join in the worship of Yahweh.[19]

The nonsegregationists immediately realized the revolutionary implications of the idea of the one God and its nullification of ethnic and political barriers: all humans are equal before the one God, and the Jews have been chosen to spread his teaching to the whole of humanity. Such ideas cannot be found in earlier, monolatrous stages.

The claim that the work of Ezra and Nehemiah, the segregationists, was motivated by nationality is at odds with the presumption that a project of national revival would have aspired to extend the community to the people of what had been Judea, not to exclude them from it. A sect excludes; a nation includes. A sect allies itself with its sister sects in other countries, as in the case of the Jerusalemite community and its attempts to enforce in Jerusalem the same rules that applied in the Babylonian mother community. A nation, on the other hand, tries to encompass all residents of the national territory, just as the Israelites and the Canaanites had merged into a single nation. From its inception, Ezra's and Nehemiah's approach is international and extraterritorial, and the temple serves only as a focus for the international Diaspora.

Weber dwells on the particular significance that the cult center holds for the internationally dispersed community:

The commandment of ritualistic homogeneity of the people, including the *gerim* [converts] was brought into a new relation with the specific ritualistic purity of the land. . . .

Thus, almost at the same moment when Israel lost its concrete territorial basis the ideal value of the political territory was definitely and ritually fixed for the henceforth developing internationally settled guest people. . . . The purely religious nature of the community, resting on the prophetic promises, determined the substitution of this confessional and essentially sharpened segregation for the political separation from the outside.[20]

The purport is that the consecration of Palestine as "the holy land" is inseparable from what Weber defines as the creation of the Jewish "Pariah caste" (a term he borrowed from the Hindu caste system). A territorial nation cannot adopt such attitudes, which are contrary to its very political-territorial existence. The ancient Israelites were tolerant toward other peoples and religions. They regarded them from a political point of view. Only after the transformation of the Israelites into Jews, into a religious exilic community, did the land of Palestine become "holy." And only under foreign rule, which takes care of all political and military problems and leaves the community free to immerse itself in its own affairs, was it possible to develop the Sabbath into a day of absolute rest, on which it was forbidden even to bear arms (a prohibition that had to be rescinded with the emergence of a Jewish political entity at the time of the Hasmoneans).

The community's structure, from its inception, is both a proselytizing and an exclusive-aristocratic one. Its proselytizing aspect is implicit in the very shift from a tribal-ethnic community to one based on contractual obligation (the covenant of Father Abraham), deriving from the recognition of the one and single God, creator of heaven and earth, before whom all are equal. But such a concept contains a revolutionary, universal potential, as realized by both Zechariah and Isaiah in his millennial vision. This is also the implied conclusion of the books of Jonah and Ruth, which were apparently composed during the same period. After all, anyone who recognizes this God and believes in him becomes thereby a member of his "chosen people." Thus emerges a permanent inner tension between the exclusivistic interests of the sect and its spiritual mentors and the universalistic logic implicit in the concept of the Jewish God, a tension which in the course of time would result in far-reaching consequences for humanity at large.

Initially, Ezra's and Nehemiah's segregation ordinances were not accepted by a large part of the Judean public, especially by the propertied classes in Jerusalem and its environs. Only the royal prerogatives that were granted to them and the Persian garrison that was at their disposal enabled them to overcome this resistance. We witness here the earliest appearance of the pattern in which the discipline of Halacha is imposed on members of the community with the help of an alien temporal force, a pattern that is to be repeated again and again in the course of the coming centuries.

Judaism, then, is essentially an exilic creation, although the nucleus of Torah and Halacha may already be found in Josiah's reform. The community's sworn obligation under covenant has no resemblance to a national-ethnic bond. It is a covenanted obligation, a religious not a national obligation.

We have few reliable documentary Jewish sources about the events that befell the Jews during the period from the conclusion of the Book of Nehemiah to the collapse of the Persian Empire. Moreover, there is hardly a single mention of the Jews in external sources.

Herodotus, "the father of history," traveled widely in the Persian Empire during the fifth century B.C. and reported on any tribe, nation, or interesting custom or event he encountered or heard of. But not the Jews. Some readers have inferred from his report about the custom of circumcision current among many inhabitants of Syria that his reference was to the Jews, but that is uncertain, since the custom was also common among the Phoenicians. This lack of mention by Herodotus seems to support the conjecture that the community was small and its influence minimal, and that would explain the small numbers of exiles reported in Kings and Jeremiah as well as the small number of exiles who returned from Babylonia. Indeed, it stands to reason that this small group of returnees to Zion, with its modest local temple, embroiled in constant provincial and sectarian strife with its neighbors in a half-ruined provincial town in a small and unimportant country, would have aroused no curiosity in the foreign traveler and would have disappeared without leaving a trace, together with its small parent Babylonian community, within two or three generations.

Ezra and Nehemiah, members of the exilic elite, wished indeed to separate their community from the people of the land. But when the district of Judea reappears in the light of history under Seleucid rule there is no longer any distinction between the returnees and the people of the land. They have all become Jews (except for the Samaritans). Since there is no knowledge of further immigration from Babylonia after Nehemiah's immigration, the most reasonable explanation of this phenomenon is that the new religion, shaped in Babylon, reconverted the inhabitants of Judea. The ancient Israelites, together with the non-Israelitic elements, must have accepted the authority of the elite who returned from Babylonia with a new religion. Despite the segregation laws of Ezra and Nehemiah, which would seem to contradict such a tendency, the new religion appears to have entered a new phase—a phase of proselytizing expansion.

But of course the two approaches, the exclusivist and the universalist, are not necessarily contradictory. The principle of covenant, of contractual obligation under treaty and oath by anyone prepared to submit to the rules and regulations of the community, is capable of indefinite extension. It oversteps the narrow limits of nation, language, and culture and creates the conditions for an unlimited expansion of the community. The extent of the expansion, as far as intracommunal factors are concerned, is determined only by the expansive or limiting interpretation of the principle. Anyone who undergoes the initiation rites, irrespective of his or her origins, becomes a part of the community.

The sudden appearance of large Jewish communities all over the Middle East and, later, all across the Roman Empire, to the extent that the Jews became one of the most powerful and populous groups in the classical world, second in the east only to the Greeks, can be explained only through proselytizing and conversion on a vast scale. This proliferation demonstrates that the ideological, religious basis permits an immeasurably larger "demographic" expansion than any biological-ethnic increase. It stands out particularly against the background of the relatively static population of the ancient and classical world, where the methods of land cultivation hardly changed throughout the period and therefore could not support a great increase in population. A population explosion such as the world has experienced over the past two centuries is feasible only if there is a growing food supply for the proliferating populace. We must therefore assume roughly stable populations and conclude that the changes in the sizes of national and religious groups resulted primarily from changes of identity and not biological factors.

Uriel Rappoport, who agrees with this hypothesis, notes that contrary to the self-segregating approach of the Babylonian exiles represented by Ezra and Nehemiah, there also existed a universalistic, missionary approach that found expression in the prophecies of Second Isaiah, Zechariah, and Malachi, as well as in Solomon's prayer (composed at about the same period). The Book of Ruth, which portrays Ruth the Moabite as the great-great-great grandmother of the consecrated hero King David, should be viewed as a polemical tract against intermarriage prohibitions and the injunction that "no Ammonite or Moabite shall enter the assembly of the Lord; even to the tenth generation" (Deut. 23: 3).

Indeed, as Rappoport notes, the universalist approach served as the basis for the Judaization of the whole of Eretz Israel at the time of the Hasmoneans. True, Jewish communities were scattered throughout the land, but the Judaization of the whole country was carried out by force—conquest and forcible conversion—and by the expulsion of the inhabitants of the Hellenistic cities who refused proselytization. Rappoport points out the class conflict between the inhabitants of the Hellenistic cities, supported by the Seleucid Empire, and the "Oriental" peasantry oppressed by them. In short, the Jewish religion had become the oppressed strata's revolutionary ideology against Seleucid imperial rule.[21] So total was the assimilation of the converts that not only did the Galilee region remain Jewish after the terrible destruction wreaked during the Great Rebellion and the Bar Kochba Rebellion that followed, but it actually became the center of Jewish life in the country during the ensuing Mishnaic and Talmudic eras.

But the most far-reaching consequences of the proselytization movement, not only in Jewish but also in world history, occurred not in Palestine but in the Diaspora. Weber points out that Jewish mobility was greatly facilitated by the location of the only legitimate Jewish temple in Jerusalem. Unlike followers of other creeds, Jews did not have to build a temple wherever a Jewish community existed. Instead, they had the synagogue, the unique religious institution invented by Babylonian Jewry as a place for prayer and reading the Torah. Baron writes:

Their decision, particularly, not to build a temple on foreign soil, forced them to establish a new, revolutionary institution: a house of worship dedicated to prayer without sacrificial offerings. Today when worshippers in the Western world attend churches and mosques as well as synagogues, it is difficult for us to imagine how deeply upsetting the abandonment of sacrifices everywhere outside a single specified locality must have been to Ezekiel's gentile as well as Jewish contemporaries. . . . Around the synagogue began to be grouped other communal institutions which, . . . in their totality, formed the nuclei for the new Diaspora community, equally unprecedented in both quality and endurance.[22]

The concept of a single, universal creator who was both a personal god and a god who acted according to moral standards generated an enormously powerful religious dynamic. For if everyone is created by the one God, the community of his believers should encompass, in principle, the whole of humanity. In Zechariah and Second Isaiah we sense the universalistic and eschatological fervor of this realization, as well as the passionate desire to carry its message to the whole world. The principle of the covenant, formulated by the strictly exclusivistic exegetes in Babylonia, is dialectically transformed into a principle permitting a universal application. The unique fusion of the various elements of the ancient Israelite deity; the fact that most of the exiles were urban, hence their ability to maintain a full communal structure in urban concentrations and to have relative mobility; the exiles' eschatology, enabling them to raise a vision of hope and redemption in the vale of tears of reality—all combined to create a soul-shaking revolutionary consciousness in the hearts of its devotees that turned them into missionaries, thereby giving birth to the first universal proselytizing religion.

Here again Weber's sociological insight is apt. He writes that this community had its origins in an urban oligarchic group. From its inception, its rules and regulations were adapted to an urban community. The ever-proliferating development of the oral law rendered its observance ever more difficult for the peasantry, and in fact became an intolerable burden on it. As a result, it was inevitable that the center of gravity of Diaspora Judaism would shift more and more toward the urban caste.[23]

Baron estimates that during the first century the total Jewish population living in the area between Persia and Rome and between Upper Egypt and the Black Sea numbered eight million and that of that number five million lived outside Palestine. He calculates that Jews constituted 7 to 10 percent of the population of the Roman Empire. Furthermore, since a considerable proportion of Diaspora Jewry was urban at a time when most people were rural and since cities have always been the centers of power, wealth, and influence, it would appear that the power, wealth, and influence of the Jews exceeded by far their proportion of the general population. It seems, then, that from this aspect too there is no ethnic continuity between the ancient Israelites and the Jewish people who spread throughout the civilized world.

Israel Levin puts special emphasis on the extraordinary support and protection which the Roman Empire extended to the Jewish Diaspora:

> The growth of the Jewish communities in the Diaspora was also largely dependent on the firm support given to them by the Roman authorities. The privileges granted to them in the Diaspora raised their standing as a group far above the average in the Empire. . . . The basic privilege granted to the Jews in Palestine and in the Diaspora was the permission to organize themselves in communities. . . . With the right to organize a community, the Jews were also permitted to create the institutions and frameworks the community needed, including the erection of buildings and the corporate ownership of property. They were also allowed to impose and collect internal taxes and to establish legal relationships between the members of the community; also, they were exempted from participation in the city's religious rituals; furthermore, they were not obliged to appear in court on the Sabbath and were exempt from military service.[24]

Thus the question of what or who are the Jews had already arisen in the Hellenistic period. Obviously, from Galilee to Idumea they constituted a clearly defined national-territorial entity—an entity that at times (as in the Hasmonean period or under Herod the Great) was organized within the framework of a single independent or autonomous political authority. But as far as other Jewish groups were concerned, the problem is more complex. As Baron rightly points out, the term *Pariah people* coined by Weber does not exhaust the subject. The Jews were "pariahs" only for limited periods. Even then they were almost always able to extricate themselves from this status by conversion. In their own self-image, they were much more "Brahmin" than "pariah," to use the Indian caste terminology employed by Weber, and were often considered as such by their neighbors. Ultimately they themselves freely determined their individual status. But in view of the exclusivity that the Jews imposed on themselves, the segregation that was imposed on them from without, and the specialized and well-defined functions that they fulfilled in their host societies, there is a measure of truth in Weber's term. On the other hand, this definition ill suits the cases of political-national crystallizations that take place in Judaism when the population as a whole adopts the Jewish religion, as happened in Palestine during the Hasmonean era and afterward.

Nor was the mass conversion in the Hasmonean kingdom the only such case. We know, for instance, of the proselytizing of several Bedouin tribes in the Arab peninsula, such as the Beni-Qureita, and of the heavy struggle waged against them by Muhammad during his early career. We know of the Jewish kingdom of Yusef du-Nuwas in Yemen, which existed until the Islamic conquest. We know of a Jewish Berber state, led by a Jewish priestess (Dahia al Kahna), in the Maghreb, which was also subdued by the Moslem conquerors. Perhaps the most famous case of all is that of the Jewish

Khazar kingdom, some of the descendants of which may have merged with East European Jews after the kingdom's defeat by the Mongols.[25]

Why did these four Jewish kingdoms collapse and disappear when, on the face of it, their starting conditions were not inferior to those of neighboring Christian or Muslim countries? Perhaps a more profound question is why North Africa, the Arabian desert, and Eastern (and Western) Europe were not swept by a Jewish wave. With their heavy proselytizing, Jews seemed on the verge of sweeping the Roman Empire. Why, instead, did all the Jewish kingdoms collapse after a relatively short period? Were these collapses due to external circumstances only or also to an antipolitical element within Judaism itself? How did Judaism differ from, say, Hellenism, its great rival in the classical world?

Some scholars compare the Jewish Diaspora to the Greek, but the analogy does not work. Unlike the Greeks, the Jews did not found cities throughout the Hellenistic empires; rather, they settled in the cities built by the Greeks. Unlike the Greeks, the Jews did not maintain a common national civilization throughout the Hellenistic and Roman empires. Unlike the Greeks, who continued to speak Greek, the Jews adopted the Greek language and culture. Greek, not Hebrew, served as the idiom of the learned. And when the Jews wished to read their own holy writings, they read them in Greek translation (the Septuagint). To the extent that Jews outside Palestine did maintain a separate culture, it was purely religious and communal.

Religion, then, remains the only common denominator of the Jews who functioned as communities in the Diaspora and those who functioned as a political nation in Eretz Israel. And that brings us back to the problem of the antipolitical element in Judaism. An outstanding example of the modus operandi of this element is to be found in the history of the Hasmonean revolt and the Hasmonean dynasty. The revolt undoubtedly had nationalistic motives, but it is highly significant that the scribes, followed by the Hasidim, the believers in and the interpreters of the Torah, were the revolt's leaders and that the first act of the revolt, as related in the Books of Maccabees, was the killing of a Hellenized Jew as he was sacrificing to Zeus. The revolt was, then, an act of civil war inflamed by a religious ideology. The Seleucid garrison of the Jerusalem citadel, the Accra, long besieged by the Hasmoneans, was composed partly of Hellenized Jews. As the Hellenizers were members of the wealthier classes, the revolt also must have been a social uprising with the Hasidic religion as its ideology.

But as the revolt unfolded, a most meaningful phenomenon emerged—a phenomenon indicative of the extent to which the religious consciousness, as defined by the returnees to Zion at the time of the Persian Empire, differed from the national-political consciousness that began to develop among the people. When the Seleucids retracted their religion-restrictive edicts, thus removing the cause of the revolt of the Hasidim, the latter began to abandon the Hasmonean leadership and return home. All that interested the Hasidim was the narrow issue of religious freedom, not the political-national aspects of the struggle. On the other hand, it was the Sadducees and the members of the upper classes, imbued with both a Hellenistic culture and a political-national consciousness, who reached an understanding with the Hasmonean leaders and undertook the leadership of both the revolt and the political reconstruction that followed. (According to Emil Schuerer, the final break with the Pharisees, the heirs of the Hasidim, and the alliance with the Sadducees took place during the rule of Yohanan Hyrcanus, 135–105 B.C.) As the political aspect was dominant in Greek thought and Greek social organization, it was the Sadducees, imbued with Greek culture, who comprehended the political aspect of the revolt and acted accordingly. Baron writes:

> Nationality had been of relatively small consequence even in the Hellenistic age. With the expansion of the Macedonian power, the new vast empires, embracing so many disparate ethnic components, emphasized still more the supremacy of the state over the nationality, of the *politeia* over the *ethnos*. The Sadducee leaders unconsciously adopted this principle. They fought the Syrian state on its own ground, erecting against it the power of the Judean state.[26]

The Hasidic sect, as well as its heirs, the Pharisees, were interested in the preservation of the Torah and not in the political state. The political element in Judaism, which existed only among the Jews of Eretz Israel, was the very same that was influenced by the foreign culture, the element that desired a state and political power, like the Hellenistic states. The historical irony is that this very element, which originally collaborated in part with the Seleucids, was the one on which the Hasmoneans could base their policy when they strove to accumulate political power and to develop a true political framework, which necessarily functioned on the same secular basis as the other political units in the region. A symptom of this process of Hellenization is that the Hasmonean rulers and members of their retinues began to adopt Greek names. Weber writes:

> The movement died ... when the Maccabean rule of necessity accommodated itself to the needs of a small secular state, borrowing the traits of a petty Hellenistic kingship. The realization that this was politically unavoidable had, indeed, led the pious to the conviction that foreign rule was preferable to an allegedly Jewish king who enjoyed national prestige but invariably failed to abide by the law.[27]

This is the cardinal point, which conventional historiography fails to emphasize: the end of Jewish sovereignty in Eretz Israel, after the conquest of the east by Pompey, was not the result of a military defeat at the hands of the Romans but of explicit and repeated requests on the part of Pharisee leaders to the Roman authorities to rid them of the rule of Jewish kings.

(Even though they were subject kings, ruling by the grace of the Roman emperors, still they had a more independent status than direct subordination to Rome.)

This Pharisee policy is typical of a religious community, not of a national society. The Persian Empire's achievement in neutralizing the political consciousness of its subjects proved to be much more durable than the empire itself. Clearly, a group motivated primarily by nationalism would always prefer its own government, fallible as it might be, to foreign rule. Moreover, Roman administration was not necessarily much more humane or just than that of the Hasmonean-Herodian dynasty, and Pharisee leaders must have been quite familiar with the world around them and known what to expect from direct Roman rule. They must also have been aware that it is far easier to correct abuses that originate at home, where one has some degree of influence, than those deriving from a gigantic imperial system, where one's weight is hardly felt. Even so, they preferred foreign to Jewish rule because the latter seemed to them religiously wanting.

Here, then, religious considerations contradicted and superseded national ones, proving incisively that the two are not synonymous. The decisive test of a national entity is the desire and willingness to shoulder full responsibility for its collective being in all its aspects—political, economic, and military—whatever the problems, dangers, and frustrations involved. As in the life of an individual, the readiness to bear the burden of freedom, to undertake responsibility for the choice between good and evil, is the test of maturity.

The abdication of the Pharisee leadership from politics in order to preserve the Halachic purity of the community was irreconcilable with the essentially political needs of a territorial nation. This abdication and the imposition of direct Roman rule on Palestine led to the direst results—the Great Rebellion against Rome and the subsequent destruction of Judea and the temple. This retreat from politics, this victory of the religious community, left the people without a generally accepted, central and responsible political authority, which might have contained the blind extremism that was leading to a headlong confrontation with Rome.

King Agrippa's speech during the initial stage of the rebellion, which according to Josephus almost succeeded in restoring the people to sanity,[28] shows just how sorely the people lacked this kind of authority. Had he been king over Judea and Galilee like his ancestor Herod the Great and not only over the Bashan in Transjordan, he might have been able to steer a course of compromise between the invincible fact of Roman world supremacy and the bitterness and rebelliousness of the people and to quell their messianic hallucinations with pragmatic firmness. Considering the caution, vast experience, and rationality of the Roman Empire's central administration, such a compromise was definitely within the realm of possibility.

Although there has been much discussion of late regarding whether the

Great Rebellion and the Bar Kochba Rebellion that followed were "justified," the question is trivial and even absurd. In principle, rebellion against an oppressive imperial regime is always "justified." The true lesson that may be drawn from these events is that disaster necessarily attends abdication from political responsibility. And those chiefly responsible for this disaster were the Pharisees, opposed to the rebellion though they were from the start. At the same time, paradoxically, it was this disaster, more than anything else, that laid the ground for their complete takeover of Judaism.

This takeover was achieved by a presumed understanding reached during the later phase of the Great Rebellion between the Roman authorities and some of the Pharisee leaders, headed by Yohanan ben Zakkai. According to this understanding (unspecified in the documentary evidence but easily deduced from the story of Ben Zakkai's escape from Jerusalem and his being granted by the Romans a center for learning and legislation in Yavneh—with his side of the bargain never specified), the sages accepted the imperial authority unreservedly, foregoing any national aspirations, and undertook to impose it on the Jewish public in exchange for exclusive jurisdiction over the latter. The Palestinian Jews thereby lost the national traits they had acquired in Hasmonean and Herodian times and reassumed the characteristics of a closed, self-segregating religious community dominated by the oral law and its Pharisee exegetes, just as it had been under Persian rule.

The basic position of historians such as Gedaliah Allon is dubious, not to say preposterous.[29] Allon argues that the jurisdiction of the Yavneh religious center was accepted spontaneously by the people and that only after this fortuitous accomplishment did the Romans give their post facto blessing to it. But it is inconceivable that victors who had recently subdued a country in a savage war, victors who were still actively engaged in rooting out any recrudescence of resistance, would absentmindedly, without prior knowledge and approval, permit the development of a national-popular authority. Reason would have it that this community, which had caused such upsets to the imperial system, would henceforth be subject to the closest observation and control by the authorities and that only circles that the authorities considered absolutely reliable would receive Roman backing and be permitted to function within the defeated population. These are the circles that created the "religious-spiritual autonomy" convenient to imperial overlordship, and that, after the last national stirring, the Bar Kochba Rebellion, saw to it that the people would henceforth submit abjectly to Roman rule.

This also seems to explain the blackout imposed in the Mishnah and the Talmud on almost all mention of the three great rebellions—the successful Maccabean-Hasmonean rebellion against the Seleucids and the two failed rebellions against Rome (apart from the Diaspora revolt during Trajan's reign). The rabbis apparently worked in collusion with the authorities to stamp out among their flock any memory of a nonreligious political activity and any favorable mention of national rebellion and independence. Apparently this also explains the strange fact that 1 and 2 Maccabees and the other books of the Apocrypha, along with the works of Josephus, were preserved by the Christian Church and not by the Jewish establishment. The latter sought to create a picture of the past in which national political existence was strictly peripheral, the center of the historical stage being occupied by the continuous chain of Halachic legitimacy, from Moses and Joshua, the elders and prophets down to the members of the Grand Knesset (sidestepping the judges and the kings, namely any extra-Halachic political and social authority). The Pharisees, the Tanna'im, and the Amora'im (the compilers of the Talmud) were only the latest links in this chain, which began with the giving of the Torah on Mount Sinai.

After the Bar Kochba Rebellion, during the reign of Antoninus Pius, the collaborative structure of the relations between the Jewish community and the empire that was established after the Great Rebellion reasserted itself, as though nothing had happened. On the contrary, relations seem to have become much more cordial than they had been in the preceding period, as though the later revolt only accelerated the process, rather than created a barrier of uncompromising hatred between the Jewish people and Rome. The rule of the Nessi'm (princes) over the Jewish community, in which any political-national aspiration was given up, continued in an almost unaltered form from the Yavneh period onward.

We have noted that, in part, the ground for these upheavals was prepared in the period preceding the Great Rebellion because the people lacked a leadership that it could trust or that could impose its will on them. The landed and priestly aristocracy was dissociated from the people and hated by it. The Pharisees, though some had origins among the common people, were largely dissociated from the peasantry and regarded them contemptuously as "people of the land." The general implication of this term (which has changed meaning since the days of Ezra and Nehemiah) was people ignorant of the Torah, but its main thrust was directed against the peasantry. Since the basis of the Pharisees' authority and social function was the learning and explication of the Torah and the development of the Halacha, the dissociation bore the nature of caste exclusivity. We thus see that within the territorial nation the dominant, antipolitical caste remained indifferent to societal problems and territorial needs, priding itself on scholarship and "purity."

This alienation is one of the main reasons for the rise of Christianity. As is evident from numerous passages in the Gospels, Christianity, from its inception in the first century A.D., was imbued with hostility toward the Pharisees. The hostility toward the Halacha and its bearers, hardly surprising, laid the ground for Paul's mission to non-Jews and the abolition of most of the commandments of the oral law.

The peasantry, mainly in Galilee, was exploited by absentee landlords and tax collectors and was generally oppressed by the high Jerusalem nobility, which even questioned their Jewishness. Baron writes:

> The Christian agitation must have inflamed the smouldering antagonisms, and the rabbis necessarily denounced more vigorously than ever that class from which had sprung the main founders of the new religion . . . it was, indeed, much more difficult for a Galilean peasant than for most members of the artisan class and petty merchants to adhere strictly to the law. Jewish agricultural regulations, not to mention the laws of purity and impurity, must have appeared increasingly burdensome.[30]

Baron notes that apart from many other taxes in kind, tolls, and customs duties, Roman taxes amounted to a quarter of the crops each year or each second year.

> From the standpoint of Jewish law, on the other hand, the farmer was supposed to put aside about 12 per cent of the remainder of the crop for the priestly tithe and heave-offering, plus a "second tithe" for the poor or for spending it in the distant city of Jerusalem. There may actually have been a third tithe for the poor every third year. All these dues, coming after the farmer had already delivered the "first fruits" to the Temple and carried out during the harvest the biblical injunctions concerning "gleanings, sheaf and corner" which had to be left on the fields, were almost unbearable charges even in the most fertile regions of the country. Superimposed upon them all was the extremely rigid observance of the sabbatical year, involving the loss of at least a year and a half of agricultural produce every seven year cycle. . . .
>
> The peasant thus simply faced the alternatives of complying with Jewish religious, or Roman civic, duties. In the face of the ruthless . . . Roman administrative methods, the decision was seldom in doubt. . . . Hence the many accusations hurled against the *am ha'ares*, whose food might not be eaten by an observant Jew, since it presumably contained grain from which the tithe and other priestly portions had not been subtracted.[31]

Despite this seething bitterness, for the next several hundred years Galilee remained Jewish and the center of the Palestinian Jewish community. It seems that even in Talmudic times the Jews and Samaritans together constituted the majority of the country's population,[32] although in Michael Avi-Yonah's estimate, their combined proportion at the time of the Persian conquest in the seventh century, which preceded the Moslem conquest by a few years, dwindled to no more than 10 to 15 per cent of the population (mainly because most of them had converted to Christianity).[33] The Jews in the Diaspora from the Babylonian period onward were largely an urban group, although there were also many Jewish farmers in Egypt and in Babylonia (as one may conclude from the farming regulations in the Babylonian Talmud). Presumably this caste-community structure, which depended on organized community institutions—which in turn necessitated a measure of population density difficult to achieve under rural conditions—was one reason for Judaism's failure as a universal proselytizing religion in a socio-economic stage when most of the population was rural. (One should also bear in mind the *collective* nature of the Jewish community, the obligation to have at least ten men—a *minyan*—for reciting most prayers, and the principle that "every Jew is responsible for every other Jew," thus submerging the individual within the group.) But this was not the main reason for Judaism's failure as a prosyletizing religion. Despite Christianity's much more moderate demands, in the beginning the new religion also spread only within (mainly Jewish) urban communities.

The great shock (Baron calls it "the Great Schism") that accompanied the rise of Christianity marked the turning point in the shaping of the Jewish caste community in Palestine, and even more in the Diaspora.

From the first century A.D. onward, the Roman Empire had been searching for a unifying ideology. A first step in this direction was the emperor cult, mandatory for all the population of the empire. But this was merely a symbolic act of loyalty, unaccompanied by inner conviction. It was therefore insufficient for the needs of imperial bonding; hence Emperor Hadrian's initiative in building the Pantheon in Rome, the temple to all the gods of the empire. The united republic of men is here reflected in the celestial republic of the gods. But even this democratic equality of all the gods under the dome of the circular Roman Pantheon, wherein none is favored above the others, was insufficient for the needs of the world-embracing empire. The framework of selfish, material institutions, interests, and power hierarchies could not provide for a spiritual unification of the population, despite the fact that by the second and third centuries A.D. the minds and worldviews of the imperial population had undergone a process of uniformization and had become ever more homogeneous. Thus, the need arose for a universal religion.

Judaism, among other Oriental cults that proliferated throughout the empire, was an obvious candidate for this role. The sense of security created by the community and the mutual support of its members; the inner laws and regulations, more humane as a rule than most of the codes prevalent in the empire; the stable system of rites and ceremonies, centered on the concept of the single, universal, invisible God, which corresponded to some extent with the philosophical conception of the deity by the Greco-Roman intelligentsia (from Plato's supreme idea to Aristotle's prime, unmoved mover); the fact that such a god suited the intelligentsia's craving for a less physical, less local religion; the fact that Diaspora Jewry was mostly urban, thus parallelling the empire's municipal structure; and finally, the unique fusion of Judaism and Hellenism accomplished by Hellenistic Jewry, which in its missionary propaganda had attempted to represent the religion of Moses as a philosophical religion from which Greek philosophy had in fact drawn its ideas, thereby allowing for Hellenism and Judaism to be viewed as two aspects of the same entity: all of these elements had a powerful attraction for the pagan population of the empire.

There are numerous explanations for Judaism's failure to attract the masses of the Roman Empire. One cause is probably the indifferent or even hostile attitude of the Jewish community, led by the Pharisees, toward the state and political authority in general. This communal self-segregation may have been the factor that prevented the necessary final step needed to create a link between the empire's political structure and the communal structure of the sect. If this conjecture has any validity, then the indifference and hostility toward politics that hamstrung the Jewish nation emerging in Eretz Israel and led to the destruction of its political existence also prevented Pharisee Jewry, fortifying itself behind the walls of the Halacha, from turning itself into the world religion that had become such a pressing need.

Although Jesus' world, according to the Gospels, was embedded in that of Pharisee Judaism, Jesus himself was a Galilean. He regarded the ritual commandments of the oral law with reserve and based his teachings on its moral doctrines. He did not refrain from eating the bread of the "people of the land." In fact, his attitude toward cultic demands is highly reminiscent of the hostility exhibited by both First and Second Isaiah toward ritual and dogma and their postulation of moral demands as the core of religion (Second Isaiah, as should be noted, was the prophet of universalism). Baron writes:

> Sharing their founder's aloofness from both state and nationality, the leaders of the early Judeo-Christian Church negated the paramount principle of the Greco-Roman world as well as that of Judaism. In this they adumbrated a synthesis of both—indeed went beyond both. . . . in contrast to Jesus the Galilean, Paul may be classified as the intellectual spokesman of Hellenistic Jewry, particularly of the type prevalent in Asia Minor. . . .
>
> From these travels and far-flung connections Paul gained wider horizons than those accessible to his average Palestinian confreres. As a rule, he thought in terms of World Jewry rather than in those of Palestine. From this standpoint, he was easily induced to abandon many revolutionary and communistic ingredients of the earlier movement. We recall how insignificant the social conflicts within the Diaspora communities were, as compared with their seething turbulence in Palestine. Similarly . . . there was a deep cleavage between the increasingly rebellious, anti-Roman mood of the Palestinian masses and the strong imperial loyalties of Rome's other Jewish subjects.[34]

Paul's solution foreshadows Martin Luther's fifteen hundred years later. He pronounces that every soul is subject to the creator, as there is no power and authority on earth but God's. The powers that be on earth have been established by God; therefore anyone opposing authority in reality opposes the arrangements established by God. Religion is thus internalized to the domain of faith. A door was thereby opened to submission to temporal authority and to the acceptance of existing reality, while reserving an avenue for an introverted retreat from it into an inner world. Such a retreat may result in a revolutionary or an ascetic negation of authority—both of which were realized in the course of the centuries. At any rate, in this manner the almost impenetrable barrier between politics and the caste-community was breached. As Baron notes,

> Even full-fledged Jews in his country must have felt the yoke of the law much more heavily than the Jews of Palestine. Those among them who were recent proselytes suffered from it to a still higher degree. It may be taken for granted that many of these Diaspora Jews, like the Galilean "am ha'aretz," could not adhere strictly to the rigid law. Perhaps the poor among them, including slaves and hired workers, often had to disregard dietary laws, the laws of the Sabbath, and other regulations. Such religious transgressors were deeply troubled, their conscience told them that they were sinners....
>
> For all these, probably constituting a majority of the Jewish people in Asia Minor and neighboring countries, Paul found a formula. All of you are Jews, he told them, as long as you believe in the spiritual tenets of Judaism. For a time the ritual law in all its ramifications was necessary, but with the advent of the messiah, "who had already come," it was nullified. Faith has now taken the place of the law.... Using the terminology of Jeremiah and of Philo, he substituted the circumcision of the heart for the circumcision of the flesh. Here was the symbol of the new covenant between man and God. In one word, the law had been abolished, and with it its bearer, the Jewish national group. Israel in the flesh had been replaced by a more univeral body of men, Israel in the spirit.[35]

The struggle of the monotheistic religions for domination of the Roman Empire was decided, as Baron states, by the mass conversion of Hellenistic Jewry to Christianity. The pagan empire recognized that Christianity was the decisive rising force and it therefore for centuries directed its efforts not against Judaism but against Christianity. Christianity prevailed wherever Jewish communities existed. The western reaches of the empire, where Jews were sparse, as well as rural areas, held out longest against its encroachment.

The reversal in the empire's attitude toward Christianity should be ascribed to the empire's crisis during the third century. The crisis, which started after the death of Alexander Severus in 234 and lasted until the beginning of the next century, involved civil wars, bitter struggles between many claimants to the imperial throne, and barbarian invasions. The disintegrative processes that resulted intensified the feeling that a unifying ideology was needed, since under such conditions particularistic paganism acted as a disruptive factor in the imperial fabric. Even prior to the adoption by Constantine in 312 of Christianity as the preferred religion of the empire, the vestiges of republicanism had faded away, and the rule of the emperors became absolutely autocratic. In 282, even the pretense that the emperor was a public appointee was abolished—Aurelian adopted the title "Dominus," and his style of government came to resemble Oriental absolutism.[36]

With the triumph of Christianity and its adoption as the Roman Empire's preferred religion, most of Hellenistic Jewry disappeared. Whereas before that development most Jews lived within the confines of the Roman Empire, after the victory of Christianity Palestine and Babylonia became Judaism's centers, although previously only a minority of the Jewish people had lived there. The majority of Jews seceded from or were rejected by the rabbinical community and joined the more open and dynamic religion that had developed out of Judaism and had created a synthesis with Hellenism. According to Baron, the decline in the number of Jews was dramatic, and little was left of the large Jewish communities of the west. He quotes Jerome's triumphant exultation that "not one in ten" had been left of the Jews.

It is no wonder that such a profound, mutual hatred developed between Judaism and its triumphant offshoot. It was from the start a fraternal hatred, which is the worst kind. When the Christian Church claimed to be "the true Israel," it was not only a doctrinal claim. On one hand this claim was based on the deliberate choice of a great part, perhaps the majority, of the Jewish people, and on the other hand it was based on its expulsion from the Jewish community by the rabbinical establishment.

That establishment reacted to the Great Schism much like the Yahwistic priesthood had previously: it sought to preserve its status and authority by preserving the Halachic-ritual basis of that authority and of the communal institutions formed around it. It appears, then, that the Pharisee establishment, crystallized in the institution of the rabbinate and in the exegetes of the oral law, the Tanna'im and Amora'im, came to the conclusion that extension by proselytism carries with it the danger of schism and heresy. World power achieved by such extension, they concluded, is not worth the risk of the challenge to rabbinical authority raised by Hellenistic Jewry and its typical representative, Paul. "Proselytes are a curse to Israel," as the rabbis put it. They preferred a small but well-disciplined and tightly knit, closely fenced-in community to a religion with millions of members, many of whom were half Jewish or less, whose various sects interpreted the Torah as they saw fit, lacking a unified authority. Circumstances now made it easier for the rabbis to develop this policy, which essentially was a reversion to the exclusivistic approach of Ezra and Nehemiah.

After the suppression of the Bar Kochba Rebellion, the emperors refrained from further interference in the internal affairs of the Jewish community in Palestine, which reverted to being just another Jewish community under the rule of the Nessi'im, without national traits. Obviously, they believed that the community no longer constituted a political danger. With the spread of Christianity, they even supported Judaism in efforts to stem the tide. On the other hand, within the confines of the Jewish community, secessionist sects were no longer tolerated. Before the rabbinical establishment became the sole authority over the Jews of Palestine, with the backing of the Roman overlords, it could not deny various sects such as the Essenes and the Christians the right to define themselves as Jews. But now the rabbinical establishment became the final arbiter in anything dealing with the Jewish community's affairs and the shaper of all its institutions. The rules of proselytization were made much harsher. A special ceremony was devised for the purpose, whereas none existed before. Special steps were undertaken to draw a sharp distinction between Jews and Christians, such as a prohibition on fasting on Sundays and the suspension of the daily reading of the Decalogue in the synagogues. This measure was adopted because the leaders of the church rejected all the laws of the Torah except the Decalogue. The suspension of its reading was meant to emphasize the equal value and weight of all parts of the Torah.[37]

After the adoption of Christianity as the state religion, it was established as principle (also adhered to in the Persian Empire, which held to the Zoroastrian religion) that it must not be imposed forcibly on the Jews, although conversion was welcomed. The Jews, as noted previously, were also the only group in Christian Europe permitted as a rule to hold to their separate religion. Jewish exclusivity also availed itself of the policy of religious separatism adopted by the later Roman emperors, in contrast to the uniformization efforts of their predecessors, for fear that Christianity might become "contaminated" by pagan and Jewish influences. Gradually there emerged in imperial society corporate bodies organized on the basis of religion (which, in the course of time, became embodied in the Ottoman "millet" system), with internal jurisdiction and taxation rights. The rabbis welcomed these developments, since they enabled them to fortify the fences around the community they led. The success of the Christian communities in wresting privileges and concessions from the imperial authorities helped the Jewish communities in wresting similar rights. The prevalent use by the Christian communities of the weapon of excommunication encouraged such use among the Jewish communities, too, and reinforced the position of the rabbinate within them, thus silencing any opposition to its authority.

The spread of Christianity, involving schisms, heresies, and violent religious disputes, such as Arianism, Nestorianism, Monophysitism, etc., down to our own day, is typical of a dynamic and growing creed, constantly renewing and enriching its contents, as Judaism had done during its great period of growth. The process of crystallization of Judaism, finally fixed with the Mishnah and the Talmud, aimed on the other hand at freezing the orthodoxy and defending it from all sides. The tension between the universalistic and the seclusive elements in Judaism, which emerged almost from the moment it was first formed in Babylonia, was then resolved by the Great Schism that occurred within it. The universalistic prophecies of Second Isaiah and Zechariah were finally realized in Christianity. Indeed, one may perhaps interpret the main development of the Halacha, which took place at this period, with its overwhelming proliferation of laws and regulations governing almost any move of the pious Jew's life, as a constant struggle of the keepers of the tradition to curb and contain the universalistic potential of Judaism, to postpone and prevent the day on which "my house shall be called a house of prayer for all peoples" (Isaiah 56: 7). By raising walls and barriers beyond reason and measure, beyond any rational explanation, they attempted to inhibit and stultify the original impetus derived from the later prophecy, an impetus that had already led to one enormous explosion within Judaism and that might erupt in the future again (as indeed has happened as a result of the work of universalistic thinkers, visionaries, and warriors such as Spinoza, Marx, Freud, and Trotsky).

One may also venture a surmise that Judaism's success in inhibiting the essential impulse of the monotheistic idea, without which monotheism becomes self-contradictory, was perhaps the cause of the petrification of historical Judaism, of the fact that the Jewish God reassumed the traits of a tribal deity. God, as imagined in the terms of Orthodox Judaism, is interested only in the fate of the orthodox community, not in humanity at large or the cosmos. Devout Jewry is no longer monotheistic in the strict sense of the term, but monolatrous. It is a fact that every period of cultural blossoming in Jewish history (the "Golden Age" in Spain, for example, or the efflorescence that took place in recent generations in Germany and the United States) was accompanied by a loosening of Halachic strictures, by a reaching toward universality.

Canonic Judaism expelled any individual or group daring to challenge the absolute authority of the Halacha and its interpreters. First were the Samaritans and the Hellenizers, then the Sadduccees, Essenes, Christians, Karaites, Sabbataians, and Frankists—all ejected. Hasidism, originally on the verge of being expelled by the orthodox, was the only reform movement Orthodox Judaism did accommodate itself to, even though very reluctantly. Thus the people "was preserved" without any change, as a kind of "historical fossil," to use Toynbee's unsympathetic but apt phrase. The spiritual content of Judaism became almost synonymous with the keeping and study of the Halacha and with the preservation of the communal structure conditional on it. In reality, then, the "preservation of the people" is nothing but the preservation of the authority of the orthodoxy in the community. Judaism, from the time it assumed its definitive form, avoids raising the "why" questions. It organized a cohesive way of life and social structure, and the whys and wherefores, which are the fructifying, revolutionary questions, are, by definition, prohibited.

But these very characteristics provided Judaism with its tremendous powers of resistance. It has dissociated itself from history and owes no explanation of it to its adherents. The historical state is a state of exile, from which the messiah shall deliver us. The immensely detailed body of the

Halacha is intelligible as a result of this state of stasis: the more a consciousness loses its contact with reality, the more there develop ritual and hairsplitting systems to form a bridge between consciousness and reality. Therefore all the disasters that befall the Jews in exile need no explanation, except the primary one that the exile was caused by Israel's sins. Thus a closed, self-reinforcing psychological structure is formed, first diagnosed by Nietzsche in *The Genealogy of Morals*: disaster is the proof of sin, instead of being a reason for questioning the ways of the creator, as Job did. Therefore the greater the suffering, the more intense is the sense of guilt. And to justify, in turn, this sense of guilt, a limitless system of prohibitions and taboos is elaborated, any infringement of which becomes a deadly sin. One can hardly breathe without transgressing against some of them, feeling as a result that one's very existence is sinful and deserving any punishment.

The community's divorce from history and its consequent petrification constitute a victory over becoming and decay. The community can exist in this permanent, unchanging form almost everywhere, in any society or age. It changes in its relation to the changing outside world, but internally it preserves its age-old institutions and outlook. Time hardly has any power over it. But this relative immortality is purchased at the cost of evading the mature responsibility for a full social existence, as an independent sovereign entity, bearing the full political, military, economic, technological, and intellectual weight that a sovereign existence entails, paying the price of the risk of decline and death. A full life is inseparable from death. Only a suspended, frozen existence can last indefinitely. The Jewish caste community can be destroyed, can disappear, but it does not change, decay, and die like an organic entity.

The community's divorce from history also means a divorce from those engaged in history, the non-Jews who are subsumed under the general term *gentiles* (or *goyim*). The result is a barrier of estrangement between those who are within history and those who are outside it. Neither can understand the other any longer. Their motivations become incomprehensible to each other. Both begin to doubt their common humanity. It is strange to hear a Yemenite and a Polish Jew speaking of the *goyim* among whom they had dwelt in the same tone of contempt mixed with estrangement, fear, and hostility, to the point that it seems that they refer to the very same *goy*, even though a Polish Catholic peasant and a Muslim nomad of the Arabian peninsula are as distant and different as human beings can be. The closed-in structure of the Jewish community also creates a uniform picture of the external world, which appears to be a vague and brutal chaos, lacking any clear distinguishing features.

The image of the gentile, then, is not a true likeness but a reflection of the preconceived patterns imaging him, shaped by the tradition. The gentile, for his part, reacts with equal alienation to this closed psychosocial system, which conceives of him as part of an essentially foreign existential framework, not a human being in his own right. Just as he becomes a stereotype in the view of the Jew looking out at the surrounding world, the Jew appears to him as a stereotype, with his unhistorical existence within his communal framework. To this is added, in the Christian world, the ancient rivalry and hostility between Christianity and Judaism. But this is not the decisive factor. Jewish aloofness exists also in the Muslim world (although there it is not accompanied by the ancient religious enmity, which may be the main cause of anti-Semitism).

The Jewish community's powers of resistance were forged by its elaborate system of charities and communal support institutions, by its emphasis on a sense of collectivity, providing each individual with a feeling of firm psychological and social support, but at the cost of his abdication of his individuality and intellectual independence. This was achieved by means of a system of rules and regulations that in previous centuries were often much more rational and humane than those of the surrounding world. Indeed, despite the inferior status of the Jews in medieval Europe, the Jewish individual was often much more protected against the vagaries and arbitrariness of the authorities and from the dangers of poverty and starvation, thanks to the community's systems of protection and charity, than a Christian individual who was not a member of the aristocracy or the clergy. The feeling that the external world is a barbarous chaos was often highly realistic. Also, there is no doubt that in former ages Jewish individuals had many more opportunities to develop their minds, thanks to the community's educational system, providing a minimal education to every member, than the vast majority of the gentile population, which was illiterate. The sense of solidarity and social warmth generated by these factors, much more than any passionate belief, preserved the community through all the strains and shocks it had undergone down to the modern age. But when the general level of education and civilization exceeded that of the community, it could not stop its members from forsaking it.

PART ONE

The Emergence of the New Jewish Nationalism

ONE

Zionist Theory
and Its Problems

There are scholars who, as a result of considerations discussed in the prologue, argue that the term *Jewish nation* is meaningless, that the Jews are a
religious sect and nothing more. But what of the indubitably national traits
developed by the Jewish community in Palestine between its return from
Babylonian exile and its decay and final disappearance during the waning
of the Byzantine period and the beginning of the Muslim era? And what of
the national traits of the Yemeni and Khazar kingdoms, which were also
Jewish? How, indeed, can we reconcile the antinational phenomena in Judaism discussed in the prologue with the emergence of a distinct Jewish nation in Eastern Europe? To find the answer, we shall examine one of the
most highly developed Jewish national doctrines, Zionism, investigate its
problems and contradictions, and try to draw our independent conclusions.

Zionism, as formulated in the late nineteenth and early twentieth century, mainly by Moses Hess, Judah Loeb Pinsker, Achad Ha'am, Theodor
Herzl, and Dov Ber Borochov, is based on the following main tenets:

- The Jews throughout the world constitute a single nation, and the
  bond that connects them is essentially national, not religious. It may
  also be claimed that in the case of the Jews the national is inseparable
  from the religious. The religious is a manifestation of a national essence that also has other expressions, such as a common Jewish mentality. Depending on the historical situations it finds itself in, the national "self" assumes various forms, including the religious. This
  "self" is the "being," the "substance," of Judaism.
- Every "normal" nation has its own national territory. That the Jewish
  nation does not is an anomaly. This anomaly is the cause of anti-Semitism, which is but the natural reaction of "normal" nations to a seemingly disembodied apparition, contrary to the laws of nature (cf.
  Pinsker's *Auto-Emancipation*). Anti-Semitism notwithstanding, the
  natural inclination of a community existing in an abnormal situation
  is to return to normalcy. In the case of the Jews, that would mean an
  inclination to acquire or reappropriate a territory of its own. And in-

deed, throughout the centuries of exile, the fathers of Zionism claim, the Jews never ceased to long for their ancestral land, as expressed in their prayers and their festivals.

- A further cause of anti-Semitism is that modern national movements have an innate tendency toward homogeneity, which involves a rejection of alien elements. The Jews, as an alien national body, were able somehow to exist within prenational feudal societies or even under the rule of enlightened absolutism, but there is no place for them within modern national societies. Borochov, a Zionist-Marxist, propounded another version of this point. He argued that the formation of the modern nation, which is synonymous with the emergence of bourgeois society, creates autochthonous middle classes that try to replace the Jews in their middleman role. Anti-Semitism then becomes the ideology of the petty and middle bourgeoisie, serving to mobilize the lower classes—which otherwise might have turned against the bourgeoisie—to create a common front against the Jewish middle classes. The Jews, ejected from their previous social roles, become a "lumpen bourgeoisie," a bourgeoisie of rags, parallel to the "lumpen proletariat." That, according to Borochov, is the origin of the "Jewish problem." Previous Jewish existence, though often accompanied by great suffering, had not constituted a "problem."

- As a result of the preceding tenets, the Jewish people must reassemble in a territory of its own, the most suitable being its ancient homeland, Palestine, where the nation was born and its culture formed. The Jewish people's right to the country is proved by its devotion to it, in custom and ritual, throughout the ages that it was kept expelled from it by conquerors and oppressors. Only in that country can it become a "normal" nation again. There is a profound, even a mystical, connection between this people and this land. In Palestine, Eretz Israel, freed from the distorting pressures of the Diaspora, the true, liberated Jewish culture will reveal itself. In it will rise the new, true Jew, a direct descendant of the ancient Jew who lived in his own land.

From an ideological point of view, Zionism was an answer to what has been defined as the failure of assimilation. This failure was made clear by the outbreak of pogroms in Russia in the early 1880s and by the contemporaneous rise of anti-Semitic movements in Germany and France. The Zionists argued that the Jews are unassimilable and will always be rejected by gentile society. Therefore, they maintained, Jewishness is not a matter of choice, of a decision to be Jewish, but an unavoidable destiny. Even if a Jew tries to shake himself loose of it, the world will force him back into it by its hostility and contempt. In certain cases, far-reaching conclusions were drawn about a different human quality of the Jew, as though Jews and gentiles belong to different branches of the human family, "circumcised and uncircumcised," as the nationalist Hebrew poet Uri Zvi Greenberg put it.

That, of course, was also the perspective, in reverse, of the racist anti-Semites, particularly the Nazis.

Zionism fed on the steady growth of ninteenth- and early twentieth-century European anti-Semitism. Not only did "progress" fail to solve the Jewish problem, the Zionists argued, but in certain respects it even aggravated it. As various Zionist thinkers pointed out, the appearance of the masses on the historical stage, welcomed by progressive thinkers, was often accompanied by an intensification of hatred of the Jews. The rise of modern anti-Semitism in the new secular national state, the Zionists claimed, was conclusive proof that the Jews constituted a separate nation. Otherwise, anti-Semitism would be completely unintelligible in political frameworks that had renounced religion as the ultimate and obligatory test of social identity. Assimilationists' claims that anti-Semitism is a result of Jewish difference from the norm have been refuted by the new variants of anti-Semitism that are aimed mainly against the assimilationists, who did try to obliterate this difference. The Zionists argued that membership in the nation, the foundation of the modern national state, is based not only on common citizenship and the removal of religious affiliations from the public domain but also is connected with much deeper and more organic ethnic affinities. The political state is only the formal expression of these affinities, to which the Jews are alien. As the dynamism of the modern nation-state—as distinct from the relatively static conditions of feudal and postfeudal societies—strives at ever clearer definitions and expression of the national personality, it will render the condition of the Jews within it ever more untenable. The ethnically based national state will sooner or later be forced, by the very logic of its being, to eject the Jews from it, or at least to limit their number to a point at which they would no longer be an irritant to the national organism. Every nation apparently has a saturation point, beyond which it cannot absorb more Jews. Once this point is reached, violent anti-Semitic reactions ensue.

The supreme vindication of the Zionist thesis, allegedly, comes from the two most traumatic events of modern Jewish history: the massacre of thousands of Russian, mainly Ukrainian, Jews by the White armies in the Russian civil war (1918–1921) and the Nazi extermination. These events seemed to demonstrate that the Jewish Diaspora had no future, that the catastrophic predictions of Herzl and Max Nordau had proved true as far as European Jews were concerned, and were also valid for any other Jewish community. The Russian revolution and the establishment of a Communist-Marxist regime had not eradicated anti-Semitism in the Soviet Union, the argument ran. And if Germany—the most highly developed nation in Europe, the land of Kant and Goethe, Bach and Beethoven—was capable of perpetrating such horrors, how much more so were less-civilized nations.

Regarding the primary assumption of Zionism—that Judaism is basically national—Herzl wrote in *Der Judenstaat:* "We are a nation, one nation." To this he added: "The enemy, by no volition of ours, forces us to be a nation." The implication is that Herzl did not consider Jewish nationhood as voluntary but as the result of external pressure, forcing a group that is not necessarily a nation to become one. Herzl made no attempt to define any distinguishing trait of the group, except to state that the Jews had already "lost their capacity to become assimilated" by the Middle Ages. But that is circular reasoning. How did the Jews lose their capacity to become assimilated? And did they have it prior to the Middle Ages? If their being a "nation" is the cause, Herzl claims that this is a result of external pressure and not the primary cause. The riddle remains unanswered, and in vain do we search Herzl's writings for a more serious discussion of the nature and character of the Jewish people. But this question, which in Herzl's time would have seemed an exercise in futile quibbling in view of the frightful Jewish misery, assumed meaning and actuality three generations later, after his predictions were borne out far more horribly than he ever envisaged—and then the pressure eased off.

We find a relatively systematic development of the national thesis in the works of Achad Ha'am. Under the influence of Darwin's and Spencer's biologism, Achad Ha'am conceived of the Jewish people as a biological organism which, motivated by the "will to exist," devises spiritual "instruments" adapted to its historical conditions. Religion is but one of the survival devices created by the national genius. Judaism consists of more than religion; it consists of all the cultural assets which the Jewish people have ever created. Therefore, not only can an atheist be a good Jew; in a certain sense, if he is a nationalist, he can be a better Jew than the devout believer, who denies the national essence of Judaism.

Achad Ha'am maintained that the Jewish people's main cultural creativity took place in Palestine, when they were a healthy nation living on their own soil. During the Diaspora, culture and religion atrophied. A spiritual rebirth will take place, he claimed, only if a part of the people becomes reestablished in the ancient homeland. The resultant spiritual health will revivify the entire far-flung Diaspora. Furthermore, he believed, the Jewish people's "will to exist" was not merely a will to exist for its own sake, like the will of other biological units, but had an end—the establishment of justice and morality on earth.

It is safe to say that Achad Ha'am's teachings have been refuted, although some of his empirical observations have proved more trenchant than those of many of the "political" Zionists. Yehezkel Kaufmann, one of the most important Zionist thinkers, rejects completely the crude analogy between a living individual and a social organism. Achad Ha'am, he says, ascribes to the "will to exist" miraculous properties, such as the divination of historical developments in advance and the preparation of "spiritual devices" in time to deal with them. Biologism, he points out, separates the national essence from its historical manifestations, thereby creating an arbitrary mystification. There is no such thing as an abstract, disembodied "will to exist" of "a national organism." The national "will to exist" is in reality the common desire of concrete individuals to coexist within a cultural framework formed by historical circumstances. There is no such thing as a biological connection with historical modes of existence, with a language or a literature or a country or a national-historical "being."

> The empirical fact, that the Jewish people has always considered its religious being as the sole reason for its struggle to keep its identity, is of decisive importance for the solution of the problem. Not an external factor [like anti-Semitism] nor an alleged biological will to exist, but the unique power embodied in the Jewish religious culture, created for it a special place among the nations. The religion in the name of which the Jewish people separated itself from all other peoples, and which the people *thought* to be the basis of its existence, was really and truly the basis of that existence. The proof of the matter is indeed the fact that all Jews who had abandoned their religion, voluntarily or under duress, were absorbed by the gentiles. . . . It was religion and nothing else which separated the Jews from the rest of humanity.[1]

As for Achad Ha'am's claim to a Jewish morality superior to other peoples', Kaufmann retorts that each nation has its own moral character and excellence, and the Jews are not superior in their morals and sense of justice to any other people. The familiar figure of the Jewish shady dealer shows that in business ethics, for instance, the Jews are far inferior to some other peoples. The difference between Jews and non-Jews is not moral but religious. Christianity or Islam can also serve as a basis for a superior morality.

Borochov took for granted that the Jews were a people and not a religion. In his essay "Zionism and Territorialism," published during the Uganda controversy (1903–1905), he discussed the possibility of the Arabs of Palestine being assimilated by Jewish immigrants, ignoring completely the religious problem—obviously, in his mind, of secondary importance—that might ensue.[2] The essay leads one to conclude that if Jews can absorb members of other religions and ethnic groups, the definition of the Jewish people must basically be national, not religious.

Borochov did make several attempts to define the Jewish people. In his essay "Problems of Zionist Theory," for example, he states that the Jews are "outsiders" wherever they are and are incapable of becoming assimilated.[3] As I have shown in the prologue, this statement is historically false, the result of short-term empirical observation. Even so, Borochov's statement does point to the disappearance of a positive religious basis for a separate Jewish identity. According to Borochov, Jews are outsiders because they do not possess landed assets, and it is the eagerness to share ownership of these assets that could motivate the majority group to be interested in assimilation. This materialistic interpretations may impress at first sight, but it is utterly without substance. Borochov evades the question of what makes Jews outsiders *as a group*. After all, many non-Jews, like the proletariat or the urban middle classes, also lack landed assets or any assets whatsoever, yet they did not become outsiders. Apparently the backward, agrarian Russian environment, where most people (after the emancipation of the serfs) had some landed property, influenced Borochov, despite his Marxist sophistication.

In another essay, Borochov argues that the difference between Jews and non-Jews is rooted in physical traits (racial thories were quite fashionable at the time). In an effort to explain why the Jews were ousted by the new native bourgeoisie, he says that it happened because the new bourgeoisie is "flesh of the flesh" of the people. To Borochov, then, the national group is a sort of extended kinship group, a "blood community." But such a definition can apply only to a tribe, not to a nation. The modern nation is not based on kinship but on generally applicable standards such as a common language or tradition. The Russian people, for example, is a mixture of Slav and Tartar tribes, to which were added over the years Scandinavian and German-Baltic aristocracies. The English people consists of layer upon layer of Celts, Romans, Angles, Saxons, Vikings, Normans, French Huguenots, etc.

But these questions about the nature and definition of the Jewish people did not interest Borochov any more than they did Herzl. Borochov took for granted that the Jews are a "people"; his analysis is aimed at prognostication and solution, at explaining the misery of this people and finding a way to improve matters. The Jews, he points out, fulfill middleman functions in their countries of sojourn and are not engaged in basic production. The branches of production they do engage in are of secondary economic importance. Also, they do not function as laborers, engineers, or proprietors; nor do they engage in agriculture, mining, or heavy industry. The rise of the local bourgeoisie squeezes them out, impoverishes them, and creates an uprooted bourgeoisie of rags. To think that "progress" will solve these problems is rootless idealistic liberalism. In any case, even before the free classless society is established, a solution must be found for the immediate, intolerable misery.

The Jews, Borochov argues, are becoming redundant in the East European socioeconomic system. Moreover, "by the counterfeiting of assets, by degeneration and decay the Jews are becoming not just redundant, but an antisocial, pernicious element."[4] Their emigration to countries such as the United States and Argentina will not improve matters much, since sooner or later, with the development of the economy and industry of these countries and the rise of an autochthonous middle class, the story of Eastern Europe will repeat itself. The only solution, he concludes, is emigration to a backward, sparsely settled country with primitive agriculture and no industry. In this country, Jews themselves can then develop industry and agriculture, engage in primary production, and fill all social strata and functions. The "overturning of the occupational pyramid" was essential for the healing and for the physical salvation of the Jewish people.

This analysis—adopted by the Zionist labor movement, which concluded from it that Jews could not continue to exist in the Diaspora and must inevitably be concentrated in Eretz Israel—has not been borne out by history. First, the emigration of Jews from backward countries in the primary stages of capitalist development to the highly developed capitalist countries of the West has shown that these Western economies are capable of absorbing much larger numbers of immigrants than the backward economies that have ejected them. These countries already have their own developed bourgeoisie, who have little to fear from Jewish rivals. The prediction that the process experienced by Russian Jewry would be repeated in the United States ignored the fact that the United States was already much more highly developed than Russia and that its bourgeoisie, from inception, fulfilled a pioneering and revolutionary role. The Jews were not the first to undertake middleman and entrepreneuring roles in the United State, and there was no need to shoulder them aside to clear the way for a new indigenous middle class.

The main fallacy in Borochov's argument seems to be that his reasoning was based on conditions in East Europe, where opportunities were severely circumscribed in comparison to the dynamic growth of the local bourgeois elements that wished to exploit them. It was this pressure that caused the ouster of the Jews from their socioeconomic roles.

Moreover, in the highly developed countries, the part of the population engaged in primary agricultural production shrank drastically, the industrial proletariat shrank more moderately, and the main emphasis shifted from heavy industry to consumer-oriented industries and services. This was accompanied by enormous growth in the proportion of the working intelligentsia, professionals of all kinds, who applied new labor-saving methods that made possible the reduction of the proportion of the population engaged in primary production. Even primary production became dependent on a sophisticated, well-trained labor force. Tolstoy's illiterate *moujik* would be a dead weight in a modern agricultural system.

The whole occupational pyramid in developed industrial nations has thus been overturned and has come ever more to approximate the Jewish occupational structure—in which most Jews belong to the working intelligentsia—rather than the other way around. Phenomena such as the *Gastarbeiter*—the unskilled or semiskilled foreign workers who perform more and more of the manual and menial tasks in the countries of the West and who can be dismissed overnight from their jobs—show that in many respects the workers in primary production have a much shakier foothold in the social structure than members of the middle classes. As a result, the present-day position of the Jews in the United States, Britain, and France is completely at variance with the Borochovian prognosis.

The vulgarization of Borochov's work in Israel and the indiscriminate fusing of it with the teachings of A. D. Gordon, the Tolstoyan extoller of physical agricultural labor as a source of spiritual renewal, has blurred one of Borochov's most incisive insights: that the Jews of Eastern Europe were at the time *dissociated* from the main economic activities, not only as workers but also as executives, capitalists, and entrepreneurs. Not only did they not participate in agriculture and heavy industry; they did not participate in modern marketing and banking, either. In short, they were marginal.

In *The Origins of Totalitarianism*, Hannah Arendt traces the decline of the importance of Jewish capital in the European economic system, which was paralleled by the development of the national state (she follows mainly Western and Middle European processes, whereas Borochov dealt with East European problems), emphasizing that this capital was mainly financial and served as an instrument of state policy, not as capitalistic-entrepreneuring capital.[5] The Rothschilds, for example, rose to prominence not as founders of industrial empires but as floaters of loans to princes and governments and as manipulators of the capital markets.

In this respect the Jews have not yet become fully integrated into the central economic activities of Western countries, particularly of the United States. They have achieved only a limited penetration of the metallurgical, machine, and chemical industries and of major banking. But they have acquired a dominant position in the U.S. academic world and are well integrated into the professions, the media, entertainment, and management, and they have established vast marketing organizations. They are also substantially represented in new sophisticated industries such as electronics and computers. In short, Jews are among the most powerful, best-integrated and wealthy groups in the United States, Britain, and France, and by no means can they be described as redundant or marginal.

Borochov's doctrine is the Marxist aspect of a tenet most Zionists share—that in the long run the development of radical anti-Semitism wherever Jews live is inevitable, and that it is therefore necessary to gather them all in Israel. Borochov tried to find a sociological, rational explanation for Pinsker's insight about the hostility of the well-rooted "gentiles" to the disembodied Jewish "ghost," a hostility that could only be eradicated by the Jews' return to their territorial base. But the number of historical factors is so immense, their possible combinations so incalculable, that the "inevitabilty of radical anti-Semitism" argument is highly dubious and unhistorical. There is a far greater probability that the Jewish Diaspora, having existed for some 2,500 years under an almost incalculable variety of conditions, could continue to exist for many centuries more.

Predictions that in the long run Jewish existence in the Diaspora is impossible are then meaningless as long as no time limit is set. Political, technological, economic, and social changes are so rapid and numerous in today's world that it is difficult to imagine what life will be like even ten years from now. If predictions made ninety years ago have not yet been fulfilled, it can easily be said that they are no longer valid.

Some space must be devoted, however, to the Holocaust, which Zionism claims is the conclusive vindication of its arguments. The Holocaust, the Zionists claim, is the highest stage of anti-Semitism, an inevitable and logical outcome of the development of nationalism in Christian countries (some include Islamic countries as well). The very fact that Germany was such a highly developed and civilized country with only a small, mostly assimilated Jewish population leads to the formulation of a basic law: as countries reach Germany's level of civilization, they will develop the same policy toward their Jews.

But anti-Semitism manifested itself in most European countries during the last century irrespective of their level of development, although primarily in close association with the reactionary elements in them (as during the reign of Nicholas II in Russia or during the rise of Boulangerism in France). From its inception, as Arendt notes in *The Origins of Totalitarianism*, anti-Semitism bore the marks of an "Internationale."[6] It appeared in both backward Russia and Romania and in advanced, liberal France (although in France it was never codified in the law of the land, except during the Vichy period, when anti-Jewish legislation was inspired by the victorious Germans). Nor can one compare the covert anti-Semitism in Soviet society, where it was banned by law, to the official anti-Semitism of the tsarist regime—and the former Soviet Union was far more developed than old Russia. Britain, which for more than a century led the world in its economic, social, and political devlopment, never developed an anti-Semitic movement, although the individual Englishman may be just as anti-Semitic as the individual Frenchman. There is no direct correlation between individual anti-Semitic inclinations and a public anti-Semitic policy. The average German during the 1920s was not more anti-Semitic than the average Frenchman, and definitely less than the average Pole.

The claim that anti-Semitism is a reaction to assimilation is equally flawed. The Russian pogroms were aimed against traditionalist Jews, and only rarely did they touch the more affluent neighborhoods where the assimilated lived. Furthermore, in Italy, where assimilation went perhaps further than in any other European country, there was no anti-Semitism, and Jews rose to prominence even in the fascist regime, until Mussolini was forced by Nazi pressure to enact anti-Jewish legislation. (In spite of this, the fascist authorities saved many Jews from the Nazis.)

Another Zionist argument claims that Jews are always hurt by political or economic upheavals to a far greater degree than the rest of the population and therefore should be protected from them in a country of their own. But this argument is also fallacious. The religious wars that rent Europe asunder during the seventeenth century and caused the deaths of over a third of the German people did not affect the Jews more than they did the rest of the population. The shocks that Russia underwent as a result of the Westernization policy of Peter the Great and his successors hardly affected the Jews. Nor were the Jews affected by the Napoleonic wars or by Napoleon's invasion of Russia (as a matter of fact, wherever Napoleon's armies arrived, the condition of the Jews improved, for the French authorities immediately legislated the legal equality of all members of the population).

The claim that Europe united in the Nazi campaign of annihilation of the Jews is utterly perverse. This "unity" was imposed by military conquest, and nobody can claim that it was the result of a European general will. That many people in the occupied countries—and in the notoriously anti-Semitic ones their number was much higher, with Ukraine perhaps the most infamous example—helped the Nazis in the destruction of the Jews does not prove this "unity." There were enough collaborators with the Nazis in other fields, too, without this proving that the occupied nations approved of them.

It is worthwhile noting that the process of assimilation in German lands, as well as the decline of the Jewish birthrate, had reached such proportions that at the time of Hitler's rise to power Germany had only 500,000 Jews, many of them *ostjuden* who had migrated from Slavic lands in the East. Germany's "Jewish problem" was in the process of being "solved." In 1911, of every one hundred Jewish women fifty years old or older, two had converted to Christianity, twenty-two had remained single or childless, three had given birth to illegitimate children, eighteen had married non-Jews, and the fifty-five who had married Jews had given birth to only 118 children. German Jewry was no longer reproducing itself biologically. Throughout the nineteenth century, the Jewish birthrate was lower than the Christian. The average number of children per married Jewish couple between 1875 and 1880 had been 4.2. Between 1920 and 1926, the average had declined to 1.69. Mixed marriages amounted in 1901 to 16.9 per hundred. In 1929 the proportion rose to 59 per hundred. There was also a drastic decline in the number of organized Jewish communities. At the beginning of the twentieth century there were still some 2,300 organized Jewish communities in Germany. By 1933 the number had dropped to 1,600. The figures for Austria, Czechoslovakia, and Hungary (but not for the Austrian areas annexed to Poland after World War I) show a similar pattern.[7] These findings invalidate the assumption that the Holocaust had "Borochovian" causes. And since German Jewry was in reality decreasing not increasing, they also invalidate the Zionist tenet that anti-Semitism is generated (or aggravated) when the number of Jews in any country exceeds a certain proportion of the population. (For further development of this argument, see chapter 4.)

A Holocaust-type occurrence is not then the result of an "organic" anti-Semitic development, a steady, evolutionary growth of anti-Semitism to the point where Jews are squeezed out completely. Such a situation has never materialized anywhere. A Holocaust-type situation comes about as a result of a comprehensive sociopolitical crisis that demolishes all norms—including anti-Semitic norms (hardly any anti-Semites had thought of exterminating the Jews, or even of expelling them; their aim usually had been to curb the Jews' influence, and, in extreme cases, to limit their civil rights).

The Holocaust will be discussed in another chapter of this book. It should be emphasized here, however, that the "final solution to the Jewish question" was inseparable from global Nazi policy. True, the Nazis selected the Jews as their first candidates for annihilation, but the Gypsies were extirpated with equal thoroughness and much larger and more ambitious plans were afoot for the enslavement and piecemeal exterminaton of the Slavs (Soviet losses during World War II are estimated at twenty-five million people, only a minority of whom were soldiers). The death camps were not necessarily a war phenomenon but were meant to serve as "peacetime" institutions as well—putting into effect the "biological policy" of the Hitlerian "New Order," the final aim of which was the total elimination of "undesirable" races and the enslavement of the "inferior" ones (accompanied by the extermination of their elites).

The Zionist prognosis was confirmed, then, not as the outcome of a specific Jew-Gentile dynamic but rather as a result of a much wider catastrophe. A specific Jew-Gentile dynamic, in itself, could not have caused such results, as demonstrated both in anti-Semitic Poland of the 1930s and in the Dreyfus Affair in France. Nor did it happen in tsarist Russia, the gravest case of all by that time.

Neither has another Zionist prognosis, predicting the inevitable failure of assimilation, been borne out by the facts. True, assimilated Jews were murdered by the Nazis as thoroughly as those who held to the faith of their fathers. Also, Jews do encounter social barriers in most Christian countries even though none of them any longer exercises legal discrimination and in most cases these barriers are very subtle. But it is a moot point whether one can term a process not fully realized a failure. Not only Jews but other population groups also encounter social barriers in ethnically heterogeneous countries without it signifying the failure of their integration within the common *political* framework. We find that the barriers facing most racial-ethnic minorities in Western countries (such as African Americans and Hispanics in the United States) are much higher than in the case of the Jews.

Most American, French, and British Jews are descendants of East European immigrants, only two or three generations removed from the Russian-Polish "pale of settlement" and still holding to the shreds of a Jewish national consciousness. These new Western Jews are in effect halfway down the road traversed by earlier Jewish waves of immigration. (In England, the Spanish-Jewish immigration of the seventeenth century had almost completely assimilated into English society, leaving hardly a trace.) The rate of their assimilation is exemplified in that Benjamin Disraeli, in the first half of the last century, had already stepped outside the confines of the Jewish religious community. The elite group of this community, men like Lord Samuel and Lord Melchett, did indeed preserve their Jewish religious heritage, largely as a matter of pride, just as old aristocratic families tend to preserve ancient rituals and heirlooms, without their having much meaning in daily life.

We find a similar case among French Jewry. The old Jewish families who had lived in France, mainly Provence, since Roman times, augmented by

Jews escaping the Spanish Inquisition, have disappeared completely. Jews were indeed expelled in olden times from some of these areas, but in the main the Jewish population became completely assimilated in the surrounding population. "Newer" Jewish families, such as those originating in Alsace, have also in their turn been assimilated.

The process is fastest among the wealthier classes, while the poor are usually a bastion of conservatism. But sooner or later the process permeates all levels of the community, with a uniform result: the blurring and erasure of Jewish identity (except for a small group that participates fully in the host population's culture but is orthodox in its religion, as we find in certain German-Jewish circles, particularly those associated with Agudat Yisrael).

In the United States, owing to different conditions, the assimilation process took on another form than it had in Western Europe. The Spanish-Portugese Jewish immigrants to early America found there a fairly homogeneous white Anglo-Saxon Protestant culture, akin to the homogeneous national cultures of Europe. Like their brethren in Western Europe, they shed their traditional traits in order to merge with it. The same is true for the German-Jewish immigrants who followed in the middle of the nineteenth century, whose "money aristocracy," the Rosenwalds, Frankfurters, Oppenheimers, and Warburgs, easily merged with U.S. high society. Later, East European immigration preserved a group consciousness within the pluralistic U.S. society, but feels equally American. In it, too, 50 percent of marriages are mixed, just as in pre-Hitler Germany.

Any claim that assimilation must eventually end in an Auschwitz is unaccompanied by any convincing argument as to why what happened in Germany must happen elsewhere. From the examples cited, it is clear that in some places the process has reached its conclusion, the complete assimilation of the Jews in the surrounding population, without being attended by any anti-Semitic reaction. Clearly, then, assimilation has failed only in certain areas of Europe, and only within certain historical spans. In other areas, inhabited by most of the world's Jews, it is proceeding successfully.

TWO

Zionism

The Product of a
Unique Historical Situation

Yehezkel Kaufmann's *Golah ve'Nechar* (Diaspora and exile), is perhaps the most ambitious endeavor yet made to put the Zionist historical perspective on sound theoretical foundations. Kaufmann rejects the popular explanations and definitions of Jewishness. He finds the racial explanation, i.e., that the Jews constitute a separate race, untenable, since Jewish law never forbade the admission of converts and a common racial origin never prevented the assimilation or loss of group identity of other peoples. He also finds the popular assumption that external anti-Jewish pressures forced group identity and exclusivity on the Jews unconvincing, since historical evidence shows that Jewish exclusivity and aloofness preceded outside hostility and were thus its cause, not its result. Kaufmann also rejects the socioeconomic explanation of group definition based on "the Jews as middlemen." Sociologically the Jews encountered little difficulty in assimilating with their non-Jewish class counterparts or once converted, in rising to the highest positions in the land.

The cause of Jewish distinctiveness, Kaufmann concludes, is the Jewish religion. But if the basic distinction is religious, how can Jewish nationalism be explained? To solve the riddle, Kaufmann propounds the existence of two parallel entities acting in a predetermined harmony: a Jewish national group fused with a universal monotheistic religion (not a national religion, which would class it with the pagan ethnic cults). The Diaspora, he maintains, has caused an "ethnic deterioration" of the Jewish national group, and only a return to the "ancestral soil" can cure this malady. In the meantime, the Jewish communities in exile, the Jewish ghettos, were in reality miniature Jewish commonwealths, within which the Jews maintained "a full national existence" under their own laws.

But there is a contradiction here. Kaufmann points out that Jewish communities were always borne by host societies, that they never shared in political, military, administrative, or technological responsibilites, which are the basics of national existence. In addition, he insists that Jewish civilization is wholly religious.

In other words, contrary to Kaufmann's thesis, the Jewish communities maintained in reality religious community, not a national existence, and this community is incapable of existing without host societies. That is not "ethnic deterioration," as Kaufmann tries to argue, but simply an unsuitable definition of the nature of the Jewish people. If the one thing that truly distinguishes Jews from non-Jews is their religious culture and all that it involves, then this culture makes Jews a religious caste, in Weber's terminology, and nothing more. That this has nothing to do with "exile from the ancestral soil" is proved by the fact that the Jewish communities of the Old Yishuv, which existed in Palestine before Zionist settlement, were typical ghetto communities. The lack of any Jewish national traits is also proved by the fact, pointed out by Kaufmann himself, that despite all the persecution they had undergone, the Jews never tried to separate themselves from their host societies to settle on their own, as they could have done in the Americas and other new territories opened by European discovery, and as other persecuted groups did. Contrary to the claim that the ghetto constituted a national enclave, experience has shown that the Jews are capable of creating a national structure only when they break loose from the traditional religious community. "Exile" then is not an accident of Jewish history. It is the very essence of Jewish existence. The Jews carry it with them wherever they settle, even in the "ancestral soil" itself.

But our arguments against the tenet that the Jews are an exiled territorial nation seem to be contradicted by the fact that a Zionist national movement did arise, that it did develop a national-territorial ideology, that it did generate political power, that it did activate great masses of people and that it did establish a national state. Such a movement could never have arisen as a result of erroneous interpretations of Jewish history. It could only have developed on the basis of a national consciousness deriving from a national entity which did not previously exist; otherwise Zionism would also have previously existed.

To understand this development, we must take a close look at modern Jewish history. First, the myth that the Jews have always longed to return to the land of their ancestors must be renounced. In the words of the novelist A. B. Yehoshua,

During the 1800 years which have elapsed from the destruction of the Second Commonwealth until the beginning of Zionism, the [Jewish] people never made a serious, significant attempt to return to Eretz Israel and recover their lost independence. This people, which has displayed infinite resource, flexibility and cunning in order to penetrate almost anywhere on the globe . . . never made a serious attempt to at least resettle in the country. Jews settled massively all around the Mediterranean basin, except for Eretz Israel. . . . Were the Jews to fight for the right to settle here as stubbornly as they had for the right to return to England, from which they had been expelled, there would be no need for all the pathetic efforts to prove that some Jews always lived in Eretz Israel. . . . After the Balfour Declaration, when the gates of the country stood open . . . the Jewish people still did not come. . . . We could have established a Jewish state

here by the twenties. We were given the chance. Hundreds of thousands of
Jews migrated from east to west, but during the years 1917 to 1921 only thirty
thousand Jews came here. . . . ²

Kaufmann argues, as we have seen, that the ghetto provided a miniature
"national existence" that afforded some outlet to the Jewish craving for nationhood and thereby enabled the national essence to exist in a state of
suspended animation, as it were. He furthermore claims that Judaism itself
is a "messianic religion," wholly focused on the realization of the national
ideal.

But the assumption of suspended animation is nothing but an inadmis-
sible analogy from physiology. The culture of the ghetto should be conceived as an entity in its own right, not as a potential state of a different
entity. And, as Kaufmann himself admits, it was a purely religious culture.
That it was not a national culture in a state of suspended animation is
proved by the violent opposition of the leaders of the Orthodox Jewish communities to the Jewish national movements, which they considered profane
and heretical. They never wanted to use this opportunity to convert the
"suspended animation" into a living reality. Even in Israel proper, the Jerusalem ghetto of Meah She'arim rejects Jewish sovereign existence, considering it to be the contradiction and denial of Judaism. Meah She'arim has as
much a right to testify to its own nature and ends as Kaufmann does.

This adamant opposition of most representatives of the rabbinical establishment in recent generations to all "salvationists" is a persuasive historical
confirmation of Yeshayahu Leibowitz's Halachic argument that the arrival
of the messiah is a supernatural event, a posthistorical and end-of-history
event. Jewish nationalism and the state of Israel, he insists, have nothing to
do with the meaning of Judaism and lack any religious significance. They
are the results of historical contingency and subject to all the accidents that
may occur in reality. They could also be destroyed and disappear, and this
would still have no significance as far as the essence of Judaism is concerned. This essence consists of the Halacha and its ordinances, which are
wholly nonhistorical and superhistorical.³ The claim that Jewish religion
has a "temporal-messianic" nature is essentially an invention of Zionist
ideology, which attempts to base itself on Jewish religion and to find legitimacy in it. To that end it cites phenomena such as the Sabbetaian movement, which was denounced as heretical by rabbinical Judaism. We see then
that to the extent that Zionism can claim that Judaism is a "messianic"
religion, it is forced, to prove its point, to resort to eccentric movements in
Jewish history, like Sabbetaianism and Frankism, which were eventually
ejected from the fold. The hostility, even today and in the state of Israel
itself, of ultra-Orthodox Judaism toward the secular Zionist movement (despite the participation of ultra-Orthodox parties in Israeli political life) is
proof enough that they consider secular Zionism the negation and corrup-
tion of Judaism.

Another popular claim is that the Zionist movement arose as an echo of and in response to the rise of the national movements in Europe, particularly after the "Spring of Nations" in 1848. That is undoubtedly true, but such a response implies a prior existence of a genuine, even if still dormant, national entity that could react to such stimuli. The stimuli could not have created something that had not existed previously. They could only serve as catalyzers of the national potential.

At first blush, this statement contradicts our line of argument—until we understand that the Jewish national movement did not manifest itself among all Jews but was essentially limited to only one part of the Jewish people—the Jews of Eastern and Central Europe, mainly the Eastern. Although we might have expected the national movement to arise among the more advanced sectors of the Jewish people, the facts do not fit such expectations. The most advanced sectors of the Jewish people dwelled in the most highly developed and advanced countries of Europe—France, Germany, Britain, the Netherlands—and in the United States. But no Jewish national movement appeared there. At most, the movement won support, not participation, among the Jews of those countries.

The assumption that the Jewish national movement is a response to anti-Semitism is also highly dubious. The two countries in which ideological anti-Semitism originated were France and Germany, but no Jewish national movement developed there. Anti-Semitism only influenced individuals such as Herzl and Nordau to adopt the national viewpoint. It seems that anti-Semitism did not suffice to cause a Jewish national movement. For that to develop, there was a need for the concatenation of several factors and preconditions.

What, then, were the special characteristics of the Jewish people in Eastern and Central Europe that enabled them to become the bearers of a national movement? It should be noted that Zionism in its various manifestations was not the only Jewish national movement which arose in that area. There was the Socialist Bund (which also came into being during the last decade of the nineteenth century); there were the movements for autonomy, which like the other ethnic groups in the Russian and Austro-Hungarian empires demanded not a homeland in a faraway territory but an autonomous status in the areas where Jews were actually living; and there were the territorialist movements, which searched for any suitable territory where Jews could establish a commonwealth of their own. By this classification, the Zionists are but one of the territorialist movements. Even Herzl, in *Der Judenstaat*, did not claim as a fundamental tenet that the Jewish state must be established in Palestine. He considered the possibility of establishing it in South America and finally even recommended its establishment in Uganda (although only as "a shelter for a night.")

Unlike other Jewish diasporas, the Jews of Eastern and Eastern Middle Europe ("Eastern Middle" refers here roughly to the area west of Russia and east of the Vienna-Stettin line; it includes Galicia, Bessarabia, White Russia, Ukraine, Poland, and Lithuania—the territories encompassed by

Greater Poland in the seventeenth century) developed distinct traits of a separate nationality: territorial continuity (mainly in the tsarist "pale of settlement"); a common (Yiddish) language and culture; and the beginnings of a common secular culture, including newspapers and classical writers (such as Y. L. Peretz, Mendele Mocher Sephorim, and Sholem Aleichem) who used this language. Discrimination and oppression directed against the group reinforced group identity. In addition, the surrounding population had a generally lower cultural level than the Jews, depriving the Jews of "identification models" outside their group. East European Jews also engaged in the widest range of occupations, including farming (mainly in the areas of Wohlin and Cherson, where they had settled with the encouragement of the tsar's government). The community was strong, prosperous, and self-confident until it was disposessed from the countryside and pressured to assimilate—both policies adoped after the ascent of Nicholas I to the Russian throne in 1825. This community's sense of separate national-cultural identity was so strong that even today it seems to many of its descendants that its culture was Jewish culture per se.

Data presented by Rafael Mahler can perhaps explain the appearance of a Jewish *nation* in Eastern Europe.[4] Toward the end of the eighteenth century the Jewish people throughout the world numbered roughly two million. Four-fifths of this number lived in Europe. Less than a tenth dwelled in Western Europe (in England, France, the Netherlands, and Italy). Approximately a fourth lived in Central Europe and two-thirds (about a million and a quarter) lived in Eastern Europe, mainly in Greater Poland and the Balkan peninsula. This proportional distribution had existed since the late Middle Ages. Jews constituted one out of every fifteen inhabitants in the kingdom of Poland; they constituted half the population in the cities and small towns. In White Russia and Ukraine the Jews were the decisive urban element in anything pertaining to trade and manufacture.

The Jews of Poland were well defined both by their economic and legal status and by their centuries-old traditions and mode of existence. They were also unique among all Jewish diasporas in their deep local roots and the extent of their legal autonomy, which included even the collection of state taxes by the communal institutions. Almost a third of them lived in the country. No other Jewish community in the world could boast such a large proportion of rural people. Many observers at the time mentioned the community's self-assurance, a derivative of its numbers and firm social base. After the partitions of Poland, most of these Jews became subjects of the tsar, but they continued to maintain their group traits.

A further significant development, as Mahler notes, was the rise of Hasidism, which could not have developed among the scattered, tiny, ghetto-enclosed Jewish communities of the West but only among the dense network of Jewish settlements in the East, which included not only cities and towns but also the villages between them.

The historian Shmuel Ettinger points out that the protonational ethnic self-assurance of the Eastern European communities was apparently also a trait of the Hasidic movement.[5] The Hasidic communities, he says, did not always collaborate with or rely on the gentile authorities, and they thus assumed an essentially independent character. This was an incipient break with Jewish tradition, beginning with the return to Zion at the time of Ezra and Nehemiah, in which the community relied on the state structure and derived its authority from it. This rare manifestation of ethnic independence among Diaspora Jews may be viewed as perhaps containing the seed of a future national consciousness.

Novelists, historians, and journalists have repeatedly emphasized the "deep national roots" of East European Jewry compared with the lack of national awareness among Western Jews. If we strip from the remarks the authors' nationalistic antecedents, regarding them as purely empirical observations, we may conclude that the difference between East European Jewry and the rest of the Jews in the world lies not in the fact that the other Jews were "less Jewish," a preposterous proposition, but that East European Jewry had demographical, geographical, and sociological traits that enabled it to develop a national consciousness.

Nationhood then is not a precondition and datum of Jewishness, but it can develop within a Jewish community under the particular conditions that we are trying to identify here. Even under such conditions, Jewish nationhood is in constant danger of slipping back and being reabsorbed by the nonnational and even antinational religious structures of the age-old Jewish community, as we shall see. The error of Zionism lies in its attempt to draw from these local and temporary conditions a generalization about Jewish history and people as a whole.

Even in Eastern Europe, Jewish nationalism contained an element of ambiguity—assimilationist trends resembling those undergone by the nonnational Jewish communities of the West made their appearance there, too. That leads to the conjecture that, given time, these trends, so powerful in Western Europe, would have gained equal strength in Poland and Russia. The educated Jewish bourgeoisie led the way in this direction, whereas in the normal course of nation forming the educated and well-to-do are the bearers of national consciousness. Among Jews the decline of religion and secular education and the rise of the bourgeoisie are all intimately connected with assimilation.

Still, there did occur in Eastern Europe a peculiar concatenation of factors. The German Jews who migrated to the East in the Middle Ages and brought with them their German-Jewish dialect, Yiddish, had a higher cultural level than the local, semibarbarous Jews. This cultural superiority obviated any possibility of assimilation in the surrounding population, particularly in view of the fact that the respective cultural centers, Russian or German, were quite distant. Few Jews were permitted entry into the inner territories of Russia, and Galician Jews had not yet migrated to Vienna. The

Jews remained in a twilight zone, peopled by various ethnic groups who had yet to develop a durable culture of their own.

Kaufmann notes that the hunger for secular culture that developed toward the end of the nineteenth century among the Jewish masses could be satisfied neither by Hebrew, which had little to offer in the direction of secular culture, nor by the adoption of the local languages, which were foreign to them. For that reason Yiddish literature and press served as the first, interim stage of the secular acculturation of the Jewish masses, before the adoption of the local language. Yiddish also served another function: the participation of the Jews in the mass movements of the time, particularly the proletarian ones, could take place only through the spoken language of the Jewish masses.

As a result, by the turn of the century Yiddish ceased being a vulgar jargon and assumed the dignity of a literary and journalistic medium. Yiddish began to replace Hebrew as the language of the educated. Extremist Yiddishists denied the right of Hebrew to be considered as a live literary language and declared Yiddish the "Jewish national language" or even the "sole national language" of the Jewish people. This was one of the forms of the disintegration of ancient Judaism. The secular began to push the sacred out of Jewish life, and with the decline of the sacred there was a parallel decline in the status of the "sacred language." Jewish secular culture had adopted the Jewish secular tongue.

It was also the expression of a genuine democratic-nationalist movement, similar to movements operating among the other European nationalities. The contempt of the Jewish intellectuals at the time of the Enlightenment toward the language of the people, which was condescendingly dismissed as a "hybrid jargon," was replaced by its careful cultivation.[6]

Thus we have abundant proof that what emerged in Eastern Europe was not an unqualified Jewish nation but something much more specific—an East European Jewish nation that had achieved such a high level of self-awareness that its intellectuals were not prepared to include other Jews in it. The very emphasis that the Yiddishists placed on Yiddish as the "only Jewish national language" implies the denial of the national attributes of Jews outside the circle of Yiddish. The Yiddishists were well aware of the existence of Jews throughout the world whose language was not Yiddish. They did not deny the Jewishness of these Jews. The only possible conclusion is that the Yiddishists distinguished between two kinds of Jews: Jews who belonged to the East European Jewish nation and "just plain" Jews, who were Jews by religion but not by nationality.

The activities of Jewish socialists contributed to this national self-awareness. The agitators of the Jewish socialist Bund party initially sought to recruit Jewish workers to the Russian revolutionary movement and to spread Russian education among them. But their activities forced them to resort to the people's idiom, Yiddish, in order to establish contact with the

Jewish working masses. That in turn forced on the Bund the recognition of the separate national character of the Jews and led it to include a demand for a Jewish national autonomy in its platform. Yiddish thus became the language of Jewish secularism and social revolution, oriented toward the present and the future. Hebrew, the language of the Jewish bourgeois intelligentsia, was rejected on class grounds, along with the religion and the legendary past.

Contrary to Zionist belief, Hebrew, when used for secular ends, had served for generations as a vehicle of transition to assimilation. During the Enlightenment and the emancipation, Hebrew periodicals and books were the first steps toward assimilation. (The violent rabbinical opposition to the use of the "sacred tongue" for mundane purposes derived from a profound understanding of this function of the Hebrew language, and also of the principle that a secular treatment of the sacred language was bound to lead to a secular, critical treatment of the sacral contents of this language. An analogy may be found in the opposition of the Catholic Church to the translation of the Bible into the vernacular, which also led to such results.) Those who wished to acquire a comprehensive secular education could not limit themselves to Hebrew, which was not a spoken language and had meager new secular contents. Inevitably, the student passed on to the local language of the country. Only the development of a complete secular civilization in a Jewish language could keep the Jews within the confines of the emerging Jewish nation and render possible the rise of an independent cultural-national entity. Consequently, the development of a comprehensive national culture in Hebrew was also impossible without Hebrew being the *spoken* language. This, however, was impossible under the conditions of Jewish existence in Eastern Europe. There was no reason for the Jewish masses to abandon Yiddish, particularly after the development of a varied secular Yiddish culture. And if one were to leave Yiddish, why should one adopt Hebrew and not the local language, which would enable one to participate fully in the country's secular life? Yiddish, which functioned from the beginning as a mundane dialect, made possible a national Jewish development dissociated from the distant, religious Jewish past. Whereas Hebrew carried with it the potential of religious culture and the romantic ambiguity—religious on the one hand and pagan on the other—of the biblical legacy, Yiddish was able to serve as a basis for a complete secularization of Jewish life.

Hebrew was not a vehicle of national revival until quite a late stage. In Germany, as noted, it served as the vehicle of the Enlightenment among the Jews and as a transitional stage to the general German culture—a course typified by the career of Moses Mendelssohn (the Jews of France traversed the course without the Hebrew way station). The Hebrew language and the firsthand study of the Bible had, as noted, a function similar to that of the translation of the Bible and the consequent access to it of any literate person in the Reformation. In both cases the appeal "to the sources" served to break the monopoly of established religion on the spiritual life of society. This immediate contact with the sources enabled everyone, in principle, to interpret holy writ, and also made it possible to discern that the Bible *contradicts* both Jewish Halacha and Catholic—or Protestant—theology. (Hence the insistence of the exegetes that the Bible cannot be taken literally but needs exegesis—by themselves, of course.)

We find then that the Jewish national movement in Eastern Europe had at least two main currents—Zionism and Yiddishist-Autonomistic. Zionism sought realization of its national aims in Palestine, with Hebrew as its language of national revival. This current was based to a large extent on the Jewish bourgeoisie and lower middle class, the only groups with enough education to know the written language of the Jewish intelligentsia, Hebrew. (A study of the biographies of most leaders of the Zionist movement from its inception in the middle of the ninteenth century down to modern times brings out this class trait.) Zionism, from the very beginning, regarded religion with forbearance. It was ready to collaborate with religious institutions, although its efforts to reactivate the Jews as a sovereign, active agent in history basically made it antireligious. The very ambiguity of the Hebrew language, with its contradictory Jewish and pagan content, and the desire to cut loose from the bonds of the East European "vale of tears" and its very Jewish atmosphere, contained from the very start the potential of a complete break with Judaism in Eretz Israel—or alternatively of the reabsorption of Zionist society by the Jewish religious tradition.

The Zionist movement, from its very inception, showed strong romantic and nostalgic tendencies—a "return to the ancestral language" and a "return to Zion." That, and the longing to escape from the Diaspora, served as an invitation to the evocation of a "golden age." The Zionist settlers saw themselves as modern manifestations of ancient models—Joshua, the Judges, David, Solomon, the Hasmoneans, the Sikarii. When spirits were low, Zionist settlers began to fear that they too would suffer the fate of the Crusaders. Common to all these conceptions is an orientation to and a search for behavior models in the depths of the past. Israeli-Hebrew society is always in the shadow of myth.

The Yiddishist-Autonomistic current had no interest in embracing a past that had ceased to exist two thousand years before. Rather, it looked to the present, seeking to solve the problem of the extant Jewish people in the places where they were living. This movement had no intention of replacing actual Jews with another, mythical people such as the conquerors of Canaan or the rebels against the Seleucids. The rejection of religion by the Bund also implied a rejection of the romanticization of Eretz Israel, which was inevitably seen as connected to the religious tradition. The very historical terminology of Zionism, e.g., "First Temple Period" or "Second Temple Period," is loaded with religious connotation, since it refers to the cult centers and not to the sociopolitical reality of the ancient Israelite kingdoms or of the Jews in succeeding eras.

The inner contradiction in Zionism derived from the assumption that all the Jews in the world constitute a single entity, an exiled territorial nation. Religion was conceived as a manifestation of this essential national trait, not as the very essence of Jewishness. But any attempt to discover extrareligious traits typical of the Jews as a whole, as Jews, has failed. The very attempt to go beyond religion, for all Jews, was trapped again in religion. The general formula defeated itself. On the other hand, Yiddish nationalism, growing organically out of the East European Jewish community, could dissociate itself completely from religion, as it was based on a well-defined community that was in actuality in the process of transition from a religious communal entity to a nationality. But this national definition could apply to only a part of the Jewish people. Zionism attempted to draw a generalization from this local, temporary fact and to reinterpret the whole of Jewish history in its light. Therein lies its failure.

Jews have only one incontrovertible feature in common: their religion. Jews may be nonreligious, even atheist, but they cease to be Jews only when they convert to a different religion (even then, according to the Halacha, they are still Jews). Historical experience shows that when religion fades, and institutional ties to the Jewish religious community are relinquished, Jews have no secular (national) culture of their own (except in the case of East European Yiddish culture); they absorb the culture of their surroundings, and within two or three generations (often even sooner) they become assimilated and fade from Judaism. Matters have reached such a pass that secular-socialist Zionist parties such as Mapam encourage religious culture in the Diaspora, knowing that this is the only way that Jews maintain contact with Judaism.

The attempt to define the Jews as a territorial nation that has become "abnormal" as a result of the loss of its territory and has been aspiring since this disaster to reassemble itself in it, does not account for the following fact: Most of the world's Jews have never tried to concentrate anywhere, either in Palestine or anywhere else, even when given the opportunity. They tend to migrate only to economic-political centers, such as medieval Spain and the United States. The definition of the Jews as basically a territorial nation should have led one to expect them to try to establish a national society somewhere in the world, not necessarily in Eretz Israel, as territorial nations have always tried to do, particularly as the opportunities to do so presented themselves many times in history. But this happened only once, in the nineteenth and twentieth centuries, with the rise of the Jewish autonomist and territorialist movements, of which latter Zionism is the most successful example. Everywhere, with the sole exception of Eastern Europe, and even there only to a partial degree, the Jews behaved as a guest people, a "Pariah people" in Weber's terminology. Never (again with the relative exception of Eastern Europe) did they create a whole society of their own. They have always been supernumerary travelers in existing societies, fulfilling "Jewish" functions within them without forming autonomous structures. (The religious community is not autonomous. It relies for its existence on the gentile political-military-economic system.) Their only previous attempts to "return to the Holy Land" were of an explicitly religious nature, like the Sabbetaian movement—similar to the Christian Crusades—which had no national meaning either.

In short, all the arguments about the "normality" or "abnormality" of Jewish existence in any diaspora or in its "own land" become dubious from the moment we cast doubt on the *original territoriality* of the Jewish people. Any kind of existence is "normal" if it suits one's desires (we have no other criteria for the measurement of normality). A medieval Jew who preferred life in the Frankfurt ghetto, where he could live in accordance with his religious beliefs, to life outside it on condition that he convert has demonstrated his free choice of this condition, which is then "normal" for him. (He was far freer in this respect than the feudal serf, living in brutish poverty and servitude, who had no hope of freeing himself, not having even the escape hatch of conversion. But the romantic notion of national normalcy would undoubtedly lead to the assertion that the peasant-serf led a "normal" life, "close to the soil and to nature," unlike the Jew. As a matter of fact, in that society only the nobility and high clergy led a "normal" life, life according to their free choice.) Rabbinical Judaism preferred this walled-in existence, in which the community was subject to the exclusive control of its rabbis and officials, to emancipation, which released individual Jews from their authority. This nostalgia for the ghetto recurs in the writings of Zionist historians and thinkers, even of the Left, as a result of their misconception that the ghetto community represented a "national autonomy." To their way of thinking, the ghetto preserved the national substance, although the vast majority of the Jews themselves, as soon as they lost their religious faith, voted with their feet against the ghetto and against this "preservation."

The popular premise that Eastern European Jewry is the "authentic" Jewry par excellence because secular-national elements made their appearance in its composition is untenable. Any Jewish community is "authentically Jewish" as long as its Jewishness is embedded in the oral law, the Halacha.

How then do we define the true nature of the Jewish people? The only meaningful way to answer this question is to proceed empirically and investigate the concrete state of each Jewish community, in its concrete setting. Before airing any "national" definition, or making the familiar statement that the Jews are "unique," that they cannot be compared with any other human ethnic group (as if any human group is not unique to some extent, as if even the nationality of two neighboring, related peoples such as the French and the Germans, both claiming the same historical hero, Charlemagne, as their founder, is identical), we should investigate not the Jew in the abstract but Jewish communities as they are in reality.

For example, Italians in Italy are incontrovertibly Italian. They have a common language, territory, history, religion, culture, and political framework. They are also self-consciously members of the Italian nation (though each Italian region maintains its particular identity). Do these Italians, when they migrate to the United States and adopt the English language, remain Italian in the same sense that the Italians in Italy are Italian? The answer is obvious. The Italian Americans no longer share a common territory, language, culture, state, or eventually even a common history with their Italian cousins. As far as religion is concerned, they become simply Catholics, as Irish and Polish immigrants do. As a group, they no longer behave like Italians but like a particular American group. During World War II, they even fought against their country of origin. After a few generations, probably only some dim family memories about "the old country" remain, along with the Italian surnames (Christian names having long since been Americanized).

Do we have here a single essence, "Italianism," with two manifestations, one in Italy and the other in the United States? If the answer is yes, then we must question the nature of this essence, which is independent of language, territory, history, and religion and dwells somehow above or behind them. Once all these elements are removed, what is "Italianism" in the pure state? The very articulation of this question makes it obvious that any attempt to define such a concept will only result in a mythical, mystic, empty entity. Furthermore, the assumption that such an essence exists adds nothing to our understanding of the specific motivations of the Italians in Italy or of the Italian Americans. It is a superfluous assumption, for we can understand the behavior of Italian Americans (or of the Italians in Italy) without resorting to it. If we assume that we are dealing not with "Italian Americans" but with an immigrant group with certain economic, educational, vocational, and religious characteristics that is living within an absorbing society with its own set of characteristics, the information that the group originated in Italy adds little to our knowledge. In the United States, the group behaves according to the dynamics of other groups in its category and not as the Italians behave in Italy (except, of course, for some traditional intragroup customs). That both groups, the immigrants and those who remained behind, are called Italians does not point to their identical essence but to a common historical past, the meaning of which wears away with time.

The origins, or historical antecedents, of a social group therefore have only a limited relevance to its present nature. Italian history and sociology is only marginally useful in explaining why Italian Americans behave the way they do. The meaning and nature of a social fact are not determined by origins but are to be comprehended by the manner in which it functions within a given system.

This principle is confirmed when applied to the Jews. The millions of East European Jews who emigrated to the United States gave up most of their emerging national characteristics almost immediately. Autonomism, Bundism, territorialism, and Zionism disappeared almost at once as operative political creeds, although lip service to them continued to be paid and their organizational frameworks continued. (As a matter of fact, emigration to the United States was the solution to the East European Jews' problem, and that is the way that the Jewish masses saw it. The intellectuals, however, for the most part failed to grasp this and continued in their stale preoccupations.) The attempts to transplant Yiddish culture to the United States held out for only a generation or two, and as a purely transitional stage. The high Yiddish culture soon died, and its practitioners indeed felt themselves in exile, cut off from their East European roots (testimonies to this effect were given by authors such as Sholem Aleichem at the beginning of the century and by Isaac Bashevis Singer in more recent years). The process is identical with that of any other group of immigrants leaving its homeland and culture and settling in a strange land. The "Jewish-national" culture belonged to Eastern Europe, was rooted there and could not be transplanted. It survived for a while as a typical immigrant culture, with its immigrant press and literature (just like the Spanish, Italian, German, and Polish press and literature in the United States), constantly yielding ground to the stronger and more vital host culture. That it managed to hold out for a full three generations is wholly because the great waves of immigration lasted until the early 1920s, when the quota system, limiting East European Jewish immigration, was imposed. As a result, the Yiddish press and theater had a public that was being continually replenished. Today very little has survived of this public, and as it dies the remnants of Yiddish culture in the United States are also dying out.

It should be noted, in this connection, that there were as many Jews in the great American centers, particularly New York, as in any Polish or Russian center. If the Jewish people does, indeed, carry its culture with it, there is no reason why Yiddish culture should have ceased to exist in America. On the other hand, if Yiddish were only a local, nonessential facet of the authentic Jewish culture—a culture that has no territorial center but Eretz Israel and changes its facets with the change of place—there would not have been the intense conviction that the loss of East European Yiddish culture constituted the loss of Jewish culture itself, the loss of Jewishness.

The language and culture of modern American Jews is by and large the language and culture of America in general. To the extent that anything "Jewish" has remained, it is more in the nature of sentimental nostalgia. In everything that matters, American Jews consider themselves as definitely and aggressively American. They do not react to the stimuli of the surrounding society as a defined group but as individuals, despite the famous "Jewish vote." In short, the Jews of the United States, or any other part of the Americas, cannot be viewed as a "people," as a national group, as they were in Eastern Europe. Again it should be emphasized that this multifarious functioning of the Jews in their present-day diasporas is the consequence of the collapse of the Jewish religious community, which until the modern era had the same structure everywhere. David Vital notes that the seventeenth-century Jewish communities in Frankfurt and Krakow, Constantinople and Cairo, were uncannily similar to those of Palestine and Mesopotamia in the third century A.D. But in the eighteenth century this stable, age-old pattern of Jewish life began to unravel, and by the ninteenth century it had vanished completely.[7]

In Israel, most of the features that characterize Jews in the countries of their dispersion (their minority status, their concentration in certain occupations, their affiliation to the communal structures, their dependence on the outside society) have disappeared, since the Jews there have created a complete political society. On the other hand, Israelis have acquired national-territorial characteristics that other Jews lack. As a result, even as the secular culture that has developed in Israel lacks any distinguishing Jewish mark, Israeli-born or Israeli-bred Jews do feel an estrangement from Jews in other countries. These phenomena refute the thesis about the existence of an exiled territorial Jewish nation, living under abnormal conditions in the Diaspora, whose return to its homeland would release the authentic Jewish-national, territory-based contents pent up within it, thus becoming more "Jewish" than any diaspora. Experience has shown that nonreligious Jews living within the Israeli political framework have in effect lost any life content that may be termed Jewish—unless living in Israel, speaking Hebrew, and leading the sort of secular life that a nonreligious Frenchman lives in France or a Norwegian in Norway is "the essence of Judaism."

Jewish sovereignty in Israel has failed to reveal any specifically Jewish trait suppressed through the eons of exile, whose release has caused a Jewish cultural revival. Israeli national traits are not "Jewish" but rather typical of young pioneering societies: a measure of egalitarianism (wearing thin with the growth and stratification of society), energy and optimism, contempt for traditional limitations, and openness to innovation and experiment. There are also negative traits, such as the arrogance, narrow nationalism, and worship of power typical of many nations fortunate on the battlefield (the same traits that were so hateful to Nietzsche in Germany after the 1871 victory over France). The "specific" Jewish contribution has a positive and a negative aspect. The positive one is the esteem in which education and knowledge are held and the low level of interpersonal violence, despite the vociferousness of interpersonal quarrels. The negative one is the attempt to clothe the negative side of the Israeli national character in a holier-than-thou mantle by reciting all the sufferings of the Jews in the past as a rationalization for and justification of any Israeli misdeed in the present and the persistence of the rigid communal separation of "Jews" and "gentiles," which creates grave problems in the social, political, and legal fields.

These theses could be challenged by citing the numerous prayers and festivals connected with Eretz Israel. But it is also a fact that these festivals never obliged Jews to undertake any worldly action. To understand a group, as I have argued, we must examine its actual behavior, not its ideologies.

The religious-communal frameworks of course inculcated typical forms of social cohesiveness, typical ways of thinking, typical ways of emotional reactions and a typical world view. All of these patterns tend to persist long after the formal communal and religious frameworks have lost their meaning for most Jews. This is why they still "feel Jewish."

Furthermore, within these frameworks, in certain geographical areas, complex kinship patterns and strong inter-Jewish affinities developed. Such affinities can serve as a basis for the formation of nationalities or protonationalities, as we have seen in Israel and in Eastern Europe. But of themselves they cannot be defined as a "nation." The "substance" of the connection betwen Jews, what makes a Jew, as I have had occasion to emphasize over and over, is not secret but open, not mystical but institutional, not racial but social-ideological. It is the religion and the religious community and civilization in all of their multifarious manifestations. The proof of the matter is seen as soon as we dissociate ourselves from the world of East European Jewry, whose common culture and complex family relationships delude us into viewing the world's Jews as a national and almost a familial-clan organization. We then see that even the Bene Israel of Cochin, India, and the Falashas of Ethiopia are considered Jews from the moment the rabbis recognize them as such. The *formal* recognition is what makes the difference, not any mystical, nonexistent "national affinity." Genetically and culturally, the Bene Israel and the Falashas hardly differ from the populations of India and Ethiopia. They are as different from German Jews as a German is from an Ethiopian. It is the Torah that makes them Jews. (In support of the myth about the common ethnic origin of all Jews, the ideologues pretend to discover in the distant past of these groups evidence that they are descended from the Ten Tribes and other similar nonsense.) National or protonational traits that develop in any Jewish group do not testify to any Jewish national potential that could materialize under suitable conditions. Rather, they show that such traits could develop within any human group under suitable conditions. The ability of Jews to create a secular-national culture completely free of religious tradition yet still definable as Jewish has never been demonstrated anywhere, not even in Israel.

THREE

Anti-Semitism

The European Background

It should be clear that anti-Semitism alone was not enough to elicit the Zionist response. Hatred of the Jews has been endemic in Christian civilization, with fluctuating intensity, since its very inception, and it never caused a Jewish national liberation movement. Furthermore, modern, "scientific," racist anti-Semitism—usually credited as the cause of Zionism—developed in Germany and France in the 1860s and 1870s without causing the rise of a Jewish national movement in either country.

But Zionism did develop in Eastern Europe, within communities that had already partly developed protonational traits. It is reasonable to assume, therefore, that anti-Semitism served as a catalyst to the rise of Zionism—as well as to other Jewish national movements—wherever the Jewish community had traits favoring such a development, but that anti-Semitism was not the only stimulus. Several objective factors were also involved, such as the enormous increase in the Jewish population, beyond the carrying capacity of Eastern Europe's backward economies. Still, it may be presumed that were it not for anti-Semitism, the Jewish national movement would not have assumed the Zionist form that proposed Jewish evacuation from Europe. In this there has always been a parallelism (sometimes a convergence) between the Zionist and the anti-Semitic arguments, since both had the same goal: the removal of the Jews from non-Jewish societies. At times this parallelism came to the point of mutual understanding between Zionist and anti-Semitic leaders.[1] That came to an end only when it looked as if anti-Semitism might not limit itself to discrimination against and persecution of Jews but could actually seek their annihilation.

What are the causes of modern anti-Semitism, as distinct from traditional hatred of the Jews, which had different causes and aims? (The goal of the traditional religious opponents of the Jews was to convert and assimilate them within Christian society. The aim of modern anti-Semitism is the opposite—to isolate and remove the Jews from the host societies.) The usual Zionist explanation of this phenomenon may be found, for instance, in the entry "Anti-Semitism" in the *Hebrew Encyclopedia*. The author, Ben-Zion Netanyahu, argues that modern anti-Semitism is a reaction to assimilation.

As the aim of anti-Semitism is to remove the foreign body from the majority population..., the more this body adheres to the majority population, the more intense the latter's opposition to this proximity. Consequently, we find (1) that assimilation not only fails to weaken anti-Semitism but even intensifies it, and (2) the more intense the assimilation effort..., the more violent the anti-Semitic reaction. The assimilation process also reinforces anti-Semitism in another way: The mask put on by the assimilated Jew enables him in many cases to penetrate areas which the non-assimilated would have been unable to. As a competitor in more numerous fields of activity, and a covert one at that, the assimilated Jew is considered by the anti-Semites to be more dangerous than the non-assimilated one, arousing a fiercer resistance to Jews as a whole.

That is the conventional Zionist appreciation of the phenomenon, which on close inspection proves to be mostly fallacious. True, as related further on in the entry, Germany provided the outstanding example of assimilationism, and that was where "scientific" anti-Semitism developed. But as noted in the preceding chapter, racist anti-Semitism never struck deep roots in countries such as Italy, where assimilation went even further than it did in Germany, nor in Britain and the United States. Anti-Semitic moods were and are indeed prevalent, to a greater or lesser extent, in all of these countries, but they never coalesced into mass political movements as happened in Central and Eastern Europe. Even in France, with its strong anti-Semitic traditions and an assimilation that went even further than in Germany, these movements have always failed to influence laws and government policy. (I omit here the Vichy regime, since it operated under a foreign will.)

On the other hand, pogromistic anti-Semitism in Russia, Poland, and Romania was aimed at a community that for the most part kept its separate communal-cultural identity. Only a small proportion of the community, mainly of a bourgeois background, had assimilated. Also, it was not this group but rather the masses who adhered to tradition that were victimized in the East European pogroms.

Even this cursory examination of the conventional Zionist thesis brings out the contradictions between its simplistic generalizations and the historical facts. One notices further that the author of the *Encyclopedia* article ignores completely the socioeconomic factors in the anti-Semitic movement, comprised primarily of petit bourgeois elements on one hand and déclassé aristocrats on the other. In addition, he ignores the fact that the socialist movements in Europe generally combated anti-Semitic tendencies among the working class, though during the first half of the ninteenth century anti-Semitic tones are clearly heard in the writings of some of the fathers of socialism. (Unlike the author of the *Encyclopedia* entry, who belongs to the right wing of the Zionist movement, Labor Zionism has always been cognizant of these socioeconomic factors.)

The assimilation of Jews within the majority population by way of conversion in previous centuries aroused no problems of anti-Semitism, even though, in the case of conversion, the "mask" assumed by the Jew was even more effective than in the case of ordinary cultural assimilation, and the convert was entitled to compete with the gentile in all fields. True, the process by which the *Conversos*, for example, were absorbed by Spanish and Portuguese societies was not smooth and immediate, and these "New Christians" suffered suspicion of their integrity as Christians, especially from the Inquisition, for several generations. In the long run, though, they were absorbed completely by the general population. According to Netanyahu's thesis, however, the closer they drew to the non-Jewish population, the more anti-Semitic it should have become and the more violently it should have tried to eject them. A similar process took place with the Frankists, who after their conversion to Catholicism in the late eighteenth century were completely absorbed by the Poles.

A serious investigator of anti-Semitism, Shmuel Ettinger, has this to say of such arguments:

> In sum it may be stated that all these explanations miss the point. They explain how individuals and groups exploit the hatred of the Jews, under conditions of general spiritual or social misery, for the attainment of political ends. But they do not deal with the problem, what caused anti-Semitism in the first place. . . .
>
> It has already been stressed that even in Nazi ideology "race fear" was not an authentic fear but a propaganda slogan. . . . The votaries of the race theory, repelled by the "foreign" as they claimed to be, were never sincere about their supposedly biological theories and distinguished between Semites and Aryans according to their affinity to a religious community and by juridical definitions.[2]

It seems that Nietzsche had better insight into the causes of modern anti-Semitism, seeing it as a symptom of a shaky psychosocial structure and a defective self-image of the peoples among whom it develops. The following is a famous excerpt from chapter 251, "Peoples and Countries" in *Beyond Good and Evil*:

> That Germany has amply *sufficient* Jews, that the German stomach, the German blood, has difficulty (and will long have difficulty) in disposing only of this quantity of "Jew"—as the Italian, the Frenchman, and the Englishman have done by means of a stronger digestion:—that is the unmistakable declaration and language of a general instinct, to which one must listen and according to which one must act. "Let no more Jews come in! and shut the doors, especially towards the East (also towards Austria)!"—thus commands the instinct of a people whose nature is still feeble and uncertain, so that it could be easily wiped out, easily extinguished, by a stronger race.

A similar conclusion may be drawn from Jean-Paul Sartre's *Anti-Semite and Jew*. Neither Nietzsche nor Sartre dwell on the role of assimilation as a provoker of anti-Semitism, and we may conclude that they do not give it much weight. The invocation of assimilation as a cause of anti-Semitism is primarily an anti-Semitic argument, and this in itself is again an instance of the uncritical way in which Zionism echoes anti-Semitic claims, without examining their validity.

The *Hebrew Encyclopedia's* explanations of anti-Semitism are also an example of such mindless copying. These explanations are surprisingly similar to the anti-Semitic ones. The definition of the Jew as "essentially alien" to his host peoples and the allegedly greater danger to the surrounding society from a Jew hidden behind his "assimilation mask"—reminiscent of the penetration of a disease microbe into a healthy body, disguising itself as harmless to fool the body's antitoxins—are typical of the dehumanization and demonization of the Jew in anti-Semitic literature and the comparison drawn between him and noxious and dangerous creatures, such as microbes and rats.

The argument that the Jews are "essentially alien" to their host societies, an anti-Semitic argument swallowed whole by the Zionists, is in reality purely metaphysical. How is one to discern an "essence" without external signs? Ettinger comments:

> The "difference and alienness" were not then a real factor in the relationships between well-defined social groups. They were aimed at a figure or "stereotype" whose depiction in literature was immeasurably simpler than in reality. In Nazi Germany, after the passage of the Nuremberg Laws, a German woman could marry a Japanese, despite his prominent racial traits, without desecrating German "blood and honor." But she was liable to severe punishment for having relations with a Jew, who sometimes looked far more "Aryan" than the average German. In such a case "Jew" was a legal fiction much more than a reality, just as the "foreignness" and "difference" of the Jew in anti-Semitic ideology is a result of the use of a stereotype.[3]

We find overwhelming support for Ettinger's arguments in the Korherr report, prepared by Dr. Richard Korherr, chief for statistics, for his boss, Nazi S. S. chief Heinrich Himmler, bearing the date March 2, 1943, and stating:

> Until recently, statistics hardly ever distinguished Jews by race but by religious faith. . . . For the establishment of racial origins, many years of training are needed, as well as the investigation of ancestry. The establishment of race affiliation has been found to be particularly difficult in southern and eastern countries, for in spite of all efforts it has proved impossible to define a uniform single Jewish race. The adherence to the Mosaic or Israelite religion cannot serve any more as a completely valid proof. Due to the Jewish missionary movement, which in the past has caused the proselyting of masses of pagans and Christians, as well as proselyting in the modern era, whether by mixed marriage or persuasion, there live today as many Faith Jews who do not belong to the Jewish race as those who do. On the other hand, the number of Jews has been reduced by forced conversion as well as voluntary conversions, which became much more frequent in recent times, and also by the phenomenon of

communally unaffiliated persons of the Jewish race. Leroy-Beaulieu, for example, estimated in 1893 the losses of Jewry to Christianity at four to ten times the number of its adherents today. According to Maurice Fishberg and Mathias Mueses, the number of Jews absorbed in contemporary Aryan Europe is three times the number of those who remain Jews today. Even Hans Guenther estimates the number of Jews in Germany as double the number of Jews of the Mosaic religion who hold German nationality. Finally, the Lithuanian Jew Bruzkus goes as far as to claim that by the composition of their blood, the Jews of Berlin are purer Europeans than the Germans of Berlin. On the basis of the above it has often been calculated that the number of race Jews, including people of mixed stock, in Europe is three times the number of Jews by faith (in Eastern Europe twice as many, in central Europe four times as many, and in the other parts of Europe even eight times as many), and it is estimated that six percent of the European population have Jewish blood in their veins.[4]

It is difficult to avoid the impression that Korherr's real intention may have been to hint that the Nazi doctrine that the Jews constitute a race, a distinct biological group, was utterly dubious and that the attempt to "uproot" all the "Jewish biological elements" from the European population was a doomed undertaking.

A historical overview of modern anti-Semitism brings to light the following points:

- From the late eighteenth century on, particularly from the period of the French Revolution to the middle of the nineteenth century, the legal attitude toward the Jews is liberalized and they are emancipated in most European countries. This process begins in Western Europe, in countries that had already undergone a bourgeois revolution (England, Holland, France), and spreads gradually eastward, although the legal disabilities imposed on the Jews are finally abrogated only after World War I and the Russian revolution.

- The opposition to the Jews intensifies steadily from the middle of the nineteenth century on. The racial ideology was developed mainly in Germany (although originally it had no anti-Jewish context). But anti-Semitic trends become increasingly apparent in most European countries, mainly in Central and Eastern Europe. The countries where they spread are by no means on an equal level of development. Anti-Semitism takes hold both in enlightened, highly developed France and Germany and in backward, benighted Russia and Romania. But only in the backward countries does it assume a violent form. (In France, even at the height of the Dreyfus Affair, Jews were not harmed in body or property).

- Anti-Semitism achieves its greatest power and influence under the fascist regimes in the interwar years (though not under the Italian fascist regime, which enacted anti-Jewish legislation only in its decline, under German pressure) and its most horrible manifestation in the extermination of most of the Jews of Europe by the Nazis. Its outbreak and rise to power are not an automatic result of the process of assimilation, as the Zionists claim, but a result of certain regimes that use anti-Semitism for their own ends. There is no "necessity" or "inevitability" about it.

- From 1945 until this writing, more than forty years later, anti-Semitism has ceased to be a serious political factor, even in Poland and particularly the Soviet Union, where a sort of anti-Semitic revival has taken place. Nor have any pogroms against Jews occurred since 1945 anywhere in the world (except for outbreaks against Jews in Arab countries, but these took place in the context of the repeated wars with Israel, so that their definition as anti-Semitic is questionable). Organized, ideological anti-Semitism has reverted to being an undignified occupation of lunatic-fringe groups.

Undoubtedly, the decline of anti-Semitism as a political force (although individual antipathies toward Jews may be as prevalent today as ever) derives among other things from the sense of shock and shame that overwhelmed the Christian world at the sight of the Nazi horror. But one should not exaggerate the weight of such sentiments. They cannot be stronger than interests and basic trends in society. Were these interests to profit from militant anti-Semitism, as they did during the century before World War II, they undoubtedly would ignore the stigma attached to it and exploit it.

These phenomena point to an array of sociopolitical factors that operated with increasing force within European society from the middle of last century down to the middle of the present one and gave birth to modern anti-Semitism. This array apparently ceased to exist in 1945.

The critical period begins roughly with the "Spring of Nations" in 1848. Until then the national movements in most European countries overlapped with the struggles for political and social liberation. The autocrats ruling most of the Continent headed multiethnic empires. The struggle for freedom of the subject nationalities, which threatened to disrupt the imperial systems, was at the same time also a fight for liberation from the socioeconomic order imposed by the empires.

From 1848 onward a new trend appears: the bourgeoisie, the main bearer of the national aspirations, achieves social dominance in most countries on the Continent but reaches a compromise with these countries' political structures, which still rest with the aristocracy. Thus the national movements become allied with the established order in the politically independent countries. In the dominant nations they provide an ideological pretext for the suppression of the subject nationalities, for whom nationalism still means social liberation. The outstanding instances of this process are Prussia-"Germany," Austria, and tsarist Russia.

Compromise with conservative elements followed disenchantment with the events of 1848–1850, which effected a transformation in the character of the movements for national liberation. As David Thomson states, "After 1850 some nationalists came to believe that what liberalism or democracy had failed to give them might be got from more authoritarian sources and by more militaristic means."[5] It thus occurred that the movements for social liberation, which until the 1848 revolution had been intertwined with the movements for national liberation, diverged toward proletarian internationalism. The events in 1848 are an outstanding example of this.

The German movement for national unity endeavored to break the autocratic power of the kings and princes who divided the country among them. In 1848 the liberal bourgeoisie caused the convening of the Vorparliament (constituent parliament) at Frankfurt am Main with the aim of uniting Germany under a bourgeois-liberal regime. With the failure of this attempt in 1854, the task of uniting Germany shifted from the popular and the bourgeois-liberal circles to the Prussian autocracy. Thus the union was achieved not from the bottom by the struggle of the masses against the old regime of privilege and oppression, as hoped by the liberal nationalists, but from above, by power politics and war.

Although part of the German working class participated in these processes, other parts, with their intellectual spokesmen who were originally members of the national movement, were pushed to the realization that nationalism had become an asset of the ruling circles and was now aimed against their struggle for political, civic, and economic rights. In consequence, these workers increasingly embraced the insight formulated succinctly in *The Communist Manifesto*: "The proletariat has no homeland."

In the Habsburg Empire, Hungary in 1848 rebelled against the imperial oppression of the Austrian-German element. The popular revolt was suppressed with the help of the Russian army. As a result of Austria's weakness following defeat in the Italian war of liberation in 1859 and defeat at the hands of Prussia in 1866 in Sadowa, the Hungarians' bargaining position was greatly enhanced, and in 1867 the Austro-Hungarian "dual monarchy" was established, recognizing an independent Hungarian kingdom with a separate parliament and government, whereas Austrian Emperor Franz Joseph was crowned king of Hungary and the two countries were linked by a "personal union." As a result, the Hungarian struggle for liberation against the Austrian Empire was transformed into a conspiracy for domination by the Austrian-Germans and the Magyars, the two dominant peoples of the empire, over its other components, mostly Slav. Here a recurrent sociopolitical pattern emerges: the so-called dominant nation is in reality subject to the rule and exploitation of an oligarchy but receives psychological and material compensation by "ruling" over other peoples, serving as the policing and coercive force that keeps them down. The liberation of the "ruling people" from its subjection to its own rulers is dependent in the last analysis on the breaking of imperial domination. Never has the condition of the masses in Britain and France been better than after the liquidation of their colonial empires.

Social liberation in a dominant nation like Russia could be attained only by internal revolution. Because of its backwardness, by the early nineteenth century Russia had not yet developed a true national consciousness. But in the course of the century, an alliance was formed between the tsarist autocracy and Russian nationalism, which turned into an oppressive, Russifying chauvinism. The solid patriotism that finds expression in Tolstoy's *War and Peace* is transformed into a messianic pan-Slav mysticism. During the reactionary phase of Alexander II's reign, from the late 1860s on, tsarist imperial sway became a Russifying pressure on the non-Russian nationalities, the Ukrainians, Lithuanians, Poles, Finns, Estonians, Georgians, etc. They, as a reaction to this pressure, began to develop their own independent national consciousness. In the case of the Jews, this policy resulted in a sharp aggravation of the official attitude toward them and in the outbreak of pogroms in southern Russia in the early 1880s.

The social significance of these pogroms is of great interest. At the time, members of the Narodnaya Volya (People's Will) movement welcomed them as a sign that at last the people were revolting against their oppressors and that, although in their blindness they had begun by attacking the Jews, eventually they would vent their fury on the true oppressor, the tsarist regime. Obviously the revolutionary elements had not yet understood that there is a great difference between a mob and a revolutionary mass and that the appearance of the mob is contrary to the revolutionary interest. As a matter of fact, the appearance and rampaging of a mob are a sign that the ruling classes have succeeded in diverting social fury and frustration toward imaginary targets.

As Hannah Arendt perceived it, the mob was created by the immense social upheaval which the countries of Europe, some to a greater and some to a lesser extent, had undergone in their transformation from agrarian to industrialized societies. This transformation uprooted many millions from stable, traditional ways of life, generating thereby an aggravated sense of insecurity and a lack of clear, self-confident social identity among very broad circles. These included artisans and members of ancient guilds rendered redundant by the new industry, petty farmers who had lost their plots of land and become proletarians without a proletarian class-consciousness, and pennyless aristocrats embittered at the bourgeoisie that had ousted them. This mob—which by its very nature is oriented to a past that it recalls in the rosy hues of a lost paradise of happy farmers and singing artisans and brave, generous noblemen—is incapable of forming a positive ideal toward which to strive, because its ideal is in the past. Its idealism appears, therefore, as a romantic nostalgia. (Thus the Nazis, for example, encouraged handicrafts, protected small businessmen, and depicted the peasant tilling his land as the foundation of the nation and its umbilical connection with the soil. All were attempts to revert to an earlier, imaginary historical stage that had never really existed.) Therefore the mob is capable only of uniting in negation, in hatred.

The mob, which constituted the mercenary army of the imperialistic and antidemocratic, antisocialist, and anti-Semitic mass movements, also became the main standard-bearer of "integral nationalism." Being hostile to existing society and all of its institutions, the mob is incapable of admitting the legitimacy of the conflicts of interests and classes within it. It considers them to be the result of "alien" divisive conspiracies, the selfsame "conspiracies" that had allegedly destroyed the fictitious paradise of the past. With this mob, nationalism turns into chauvinism, which becomes ever more xenophobic when it allies itself internally with social and religious reaction, and feeds externally on the growing friction with the other European nations, particularly with the rise of imperialism during the second half of the ninteenth century. During the first half of the century nationalists were prepared to support each other (although from the start we hear the notes of xenophobic nationalism, as in Fichte's 1806 "Addresses to the German Nation"). But by the end of the century patriotism implied hatred of foreigners and their depiction as inferior, as apostles of the devil, or both.

Another decisive factor in the creation of the mob was the demographic revolution that swept Europe. Thomson ascribes this to the fact that the absolute monarchies that emerged in Europe at the end of the seventeenth and the beginning of the eighteenth centuries created stable conditions of life, put an end to the frequent internecine wars, extirpated banditry, and made possible the establishment of developed health and other public services. The development of medicine eradicated illnesses and epidemics that had plagued humanity immemorially, and the revolution in farming and transportation made possible vast increases in crop yields and provided the means of shipping them to the ends of the earth.

As a result, in the two hundred years between 1750 and 1950 the population of Europe increased fourfold. That is a novel phenomenon. Moreover, these figures do not take into account the approximately forty million Europeans who emigrated overseas between 1815 and 1914. The population of Britain alone doubled between 1811 and 1891. The only European country whose rates of population growth exceeded even Britain's was Russia, which doubled its population during the first half of the century and doubled it again during the second half. The smallest continent held a third of the human race, and its civilization spread all over the globe.

Even more dramatic was the growth of the Jewish people, mainly in Europe. Between 1800 and 1939 the Jewish people increased almost sevenfold, from 2.5 to 17 million,[6] even though during the same period assimilation and conversion grew to an extent unseen for centuries, so that the natural increase was even larger than appears from these figures. Emancipation opened to Jews the gates of the professions and economic fields hitherto closed to them. This phenomenon, coupled with the socioeconomic changes that reshuffled the populations of Europe, added to the status anxiety of the traditional petit bourgeoisie the fear of competition from the increasing Jewish population. During the ninteenth century the Jews, who previously had been a marginal factor in European society, became a central one. This demographic jump also explains, in part, the anti-Semitic images of Jews spreading and taking over society—images that reflect fear of the Jewish demographic energy, a subject which was also a preoccupation of the Nazis. Jew hatred in previous centuries did not employ such dynamic imagery.

The demographic revolution was accompanied by an industrial one, which spread from England to the Continent. The first countries to industrialize were France and Belgium. Germany and Italy, before they could start an industrial revolution, had to complete their political unification, although parts of them, like Prussia in Germany and Piedmont in Italy, had already achieved a high level of industrialization and a modern socioeconomic and financial structure. In Eastern Europe, Austro-Hungary, Russia, and the Balkans lagged behind the lands to their west down to the end of the century. Germany, on the other hand, once it united, and owing to its central position in Europe, became the center of the European communications system and the hub of east-west transport. By the end of the century it had already become Europe's richest and mightiest industrial power. In the military sphere it became the foremost land power in the world.

Let us now consider the phenomenon of nationalism not in the conventional manner, as the product of autochthonous cultural, historical, and ethnic dynamics, but from the structural point of view. Only such an examination can account for the astoundingly rapid and universal spread of the phenomenon. Each population and economic crystallization in Europe was formed within a political framework that enabled it to have reciprocal relationships with similar units within the same European force field. The advent of nationalism meant the rise of European society and the world awareness of the individuals within it from a lower to a higher plain of organization.

Until the emergence of the absolute monarchies, the horizons of the vast majority of Europeans were limited to the local parish. To a large extent, this situation existed until the French Revolution. The individual was not involved in activities that went beyond these limits, except in the sense of being a member of the Church and a passive subject of a sovereign. The fact that he spoke a dialect of Russian, German, Polish, or Italian, was not of cardinal importance, though he was well aware of it. It seemed right and proper that German-speaking soldiers, subjects of the House of Habsburg, should fight shoulder to shoulder with Hungarian- and Czech-speaking subjects of the same dynasty, against other German soldiers, who were fighting side by side with French-speaking subjects of the House of Bourbon.

The power that the old-style sovereigns could extract from their subjects was strictly limited. The states they ruled were to some extent abstract formal arrangements, touching only peripherally on the daily life of most of the population. For that reason those dynasties could augment their holdings or trade them by marriage, since in most cases these holdings were not centralized organic structures. Few countries approached the level of political-economic organization of England, Holland, or France. The subject, for his part, could unhesitatingly vow allegiance to the new sovereign to whom the territory he lived in was ceded without feeling thereby that he had "betrayed" his nation.

But the modern state penetrates directly to the plane of the individual, without the mediation of hierarchical structures. It extricates him from his traditional communal frameworks in order to reintegrate him in its own mass organizations, using him as an industrial worker, entrepreneur, bureaucrat, or soldier. In doing so it succeeds in extracting from him energies and abilities which hardly found expression within the previous communal structures, and which the older state structures could not reach. The modern state thus atomizes its citizens, who become isolated individuals confronted by the state's systems of influence, manipulation, and control. On the other hand, the far vaster size of these systems and their openness provide the individual with opportunities for development and social mobility unknown in the past. For the purpose of dissolving the local communal structures the state uses the solvent of national consciousness and loyalty. The creation of a national consciousness thus becomes a necessary stage in the generation of social energies on a scale undreamt of in the past. Only a national consciousness and the proliferation of intranational and intrastate connections could maintain a measure of loyalty and discipline in the heavily exploited "industrial armies" mobilized for the industrial revolution without the class conflicts in each country snowballing into an overt or covert civil war.

The national idea served that purpose on its first appearance in modern history, in 1793. Facing the crusade of European monarchs against revolutionary France—the revolutionary convention initiated the Terror to liquidate the enemies within and raised the national idea in order to unite all classes of French society for war against the enemies without. On the other hand, in reaction to the appearance of the French nation-in-arms, France's neighbors concluded that only a national mobilization could provide the forces that would be able to defeat French might.

The price the nation-state had to pay for this higher energy yield was the exclusivity it involved. An absolute monarch could unite several nationalities under his rule, and none would consider this intolerable as long as he refrained from exploiting them unduly or interfering in their religious affairs. But the development of the ethnic-national consciousness meant the exclusion of all who were not members of the ethnic community, thus presenting the multiethnic structures with a destructive contradiction.

The centralized authority of the nation-state recognizes only individual citizens, equal in rights and duties, and demands from them a uniform identification with it. Any connection between them must be subject and secondary to the civic one and never stand in conflict with it. No other connection between them may be of a political nature. The new political structures, which demanded absolute identification (even the Church became "national," and its priests became interpreters of Scripture according to the new national spirit and interersts) penetrated into areas that had never been within the scope or even within the capacity of the state to influence. The state had never before had such means to reach the individual. Its communications systems had not permitted quick access to any corner of the state or society; nor had its machinery of registration, classification, taxation, and documentation been capable of keeping track and control of all subjects and of making an effective assessment of their income.

We must distinguish here between two types of political-national development within Western civilization. The first took place mainly in England, the Netherlands, France, and the United States and is founded on the assumption of a social contract, namely on the tenet that the individual precedes society, that he is essentially free and endowed with a capacity for independent discrimination and choice, hence he is sovereign and above any social, ethnic, or biological determination. The second became pronounced in Germany, Russia, and most other countries of Central and Eastern Europe and has been defined as "integral nationalism." It assumes that society precedes the individual, that the individual is a mere fragment of the whole and has meaning only insofar as he belongs to the whole, and is wholly determined by national, biological, or class factors (the "national essence" is conceived perforce as a mystical unity). It should be noted that traces of this current of thought are apparent also in Western liberal countries, and reached their fiercest expression in France during the Dreyfus Affair. Indeed, the anti-Dreyfussards were the very same forces that in retrospect rejected the French Revolution and were never reconciled to it; they were also the upholders of the Vichy regime. The Dreyfussard victory was in a sense a continuation and completion of the revolution started in 1789.

Walter Grab contends that the victory of the liberal-individualistic political philosophy in some Western countries was achieved because in those countries the bourgeois revolution had preceded the industrial and had imposed its concepts of individualism and free competition. No industrial proletariat had yet arisen there, and so the bourgeoisie became the standard bearer of the struggle of the underclasses against royalty and aristocracy. Its triumph created the institutional and social basis for liberal institutions and a deeply rooted sense of individual liberty, and for the industrial revolution which was to follow. Moreover, this political philosophy assumes that the citizen cedes to the state only a part of his personality, the part needed for the state's proper functioning, while the other parts of his personality and identity remain his private domain. This view leaves a broad margin for differences of opinion, for variations in ways of living, and even for differences of ethnic affiliation—as long as they have no political bearing. The state exists, as the U.S. Constitution puts it, to ensure its citizens the right to "life, liberty and the pursuit of happiness," hence it is a voluntary association for the achievement of these ends. If a national ascendancy is achieved, it is not the result of an innate superiority of that particular people, for they had nothing in common prior to the pact they contracted among themselves. It is the result of conscious effort and achievement. Thus, the French people were not "by nature" freer than the German; they had *become* free once they had decided to take up arms and conquer their freedom, overthrow the old ruling classes, and establish freedom as the basis of the state. They had achieved it by action, action generated by the mutual consent of individuals to carry it out, not as a result of some mystic potential trait of freedom innate to the French people. But if, as Fichte argued in his "Addresses to the German Nation," the Germans are innately superior to the French, even without doing anything to realize their potential superiority, then this superiority is implicit in the mysterious trait that constitutes their Germanity. To share it, one must be born a German; it cannot be achieved by effort and action. To take Fichte's thought a step further, if the Jews are peddlers and financial speculators by nature and the Germans are poets and thinkers by nature, then a German peddler or speculator is really, in the depths of his being, a poet and thinker, while Spinoza the philosopher and Heine the poet are in the depths of their beings peddlers and speculators, albeit in the field of the spirit. The organistic conception of innate traits had arisen half a century before the elaboration of the concepts of genetics and race.

Such ideas, clearly designed to compensate for feelings of national inferiority, gained the upper hand in those countries where national movements had allied themselves with social reaction. The triumph in Central and Eastern Europe of integral nationalism, with its insistence on complete identification of the individual with the political framework and the dominant nationality, aroused among other ethnic groups the resistance of hitherto dormant cultural and psychological levels. As long as Russia was the domain of the Romanovs, the subjects would grit their teeth and bear it even when a tyrant like Nicholas I occupied the throne. But the moment the tsars are obliged to mobilize Russian patriotism to enhance the country's power, the moment they free the serfs and start a process of industrialization and urbanization, Ukrainians, Poles, Georgians, Lithuanians, Finns, Estonians, and Jews rise and claim their separate national rights. This demand threatens the organic, conformist cohesion required for developing the new socioeconomic-military forces, and the state tries to suppress and digest the disparate ethnic elements or to get rid of them. In countries that contain several ethnic elements but are dominated by one nationality, the demand for total identification with the nation-state contains the seed of disintegration of the polity.

The totality of national identification raised dividing walls between the

Continent's nations, nations that had hitherto been integrated in monarchical, ecclesiastical, and feudal frameworks. Each group tried to develop its specific national personality by treasuring and preserving traditions and folklore hitherto ignored by civilized individuals. The real purpose of this evocation of the past, sometimes a wholly fictitious past invented by nationalistic ideologues, was the creation of frameworks and focuses of identification for the present and the future. We thus come face to face with the inner contradiction that characterizes the European structure during the ninteenth and first half of the twentieth centuries.

On one hand, we see the emergence of the national sociopolitical-economic entities, which make possible the development of modern society and economics. Without such unified systems of currency, finance, customs, banking, taxation, marketing, legal rights, and political organization, no industrial revolution could take place. On the other hand, despite the continued existence of customs barriers and economic nationalism, the Continent became a single trading area. All its political units became interdependent, and its intellectuals were united by an awareness of a common cultural heritage that transcended national boundaries. Indeed, the national differentiation of Europe could only take place on the basis of such common ground. With the emergence of this trading area, international organizations were formed whose members were cognizant that their interests went beyond political borders. First, financial organizations such as the House of Rothschild arose, with family members settling in all European money centers and creating a Continentwide financial network. At a later stage the First and Second Internationales made their appearance, based on the awareness of their members that what unites them as proletarians outweighs what separates them as members of different nationalities. Similarly, there emerge the industrial and financial arrangements of the great international concerns, the intergovernmental accords such as the reciprocal adjustments in the fields of communication, patent and copyright agreements, and international organizations of all sorts in the fields of science, art, and technology.

If we consider Europe as a single system, we find that transition from one level of organization and power to a higher level necessitates the advent of numerous competitive nodes of organization within the civilization that unites them, covering roughly Western Christian (Latin) civilization with its Balkan and Slav (Orthodox) peripheries. The unity of this civilization had already been proclaimed in the early Middle Ages, but at that time, when most of Europe had hardly reached the feudal level of organization, it was a declaration of an abstract ideal based on memory of the Roman Empire and the actuality of the Catholic Church. Each step in the course of the unification of this civilization involved a higher level of organization, which also led dialectically to a different level and type of conflict. The national stage of this process, beginning at the end of the eighteenth century, which in two world wars almost wrecked the civilization itself, reached its climax and denouement in 1945. This stage gave birth to both modern anti-Semitism and Zionism.

The Zionist claim that the development of nationalism breeds anti-Semitism is valid only for integral ethnic nationalism. Essentially, that is how most Zionist thinkers view the Jewish people. And the tenet that Judaism cannot be summed up in religion, that there is an indefinable Jewish essence to be found in every Jew, is tantamount to integral nationalism. This conception of the nature of the Jewish people inevitably dictated the Zionist conception of nationalism in general and its fundamental misunderstanding of the liberal-democratic type of nationalism, which the Zionists claim to be merely a mask of the other, true, integral nationalism of the peoples involved. This attitude has also dictated the legal and political treatment of non-Jews in Israel.

Integral nationalism cannot, of course, tolerate any group—such as the Jews—that does not belong to its "mystic union." It may be added parenthetically that in the final analysis integral nationalism is incapable of applying its own criteria, as there can be no connecting link between the universal nature of the law of the state and the mystic intuition as to the "belonging" or "nonbelonging" of any particular individual to the "folk community." Integral nationalism, when embodied in the law of the land, is therefore forced to resort to "external" formal criteria to define the limits of the "folk," such as language or sojourn in the national territory. Even the Nazis were forced, in the final analysis, to define the Jews by religious-communal, not racial, criteria. Membership in the German people and the Aryan race was proved by a family's sojourn in Germany for several generations and by its being Christian—both external, formal criteria. In Israel, too, Jewishness is determined by the purely formal criteria of the Halacha, as interpreted by orthodoxy. Therefore it is not the predilections of individuals in a society that determine its attitude toward the Jews (or other minoritites) living in it, nor the Jews' own readiness to adapt themselves to the prevailing social norms, but rather society's basic conception of itself.

Whenever integral nationalism is on the rise, the danger of anti-Semitism becoming an active political force increases. The Jews, being largely foreign to the "folk" in such societies, disturb the collective unity of the tribe, without any reference whatsoever to whether they are orthodox, agnostic, or assimilated. The average pre-Hitler German was hardly more anti-Semitic than the average Englishman. The difference was not in the level of dormant anti-Semitism in the populace; it was rather that a political force had emerged in Germany that had decided to exploit anti-Semitism by making it a part of the fundamental tenets of the state.

We must also take into account the basic assumption of Western civilization in which the nation-state first made its appearance. This almost unspoken assumption—that it is Christian—is also the line of demarcation between the Jews in any European country and the rest of the population.

Even the separation of church from state, achieved by most European countries, has not erased the typical traits of the Christian ways of thinking and European Christian history. On the contrary, this very separation echoes the ancient struggles between emperors and popes. Christian and Roman conceptions are implicit in the secular notions of the freedom and sovereignty of the individual, in law, architecture, language, etc.

Even the secular state developed out of the basic patterns of thinking and feeling and world view, out of the legal, historical, and aesthetic notions implicit in the cultural synthesis of the Christian (some would add Judeo-Christian) tradition and the Greco-Roman world. For that reason, when religion was separated from state in the modern European states and they became secular structures, society, as distinct from state, did not become culturally and ethnically indifferent. The implicit foundation of these societies continued to be Greco-Roman-Christian civilization, in addition to their autochthonous traditions. Thus a gap exists between their formal political structures (for which these foundations are largely irrelevant) and their concrete cultural accretions. The assumption that Jews could be accepted in these countries as "Frenchmen (or Germans or Englishmen) of the Jewish faith" ignored the fact that Judaism is not just one more religious sect in the list of Christian ones, all based on the same Greco-Roman-Christian traditions, but that it is substantially foreign to the others (though much closer than Islam or the East Asian religions). The Jews were caught in a halfway house: their formal civic status was that of natives of the country, equal citizens before the law. But in terms of the implicit assumptions of cultural and social life, they were outsiders.

Thus a fundamental difference exists between Jewish interests in either a feudal society or an absolute monarchy and between Jewish interests in the nation-state. In the earlier forms of society, the Jews, holding to their religion and separateness, aimed at keeping themselves apart and succeeded in it. They relied on tradition and authority, won various privileges (and suffered grave disabilities), and the traditionalist basis of the societies in which they lived helped them to keep apart. They were protected by kings, bishops, and princes and feared the steady rise of the masses (often accompanied by anti-Jewish outbreaks).

The interest of those Jews who accepted the basic tenets of the nation-state and strived to fully participate in it was to advance the universalistic elements implicit in the formal framework of the state. These elements included them, whereas the traditionalist folk background did not. Thus, contrary to what had transpired in previous periods, when the Jews had a vested interest in social conservatism, an objective community of interests arose between emancipation-seeking Jews and radical uniformizing social forces, such as big business on one hand and the labor movement on the other. These are forces that demolish, each in its own way, the traditional conservative social frameworks. There is, therefore, a measure of truth, though a grotesquely distorted one, in the anti-Semitic diatribes about

"Jews lurking behind both Plutocracy and Bolshevism." The traditionalist, conservative elements of society—small merchants, peasants, artisans, and the other varieties of the petit bourgeoisie—are fighting a defensive battle against the social dynamic that finds expression in both great entrepreneurial capital and giant corporations and in the socialist-labor mass movements. The constantly radicalized antitraditional general frameworks created by these mighty forces are the ones that permit a more complete integration of the Jews in society. The Jews, an essentially urban element free from any unambiguous loyalty to any particular country, become ever more integrated into society as it increasingly develops into anonymous urbanity. The Jews can then merge with it and disappear. The factors conducive to a full Jewish integration in society, then, are the city as against the village and small town; industry as against agriculture and handicrafts; rationalistic individualism as against the romanticism of the collectivist-integral tradition. The foreignness of the Jews to the traditional basic stratum of European civilization turned them into a radical and egalitarian factor in it, even when they were conservative by personal inclination. In addition, their vested interest in the radicalization of society prompted Jewish ideologues to emphasize those elements in Jewish tradition that could be interpreted in the spirit of humanistic universalism, suppressing its exclusivist and xenophobic aspects.

The Jew, then, inasmuch as he preserves anything of his ethnic-religious specificity (and nothing but conversion can remove him from it), can integrate himself into the host nationality to the extent that the latter (to use Hegelian terminology) approximates the concept of the state. A well-known joke has it that a gentile is either a Czech or a Slovak. Only a Jew can be a Czechoslovak. The joke contains a great deal of truth. The greater the prestige and the deeper the roots of the formal constitution of the nation-state, the easier it is for Jews to become integrated into it. The formal structure of the English-speaking countries—which developed organically out of English history and the immense importance English society ascribed to the rule of law and the state, as part of society's traditional foundation—forged a social framework far more capable of absorbing Jews than, for example, the Germans, whose framework placed particular emphasis on the tradition of the "folk," of German tribalism. It is well to remember that the British political system unites as equals four different nationalities, English, Scot, Welsh, and North Irish, who have fought each other in the past and even have different languages, and that three of them harbor a measure of bitterness against the biggest and strongest, the English, who conquered them. Still, except for marginal minorities, they have no intention of cutting themselves loose from Britain, and today they all use English as their main cultural idiom. The Crown, in the sense of a supranational legal-political authority (the queen is the sovereign of the United Kingdom, not of the English people), is a political reality with a profound, ancient tradition dating to times when the country was ruled by French-speaking Norman kings. The social content of the British political framework, the *pays réel*, can hardly be separated from the *pays légal*. The result was that even though the instincts of the average Englishman are no more or less philo-Semitic than those of the average German or Frenchman, the rights of the Jews and their equality before the law have always been sedulously preserved within the confines of the United Kingdom, ever since they were permitted to return to it at the time of Cromwell's protectorate in the mid–seventeenth century. British overseas colonies, like those in North America, had from their inception not instituted discriminatory legislation against the Jews.

The modern French state is founded on the myth of the revolution—the smashing of tradition in the name of the abstract principles of equality, liberty, fraternity, reason, and atheism. This means that the myth of the revolution, an essential and sanctified part of the French political tradition, lies at the foundation of the state's constitution and is itself a contradiction of the autochthonous traditions of the various peoples of France. This brought about a highly significant phenomenon: from Napoleonic times on, French law never veered from the principle of the equality of all citizens before the law. Nevertheless, Jews have repeatedly encountered anti-Semitic manifestations from precisely those circles that never reconciled themselves to the revolution. These manifestations resurface again and again—in the Dreyfus Affair, in the Action Française movement, in the Vichy regime. Nevertheless, time has shown that the principles of the revolution, the *pays légal*, have always proved stronger than popular anti-Semitism. The French attitude toward the Jews is a reflection of the tensions between the tradition of the revolutionary state and the organic traditions of the peoples of France. In English-speaking countries, where the formal conception of the state is itself an ancient tradition, one hardly encounters such tensions.

Jews' prospects of becoming integrated in the surrounding society are greater in a multiethnic state, the unity of which can be preserved only by insistence on their supraethnic formal frameworks. Britain is one case in point. France is not founded on "the French people" but on the monarchy that united the people of Languedoc and Savoy with Burgundians, Normans, and the people of Alsace-Lorraine. France was an abstract supraethnic concept even before the revolution. Its unity derived first and foremost from the Crown, and the political association thereby created led to cultural and linguistic unification, which in its turn created the French people—just as later the unity of France found expression in the revolutionary constitution.

These remarks are doubly valid for countries whose very essence is federal and pluralistic, like the United States. The authority of the U.S. Constitution, as argued brilliantly by Alexis de Tocqueville in *Democracy in America*, derives not only from its organic nature, its being based on ancient English traditions; it also derives from the functional fact that without this constitutional structure the entire vast edifice of the United States, which unites many lands, climates, peoples, and races, could collapse. Today the United

States has hardly any ethnic subjects (the white Anglo-Saxon Protestants are by now a minority). Any attempt by one group to infringe on the rights of the others and declare itself the "true Americans" could blow the whole country apart, leaving no clear ethnic carrier of continuity. In addition, any attempt to limit the rights of one minority would immediately activate a united front of other minorities that would rush to its aid in order to preserve their own rights.

Emancipation placed the Jews in a highly contradictory position. The demand to identify completely with the nation addressed to them by the nation-state was ambiguous from the start. They were prepared to identify with the state, but with the best will in the world they were outsiders and could not identify with the ethnic nation. Attempts of some Jews to identify with an alien ethnic tradition usually encountered derision and anger. This tradition is organic, instinctive, familylike, and can absorb strangers only very slowly and with great difficulty. Therefore any attempt to identify the state with this tradition will inevitably result in a negative reaction-formation toward any group alien to the ethnic tradition. The legal identification of the state with the ethnic nation, a process legitimized by the struggles for freedom of the subjugated European nationalities and recognized as the right to self-determination of all peoples, created a highly menacing potential, reaching its extreme in the fascist regimes established after World War I.

FOUR

The Transition to Continental Systems and the Decline of Zionism

The nation-state is one stage in the development of European civilization. By making possible the establishment of democracy and socialism, it paved the way for the entry of the masses onto the stage of history. The Romantic movement's appeal to the people's ethos and the idealization of the people and its "closeness to nature," as expressed by Herder in Germany and Rousseau in France, meant the discovery and emergence of strata of society that had been historically and politically passive, and a legitimation of their world view and culture. Previously, culture had been the preserve of the upper classes. This is the moral aspect of the advent of the nation-state—the possibility it opened for the growing realization of human equality. In addition to its moral aspect, however, the nation-state is also a higher and more efficient form of organization than those that preceded it. And when the history of Europe is considered as a process within which higher, more efficient, and more comprehensive levels of organization replace more backward ones, we must conclude that the overdevelopment of political individualism involved in the cultivation of the separate national personality was bound to undermine the field, the system within which the nation-state had its birth.

The European nation system was inherently unstable. The nurture of national sacred egoism toward the end of the nineteenth century and the nationalistic credo that the nation owes everything to itself and nothing to others were largely a reflection in the international arena of the doctrines of Social Darwinism and the laissez faire of the new bourgeoisie.

The nationalist world view is solipsistic. It dissociates the nation from the civilization within which it functions. Nationalists, in their introversion, were incapable of realizing to what extent their country and nation were inseparable parts of a whole continental civilization, to which each nation was connected by a million cultural, economic, and communications threads and without which it could hardly exist. This understanding of the organic and holistic nature of European civilization led many thinkers at the beginning of the twentieth century to argue that in view of the intricately knit web of the life of the Continent, a European war was simply impossible. At first sight they were wrong, but in a deeper sense they were right. The two great wars that did erupt showed the instability of the system and led to its profound transformation. As a result, the developed world has entered the postnational era. And when one considers these processes carefully, one realizes that they have also brought Zionism to an end.

As described in the preceding chapter, the nation-state mobilizes ethnic-linguistic loyalties that had little political application in the past. But this mobilization immediately highlights the distinctive difference of those groups which do not belong to the dominant group, who then become subject to pressure by the state, which tries to obliterate their distinctive traits and assimilate them within the majority population.

The minorities, in reaction, develop their own ethnic consciousness, and in combating the assimilatory pressures of the nation-state, they raise a demand for the establishment of their own national state. That is the paradox and internal contradiction of the nation-state: since most states were not established by nations but by feudal, dynastic, or religious processes or by military conquest, the borders of few states correspond with ethnic distribution. As a result, the pressure for ethnic conformity causes divisive stresses within the nation-state. The right to national self-determination thus became a primary, obvious principle of European liberalism. It was a main plank in President Woodrow Wilson's program for settling European affairs after World War I. But the settlement shaped by the victorious powers at Versailles only aggravated the system's inherent instability.

It seemed that the national tensions were being finally settled by the establishment of a group of nation-states out of the ruins of the multinational empires of the Romanovs, the Habsburgs, and the Hohenzollerns. But the outcome was not a system of liberal-democratic states living in peace with one another, as had been hoped for by idealists like Wilson and as was inscribed in the liberal constitutions adopted by these new states. The newly liberated peoples for the most part lacked democratic or self-rule traditions. Apart from Bohemia and Moravia, the heart of the new Czechoslovakia and some areas of Poland, like Silesia and Lodz, these countries lacked a developed industrial base. Being mostly backward agrarian societies, lacking a developed bourgeoisie, and with mainly agricultural exports, they were extremely sensitive to any decline in the price of agricultural goods. When the Great Depression began in the late twenties, they were all heavily affected. The impoverishment of the middle classes, the bitterness of the working class, and the fear of both the upper and middle classes of the spread of Bolshevism to their countries, most of which had common borders with the Soviet Union, engendered in most of them authoritarian and despotic, sometimes fascistic, regimes. These regimes shook off constitutional restraints and resorted to the inflammation of the instincts of integral nationalism.

Despite the solemn obligations which these "successor states" undertook under the peace treaties to respect the rights of the minorities still dwelling within them (though great efforts had been made to draw borders according to ethnic lines of demarcation), almost all of them began to oppress the minorities. The attendant mutual hatreds hastened the fragmentation of the area.

In this disintegrating system, corroded by mutual hatreds and irredentas, the Jews found themselves in a particularly difficult position. First, they were a minority everywhere. Unlike the Magyar minorities in Czechoslovakia and Poland who could turn to Hungary, the Jews had no mother country to turn to in their quarrels with the majority population. Also, the intensification of integral nationalism in most of these countries and the denigration of the democratic-individualistic world view as "artificial," "abstract," "contrary to the healthy instincts of the people," rendered the Jews doubly suspect on all these counts. Not only were they ethnically alien; not only did they hold to a different religion; not only did they compete with the autochthonous bourgeoisie and intelligentsia, but they also were a universally distributed group, and as such they symbolized the universal forces that the introverted nation-state seeks to hide from. In most of these countries the fascist and anti-Semitic movements won a mass following. The "plight of the Jews," which before World War I had been mainly an East European problem, now spread westward with Europe's rush to fragmentation and reached its climax with the Nazi rise to power in Germany.

The Nazis did not conceive of anti-Semitism in the old clerical or petit bourgeois terms but rather in totalitarian terms with totalitarian solutions (like the "solution of the kulak problem" in the Soviet Union). Anti-Semitism was not only a recommended domestic policy; it was conceived of as a weapon in the struggle for world domination and a means for undermining the countries marked for annexation from within. The extermination methods applied to the Jews were meant to be extended (and began in fact to be extended) also to the Slavs in order to "purge" Eastern Europe of them and prepare it as *Lebensraum* (living space) for German settlement. Although many of its causes were similar, anti-Semitism in Nazi Germany had a totally different nature and significance than it did in all other European countries. However, a detailed analysis of the meaning of the Nazi revolution—for a revolution it was, and Nazi anti-Semitism was also revolutionary—lies outside the scope of this book.

Thus the acuteness of the Jewish problem reached its highest point in the interwar period. Its aggravation was inherent in the development of integral nationalism. The disintegration of the Central European system was synonymous with the collapse of the position of the Jews there, just as the intensification of anti-Semitism as a government policy in most of these countries was also a symptom of the same disintegration. The plight of the Jews was also the plight of Europe.

Such a fragmented system could not survive for long. It was doomed from the moment that Germany and the Soviet Union regained their strength. The only chance the small countries had of maintaining their independence vis-à-vis the giants reviving to the east and west of them was their cooperation in all fields, including the military, and a readiness on their part to forgo certain national prerogatives for the sake of their common interest. In short, there was need for some sort of a confederacy that would replace the Habsburg Empire and reestablish the balance of power upset by its collapse, a new system that would ameliorate and reconcile national grievances. Had such a confederation existed, it is doubtful whether Nazi Germany would have been capable of launching its campaign of conquest.

The collapse of the system in the thirties, culminating in the outbreak of World War II, led to its replacement by another. The collapse also put an end to the Jewish people as it had been until then. The new structure of the Jewish people, and the reshaping of those parts of the world where most Jews live, rendered Zionism largely meaningless. It can be argued—and in the chapters to come I shall try to prove it—that perhaps by as early as 1945, but most definitely shortly after the establishment of the state of Israel, Zionism no longer had a raison d'être. The East European Jewish people— the only sector within which processes of transformation into a nation had begun to take place—had been split since 1917. One part was in the Soviet Union, cut off together with the other Soviet peoples from contact with the outside world. The other part was scattered all over the successor states. Soviet Jews underwent accelerated processes of assimilation and became integrated in all the aspects of Soviet state and society. Despite the anti-Jewish reaction that began to set in during the thirties, peaking by the late forties and early fifties with the murder of a part of the Jewish intelligentsia, there was no return to tsarist oppression. As a result, neither was there a full recovery of Jewish nationalism, even after the gates were opened to Jewish emigration in the wake of Gorbachev's perestroika. The occupational structure of Soviet Jewry became increasingly similar to that of Western Jews, and its secularization processes became intensified. It seems, despite the upheaval that had been shaking Eastern Europe and the Soviet Union in particular, that the greater part of Soviet Jewry had become completely integrated in the society of what is now the Commonwealth of Independent States (CIS). Those who now wish to emigrate do not do so in most cases as a result of national motivation but simply in order to start a new and better life somewhere else, or because they fear that the crisis of the system may lead to incalculable results and to rampant anti-Semitism. Most of them, had the United States not imposed strict limits on the number of admissions from the CIS, would have chosen to emigrate to America.

Most Jews of the successor states (as well as many Soviet Jews) and of Western Europe were murdered by the Nazis, except for a few groups that survived thanks to particular circumstances—like many of the Jews of Bulgaria, Romania, Hungary, and Italy. Most of them left their countries of origin for Israel, the United States, or Western Europe. The result is that through assimilation, emigration, and physical extermination the great Jewish people of Eastern Europe—which 150 years ago began to develop national traits, wherein Zionism was born and from which it drew its sustenance and ideas—has virtually ceased to exist. The other large Jewish groups, in the United States, France, and Britain, have no intention of emigrating to Israel; nor do they possess national traits in the sense that East European Jewry did. They do not view their condition as a problem calling for a solution. Their Zionism is merely a financial and political support of Israel.

Another factor in the demise of Jewish nationalism in Europe has been the collapse of the nation-state system. The new world order established after World War II also put an end to the external pressures that created the "plight of the Jews" and led to Zionism. The world order I refer to is mainly the new *European* order. Europe (together with North America, and lately also the Pacific sector, where Japan is most prominent) is still on all counts the world's leading sector. This area (taking into account Eastern Europe, too) contains most of the world's production facilities, the vaster part of its scientific and cultural potential, and most of its military force. For the past four hundred years the world has been dependent for its ideas, its social, economic, and political structures, its literature and art, on the European–North American region. What happened in Europe and North America yesterday happens in Asia today, and it is reasonable to assume that it will happen in Africa tomorrow. For that reason, a new European–North American structure presages (to the extent warranted by historical predictions) a new world structure. As against the argument that in Southeast Asia (and recently again in Eastern Europe, with the dismantling of the Soviet empire) there exist national conflicts, and in western and Central Asia religious wars are still raging, one can only reply that these areas are lagging behind the historical level of our time. One could once argue with equal plausibility that the idea of the nation-state is an absurdity, in view of the fact that primitive tribes in New Guinea still practice head hunting. If the nation-state has been spreading throughout the world, there is no reason why the postnational structures will not also spread to an equal extent.

By 1943–1944 it had become clear that the European continent was incapable of determining its own fate. The decision in World War II, begun by the West European powers, was achieved on one hand by the Soviet Union—a semi-Asiatic power—in the battles of Moscow, Stalingrad, and Kursk, which were the greatest and most decisive land actions of the entire war, and on the other by the air and sea forces of the English-speaking powers, mainly the United States, in the battles of the Atlantic and the Pacific and in the devastation of Germany and Japan from the air. The failure of the Germans and the Japanese to achieve a quick decision sealed their fate, since their industrial potential, their economic resources, and the size of their populations were greatly inferior to those of their opponents.

It is highly significant that neither of the two superpowers that assumed world leadership after the war was a nation-state. Both were multinational, multiracial federal systems, occupying continent-size areas and numbering their populations in the hundreds of millions. The war proved that no nation (except the Chinese nation, which itself is a conglomerate of peoples and tongues united by a common civilization) is large or powerful enough to maneuver independently in the system of world power relations. It transpired that even the greatest European nation-states, like Britain, Germany, and France, which had but yesterday ruled the world, were not large enough to generate global power. The Common Market developed as a result of this reality.

The innovation of the Common Market is that this is the first European organization that is not international but supranational. The Coal and Steel Authority was authorized to organize the production and marketing of these goods in all of the members' area, not by multilateral international agreements but as a supreme authority. Around this authority there began to emerge in Brussels and Strasbourg the various bodies and organizations that owe loyalty not to this or that state but to the system as a whole. The age of the Eurocrats had arrived.

Joint international ventures such as the Concorde passenger plane and the Euratom nuclear agency have shown that an increasing proportion of the basic technological ventures of the late twentieth century is on such a scale of technological and financial organization that it taxes the resources of even the largest and wealthiest nation-states. A reversion to separatist nationalism in the age of the new expensive technologies, the multinational corporations, and the new capital structures is inconceivable. Both the rebuilding of Europe from the ruins of war and the development of the various national economies could be carried out only on a multinational basis, the more so when it transpired that an event taking place in one of the Continent's countries has immediate effect on all. It became clear that the national political unit has only limited influence on economic developments not only around it, but even inside it; that its own greater control of such developments depends on participation in supranational bodies, in coordination and agreement with other countries.

Only such a system of control made it possible to offer an alternative to fascism (which failed and was discredited in the war) and communism. This alternative goes under various names—the affluent society or the welfare state. Under capitalistic market conditions it calls for a constant expansion of production and consumption—and this depends in turn on the maximal elimination of customs barriers and the creation of the broadest possible market within which men and goods can move freely. The welfare state and the creation of regional, multinational economic unions are then two aspects of the same coin.

Modern military structures are also on a scale that strains the resources of the nation-state. The development of new warplanes, tanks, and other weapons systems necessitates international financing and cooperation. The costs of weapons development are only one aspect of the modern military scale. The decisive factors are the military alliances that have occupied the international political arena. No single state, not even a superpower, can be dissociated today from a military alliance system. But the difference between the traditional military alliances and organizations such as NATO and the now-defunct Warsaw Pact is that these are not only agreements for cooperative military action but also integrated military systems, subject to unified commands, whose weapons systems, fighting doctrines, and communications systems have been made uniform. Although they do not yet constitute a single army, they are no longer separate armies.

These developments seem to be contradicted by the revival of separatist ethnic movements in many advanced countries (to say nothing of the nationalistic reaction in Eastern Europe following the demise of the Soviet empire). We witness the rise of the Scot and Welsh national movements in Britain, the Basque and Catalan in Spain, the Breton and Gascon in France, the substitution of ethnicism and cultural pluralism for the melting-pot ideal in the United States, the centrifugal pressures of the Soviet peoples, the civil war in former Yugoslavia.

A number of these movements, such as the Catalan, Ukrainian, and Scottish, have existed for more than a century. Under different historical conditions, some would undoubtedly have established independent states (as the Ukrainians have). But the different conditions of the world today have also effected a change in these national demands. First, in the new supranational systems the pressures for cultural and ethnic conformity have been greatly relaxed; with the dissipation of conflicts with other states, the need for it has largely disappeared. Ethnic movements are now more at ease within the existing states and their demands have been moderated to an insistence on a degree of autonomy, or on confederate or even lesser arrangements. Second, movements that were of a mild or even eccentric nature until 1945, like the Scottish or Welsh ones, have since gathered strength. Until 1945 it had paid to identify with a global power and to share with it the accruing benefits; but the advantages to be derived therefrom have greatly dwindled with the decline of the British Empire. Furthermore, as more and more functions which were traditionally performed by the nation-state are being transferred to the multinational systems (such as determining economic and military policies for the system as a whole), these national minorities are of the opinion that they are less in need of the framework of the existing state and can manage very well on their own as junior partners in the regional systems. A case in point was the demand for independence in the early part of 1990 of the Soviet Baltic republics, which hoped to join the Common Market once they seceded. This "ethnicity," then, is itself a by-product of the emergence of the supranational systems.

A different case is the emergence of ethnicity in the United States. There it is the result of the progress of various cultural and ethnic groups and their seizure of vantage-points from which they can challenge the dominant WASP culture, once the ideal of the melting pot. The flexibility of the U.S. sociopolitical structure enabled it to adjust to this new reality and to adopt a new ideal—one of an open, pluralistic society. To be precise, ethnicism had existed in America previously. The Jews, Italians, Chinese, Mexicans, Africans, Poles, and Irish differed much from each other and from the dominant group. But in the past, everyone had tried to shake off distinctive ethnic traits and to resemble as much as possible the blond demigod of Anglo-Scottish extraction. What happened in fact was that with the growth of their self-confidence these groups finally realized that this ideal is not theirs, that their own human type is just as valuable and legitimate as the Anglo-Scottish. The emphasis on ethnicity surfaced just as the differences between the various ethnic groups began to diminish.

As for the Jews in the new world order, the cornerstone of Borochov's analysis of the Jewish problem was the "inverted pyramid" theory (see chapter 1). It seems, though, that Borochov had an incomplete understanding of the problem of the Jewish occupational structure in Eastern Europe. He was correct in his insistence that the Jews were trapped in the backwater of light, backward industries, without reserves of investment capital, and that they had little to do with modern heavy industry, either as owners, managers and planners, or as laborers. He was right in denouncing the Jewish lumpen bourgeoisie, a rabble of starved peddlers and middlemen without any skills, without any access to modern marketing and finance networks. But the necessary conclusion from his insight was that basically, the Jewish occupational anomaly did not derive from an inverted occupational pyramid, a surplus of trade and services on too narrow a basis of agriculture and industry. The problem was the basic dissociation of East European Jewry from the modern economy as a whole—from industry, from agriculture, even from commerce and finance. The cure was not an inversion of the pyramid but integration of the Jews into the modern economy.

And indeed, as noted, the vast majority of Jews in both the capitalist West and the socialist East did not change their occupations from light industry and middleman functions to physical labor in agriculture and industry; rather, they made a gigantic leap out of their backwardness and integrated themselves into the leading sectors of modern economy. The traditional Jewish emphasis on learning, when it was translated from arid Talmudic scholasticism into scientific and technological research, enabled Jews to crowd universities, laboratories, and research institutions in all advanced countries, thus establishing a deep involvement in most industrial fields and in agriculture, too (to say nothing of agricultural achievements in Israel). Furthermore, highly developed societies have a legitimate need for the commercial and financial services that Jews have specialized in for centuries. A redundant activity in a backward, impoverished society may well be a necessary function in a developed one. Unskilled manual labor is what is becoming increasingly redundant in such a society.

The proportion of unskilled laborers or peasants among the Jews has not increased (and perhaps has decreased). But with the development of technological sophistication, the number of manual workers and agriculturists has been drastically reduced in all advanced countries. The celebrated pyramid has indeed been inverted, but not by the *proletarization* of the Jews, which would have truly dissociated them from real productivity, but by *productivizing* them, by integrating them fruitfully into all the scientific and economic arrays of modern developed societies.

Modern technology and the relatively high level of education of most Jews put an end to their redundancy in advanced societies. In addition, the fear of Jews' "seizing control" has also somewhat eased; contrary to the pre–World War II situation, Jewish rates of natural increase are now quite low, substantially lower than those of their host societies. This low rate is largely a result of their belonging to the middle or upper middle classes and having the typical family structures of these classes, namely two children at most. Furthermore, in all advanced countries the Jews are undergoing a massive assimilation process, steadily reducing their visible number. Thus the immediate stimulus to anti-Semitism has been substantially blunted.

Another cause of the Jews' increasing integration into their host societies is, as noted, the total victory of the urban-cosmopolitan civilization, the atomization of society, and the collapse of organic social systems. All these are forces that undermine ethnic inwardness. It is also obvious that within the continental systems described here, nationalist self-segregation is impossible. Their ethos is necessarily pluralistic; otherwise they are bound to collapse. All these elements seem to explain the fact that although anti-Jewish prejudices may still be widespread among the European and American populations, mainly among the more backward elements, anti-Semitism as a political force, as the platform of a serious political movement, has largely disappeared. There still exists a measure of social discrimination against Jews (like nonadmittance to certain clubs or economic fields), although to an immeasurably lesser degree than before World War II—and also to a much lesser degree than against other minorities, like Africans and Asians.

The very fact that many Jews have ceased to be ashamed of their Jewishness and even display it may be a sign of successful assimilation. Apart from the opening up of national societies and the recognition of the legitimacy of the alien and the different within the supranational systems, to be a Jew in the West today confers the prestige of belonging to a group of a substantially higher cultural and economic status than the rest of the population. Jews have ceased to be be derided, contemptible creatures. On the basis of their consciousness of power and self-confidence they can afford to be themselves, and can be more easily absorbed into non-Jewish society.

Is a massive outburst of anti-Semitism possible, this time on a continental basis, in the new world order I have described? Do manifestations of Soviet and other East European anti-Semitism (and recently in Western Europe, too) not presage such a development? Does the fact that anti-Semitism did appear from its inception as an international movement not indicate such an outcome?

Predictions are of course impossible, and some people point to new manifestations of anti-Semitism that generally camouflage themselves as anti-Zionism. Still, the anti-Semitic international of the ninteenth and early twentieth centuries did rise on the background of a nationalistic fragmentation of Europe. Since the Continent has changed immensely since 1945, no simple "revival" is possible of a phenomenon born under different sociopolitical conditions. If anti-Semitism does appear again as a political force, it may be difficult to identify it clearly as such, just as anti-Semitism differs from the hostility toward the Jews prevalent in earlier eras. The attempts to brand anti-Zionism, or even criticism of the Israeli government's policies, as anti-Semitism are clearly misleading and propagandistic. As the well-known Israeli thinker Professor Uriel Tal commented, anti-Semitism and opposition to Israel's policies do not derive from the same source.

> The World Council of Protestant Churches, based in Geneva, fights anti-Semitism—but at the same time it is one of the main forces in the world opposed to Israel's policy in the Israeli-Arab conflict. . . . The bitter cries about anti-Semitism which allegedly raises again its head all over the world serve to cover up the fact that what is disintegrating in the world is Israel's position, not Jewry's. The charges of anti-Semitism only aim to inflame the Israeli public, to inculcate hatred and fanaticism, to cultivate paranoid obsessions as if the whole world is persecuting us and that all other peoples in the world are contaminated while only we are pure and untarnished.[1]

It seems then that under the present world constellation—with the exception of events in the former Soviet Union, which appear to evoke a desire by members of all the nationalities there (including Russians), not only Jews, to emigrate—there are no factors prompting Jews to emigrate, particularly to Israel. The only immigrants who would prefer Israel above all other places are those who are motivated by Jewish sentiments, who wish to live in a Jewish society. Immigrants of this kind are necessarily few, as the masses are moved only by fear of persecution or by hope of improving their lot. But this desire to live a Jewish life that prompts some Jews to emigrate to Israel clashes with the Israeli environment, one of whose outstanding traits is that it is non-Jewish in character, except for the religious sectors within it.

In sum, neither the inner conditions in the present-day Jewish people nor the historical conditions under which the Jews live are capable of generating a national consciousness and a desire to solve a problem which today is largely nonexistent—which causes me to conclude that Zionism largely lost its raison d'être in 1945.[2]

A few words are in order to describe a phenomenon that on the face of it appears to contradict what I have said: the mass immigration to Israel of Jews from Islamic countries. This immigration has often been described as motivated by a deep national sentiment. I shall deal with this immigration in greater detail later. But for the moment it should be noted that religiously inspired immigration was common for centuries among both Eastern (Oriental) and Western Jews. In both cases it was limited to very few and had a purely religious, not national, motivation. Indeed, a systematic attempt is now made to represent any past immigration as national, but such a presentation is clearly false. The argument that the nationalism in these cases was unconscious is negated by the anti-Zionist ultra-Orthodox Neturei Karta group, which furiously rejects any nationalist interpretation of its presence in Palestine.

One should also take into account the natural distribution of Jews in the Ottoman Empire, including Palestine. Just as Jews from Morocco reached Egypt and Syria and Jews from Syria and Turkey reached Algeria and Morocco, they also arrived in the Holy Land not out of national or religious motivation but for the same economic or other considerations that led them to settle in Beirut or Damascus. Messianic waves would sometimes shake some of these communities, as occurred among the Yemenite Jews over the past century. But these waves, just like Christian pilgrimages, have always been guided by messianic religiosity and not by a modern political program. Only a political, self-aware movement may be defined as nationalist.

The proof of the low level of national awareness among the Jews of Islamic countries lies in the fact that Zionist organizations active in these countries have always been small and weak, contributing little to the Zionist leadership. (In Egypt as well as in Algeria, a considerable proportion of the membership of these organizations consisted of Ashkenazi Jews, with their more highly developed national consciousness, although in Iraq the organization was more autochthonous.) Indeed, until the establishment of Israel, immigration from these countries was practically nil (with the exception of Yemen, whose Jews were among the most backward of the Jewish communities in Islamic countries, which goes a long way in explaining their messianic drives).

Mass immigration from these countries began only after the Israeli War of Independence and the establishment of the state. This war, which inflicted a humiliating defeat on the Arab armies, combined with the rise of nationalist movements in the Arab countries, provoked a reaction typical of countries passing in a "catastrophic" manner to the national stage of development. The Jews were uprooted and expelled (just as some African countries, upon gaining independence, expelled most whites and Asians, and as the Indonesians butchered their Chinese minority), and as is well known, this was not unwelcome to the Israeli authorities, who were avid to receive the expelled Jews. In short, the Oriental immigration was not motivated by a national consciousness or initiative. It was caused by external forces. The Jews themselves were almost completely passive in the process. North African and Egyptian Jews, who had a measure of choice about the destination of their emigration, were roughly divided in their decisions. The intelligentsia and wealthier classes emigrated to France, the poor mostly to Israel. To the extent that free choice was exercised in this matter, the preference was France, not Israel. Iraqi and Yemenite Jews did not have a choice.

The political passivity of the Jews from Islamic countries was apparent again in their posture in Israel. Until recent years they have been politically passive, without a true political or class consciousness (Polish-born Menachem Begin paradoxically served at one time as the focus of the Orientals' communal frustration, as their "savior") thus perpetuating their secondary socioeconomic status in comparison with the dominant position of the Ashkenazim.

In short, the immigration from Islamic countries cannot be viewed as a result of the development of a national consciousness and movement among their Jews; nor can it be interpreted as proof that the Jews from those countries constitute a "nation" and not a religious-ethnic community like the Jewish communities in Europe before emancipation.

PART TWO
A New Homeland

FIVE

Creating a New People

In the preceding chapters we established that contrary to Zionist theory, Jews could become productive within advanced host societies and that this need not have any national significance. Indeed, throughout their history, except for brief interludes such as the mass impoverishment of East European Jews during the nineteenth century, the Jews fulfilled vital functions for their hosts. They were productive.

The national movement that arose in Eastern Europe was aware from the outset, albeit somewhat romantically and not always clearly, that the realization of Jewish national potential depended on changing the nature of the Jewish people, on transforming the Jewish people from a caste into a nation.

In this respect, the territorialists (including the Zionists) were on target. For despite the numerous national traits of East European Jews (separate culture, dense territorial distribution, broad range of occupations, etc.), they were not a self-supporting nation in the full sense of the word. They were a caste, fulfilling various functions within their host societies. Any political or cultural autonomy they could have achieved, short of a sovereign territorial concentration within which they fulfilled all national functions, would fail to release them from their caste status. For proof, we need only look at the accelerated rate of assimilation of Soviet Jewry during the first two decades following the 1917 Revolution—despite official recognition of their separate nationality and official encouragement of the Yiddish language and Yiddish cultural and educational institutions, and extending to the establishment of the Jewish Autonomous Soviet Region in Birobijan. Soviet Jews, then, had been granted conditions of cultural autonomy within the Soviet system and had been offered the choice of territorial concentration. But they failed to take advantage of either opportunity and preferred to assimilate within the Russian Soviet culture—just as Jews elsewhere always opted to join the culture of the dominant ethnic group as soon as they were permitted to do so. I, therefore, define the situation of the Jews of Eastern Europe as *protonational*, not national in the full sense of the word. To achieve full nationhood they would have had to develop a full national system. That was impossible even in Eastern Europe, for the Jewish communities there were still inseparably interwoven with the surrounding population.

In order for Jewish national potential to be realized, a complete dissociation from the old Jewish framework was required—from the Orthodox community and also from the caste, for in many cases even those who had left the religious community still belonged to the caste. The dissociation had to be territorial, cultural-linguistic, and psychological. It was necessary to create a new mentality, the mentality of a territorial nation. It is difficult if not impossible to create such a mentality ex nihilo. It is much easier to shed the old, unwanted existence if there is an ideal model to emulate. It was, therefore, necessary to create a new national myth, a new human ideal, an ideal diametrically opposed to the existing reality. This need for an opposed mythical model could not be fulfilled by the "folkist" Yiddishist ideology, which romanticized the existing "plain everyday Jew."

For people to make such a leap, to persuade themselves that this particular leap was feasible at all, another assumption was needed—that potentially, the ideal already exists within them, and that it need only be realized. There was a fundamental and absolute need for the Zionist myths of an "exiled territorial nation" ever longing to return to its soil, that only on that particular soil could "true" Judaism, free of exilic deformations, blossom forth. The desire for and need of a transformation required a myth of restoration that transforms potential into actuality. Hence the need for a myth of ancestral soil whose magic touch turns pauper into prince—a soil whose mystic properties do not exist in any other land.

The myth was supplied by the Old Testament and the Hebrew language, both of which are connected first and foremost to the pre-Jewish, Israelitic era. The pagan, political, earthy, and open character of the period—the times of the Judges and the Kings, the Song of Songs and the Book of Ruth, as opposed to the Jewish caste-community existence, based on religion and estrangement from the world—was obvious from the start, even before the spread of modern Biblical criticism. We find it in the poetry of the young Shaul Tschernikovski (1875–1943), turning his back on Jewish existence at the time ("The people is old / and its god has aged with it!") and evoking "the mysterious God of the deserts, Lord of the hosts conquering Canaan by storm, lately bound and gagged by phylactery thongs" ("Facing the Statue of Apollo"). We find a total rejection of Jewish life as then lived in the prose works of Yoseph Chaim Brenner and Micha Yoseph Berdichevsky, and earlier, in the works of Peretz Smolenskin, J. L. Gordon, and Mendele Mocher Seforim. The romantic dreams of Abraham Mapu evoke the period of the First Commonwealth, not the Judaism-dominated Second. One of Chaim Nahman Bialik's most important tales, "The Tale of Three and Four," deals with King Solomon, lover of a thousand wives from all corners of the earth, and the love of a Hebrew youth for the daughter of a foreign king (obviously non-Jewish), whose marriage becomes a celebration of the triumph of love and nature over the artificial barriers raised to separate them (namely, the barriers raised by the teachers of the Halacha on one hand and the anti-Semites on the other). Obviously, no such tale could have been told about any period after the Babylonian exile. The romantic nostalgia for the ancient national past is then mostly for a pre-Jewish past, and could, as far as halachic Judaism is concerned, even be termed anti-Jewish.

At the same time that these literary works were being written, the ideologues portray the ideal figure of the liberated Hebrew (*Hebrew* is emphasized as distinct from and the opposite of the rejected *Jew*, being both a desired future state and an evocation of an ancient past, in the usual pattern of myths of renewal, harking back to a lost golden age). This ideal undergoes several transformations over the years, though it is always contrasted with the stock figure of the exilic Jew in Zionist literature, which is not much different from anti-Semitic caricatures. (Religious Zionism, with which we shall deal later, saw things differently, but it was only an appendage to the main body of the Zionist movement.) Ze'ev Jabotinsky, the rightwing Zionist leader, depicted the ideal with Nietzschean strokes, poeticizing about a "proud, generous and ruthless race." Members of Hashomer (Watchman, the first Jewish self-defense organization in Ottoman-ruled Palestine) wore Bedouin robes, rode thoroughbred Arabian mares, and affected Bedouin customs and vocabulary. In *Exodus*, Leon Uris portrayed another manifestation of this ideal in the figure of Ari ben Canaan, whose very name, Ari, betrays an admiration of the Aryan type. (Uris, of course, wrote his novel for the consumption of the Jews of America, whose popular culture is dominated by this ideal.) This type is but the incarnation of the Nordic demigod in European (not only Nazi) racist literature: blue-eyed, blond, hardy, calm, uncomplicated, fearless, unintellectual. The figure of Elik, in Israeli writer Moshe Shamir's *Telling of Elik*, also partakes of this naive self-abasement before the mythical ideal of the enemies of Judaism. But for the anti-Semites, too, this figure represents a romantic nostalgia of effete intellectuals for the primeval, natural ferocity of the pre-Christian Viking sea-raiders, just as the Hebrew ideal is pre-Jewish.

The realization that the transition to Eretz Israel must be a transformation of personality, an amputation of one essence and the adoption of another (with the implication that the other is really the true self, which blossoms forth on contact with the mysterious properties of the ancestral soil); that this transformation must be effected by an effort of will, in which one overcomes the false, external, exilic being; and that this true being is organically connected with the new land, which is one and the same with the ancient one, both true being and soil linked in a mystic union—all this achieves a typical expression in the works of the early Zionist visionary and pioneer A. D. Gordon.

On making Aliya to Eretz Israel we expect to have a certain sort of impression. But I, coming to the Holy Land, felt far, for whatever reason, from what R. Yehudah Halevy [the renowned medieval Jewish poet] felt on such an occasion. Even later, on visiting the settlements, I did not feel what any good Zionist should feel. . . . True, nature here . . . is wondrously beautiful, but I feel something lacking in this beauty, perhaps because there is too much of it. It looks artificial, not natural. . . . In the landscape of Eretz Israel, I feel like an alien. . . . It is not like nature in Russia, to which one is accustomed and for which one has an affinity of the soul. Nature in Russia not only understands you, but you also understand it completely, in all its simplicity and naivety, sometimes punishing and sometimes caressing you—and all in a simple way, like a simple, naive and loving mother. Not so nature in Eretz Israel. It is also a loving, compassionate mother, and perhaps its love is even deeper, but it is incomparably more sublime in its spiritual greatness. . . . [1]

This highly personal confession is a concentrated expression of the mood of the revolutionary pioneers who chose to go to Eretz Israel. This mood is quite distinct from those of the Jews who arrived as refugees or who came as a result of religious motivations. For the latter, who settled in one of the "Four Holy Cities" (Jerusalem, Hebron, Tiberias, and Safed), there were no problems of adjustment to the country's landscape. Just as they paid scant attention to the landscape in their countries of origin, they scarcely noticed that of the Holy Land, except for feeling edified by the holy air. The aim of their pilgrimage was spiritual-religious, and they felt no compulsion to develop an emotional affinity for the country's physical landscape. In their few descriptions of the landscape, however, they provide an immediate and perhaps franker account of their real feelings about it than the ideological, Zionist immigrants, who felt compelled to love it physically, not spiritually. (A founder of the Meah Shearim quarter in Jerusalem, writing in the 1880s, had this to say: "Jerusalem was surrounded by a wasteland, overlooking the desert, bandits sometimes being seen in broad daylight among the terrible rocks and bluffs wrapped in eternal desolation.")[2]

Gordon admits that the landscape of the country fails to excite in him what "any good Zionist should feel," namely, an immediate attachment to the "homeland landscape." It may be assumed that very few Zionists really did feel it. Further on in the passage, Gordon makes a conscious effort to appropriate this landscape. To that purpose, he indulges in naive, ridiculously artificial anthropomorphisms. Obviously, he loves the Russian landscape, feeling comfortable only in it. So he anthropomorphizes it into a "mother" (certainly not a "father," for earth is a "mother"). Eretz Israel is also a "mother," of course. On and on he goes, ascribing to soil, trees, and stones qualities of "spirituality," "sublimity," "greatness," and "love"—all to explain why it is so much more difficult for him to feel attachment to it than to his native Russian land. This strange exercise in mystification, this bizarre search for an "organic" connection to this particular piece of territory (presumably, had he been unknowingly transferred to a similar landscape, say in Anatolia, Greece, or Sicily, he would have contrived to discover in that vista too the same "spiritual" qualities he pretended to himself to find in the geological formations and flora of Palestine at the beginning of the century), was, despite its artificiality, necessary for the attempt to change one's inner nature in order to create a "new man." In short, the Zionist pioneers knew from the outset that a simple physical move to the country they had chosen as a homeland would be no salvation at all. They saw that all that the religious Jews of the Old Yishuv, who had not undergone any such transformation, had managed to establish in the country was another Jewish exilic community, and a beggarly one at that, living off the handouts of other Jews abroad. In 1907, Chaim Weizmann, on his first visit to Palestine, garnered the following impression of Jerusalem, the heart of the Old Yishuv:

> Jerusalem was a city of alms distribution, living on charity, on letters of petition, on handouts. . . . The hotel to which I was introduced was a tottering ruin, infested with vermin, where peculiar-looking people went in and out at all the hours of the day, all seemingly engrossed with one thing—wasting their own and other peoples' time.[3]

There is a similar revulsion toward the "exile" in Eretz Israel in the writings of David Ben-Gurion. In describing his impressions upon arrival in the country in 1907, he wrote:

> When the intoxication of our first enthusiasm wore off, we glimpsed an old picture within the new frame—the picture of the "Galut," the exile. The skies were new, the skies of Eretz Israel, and the land was new—the homeland. But the people, the members of the Yishuv, were people of the "Galut," engaged in "Galut" occupations.[4]

It may be concluded, then, that the concentration of Jews in any place, including Eretz Israel, does not in and of itself give birth to a nation. It creates a caste community. For a nation to be created, the Jews must undergo a mental and social transformation and establish a society that is in diametrical opposition to the concepts and values of the Jewish caste community.

This very change, the transformation of a member of a caste community into a member of an emerging territorial nation, is exemplified in the life of A. D. Gordon. Eliezer Schweid writes:

> When in the Diaspora he [Gordon] lived as an observant Jew, but did not feel quite "at home" in his orthodox environment and was attracted to the young people [the pioneers]. When in Eretz Israel he lived with the young people, but again did not feel at home among them, and described himself as "an old-fashioned Jew, not only by upbringing but also by my very being, by the root of my soul" (from a letter to J. Fichman). . . . One way or another, it was as if he were always standing at the threshold of the society to which he belonged. Again and again he had to make an effort of will in order to belong. . . . Striking roots in Eretz Israel was then, for him, an ordeal which lasted throughout his life.

Every day he had to renew within himself the decision to "make aliya," to desire it and justify it. . . . No gain in this struggle was ever permanent.[5]

It is obvious that the Orthodoxy Gordon grew up with and the new national existence into which he wanted to become integrated were sharp and clear opposites. To change from one to the other, he felt that he would have to break away from traditional Orthodoxy. This, as Schweid notes, was a struggle Gordon waged all his life—a struggle that was not primarily political or social (although a member of the petit bourgeoisie had to transplant himself to another class, to become a manual worker, in order to tear himself from his former social environment), but an internal one.

> One must begin with the individual. For him, this sentence was the cornerstone of Zionism. It had already been said that his decision to go to Eretz Israel and engage in manual labor was not a romantic act or an act of self-immolation, but an attempt to reorient his life.[6]

The emphasis on the individual means a change of character, a change of the "Jew" into something else, into a man with a national territory. Otherwise Gordon's thought, or the following excerpt from a biography of Ben-Gurion, remain incomprehensible:

> [Israel Shochat] was impressed by David [Ben-Gurion], by his "Eretz Israelian" quality, from his very first day in the country. This quality has never been fully clarified; it was more an intuited trait than one that could be grasped rationally. Essentially, it indicated the reversal of the "exilic" mentality and implied Hebrew rootedness in the soil, pride, courage, a pioneering spirit and a love of independence. The term "Eretz Israelian" can mislead, because some people whose families had dwelled in the country for generations were defined as "exilic," whereas some newcomers possessed the "Eretz Israelian" quality even before arriving in the country.[7]

This awareness of an inner transformation is typical of the pioneers of the Second Aliya (the second major wave of Zionist immigration, which began around 1905 and lasted until the eve of World War I). They were also under the influence of the 1905 Russian Revolution, and many of them had a highly developed socialist world outlook. They had a combined craving for personal transformation into the seeds of a new nation and for a social revolution that would bring about the establishment of an egalitarian, toiling, and just society.

As described in the biographies of Ben-Gurion and Berl Katzenelson, the number of individuals who actually underwent this transformation was quite small. But the institutional and attitudinal patterns that they set had a decisive influence on the psychology of succeeding generations. At that time, however, the vast majority of Jews in the country were members of the Old Yishuv, mostly extremely Orthodox, or of the First Aliya village settlements (the *moshavot*) whose farmers were markedly petit bourgeois in outlook and largely traditionalist, or of small towns like Tel Aviv, whose population was middle class and provincial. Basically, they still maintained most of the traits of exilic Jewry.

To realize more fully the broader significance of the sociopsychological changes that were taking place within the Jewish people, it should be noted that the so-called Eretz Israelian traits have nothing to do with Palestine or Zionism. From Ben-Gurion's biography it is clear that the Aliya did not create this change; on the contrary, this change caused the Second Aliya. Those who came with the Second Aliya possessed the Eretz Israelian mentality on arrival in Palestine; they had already undergone the inner transformation while still in Russia. This transformation basically meant the severance of the psychological and cultural nexus with the Jewish caste community and the adoption of a territorial-national, even non-Jewish, self-awareness. This occurred either as a result of assimilation or the burgeoning of a nonreligious national self-awareness. In this way, assimilated German-Jewish youth, who had but the vaguest notion of Judaism and who had previously considered themselves full members of the German nation, became the elite of the pioneering and fighting Eretz Israel youth after immigrating to the country in the 1930s. They had simply translated their identification with the German people and the German land into an identification with Eretz Israel, both with the people and the land—sans any Jewish spiritual content. The Russian war hero Yosef Trumpeldor (1880–1920) was in a similar fashion transformed into a Zionist-socialist activist.

Out of the same national transformation of part of the East European Jewish community came revolutionaries, officers, generals, and commissars of the Soviet Union—a large gallery of outstanding personalities including Leon Trotsky, Karl Radek, and Maxim Litvinov among the revolutionary politicians, Lazar Kaganovich among the commissars and Yona Yakir among the generals. In point of fact, David Ben-Gurion, Mordechai Namir, and Zalman Aranne could just as easily have become Bolshevik or Menshevik leaders as Zionist ones. The backgrounds of the two groups were much the same. Ze'ev Jabotinsky's social and educational background, for example, in many respects resembled Trotsky's. Both were equally removed from Jewish culture and equally infused with European civilization (though Trotsky's seems to have been the deeper and more brilliant personality). Only differences of chance and temperament caused the one to become a Zionist and the other a revolutionary socialist. (In a graceful autobiographical sketch, Jabotinsky makes a point that he never felt any particular sentiment for Eretz Israel.)

Pinhas Rutenberg, who embodied both alternatives in a single personality, is perhaps the most significant and best example of all. He had no Jewish background, was supremely comfortable with the cultures of Russia and Western Europe, was a grand entrepreneur and an engineer of genius. At first he aligned himself with the revolutionary Russian parties and was one of the persons responsible for the execution of the priest cum agent provocateur Gapon (in the abortive 1905 revolution). For a while he was military governor of Petrograd (later Leningrad) under Kerensky's Provisional Government (after the 1917 February revolution). Then he converted to Zionism and became one of its most dynamic and constructive figures, founding the Palestine Electric Company. Weizmann described him thus:

> Rutenberg was a man of immense energy, tact and ability in dealing with the many Jewish factors he encountered, which was the more surprising in view of his lack of Jewish background. He came from the revolutionary school, and had been trained in adversity. It is my impression that if Kerensky had remained in power, Rutenberg would not have come back to Jewish life.[8]

Similarly, the gap between the unqualified assimilationist Arthur Koestler and Zionism was immeasurably smaller (in his youth, he sought admission to a kibbutz) than the distance between Zionism and a denizen of Jerusalem's ultra-Orthodox Meah Shearim quarter. Zionism and assimilation are on the same plane, and transition between the two is easy. This plane is completely divorced from that of the Jewish caste community, which is alien to it and detests it.

The polemics of Ben-Gurion and Katzenelson—particularly the latter—and other leading figures of the Second Aliya and Third Aliya (which took place after World War I) are replete with a characteristic bitterness directed against the Soviet Union and the Yevsektzia (the Jewish branch of the Soviet Communist party) on one hand and the Jewish socialist (autonomistic) Bund on the other. The causes for this vindictiveness seem to be both sociopolitical and psychological. Politically, they wanted to influence the primarily young and revolutionary Jewish audience that had shaken off the shackles of the religious community and also cut itself loose from its parents' petit bourgeois background. This group stood at the juncture of three equally tempting political courses: socialism in the service of world revolution, Jewish-socialist nationalism fighting for the autonomy of the Jewish people and the Jewish working class within Eastern Europe, and Zionism. But the obsessive bitterness we find in the writings of Katzenelson, for example, seemingly points to a further cause: each of the leaders of labor Zionism found himself at one time at this juncture and waged within his own mind the debate between these three possible options, each with profound and decisive arguments in its favor and to the detriment of the other two. Katzenelson decided in favor of Zionism, but even after the passage of many years, he was still troubled by the gnawing doubt that perhaps the Communists or the Bundists were right or partly right after all. The bitterness of his polemic could have stemmed from the effort to silence the doubts in his own heart.

We thus come to draw several distinctions between the character of the prestate Yishuv population and that of the population once the state was established. Those who had undergone what I have defined here as the national transformation, the metamorphosis into a territorial nation, and their descendants in particular, felt a growing alienation toward the Jewish people in the Diaspora and an increasing conviction that its history had no relevance for them.[9] The young descendants preferred the adventure stories of Rider Haggard and Rudyard Kipling to stories about the shtetl. They identified with the young Germans in Erich Kaestner's *Emil and the Detectives* or with the young Americans in Mark Twain's *Tom Sawyer* rather than with Sholem Aleichem's East European characters.

The growing estrangement toward the Jewish caste community's history and identity, inseparable from the transformatory process, created a need to find a term that would specifically define the Jew who had undergone the transformation and ceased to be Jewish in the former sense. From the beginning of the twentieth century the term *Hebrew*, which also implies a connection with the pre-Jewish past, gained currency (although in European languages *Hebrew* is synonymous with *Jew*). The term was prevalent until the early fifties, when a deliberate effort, guided by Israeli state educational institutions, was made to blur the Israeli sense of separate nationality in the name of the broader "Jewish fraternity," under the slogan "We are all one people." Undoubtedly, there was a need in Israel to identify with the victims of the Nazi massacre of European Jewry and not to to treat them condescendingly from the height of an arrogant "Hebraism." But the basic reason was different: the Zionist leadership never dared to draw the logical conclusions called for by its premises, never had full faith in its own ideology.[10]

The alienation from Jewish historical consciousness also resulted in an alienation from Jewish historical suffering, and with it also from Jewish "ressentiment."[11] Long historical memory, delving endlessly into centuries-old, even millennia-old, disasters, massacres, and wrongs (accompanied by the convenient forgetting of wrongs and atrocities perpetrated by one's own people against others), lachrymose self-righteousness, are all characteristics of groups whose experience is basically passive, as the Jews have been politically for thousands of years. In such groups, the consciousness of being victims accumulates and poisons the very being of the members. At times these characteristics become the primary content of their self-awareness as a group, a perverted focus of their self-identity. Finally, this suffering becomes a source of pride ("I am persecuted and hated, a sign that I am valuable and unique, for which I am envied and hated"), rather than engendering a desire to be rid of it. Active, sovereign groups immediately externalize the damage done to them and accept the wrongs as an almost inevitable part of the historical experience. They do not entertain unending resentment toward those who wronged them in the past (they are well aware of being capable of perpetrating similar deeds, and in the past may indeed have committed them). The Germans harbor no desire to avenge themselves on the Swedes, who spread death and destruction throughout Germany during the Thirty Years War. The English absorbed the Vikings and Normans, people who devastated whole counties in England, and made them part of themselves. The Russians overcame their resentment of the servitude and humiliation imposed by the rule of the Mongol Golden Horde. Similarly, that segment of the Israeli population which underwent a full national transformation feels completely at home in its country, and its emotional and cognitive connections to the age-old Jewish experience are blurred and lacking in bitterness. A case in point is also the ease, compared with Diaspora Jews, with which a large part of the Israeli people made its peace with the Germans.

Neither do Orthodox Jews suffer from ressentiment. The rigid framework of the community and the Halacha, which create a total separation between Jews and *goyim*, accompanied by an absolute certainty of the infinite superiority of the Jew over the *goy*, leaves no room for such a psychological development. To develop ressentiment, the victim must feel inferior to his persecutor. The Orthodox Jew does indeed have a physical fear of the *goy*, just as a man might fear a tiger, but he does not as a result feel ressentiment toward the tiger or feel he is its inferior. Indeed, to a certain extent the Orthodox communities in Israel regard the state, just as any Orthodox community abroad regards the state in which it lives, as an alien "gentile" state (and in Israel this is accompanied by a particular hostility, for the very reason that the state claims to be Jewish).

Ressentiment, then, occurs among Jews who have lost the social and value framework of the caste community but retain their caste characteristics. At the same time, their values are in effect those of the non-Jewish European-American world, although they hardly identify with that either. This complicated description of their placement and character parallels the identity crisis that is their main psychosocial trait. I refer here mainly to those circles in Israel that originated in the Central European middle classes, who in thinking and way of life continue the caste existence of their original milieus. These are the Ashkenazi groups connected mainly to the right-wing Likud party (the Oriental circles connected with this party have different characteristics and their connection results from a somewhat different motivation) and the bourgeois circles connected with middle-of-the-road religious Zionism. Typically, these characteristics also apply to a large part of the Jewish petit bourgeoisie in the Diaspora, mainly in the United States, which feels an obligation toward Israel.

These Jews are suspended between different worlds, unable or unwilling to belong and be completely committed to any of them. The discrimination against and persecution of the Jews left an open account between them and the society within which they had lived (or from which they had been ejected). They carry this grievance even after emigrating to Israel, and it torments them even more if they stay in the Diaspora. Israel, for them, is not, therefore, a political-territorial space devoted to the cultivation of a normal national life, but a historical revenge. Even in Israel they continue to suffer from the identity crisis that haunted them in the Diaspora. In this respect, despite the political independence they enjoy, they have not undergone a transformation into an autonomous national identity. Their independence is purely external. Their political-public being is reflexive. It is not dictated by their autonomous interests (which they are unable to identify) but by their burning urge to pay the *goyim* back in kind.

Thus, through the Israeli army, they want to square accounts with the *goyim* for all the humiliations and persecutions they have suffered personally or in their historical memory—even if that score is not settled with the Christian gentiles who, as a rule, were the actual persecutors, but with their Arab neighbors and more particularly the hapless Palestinians subject to Israeli rule (conveniently defined as "partners of the Nazis"). This kind of Jew still suffers from the inclination of the caste-community member to view all non-Jews as *goyim*, all of whom are anti-Semitic, all—black and white, red and yellow—falling into a single, undifferentiated stereotype of a hostile, menacing foreignness.

To be sure, this commingling of Arabs with Cossacks and Nazis is highly tendentious, and on one level these Jews are quite aware of the enormous differences involved. They perceive European and American Christian *goyim* as powerful; any attempt to take direct revenge on them would be too risky. In addition, these Jews harbor toward this sector of *goyim* the hidden admiration a victim has for his tormentor. They desire to emulate him. They desire to demonstrate to the European-American "Nordic supermen," whose claim to superiority they tacitly accept, that Jews too are brave, they too are blond, they too are Panzer troops and combat pilots, they too are well-rooted farmers, they too have a landed gentry—and thus restore their self-respect and respect in the eyes of the *goyim*. Moreover, they wish to demonstrate, again to the same *goyim*, that they too know how to trample others into the ground, just as they themselves have been trampled. The Palestinian Arabs under Israeli rule, on the other hand, are powerless, so these Jews select them as objects of victimization.

Finally, it should be emphasized that in the vast majority of cases, the pilots, farmers, and warriors are not the same Jews as those who boast of them. Most of the former come from the ranks of those who have undergone the national transformation; their motivations are not historical revenge or a show for the benefit of the *goyim*. Their only wish is to live their own lives, without burdening themselves with history. They wish to live in the here and now and not on a historical stage in which accounts are symbolically settled with all the enemies of the Jews, from Amalek, Pharaoh, and Sennacherib down to Bogdan Chmelnitzky and Adolf Hitler. Theirs are not the souls of slaves, daydreaming of vengeance.

Perhaps a main factor in Israel's psychological hold on the Jewish Diaspora is that that part of the Diaspora that has lost its religious framework but has remained locked within the Jewish caste uses Israel as a means of venting its complexes by proxy. These Jews imagine themselves to be part of the Israeli people, while maintaining their own comfortable caste existence in the Diaspora. To that end they also pay Israel handsomely to enable them to maintain this imaginary, vicarious existence. They magnify themselves in their own eyes without having to share in the toil of farming or the dangers of battle. The obvious aim of the slogan "We are all one people" is to enable them to imagine that they and the "Israeli heroes" are one and the same.

Thus Israel deliberately helps Diaspora Jews maintain an illusory existence rather than face their own problem of identity. It is in the obvious interest of the Israeli leadership to prevent such an honest self-appraisal, which might lead to the creation of a different, genuine Jewish identity. In the present state their externalized, false identity is focused on Israel and serves it as a source of financial and political support. And it is false because it has nothing to do with their daily lives. An identity is shaped by the real relationships of a person with the surrounding world, not by his or her daydreams.

That may also provide an explanation of the peculiar connection established with this element of Diaspora Jewry by a person like Menachem Begin. The Zionist revisionist movement, in which he grew up, emphasized grand gestures, uniforms, theatricality, dramatic military and political acts, and resounding declarations, and was contemptuous of the true, bitterly difficult processes which are the only means by which people or groups change their nature. A petit bourgeois Jew in Poland, the United States, or Israel could imagine, by donning a uniform and listening to inflammatory rhetoric, that he had become a hero and a conqueror—without having been obliged to do anything to achieve this status. Zeev Jabotinsky poeticized about "hidden glory," declaring that every Jew is a potential "prince"—in other words, that Jews are noble by their very nature (just as the Germans imagined themselves to be innately superior). He had already become what he wanted to become by the very fact that he wished to become so. There was, therefore, no need for him to change. He could secretly bask in pleasurable daydreams about his inborn nobility and superiority, without having to prove their existence by realizing them.

One can understand Jabotinsky's motives. He wanted to instill in the miserable Jewish masses of Russia, Poland, and Galicia a self-confidence and pride that would enable them to pull themselves out of the mire. But when self-confidence and pride are not based on reality, on true work, achievement, and struggle, they are false and empty, a mere pretense. Indeed, this belief in innate superiority is the basis of racism and of all the varieties of fascism, which is also a reason for classifying revisionist Zionism within the general category of fascist psychology, even though personally Jabotinsky was an exemplary European liberal.

Because they did not undergo a true transformation, despite all their nationalistic muscle flexing and theatrical displays of force and pride, these Jews remain unchanged, consumed by an unconsummated ressentiment. They simmer in the bitterness and fury and hatred caused by past injuries, without being able to change and overcome themselves. They remain imprisoned within themselves, repeating obsessively the same shopworn clichés that they took for truths in their youth and that still frame their whole world outlook, oblivious of their utter unreality. Thus a bond was formed between a large section of world Jewry and those who arrayed themselves with the revisionist movement in both Yishuv and state. Neither achieved redemption, because they are incapable of understanding that redemption does not depend on these or other borders or a more nationalistic political setup, but on inner change and liberation.

From the very beginning of Zionism a tension has existed between these circles and those concentrated around the Labor movement (as well as that part of the middle class that cooperated with it), who believe that sovereignty and independence cannot be achieved by shortcuts but only by hard work and personal and social transformation. That was the basis of their alliance with Chaim Weizmann, a man who carried out in his own life the transformation from the aimless futility of small-town Jewish existence in Russia to the solidity of personal, professional, and political achievement. Weizmann defined the difference as follows:

> It was a conflict between those who believed that Palestine can be built up only the hard way . . . who believed that in this slow and difficult struggle with the marshes and rocks of Palestine lies the great challenge to the creative forces of the Jewish people, its redemption from the abnormalities of exile, and those who yielded to these abnormalities, seeking to live by a sort of continuous miracle. . . . I felt that all of those political formulas, even if granted to us by the powers that were, would be no use for us, might possibly even be harmful as long as they were not the product of hard work put into the soil of Palestine. Nahalal, Daganiah, the University, the Rutenberg electrical works, the Dead Sea Concession, meant much more to me politically than all the promises of great governments.[12]

Jabotinsky did not introduce this theatrical attitude. Theodor Herzl, the founder of political Zionism, did. It was Herzl who put his trust in a charter for Palestine. It was he who insisted that delegates to the Zionist congresses dress and behave with decorum, with suitable, respectable, restrained manners, "like the gentiles," which earned him the ire and derision of the East European Zionists, mainly Achad Ha'am. Herzl's route from total assimilationism (he lacked any Jewish background), his idea of solving the Jewish question in a single blow, by mass conversion to Christianity, to Zionism, which is allegedly the opposite pole (but both aim at ending the existence of the Jewish caste community), testifies to the absence of any positive Jewish values in his world view. All of his values (and in this he resembled Jabotinsky) were those of the non-Jewish world in which he had grown up and into which he had failed to gain unqualified admission. We find a most interesting illustration of this in his utopian novel, *Altneuland*, in which he depicts the future Jewish Palestine. Significantly, the hero's employer is an

arrogant, self-assured Prussian nobleman—the very opposite of the Jew—
and most of the pictures Herzl draws of future life in Eretz Israel seem
designed to impress and win his praise.

Rather than possessing independent Jewish values that the new Jewish
society was supposed to realize, Herzl played a game of charades before a
mirror, squinting all the while to see how the performance appears to the
Prussian, the Jew's opposite. All the big talk current now too of "Jewish
pride" and "proud Jews" (cf. the description of Golda Meir as a "proud
Jewess") is the pathetic expression of a desperate feeling of inferiority, a
feeling that there is nothing to be proud of, a desperate effort to display
freedom and pride instead of being truly free and proud, and therefore
without any need to display it.

SIX

Holy Land versus Homeland

Jewish settlement activities in Palestine during the nineteenth century reveal a surprising simultaneity: the expansion of the Orthodox Old Yishuv, with its emergence from behind the walls of the holy cities, mainly Jerusalem, and the First (Zionist secular) Aliya. On the face of it, it would seem that there was no connection between these two occurrences and no common motivation.

Indeed, the two were not quite simultaneous. Mishkenot Sha'ananim, the first Jewish Orthodox quarter outside the walls of Jerusalem's Old City, was built with the help of Sir Moses Montefiore in 1860. Two other quarters, Nachlat Shiv'ah and Machane Yisrael, were built in 1867, and Meah Shearim was built in 1874. This expansion was not motivated by Zionism; it was a simple result of the growth of the Jewish (and non-Jewish) population in Jerusalem during the mid–nineteenth century. As the population increased, the Arab landlords in the Old City raised rents, and settling outside the walls became the only means of alleviating congestion. Still, it took courage to move out into the lawless wilderness beyond the walls. The early settlers of Mishkenot Sha'ananim lived in their new, spacious homes only during daylight hours, returning to the Old City to spend the night in their old, overcrowded flats. Montefiore even paid people to live in the quarter he built for them. There wasn't much Zionism here.

The first true Zionist step taken by members of the Old Yishuv was the establishment of the Motza (1873) and Petach Tikva (1878) agricultural settlements. Unlike the settling outside the walls (which did not press for the coming of the messiah), these ventures, which ultimately failed and were revived only later by members of the First Aliya, provoked the fury and intense opposition of leaders of the Orthodox religious community. The national potential within the Old Yishuv, shackled by its communal-traditional institutions, was indeed very limited.

It should be emphasized that these settlement activities by members of the Old Yishuv were not Zionist in the same sense as those of the Zionist immigrant settlements. The founders of the former were ultra-Orthodox Jews who never intended to work for Jewish independence in the political, secular sense. They simply were fed up with living on charity from abroad and of leading nonproductive lives. Essentially, the Old Yishuv may be summed up as follows:

> The Old Yishuv was based on the traditional view which conceived settling in Eretz Israel as of a religious-spiritual value for the Jewish people as a whole.... The concept, "Eretz Israel," was thus connected [in the eyes of Jewish traditionalists] to a group which devotes itself to the fulfillment of a metaphysical-spiritual function—the study of the Torah and prayer—and which demands that the Jewish Diaspora take care of its material needs.... Whereas the Old Yishuv considered the anomaly of its economic structure a positive phenomenon, justified by the supreme values of its culture, the new [Zionist] Yishuv considered its existence justified only to the extent that it succeeded in creating a society with a "normal" structure, independent and living off its own labor.[1]

Those members of the Old Yishuv who settled on the land in order to farm were not representative of but exceptions to the norm. That they failed shows that they had no followers, no human reserves.

There was of course no direct connection between this expansion of the Old Yishuv and the establishment in Russia of the Hibbat Zion and the Bilu (a Hebrew acronym for a pioneering group intending to settle in Eretz Israel) movements in 1882 and the subsequent founding of the Bilu settlements in Palestine a few years after the agricultural ventures by the Old Yishuv settlers. These movements came about as a result of the outbreak of pogroms in southern Russia. But there did exist a common factor, a factor which contributed on one hand to the growth of the Old Yishuv and which enabled the Bilu settlements on the other hand to strike roots in the country and which made possible the very flow of immigrants to both the Old Yishuv and Zionist settlement.

This factor may be described as Palestine's return to history. Starting with Napoleon's invasion of Egypt and the siege of Acre in 1798, Palestine became increasingly more interesting to European powers that were channeling great sums and diplomatic effort into the search for protégé communities that would serve as footholds in the struggle for the heritage of the crumbling Ottoman Empire. This was the basis of the century-long alliance between the Jewish community in Palestine and Great Britain—during which time the Balfour Declaration was issued—and which finally collapsed with the publication of the British White Paper in 1939.

The conquest of Palestine by Egyptian ruler Muhammad Ali (with the support of the French) and its occupation by Egypt from 1832 to 1840, when the Turks succeeded (with British help) in reestablishing their rule in it, marked the country's return to the field of international power struggles. Following the more progressive Egyptian occupation, the Turks introduced certain reforms that improved the conditions of the population, including those of the Jews, and, in comparison with the past, created conditions of relative security. The great powers' growing involvement was also connected to the development of sea and land steam-power communications, which began to extend their lines to the Middle East, thus restoring the area's ancient importance as an international crossroads. The idea of excavating a canal through the Suez isthmus, which began to gain currency following the Napoleonic invasion, also served as a magnet to world interests, which began to focus on the area and mainly influenced Egypt's standing in it. With the improvement of communications, the flow of pilgrims and tourists to Palestine increased (with the active encouragement of their governments, which considered this as a means of penetration). The British opened their first consulate in Jerusalem in 1838, and its function was not only commercial but also to protect British interests in this part of the Ottoman Empire. The British were followed by the French and Prussians (1843), the Russians and the Austrians (1849). Alongside the consulates, religious and cultural organizations sponsored by the powers commenced operations. They initiated missionary activities, established churches, schools, and hospitals, and acquired land. The first hospital in Jerusalem was established by the British in 1842, and others followed. These hospitals, which served the general population without discrimination, improved the health situation of the city, which then and also later, down to World War I, contained half the Jewish population of the country.

Furthermore, the powers, in their rivalry for influence, undertook the protection of the various local communities. The French assumed the guardianship of the Latin Catholics, the Russians of the Greek Orthodox; beginning in 1868, the German Templar religious movement established settlements in Jaffa, Sarona, Haifa, and Jerusalem under German protection. The British had no "natural" protégé community in the country, so from the 1830s on they undertook the protection of the Jewish community (the Russians protected their Jews in Palestine, too, even though they persecuted them at home). This policy was initiated by the first British consul, William Tanner Young, who was instructed in the letter of appointment issued to him by the Foreign Office in London on the authority of Lord Palmerston to provide protection to the Jews in general, and also to provide the foreign secretary with reports on the situation of the Jews of Palestine.[2] This policy was also enforced by his followers. The activities of Moses Montefiore and Lawrence Oliphant should be viewed within the framework of British interests (Montefiore obviously had Jewish interests at heart, but these meshed well with British intentions in the area and as a result he won understanding and support in London). Protection of the Jews was also provided by the consuls of Germany and Austro-Hungary until the country's conquest by the British in 1917.

As a result of the general improvement in living conditions in the country, the Jewish population in Jerusalem alone increased from 3,000 in 1838 (according to a census initiated by Montefiore) to 10,500 in 1873–1874. Jews accounted for more than half of the city's population, which then numbered 20,500; in 1876 their numbers grew to 14,000.[3] Jewish communities began to crop up in Haifa, Nablus, and Jaffa as well.

It is true that most of the Jewish immigration was religiously motivated, but improvement of conditions was also a factor. (Jews, like other people, always migrated from areas where their living conditions were difficult—and in the nineteenth century this meant mainly Eastern Europe, particularly Russia—to more hospitable places. It should also be noted that at that time, as a result of the economic prosperity which attended the opening of the Suez Canal, many East European Jews settled in Egypt.) The assumption that any Jewish immigration to Palestine was motivated either by religion or nationalism ignores normal, nonideological population movements. Many of the Jews who moved to the port city of Jaffa after its restoration at the beginning of the nineteenth century and those who settled in Haifa did so for nonideological reasons. Had their motives been primarily religious, they would have settled in one of the four holy cities. The growth of the Jewish population of Jaffa, for example, was connected with the increasing volume of Christian pilgrims moving through Jaffa to Jerusalem:

> The [Jewish] community in Jaffa began to grow only after the end of the Crimean War in 1857. Many Christians began to arrive in Jaffa harbor to visit their holy places. At that time commerce in Jerusalem increased and many of its inhabitants moved to Jaffa, including also Sir Haim Amzalek, who established a trading house with other partners. . . . About ten years later several Ashkenazis also moved from Jerusalem to Jaffa, and the first Ashkenazi congregation was thus founded in Jaffa. The community increased by slow stages until the immigration wave from Russia and Poland which arrived in the early 1880s, simultaneously with the First Aliya of Hibbat Zion. The emergence of Jewish Jaffa was then connected with the idea of agricultural settlement, and it grew with the development of the settlements in Judea. . . . By the end of the century the Jewish quarters, Neve Zedek (1888) and Neve Shalom (1890), were founded, and they served as a basis for the new Jaffa and later of the city of Tel Aviv.[4]

From the very beginning, then, Jaffa and Tel Aviv were characterized by a productive commercial and industrial activity far removed from the sanctified but beggarly atmosphere of Jerusalem.

The growth of the Jewish population in Palestine thus became possible only thanks to the general development taking place in the country as a whole. This may be obvious in so far as the Old Yishuv is concerned. But if we examine the motivations and composition of the First Aliya, which is the first Zionist wave of immigration in the sense of its being national-secular, we find that in many cases Zionist convictions played only a secondary role in the decisions to emigrate to, of all places, Palestine.

In *The Bilu Movement*, Shulamit Laskov notes that organized attempts to found Jewish farming settlements, as a result of the growing discrimination by the tsarist government against Russian Jewry, were made in the United States even before the establishment of Hibbat Zion and the Bilu movements, which aimed to do so in Palestine.[5] These took place in New Jersey, Louisiana, Kansas, and Oregon (the latter, named New Odessa, had non-Jewish members as well, was communal, and preached free love). A well-known case is that of the Jewish American journalist, Mordechai Emmanuel Noah, who at the beginning of the nineteenth century proposed to establish a Jewish state as part of the United States. We see then that from the outset Palestine was not the sole objective of Jewish nationalism. These attempts, which preceded by many years the mass Jewish emigration to the United States, generally failed owing to lack of support and guidance and the absence of absorption mechanisms. In 1881, Laskov writes,

> a wave of panicky immigration reached Palestine too, unorganized, without any ideological motivation and without any support. . . . It is almost impossible to estimate its real size, as no organization supported it and no lists of the immigrants were kept. . . .
>
> This immigration wave had varied causes. Toward the end of 1881 rumors spread about Sir Lawrence Oliphant's plans for the settlement of Palestine by Jews, greatly exaggerating the sums at his disposal. . . . There were also rumors about a vast sum collected by eminent Englishmen for the Jews, which led many to surmise that the British government was interested in helping the Jews to settle in Palestine. [Indeed, in view of British middle eastern policy, as we have seen it beginning to take shape, there was a kernel of truth in these desperate rumors]. . . . Anyway, among the Jews these rumors aroused . . . great hopes to settle in Turkey, where Jews lived honorably and opulently.
>
> Although it was a panicky migration, the idea of the return to Zion did play some role in it. Furthermore, the bitter disappointments encountered by the emigrants to the United States forced the refugees to seek another haven. There was also a practical reason. . . . The cost of a trip to Palestine was only an eighth of the price of a ship's ticket to the United States. As a result, the refugees did not consider the trip to Palestine as an irreversible step, unlike a journey across the ocean. . . .
>
> It is an outstanding fact that the two phenomena which effected a profound change in Jewish life—the migrations to the United States and to Palestine— manifested themselves at first in ideological-practicing organizations which were tiny compared to the migrations themselves and to the intensity of the debates of principle which took place among Russian Jewry in this matter. The number of people who intended to settle in person in Palestine, convinced that this was the right course, was even smaller than their brethren who emigrated to America.

Under these circumstances, Laskov's observation that the idea of the return to Zion "did play some role" in this emigration is hardly more than lip service to her preferred ideology. One of the most salient facts here, which she ignores, is that emigration to the United States soon reached a volume greater by a factor of tens and hundreds than emigration to Palestine, even though the cost of a trip to Palestine amounted to only an eighth of the price of a journey to America. One wonders what would have happened to even the modest emigration to Palestine were the costs equal. The main conclusion apparently to be drawn from Laskov's description is that the volume of migration is not determined by "idealistic motivations," which in any case affect only a small minority (and when they affect many, then not for long), but by two variables: the pressure at home to emigrate and the absorptive capacity and powers of attraction of the destination of emigration (the life of the new arrivals in the United States was sometimes even harsher, at least at first, than the life they left behind them, but America's attractive powers were not diminished thereby, the reason being the vast range of opportunities and high mobility that characterize U.S. society). Laskov does refer further on in her book to Bilu members' fears that emigration pressures might ease as a result of improved conditions in Russia stemming from Prince Tolstoy's appointment as minister of the interior. The absorptive capacity of the emigration destination, particularly when it becomes highly attractive, as happened in the case of the United States, sometimes becomes the decisive factor affecting immigration, even when pressures at home diminish. Jews were not the only people to emigrate to the United States; nor were miserable conditions or persecution in the country of origin the only motivating factor. More often than not, emigration was the result of impatience with the limited opportunities in the mother country and of the hope of conquering new worlds beyond the ocean. The abundant opportunities, the open and nondoctrinaire society, and the wealth of the new world were magnets of attraction which Palestine could never rival, even after it had been developed and major absorptive opportunities had been created—despite the nationalistic verbiage used to try to attract Jewish immigration.

The decisive factor in attracting immigrants, namely Palestine's absorptive capacity, was a consequence created by the improvement of the machinery of government and internal security, by the protection of foreign nationals and religious and ethnic minorities from the arbitrariness of the local authorities by the "capitulations" regime of the great powers, and by the channeling of large sums of money to the country by the same powers, which created new sources of livelihood and established health and educational institutions open to all elements of the population. To some minor extent the New Yishuv and the First Aliya relied on the Old Yishuv for livelihood. The First Aliya agricultural settlements, however, insufficiently supported by funds from Russia, failed to strike firm roots until they were rescued by Baron Edmond de Rothschild's massive infusion of capital. And the same "Baron settlements" and their periphery became in their turn the absorptive basis of the Second Aliya pioneers, despite all the bitter friction between the new pioneers and the settled farmers.

Agricultural settlement in Palestine was seen as more national than any other form of settlement. The reasons are obvious: there was no sense of national audacity in the establishment of suburb such as Meah Shearim and Nachlat Shiv'ah in Jerusalem. This was what Jews had always done, both in the Diaspora and in Eretz Israel. On the other hand, agricultural settlement, particularly at a time when the majorities of the populations of all countries were engaged in agriculture, carried with it the implication of becoming a complete national society rather than of being a caste that derives its livelihood from traditional Jewish occupations. (Nevertheless, a distinction should be made between ideological agricultural settlement like that of Bilu, with its deliberate national goals, and settlement motivated by purely local conditions, with no national motives, which eventually could become enmeshed within a national system, such as that which the Jewish community of Safed wished to establish in a communication with Moses Montefiore.) Land settlement also had a further meaning essential to nation building, namely the seizure of territory, without which the nation remains disembodied. The psychological aspect is equally important: the transition from "easy" urban occupations to hard farm labor carried with it the same message—the building of a new consciousness, national-territorial in nature, which I described in the preceding chapter.

Even so, agricultural settlement in Eretz Israel was a necessary, although not a sufficient, condition for the creation of a national society. Jewish agricultural settlements, albeit without ancestral Biblical homeland romanticism, were established in Argentina, too. Jewish villages were established in tsarist Russia itself during the first half of the nineteenth century, in the Cherson and Wohlin districts, and many Jewish farmers could be found in Bessarabia. The utter dedication of Old Yishuv, leading Orthodox settler Yoel Moshe Salomon and of the secularist Bilu pioneers could not save the early settlements from failure. There are numerous reports of the waning of national enthusiasm in the New Yishuv around the turn of the century, and a number of its members supported the British government offer in 1903 to establish an alternative Jewish homeland in Uganda. The ideal of national renaissance moved Salomon and his associates among the Old Yishuv no less than the Bilu pioneers, but that was not the decisive factor that gave birth to the national nucleus that began to form in the country.

This national formation had two causes, one external and one internal. The external cause was that Palestine was a backward, neglected part of a decaying empire, a country with a sparse, largely backward population lacking political or national consciousness. Had the country been organized as a reasonably developed Arab national state, it is unlikely that it would have permitted the growth of a Jewish national society within it. The East European Jewish national effort would have then turned in a different direction. The Argentinian parallel is instructive: large-scale Jewish agricultural settlement could not have developed into a nation there either, for the country was already an organized national state. In this respect, Zionism was very fortunate. Had the national effort begun after World War I, a delay of only forty to fifty years, it would haved missed its opportunity.

The second, internal cause was the type of organization established by the Second Aliya in Eretz Israel. True, the First Aliya, as well as the Old

Yishuv pioneers, had been guided by a national ideal. The Bilu members had even begun to think in political terms, as can be seen from the wording of their articles of association. Their stated aim was "a political, economic, and national-spiritual revival of the Hebrew people in Syria and Eretz Israel." But their activities lacked this declared political dimension. It is, therefore, the general opinion among historians that the origins of the political consciousness in the New Yishuv are to be found in the crystallization of a leading group from among the members of the Second Aliya, the wave of immigration that began to arrive from Russia in 1904 and continued through to the eve of World War I.

Many of these immigrants, who began to arrive shortly before and immediately after the abortive 1905 revolution, were imbued with socialist-revolutionary ideas.[6] They emigrated from Russia to achieve the inner transformation described in chapter 5, and also to effect a proletarization and productivization of the Jewish people. To achieve these aims they hired themselves out as farm workers in the Jewish settlements (thus combining the ideals of the return to the land with socialist values). But here they found themselves trapped in an economic vise: the early Rothschild-supported settlements largely switched over to plantation-type farming (except in Galilee) and employed for this purpose neighborhood Arab labor. In spite of their awareness of the importance, from a national perspective, of employing Hebrew pioneers, the veteran farmers were reluctant to employ people who were often inferior to the Arabs as laborers, and who both demanded higher wages and fought from the very start for the right to organize. Economic expediency generally defeated national ideals.

The economic weakness of the workers vis-à-vis the farmers in the old established settlements forced them to set up mutual aid institutions and to organize in order to struggle for their interests. As most of them were unpropertied farm laborers, they moved freely all over the country and coordinated their activities (or just looked for work) from Rosh Pinah in the north to Gederah in the south. Their organizational work was facilitated in that many of them had originally been members of Zionist-socialist parties and shared common ideologies. In this way their organizations, which at first numbered only a few dozen members, became the first countrywide voluntary organizations to be established in modern Palestine, not only among the Jews but among the country's population as a whole. Furthermore, from the beginning these organizations had a definitely political character. The pioneers sought to establish a socialist Hebrew society and were well aware that only control of the machinery of a state can create a basis for socialism. The "natural" development of Jewish settlement in Eretz Israel would never have resulted in socialism but rather in the emergence of an ordinary bourgeois society, as had been predicted by Borochov. Their national and social views, then, constituted a single integral whole—as opposed to the romantic and individualistic outlook of the members of the First Aliya.

The leadership group of the agricultural laborers—which in the course of time established the Achdut Ha'avoda (Labor Unity party), later transformed into Mapai (an acronym for Eretz Israel Workers' party), and became the core of the country's labor movement—is the body which created, in collaboration with the liberal bourgeois elements, what came to be known as the organized Yishuv, the basis of the new Israeli society.[7] The process by which this organization amassed power and achieved domination in the Yishuv and the World Zionist Organization was the struggle for Hebrew labor in the Hebrew farming settlements.[8] And it is a profound paradox that the struggle for Hebrew labor, by which this domination was achieved, in itself had largely failed. But this paradox is highly symptomatic of the deeply paradoxical nature of the Hebrew Yishuv and the state that followed it. It is a dialectical process in which weakness is a lever of power, whereas power contains its own disastrous structural weaknesses.

The agricultural settlements established by the First Aliya in the Judean Plain and in Galilee could never, of themselves, have led to the establishment of a Jewish society and state. As Anita Shapira has written,

> the members of the First Aliya were very few in number. For a variety of reasons, farmers in the Judean Plain developed a monocultural plantation system, employing numerous workers for brief, intense periods. The Jewish settlers were too few to work the plantations alone, whereas they found in the neighboring villages Arabs who were prepared to work for low wages. . . .
>
> From the very beginning of the Zionist settlement the dialectical nature of the development of the Jewish and the Arab populations became apparent. The growth of the Jewish population fed the growth and strengthening of the Arab population. As A. Munchik put it, "By settling a single Hebrew farmer in the Galilee we helped settle two Arab fellahin, and each [Jewish] planter settled in Judea created sustenance for five foreign workers." Around the Jewish settlements, the Arab villages abandoned during the nineteenth century were repopulated. The foci of Jewish settlement became the nodes of an Arab population relying for its living on the Hebrew settlements.[9]

Arthur Ruppin therefore drew the conclusion that

> it was necessary to shift into mixed farming, to deal not only with plantations but also to grow cereals. . . . In this way, one of the most important problems in the settlements will be solved—the problem of labor. Until now the farmers in the plantation communities have been unable to employ Jewish labor throughout the year, only during a part of it. When seasonal work intensifies, there are not enough Jewish workers and the farmers hire Arab labor from the neighboring villages. . . . If the settlements cultivated both cereals and plantations, the farmers would be able to employ Jewish workers throughout the year.[10]

This was not a suitable basis for the development of a large-scale Jewish population. The agricultural sector consisted of a very thin layer of Jewish landlords and the Arabs who worked their estates. True, Jewish villages and small towns such as Petach Tikva, Rishon Le'Zion, and Zichron Ya'akov, inhabited by Jewish craftsmen, skilled workers, merchants, and professional people, did develop around these estates. But because the plantations created belts of Arab settlement around the Jewish communities, the Arabs would undoubtedly have developed in the course of time into an urban work force, as apprentices, servants, and ordinary labor. Indeed, in the period preceding the establishment of the state of Israel such phenomena were in various stages of development, and they resurfaced, particularly after the West Bank and the Gaza Strip were conquered in the Six-Day War. As Shapira writes,

> Arab labor in the settlements caused a contradiction between Zionist ideology and the conventional Zionist methods of its application. Instead of giving birth to a new type of Jew, it recreated in Palestine the figure of the big leaser of Polish estates—but here he is also the owner of the land, and has shed the caution, bred by age-old wisdom, in his relationship with his inferiors. Instead of leading to a growth of the Jewish population in Eretz Israel, the plantation system led to a Jewish minority and an Arab majority; instead of reinforcing the Jewish hold on the land, it limited Zionist freedom of maneuver.[11]

The majority of Second Aliya pioneers may not have been conscious of all the economic, social, and political implications of this situation. But they were fully and immediately aware of its consequences: unemployment and starvation. They tried to compete with the Arab laborers under the same conditions and for the same wages. But even when they were able to match the experienced Arab worker in productivity, they could not subsist on the wages paid him. Their consumption habits were different and more expensive; they also had cultural needs that the Arab worker did not have. And above all, Arab workers could maintain a higher standard of living on the same wages, since they usually had their own farm which they could cultivate in the off seasons. The Jewish farmers, for their part, felt as Zionistic and nationalistic as the workers—even more so, for the workers' internationalist outlook and atheism were anathema to them. The farmers also claimed that the higher wages demanded by the Jewish workers undermined their farms' profitability, thus harming the national enterprise. But above all, the farmers were motivated by the natural preference of an employer for the unorganized, submissive Arab worker who lacked the elementary concepts of organized struggle, to the Jewish worker with his militant-socialist class consciousness, ready to fight the Jewish bourgeoisie of the country before it barely existed.[12] The ensuing struggle for Hebrew labor in Jewish agriculture, which lasted in various forms down to the establishment of the state of Israel (and in the privately held agricultural sector was never completely won), had a decisive influence on the character of the Hebrew Yishuv—on the structure of its institutions, its political makeup, and its geographical distribution. It may not be an exaggeration to assert that this struggle created the conditions that made it possible to establish the state.

As explained, the plight of the Hebrew workers drove them to organize. The primary organization focused on the primary necessity, food. The initial nucleus of the laborers' collective was the kitchen established in the freeholders' settlement (the *moshavah*) to ameliorate the life of the Jewish farmhands, who owned it collectively. The kibbutz and the moshav, the collectives that grew out of this nucleus, came about as a result of the search for the most effective way to organize in order to gain employment.

But an association of the penniless, in itself, is powerless unless it controls or owns some needed resource. The Hebrew workers were hardly needed as a labor force. There also seems to be some exaggeration of the importance of the Hashomer (Watchman) organization, which peddled security to the Jewish settlements against pillage and theft by the neighboring Arabs and tried, not always successfully, to tie it to an obligation to employ Jewish labor. Indeed, there were more takers among the Jewish farmers of this commodity, security. Still, the largest moshava, Petach Tikva, which even under the British mandate supplied some 50 percent of the total citrus export of the Jewish economic sector, made do without Hebrew watchmen. Only the chief of security there, Avraham Shapira, was a Jew.

Thus the realization grew that the struggle for Hebrew labor could not be won either by competition with Arab labor or by class struggle against the plantation owners. Furthermore, it was recognized that this course offered the workers no hope of striking roots in the country. Now, considering that the vast majority of the immigrants in the Second and (post-World War I) Third Aliyas were penniless and sought employment as manual laborers, the failure of the struggle for Hebrew labor was not merely a personal or class failure but also the failure of immigration itself, the failure of Zionism.

From this very failure, labor's emerging leadership derived its power. It could present the World Zionist Organization, dominated by the Jewish middle and upper middle classes in the Diaspora, with two alternatives: either support the immigrant workmen, even against the Yishuv's middle class, or resign itself to the failure of Zionism.

The maneuvering of the labor movement's leadership within this network of relationships, as described by Yonatan Shapiro, was complex and multifaceted. On one hand, the labor leaders' influence on the rank and file and their ability to organize them effectively depended on the leadership's ability to supply them with work and minimal living conditions, something which only the financial resources of the Zionist organization could provide. On the other hand, the leaders' standing vis-à-vis the Zionist organization was dependent on the degree of control they had over the workers and their ability to organize them as an effective body. Furthermore, to maintain their position, the labor leaders had to make sure that Zionist organization funds earmarked for the workers would pass through their hands. They provided an ideological justification for this by arguing that only they were fully cognizant of the long-range objectives of the Zionist enterprise and that only they could focus on them beyond any considerations of profit (which guide the middle and upper middle classes) or of daily hardships, which force the workers into hand-to-mouth decisions. The realization of Zionism, then, depends on a leadership that knows how to rise above the short-term calculations of both the bourgeoisie and the proletariat. Anita Shapira writes:

> From the start the labor movement's power as a body was aimed outward—toward the institutions of the Yishuv and the Zionist movement, and toward the employers; and inward—toward its own membership. Constructive socialism needed the ability to exert political pressure to gain its ends as regards land settlement and Hebrew labor in the moshavot, as well as the ability to exert pressure on the workers, to prevent their indulging their particular interests. To that end the labor movement imposed its discipline on the individual in a hundred ways, on the basis of the conviction that only the continuous control of the individual by the community can prevent the erosion of his idealism and preserve the national goals.... All this led to the conclusion that the labor movement and its executive body—the Histadrut—must be a centralized organization. In the view of the workers, the Histadrut's centralized power seemed to ensure the future of Zionism in the country. In the eyes of others, it was a force scheming to seize power over the entire country.[13]

The Achdut Ha'avoda party, which founded the Histadrut, wrested in 1920 from the World Zionist Organization a recognition of the principles of national land and national capital. The settlement of self-employed Hebrew workers was recognized as preferable from a Zionist point of view to private settlement, particularly since there were among the immigrants not many who possessed capital.

The labor leadership could then claim, with considerable justification, that the working class was the main bearer of the Zionist enterprise. Only the unpropertied workers, supported by national capital and guided by their leadership towards the realization of national aims, would be capable of disinterested action. The Zionist organization largely acquiesced in this argument, and as a matter of fact it was also accepted by the leadership of the urban bourgeoisie. (That the independent farmers could find no ideological counterargument was one of the main causes of their political weakness.)

The support extended by the Zionist organization to the Histadrut and the temptation created thereby for noneconomic expenditures aroused sharp criticism among important circles in Diaspora Zionism.

Zionist circles in the United States, headed by Supreme Court Justice Louis Brandeis, argued that too much aid could corrupt its recipients. The European Zionists argued to the contrary. Since people of means were not emigrating to Palestine, they claimed, the pioneers who were prepared to do so should be given all possible help. Chaim Weizmann explained that since the pioneers were young and believed in socialism, they would not consent to work for the profit of private entrepreneurs but only for the good of the nation as a whole. Therefore, support for the building of a nationalized economy was dictated by necessity. The victory of Weizmann and the Europeans in this debate made the Zionist movement's leaders shift their policy to support of the workers and their enterprises.

The main confrontation in this dispute took place in 1928. The head of the Zionist executive of the 1927 Zionist Congress, Harry Sacher, undertook to change the economic policy of the preceding executive. He decided to enforce efficiency and eliminate deficits by, among other means, canceling unemployment benefits and financing public works. A Report of the Experts, written by three economists appointed by a group of eminent Jewish businessmen, was published in 1928. The report sharply criticized Zionist economic policy in general and the Histadrut enterprises in particular. It claimed that the latter's primary aim was not economic but rather the establishment of a new socioeconomic order. The experts proposed to finance the settlement of people of means and not of unpropertied workmen and recommended an end to the Histadrut's involvement in economic activities.[14]

The report aroused the ire not only of the workers but also of the bourgeoisie. The Eretz Israelians felt that the entire Yishuv was being arraigned, and most of them rallied to the labor leaders' demands that the Zionist organization invest according to national considerations, not profit and loss calculations. It soon became clear that all the Zionist parties were united in their opposition to the report. In consequence, the Zionist organization's leaders began to withdraw their backing from the report. The meeting of the Zionist executive ended with resolutions that satisfied the labor leadership. It was decided to allow settlers themselves to decide which form of settlement they preferred. Reaffirmation was given to the principle that land acquired by the Zionist organization would remain national property and not be transferred to private ownership.

The Zionist organization now officially adopted the principle of the ideological dominance of Achdut Ha'avoda in the Zionist movement and the precedence of its approach to the realization of Zionism and the building of the land. A public statement in the Zionist organization's organ, *Die Welt*,

asserted clearly that all Zionists, even nonsocialist, must accept the socialist principle as central in the building of the country, because the socialist Zionists are the most devoted builders of Zionism. This statement implied the acceptance of a paramount ideological tenet of Achdut Ha'avoda, asserting the identity of the class interests of the [Jewish] workers and national interests of Zionism and socialism.[15]

The waves of immigration in the twenties and thirties, which included many capitalists and members of the middle classes, prompted the main labor party, Mapai, to adopt a moderate, reformist stance, displaying a readiness to participate in coalitions with the middle class in the Zionist organization.

> This decision was based on the [party's] realization that under the new conditions created by the Fourth Aliya, a policy of a pressure group limiting itself in advance merely to the procurement of financial support cannot serve the party's aims any longer. The best way, then, to defend its positions was to join the Zionist executive, where the middle-class parties had a majority, and thus defend the economic interests of the labor organizations from within.[16]

There was much support among the country's middle class for the labor movement. Arthur Ruppin repeatedly insisted that only the workers could establish the Jewish state, since the middle classes were not prepared for self-sacrifice. The leaders of the middle-class General Zionists party and their organ, the Ha'aretz daily, also admitted this. The recognition of labor's superiority spurred the labor leaders to collaborate with the middle class, once the former reached the conclusion that if they joined the coalition they could become the dominant force in the Zionist leadership even without winning elections.

On this basis the labor movement succeeded in gaining control of the Zionist movement as a whole. The opposition to its ascendancy by the New Zionist Organization (the "Revisionists"), founded by Ze'ev Jabotinsky, proved ineffectual, due to the Revisionists' radical, protofascist, and populist positions, which could not win the support of the liberal and conservative elements among U.S. and West European Jewry or form a common front with the Eretz Israelian bourgeoisie. Thus the labor movement gained national hegemony, and its leaders—David Ben-Gurion, Berl Katznelson, Yitzhak Ben Zvi, Yitzhak Tabenkin, Eliyahu Golomb, etc., together with Chaim Weizmann and his circle—became the leadership of the Yishuv and the World Zionist movement.

The triumph of the labor parties and the principle of Jewish labor in the Zionist movement necessitated a separation between the Jewish and the Arab economic sectors. As detailed above, Jewish agricultural labor did not fare well in competition with Arab agricultural workers. Since agriculture was the main economic field of the Yishuv until 1935, it became necessary to subsidize Hebrew workmen so they could survive the competition. That meant subsidization of the employers as well, and hence of the Yishuv as a whole. The various attempts to establish joint Jewish-Arab labor unions failed because of the utterly different sociocultural structure of the two national groups and the national opposition between them, as a result of which the workers' primary loyalty was to their respective national groups. A separation was thus inevitable.[17]

The realization of this inevitability prompted Ben-Gurion to propose cantonization of the country, a territorial and economic separation between the Jewish and Arab sectors. He opposed connections between Jewish capital and Arab labor but favored connections between Jewish and Arab capital and Jewish and Arab labor, namely contacts between Jews and Arabs of the same class. This general tendency was strengthened by the growth of a Yishuv urban industry, which gained significance from the mid-1930s on. Here there was no problem of Arab labor, for it was found that the Arab worker was as yet unsuitable for industry. But there arose a problem of a different kind, that of marketing the Hebrew industrial product, which was usually both inferior in quality to and more expensive than industrial imports. Thus began a campaign to "buy Hebrew," meaning the Yishuv product manufactured by Jewish labor. This was a campaign in which workers and urban employers had a common interest. It led to the conclusion that a separation between the two national economic sectors of the country was mandatory.

The Arab sector began to reach the same conclusion. Just as Jewish workers formed picket lines against the employment of Arab workers by Jewish businesses, Arabs formed picket lines against the employment of Jewish workers by Arabs.[18] The Arabs also began to accept the territorial principle of separation of sectors and the identification of the areas of national settlement with the right to work.

As a matter of fact, starting with the 1929 Arab riots, the Zionist leadership accepted the validity of the approach that called for territorial entrenchment in solid areas of settlement, ensuring maximum security for their inhabitants. That provided further impetus to the tendency toward residential and economic exclusivity first manifested in the ideology of Hebrew labor. The boycott imposed by the Arabs after the riots also reinforced the trend toward separation, with the Yishuv functioning as an independent economic unit as far as possible under the circumstances.

Ben-Gurion, who recognized the existence of an Arab national movement, strove now more than ever for the development of a continuous zone of settlement—along the coastal plain from the south of Jaffa northward to Haifa, eastward along the Jezreel Valley from the plain of Acre to the Jordan Valley, and northward from Migdal to Metullah in Upper Galilee. Two years after the 1929 riots he explained the reason for this configuration: "In these valleys it is possible to achieve an absolute Jewish majority without displacing a single Arab family." It is worth noting that the establishment of this zone of settlement was possible because Arab lands in flat lowlands with high settlement potential, mainly large estates owned by absentee landlords, were put on the market. "It may be stated that to a large extent, the map of the lands offered for sale in 1891 corresponds to the map of lands in actual Jewish ownership in 1936," writes Shalom Reichman.[19] It is clear from Reichman's book on the shaping of The Yishuv settlement map that as a rule more Arab lands were offered for sale to Jews than there were funds available to the Jewish settlement authorities to buy them. This means that the settlement authorities could largely determine the direction and nature of their land acquisitions, according to their own list of priorities.

This policy led to the formation with the Jerusalem area of the backbone of the modern Hebrew Yishuv. The population of areas added after the establishment of the state (such as Beersheba and the northern Negev, Lachish, the Arava and Eilat) is still small in comparison with the preponderance of the backbone. In fact, this policy determined in advance the structure of the country's partition, although the two national movements refused to recognize this fact and each continued to claim the whole area of Palestine.

It follows, however, that this separation—effected for reasons of security and demography but chiefly, it seems, because of the inability of the Yishuv to face open economic competition—also created the need for permanent subsidization of the Hebrew community. As long as this community remained at a relatively low economic and technological level, it would not survive open competition in the regional and the world markets and would be forced to subsist partly on the support of the Zionist movement in the Diaspora. As this support was now being administered under the control of the labor movement, the whole Yishuv, to a greater or lesser extent, became dependent on it. The hegemony of the labor movement, then, was achieved by its superiority in Zionist ideology and practice, which enabled it to wrest control of the world Zionist movement. On the other hand, its control of the financial resources of the Zionist movement and its economic and political ascendancy enabled it to shape the Yishuv as a separate, economically dependent entity; and this, in turn, ensured and perpetuated the Yishuv's dependence on the Zionist apparatus.

We have here then a paradoxical, dialectical situation. The realization of Zionism, involving the territorial-national concentration of the Jews and their conversion into a normal nation among nations, could not take place without a separation between the Hebrew and the Arab economic sectors and the isolation of the Hebrew economy not only from the Palestinian but also from the world economy. Had this not been done, the Yishuv might well have developed into a planters' economy employing Arab labor, unable to absorb Jewish workers. But the isolation of the Yishuv forced it into a dependence on Diaspora Jews, and the more it developed the greater its dependence became. The existence of the Yishuv (and of the state that followed) was then predicated on the existence of a rich, large Diaspora, since only such a Diaspora could muster the financial (and political) resources needed for the support of the Yishuv. In short, the existence of the Yishuv and of the state that followed necessitated the nonrealization of Zionism, if Zionism means the concentration of all Jews in their country, as well as making the Jewish people in its country economically and politically independent, like other nations. A structure emerged within which Western, particularly U.S., Jews supplied the Zionist movement and the Israeli leadership (which in the course of time became synonymous, when the Israeli leadership became the sole arbiter in the Zionist movement) with the economic means and political support needed both for the functioning of the Yishuv (and the state) and for the immigration and absorption of the Jews from Muslim and East European countries. The basic interest of the structure then is to prevent a drastic diminution of Western Jewish communities, whether by assimilation or by immigration to Israel. (The immigration of a few thousand U.S. or British Jews to Israel has negligible weight, so that one can continue to preach immigration from those countries and call for the abolition of the Diaspora without any fear that this would lead to real results.)

In other words, the concrete conditions under which Zionism developed made its survival dependent on the perpetuation of the situation which it ostensibly aimed to end. Furthermore, these conditions meant that the original aim of the Zionist movement—the normalization of the Jewish people and its transformation into an independent territorial nation, functioning as an equal member of the family of nations—could not be realized. The Yishuv and the state remained dependent on outside aid and donations, somewhat in the style of the Old Yishuv. But whereas members of the Old Yishuv received money to pray for the Jews around the world, the Israelis receive money and political support from world Jewry in order to act out the daydreams of Jews in the postemancipatory era. However, the division of roles between the Jews in Eretz Israel and those abroad remains essentially similar. In both cases, the Jews of Eretz Israel serve in a vicarious capacity for Diaspora Jews, according to the changing values of the times. In chapter 5 I discussed the false identity a Diaspora Jew acquires by his illusory identification with Israel. But this potential Israeli identity is utterly imaginary; there is no such thing. A person is what he is and is not what he is not. The Israeli, required to act out a role for which he is paid and to adopt affinities which are foreign to his nature, is also unable to realize his true identity, whatever it is. The slogan "We are all one people" is a cliché that hides from both sides their problems of identity. It also creates a state of collective neurosis, if one may be permitted to use such a term in a work with a sociopolitical bent.

Another paradox is that had the Hebrew economy developed according to pure economic logic, a viable capitalistic economy might have resulted, needing no outside aid—but most of the workers would have been Arab, and the relatively low standard of living it could have provided would have repelled Jewish immigration even further. In truth, no distinct Hebrew sector would have been formed and a single Palestinian economy would have emerged, without the autonomy and independent organization that were an essential prerequisite for the eventual achievement of independence. On the other hand, this autonomy, created by the Hebrew labor organizations, was always dependent on the support of the Jewish bourgeoisie abroad and resulted in a permanent structural dependence of Yishuv and state on outside support.

This structure of dependence became a central power source of Israel's governing elite. After the failure of the Zionist organization to control, via the Report of the Experts, the ways its money was spent by the Yishuv, the leadership of the Yishuv (and later the state) became the only effective authority deciding on the uses of these funds. The Zionist organization's control of these expenditures was and is purely nominal. The same is true of U.S. government financial support and of German reparations. These are immense sums, not subject to the control of either the donors or Israel's citizenry (for they are not tax moneys collected within the country), and they are all subject to the discretion of Israel's power elite. This means that contrary to the practices of countries whose governments are truly account-able to their citizens for all income and expenditure, the Israeli establish-ment is largely exempt from submitting a detailed account for a very large part of the country's income, though not to the extent of the ways these funds are being spent. This situation provides the executive branch with a freedom of action and maneuver unparalleled in democratic societies. The only control exercised over it is by the Zionist parties, who see to it that the party in power does not appropriate all the funds for its own use but di-vides it among them according to an agreed ratio.

This dependence of the Yishuv and the state on external financial sup-port, as against the elite's independence in the use of this money, was es-tablished by the labor movement in the 1920s and 1930s and shaped all of the Yishuv's institutions and internal relations, becoming a governmental asset in its own right. When the labor movement was defeated in the 1977 elections, this asset passed into the hands of the Likud. It should be stressed that this arrangement also provides the elite with an immense ad-vantage in its relations with the electorate. Funds that were not collected as taxes from the public can be manipulated to bribe and influence it to an extent beyond the powers of ordinary governments. This is due to the pub-lic's feeling that since this money is not the public's, any of it which does reach the public is in a sense a gift from the authorities. This means that the power elite has a vested, inherent interest in the continued dependence of the country on foreign financial sources, in the thwarting and postpone-ment of economic independence. For if ever such independence is reached and foreign support dispensed with, the establishment stands to lose a most important power base. It should be assumed, therefore, that such an evil day will never come to pass, insofar as this depends on the power elite. The latter can ensure that it never does, since the elite controls the volume of public spending in the country.

On this background, it is clear why the idea of neutralism—much dis-cussed at the time of the establishment of the state—in spite of sympathy toward the Soviet Union as a result of its triumph over Nazi Germany, its determined support of the establishment of Israel, and its vital military aid during the decisive stages of the War of Independence, could not be accepted by the leadership of the labor movement and other sectors of the Yishuv establishment. The financial sources of the Zionist movement were at the time almost exclusively in the United States. These sources were a vital base for the continued functioning of the Yishuv, which now became a state, and for the continued control of the establishment. This dependence became even more absolute owing to the mass immigration and the enormous problems of its absorption. It may be assumed that even if the leadership had been interested in conducting a neutralist policy and had asked for help from the Soviet Union, it would not have been granted, as Russia was then in the midst of postwar reconstruction efforts. It may be further assumed that even had such aid been offered by the Soviets, Israel would have refused it, for it could have no influence on the sources of the aid, unlike the influence it could wield over the Zionist movement and the powerful Jewish lobby in Washington.

Finally, the Zionist movement, from its inception, viewed itself as an ally of Britain. The conflict with Britain, which began to develop in the 1930s, was thought to be a superficial difficulty marring a fundamental identity of interests. When the alliance with Britain finally collapsed, the Zionist leadership hastened to ally itself with Britain's successor, the United States. Zionism never veered from the basic tenet that it needed an alliance with a big power with vested interests in the region to back it against the resistance of the local population.

SEVEN

The Hebrew People versus the Palestinian People

The Hebrew Yishuv and the state of Israel were shaped and structured by a continuous struggle against the Arab-speaking population of Palestine and the neighboring Arab countries supporting it. This process also shaped the character and consciousness of the Arabs, who now began to regard and define themselves not only as Arabs but also as Palestinians, although a separate Palestinian national consciousness had arisen among them even before the intensification of this struggle.[1]

The various currents in Zionism have always been reluctant to admit the existence of a Palestinian Arab nationhood, since such an admission would imply that the Palestinians also have national rights to the country. They argued that since the Arabs of Palestine are part of the greater Arab nation, which already has several states on vast land areas with immense natural resources, it is not unjust to demand that this great nation evacuate a tiny corner of its holdings to make room for the homeless Jewish people. Presumably this frame of mind is what prompted Israel's prime minister Golda Meir to declare "I am a Palestinian, too," in order to ridicule the very notion that such a people exists. But any account of the debate that raged in the Yishuv from the turn of the century onward, and particularly after the issuance of the Balfour Declaration, about what has been defined as "the Arab problem," would lead any fair-minded person to conclude that Meir's declaration was less than ingenuous.

The Palestinian nation is a new entity, largely shaped by the conflict with Zionism. As Yehoshua Porath points out, the name *Palestine* had been used primarily in defining the jurisdiction of the Greek-Orthodox Patriarchate that existed "uninterruptedly since the days of Roman rule, and apparently exercising its authority originally over the three Roman subdivisions of Palestine: Palaestina prima, secunda and tertia."[2]

But an awareness of a distinct population-territory Palestinian entity was already manifest, though ill-defined, at the beginning of the twentieth century. This is testified to by the appearance of the nationalistic newspaper *Falastin*, published in Jaffa in 1913 by the Christian Al-'Issa brothers. This budding nationalism arose even though administratively and from the point of view of the continuity of population and language, Palestine was a part of the Syrian province of the Ottoman Empire. Porath writes:

> This conception of Falastin as distinct from Syria is also found elsewhere. During the years 1915–1916, a Jerusalem Muslim youth, apparently a member of the Al Khalidi family, kept a diary in which he describes his activities, feelings, and contemporary events. He also relates conversations he had with other Jerusalemite youths about the war and the future of the Ottoman Empire. The fate of the Arab lands under Ottoman rule was a constant subject of these discussions. It transpires from them that the existence of Falastin as a distinct area, not part of a broader region, as distinct as Syria and Egypt, was taken for granted. An identical picture emerges from another journal kept at the time, by Khalil al Sakhakhini. . . .
>
> In addition to the contribution of historical-religious factors (both Muslim and Christian) to the formation of the term *Falastin*, a later factor was also operating, Zionism. . . . It influenced profoundly the development of an awareness of Falastin's uniqueness even before World War I, but mainly after it.
>
> The new Jewish settlement encompassed already before World War I the whole of Palestine, from the Galilee in the north to the Judean Plain in the south. The negative Arab reaction to it also embraced all parts of the country, the Galilee, Haifa, Jaffa and Jerusalem.[3]

Porath notes that such Palestinian opposition had already emerged in 1891, when the Jerusalem notables presented a petition to Constantinople demanding the cessation of further Jewish immigration and land purchases. That the Jerusalem notables presented the petition indicates a further point: owing to the special status of Jerusalem, which had been elevated to administrative equality with Damascus (the Jerusalem Sanjak), the status of the Jerusalem notables had also been elevated to equal that of the Damascus notables—in preference to, say, the Nablus notables. Thus a node of national leadership was formed for the embryonic Palestinian national consciousness. The great Jerusalem families—the Husseinis, Nashashibis, etc.—became the leaders of the Palestinian Arabs. That apparently made it easier for many in the Zionist movement to delude themselves that the Palestinian national movement was a malicious invention of the aristocratic effendi class, inciting the masses to divert attention from class exploitation. These Zionists conveniently ignored the fact that in a society that is largely feudal, the aristocracy is the "natural" leadership and is entitled to speak for society as a whole. (For example, nobody contests the authenticity of the Hungarian national movement in 1848, led as it was by the aristocracy.) But the most salient expression of Palestinian Arab nationalism is the continuous struggle it waged against Zionism and later (for as long as they supported Zionism) against the British authorities. This struggle was conducted both by political means and by recurrent and ever-intensifying cycles of violence. It united most segments of the Palestinian population, so that in times of decision it gave its leadership full support and obedience

even though it had not been democratically elected. All joined in the struggle—the wealthy, the urban proletariat, and the peasantry.

Some observers, including the Jewish philosopher Yaakov Klatchkin,
warned the Zionist movement at the beginning of the Mandate period
against being overenthusiasic about the Balfour Declaration. He pointed
out that Zionism was at a crossroads. One road, he claimed, led to collaboration with the imperialist power against the local inhabitants. Sooner or
later these local inhabitants would liberate themselves from their masters
and send them packing—and the Zionists with them. The second road led
to making common cause with the local inhabitants for the purpose of a
joint struggle against the foreign occupier.

In fact this was an imaginary choice, for, as Porath shows, the Palestinian Arabs had already expressed their opposition to Jewish settlement and
to Zionism even before the Balfour Declaration. It is inconceivable that they
would have welcomed the influx of a powerful, organized population with
an alien national consciousness, which would perforce strive to establish a
sovereign political entity within a territory which they viewed as their
own. It is, therefore, highly unlikely that Zionist settlement could have developed in the face of Arab opposition without the protection and patron-
age of a great power. The very structure of the Zionist movement and its
national aspirations in an already populated region necessitated an alliance
with an external imperialist power seeking to impose its rule over the area
with the help of a loyal local ethnic group. On the other hand, it was in the
interest of the imperialists to achieve a modus vivendi with other elements
of the ruled population as well, or with key groups within it, in order to
avoid an exhausting struggle against an uprising of the native population.
As detailed in the preceding chapter, the connection between Britain and
the Jews had already begun by the first half of the nineteenth century. But
the nature of this connection necessarily changed when Britain ceased to
be an external power seeking a toehold in the country and assumed direct
rule over it—with the explicit interest in maintaining power with a minimum of friction with the various elements of the population, and without
arousing undue opposition in the other parts of the Middle East under its
control. These constraints necessarily militated against the obligations undertaken by Britain in the Balfour Declaration and in the terms of the Mandate for Palestine. The Zionist movement, for its part, and despite its eagerness to keep to the terms of the treaty which it assumed it had contracted
with Britain, was forced within a few years to realize that it could not trust
Britain to do its job for it. The British had much broader regional interests.

Nevertheless, it seems that the Zionist movement was not particularly
eager to explore the possibility of a negotiated agreement between Jews and
Arabs in the country. Berl Katznelson, for example, rejected out of hand the
idea of negotiating with the Arabs. "What agreement can they conclude
with us," he asked, "unless it is one aimed at our restraint and diminution?"[4] Jabotinsky opposed all negotiations with them (in his article "A

Round Table with the Arabs," published in 1931) with arguments very similar to those of Katznelson. Ben-Gurion relates his meetings with the Palestinian leader Moussa Alami (who reported his proposals to the Grand Mufti of Jerusalem, Haj Amin Al Husseini):

> At 10 A.M. on August 31, 1934, I met with Moussa Alami at his home in Jerusalem. He had visited the Mufti in the latter's village and reported to him the contents of our talks. This was like a bombshell for the Mufti. He never imagined that there were Jews who sincerely desired understanding and agreement with the Arabs. There has never been anything like this before.[5]

Ben-Gurion, by quoting the Mufti's surprise statement without any comment, seems by implication to confirm it, although he himself had often urged his colleagues to recognize the fact of Palestinian nationalism.[6] Indeed, in view of the constant attacks by both right-wing Revisionists and the labor movement on B'rit Shalom (composed primarily of intellectuals and academics who advocated the establishment of a binational federated state in mandatory Palestine), the only group which throughout that period had tried to reach an understanding with the Arab leadership, and aside from Histadrut attempts to organize Arab workers and help their independent organizations, it appears that little was done by the top echelons of the Zionist movement during that period to establish contact with the top level of the Palestinian national movement in order to achieve a negotiated compromise with it. For many years the Zionist leaders, including Weizmann, did not consider the Arabs as potential partners in negotiations on the future of the country. They concentrated all their efforts on the British.[7]

To these publicly documented facts, I add a personal memoir. My late father, David Hamburger, a lawyer by profession, acquired his legal education under the mandatory government's Council of Legal Studies in the early 1920s. He told me that during his studies a nationalistic Arab Muslim-Christian students' association was established in the school. My father and some of the other Jewish students initiated a counteraction. They approached the Arab students with the argument, "All of us, Muslims, Christians, and Jews, are natives of this country, and an association should be formed to include members of the three communities." A counterassociation, on the lines suggested by the Jewish students, was indeed established and commenced activities. (Because at the time this was the only institution of higher learning in the country, preceding the founding of the Hebrew University in Jerusalem, and also the only such institution attended by members of all the country's ethnic-religious communities, it obviously concentrated many members of the intelligentsia and future leadership of mandatory Palestine, so that the importance of this initiative was much greater than it might seem at first glance.) But shortly after the establishment of the tripartite association, one of the Jewish students who worked as an official of the Zionist institutions requested a closed meeting with only the Jewish activists and told them that he had reported their activities to Menachem Ussishkin (one of the most prominent Zionist leaders at the time), who had sent him to instruct them to desist immediately from their activities and to disband the association: "The English will take care of the Arabs for us. We need no contact with them."[8]

I have not investigated this story beyond what my father told me. But it seems to give a true reflection of the disregard and disdain harbored by large segments of the Zionist movement toward the Arab population. This was particularly true of recent arrivals from Europe, who were imbued with a sense of European superiority over the "backward Orientals," unlike members of the Old Yishuv, such as my father, who grew up with Arab neighbors and were familiar with them. That may have been one of the causes of Arab bitterness and hatred toward the Zionist enterprise. The very fact that Ben-Gurion's first meeting with an Arab leader, Moussa Alami, took place only in 1933, sixteen years after the Balfour Declaration and twelve years after the first round of Arab violence against the Zionist enterprise, indicates a lack of interest on the part of the Zionist leadership in establishing contact and reaching a compromise with the Arabs. Ben-Gurion notes that he initiated his contacts after being elected to the Zionist Executive Committee in 1933. But the implied excuse—that previous to that date he had no authority to initiate such steps—is hardly convincing. From the early 1920s on he was the outstanding leader of the Achdut Ha'avoda party, with enough weight to send out feelers toward the Arab side even without prior approval by the highest Zionist institutions. It therefore seems that he reached the decision to open negotiations with the Arabs only after concluding that their opposition could put an end to the mandatory government's support of Zionism, or at the very least hamper it greatly, and that one could no longer ignore Arab opposition on the naive assumption that it would be taken care of by the English. This is stated almost explicitly in Ben-Gurion's speech to the Zionist executive on May 19, 1936, when he predicted a pro-Arab shift in the policy of the British government, adding that "nevertheless, we shall strive to achieve a Jewish-English agreement, and in order to facilitate it we must outline a plan for a Jewish-Arab agreement."[9]

This tardiness does not, however, mean that a continuous debate was not held in the Hebrew Yishuv and in the Zionist movement abroad about the attitude that should be adopted toward the Arabs of Palestine—a debate that also meant a discussion of the nature of the future Jewish state. The outstanding cause of this debate was the continuous Arab opposition to the Zionist enterprise. As Anita Shapira notes, the educator Yitzhak Epstein had recognized in 1907 that the Arabs of Palestine constituted a people. He asserted that there were no empty areas in the country fit for cultivation and proposed that at first the Zionist movement not acquire settled lands but rather areas that must be improved for cultivation. At a later stage, when Jews began to purchase settled lands, too (which under the existing system of land tenure in Palestine were owned in many cases by the effendis, feudals who leased them to their tenants), he suggested that they not drive the tenants off the land but give them a part of it and develop it for them. At the same time, Epstein recognized that "the employment we give to an Arab will never seem to him compensation enough for the field taken from him. He will accept the good, but never forget the evil." Shapira adds this significant comment:

> The dichotomy between Epstein's sober appraisal of the Arab problem and his effective disregard of it, by suggesting palliative solutions, symbolizes the whole Zionist dilemma as regards the Arab question. . . . The settlers' realization of the nature of the Arab problem led to no real action in this matter, as the root of the problem was the very act of Zionist settlement in the country.[10]

In his public positions, Herzl hardly referred to the subject. In *Altneuland* he depicts an Arab notable, Rashid Bey, who welcomes Jewish settlement, which he feels benefits his people. In the Jewish Diaspora the naive slogan "A country without people for a people without a country" gained currency, but it never struck roots in the Yishuv. In Palestine itself it was impossible to ignore the existence of the other nation.

The figure of Rashid Bey is a fascinating example of the ability of a nationalist visionary to ignore the national impulses of other peoples. Herzl was well aware that the root of the problem of the Jewish people in some of its main diasporas was not economic but socioethnic and that the solution of this problem was not basically economic but political. As far as the Arabs of Palestine were concerned, however, he deluded himself (and many, many others, both then and later, deluded themselves with him on this question) that Rashid Bey would be satisfied with economic gains and forgo his political being in exchange.

If truth be told, Herzl's *economic* prediction as regards Rashid Bey was largely fulfilled. Jewish settlement brought economic prosperity to the Arabs of Palestine, though it was not equally distributed among all strata of the population. The most reliable and objective evaluation of the condition of the Palestine Arabs and the influence of the Zionist enterprise on them is by all counts that of the Palestine Royal Commission of 1937, headed by Lord Peel.[11] The commission established that the Arab population in Palestine had increased by 50 percent from 1920 until the date of the report, from 600,000 to 950,000, and that it should be assumed that nine-tenths of the growth was by natural increase. During the Ottoman period, the Arab population had increased at a much slower rate. The commission stated further that in view of the growth of the country's wealth, "it is difficult, on the face of it, to believe" that the Arab population did not benefit from it, although the Arab witnesses who appeared before the commisssion tried to deny this. The commission found that the rise of the indices of commerce and industry in the country, coupled with the rise of government revenue and expenditure, were in direct correlation to the growth of Jewish immigration. The effendis, who sold their land at very high prices, invested a large part of the proceeds in the improvement of their plantations on the remaining land, and as a result "at least six times more Arab-owned land is now planted with citrus than in 1920."

The daily wage paid to an Arab for skilled labour is now from 250 to 600 mils, and for unskilled labour from 100 to 180 mils. In Syria the wage ranges from 67 mils in older industries to 124 in newer ones. Factory labour in Iraq is paid from 40 to 60 mils.

The commission noted, on the other hand, that the increased population undermined the conditions of the fellahin, since less land per capita was left in rural areas, and this caused a flow of population to the cities. The fellahin who migrated to the cities were absorbed in industry.

The official estimate for Arab unemployment, admittedly a very rough one, was 6,000 at the time of our visit to Palestine, which in the circumstances and especially in view of the "disturbances" is not an alarming figure.

As regards the problem of the dispossession of tenant farmers, the commission stated:

Although 3,271 applications for resettlement were received from landless Arabs up to the 1st January, 1936, only 664 were admitted to the Register, 2,607 being disallowed. Government purchased lands at a cost of 72,240 pounds for the resettlement of these proved displaced Arab cultivators, and at the time of our inquiry more than half of the 664 families had been provided with land. Some of the remainder declined the land offered them on the grounds that they were accustomed neither to the climate of the new area nor to irrigated cultivation.
    The Jews also submitted evidence that they too had made a careful inquiry into the matter of landless Arabs and they had discovered only 688 tenants who had been displaced by the land being sold over their heads; and that of these some 400 had found other land. This inquiry related to the period 1920–1930.[12]

Among the commission's findings were the following:

1. The large import of Jewish capital . . . has had a general fructifying effect on the economic life of the whole country.
    2. The expansion of Arab industry and agriculture has been largely financed by the capital thus obtained.
    3. Jewish example has done much to improve Arab cultivation, especially of citrus.
    4. Owing to Jewish development and enterprise, the employment of Arab labour has increased in the urban areas, particularly in the ports. . . .

7. The general beneficent effect of Jewish immigration on Arab welfare is illustrated by the fact that the increase in the Arab population is most marked in urban areas affected by Jewish development. A comparison of the census return in 1922 and 1931 shows that, six years ago, the increase percent in Haifa was 86, in Jaffa 62, in Jerusalem 37, while in purely Arab towns such as Nablus and Hebron it was only 7, and at Gaza there was a decrease of 2 percent. . . .

The further claim, based on the Jewish contribution to revenue, seems to us indisputable. . . . But it is certain that much the greater part of the customs duties are paid by them, and the rising amount of customs revenue has formed from 1920 to the present day the biggest item in the rising total revenue.

Whereas most of the revenues of the mandatory government were collected from the Jewish sector, most of the outlay was in the public and relatively backward Arab sectors. The British justified this with the weighty argument that social justice demands that more should be taken from the rich and spent on the poor. Thus, for example, the government's school system served only the Arab population, whereas the Hebrew school system was supported by the Yisuv's own funds. There is no doubt that from a purely economic point of view, Jewish settlement was highly beneficial to the Arab population in Palestine and that even the few displaced tenant farmers were easily absorbed into the rapidly developing Palestinian economy. It is difficult to claim that the Arabs were "exploited" by the Jews. The Jews could easily counter with more justification that the use of their taxes for the benefit of the Arab population constituted exploitation of the Jews in the Arabs' favor.

The Arabs countered this argument with the claim that the tax burden in Palestine was heavier than in any Arab country and that they should not be responsible for sharing the burden of expenditures for security caused by the friction between the two peoples that was created by Zionism. And when, in his conversations with Moussa Alami, Ben-Gurion raised the Zionist argument about the wealth the Jews were bringing to the country, the latter replied: "I would prefer that the country remain poor and desolate even a hundred years more, until we Arabs shall be able to develop it by our own efforts."[13]

Moussa Alami stated a fact which the Zionist movement repeatedly tried to ignore: that the struggle between Jews and Arabs in Palestine was a *national* struggle. Economic and social progress did not blunt the clash of nationalities. On the contrary, it aggravated it. Among the Arabs it spurred organizational efforts on higher levels than those of the traditional rural society and stimulated the political education of all levels of society. That the Hebrew Yishuv functioned as a coherent, organized national body made all Arabs who came into contact with any sector of the Yishuv quickly aware that this sector did not operate solely according to its own immediate interests but as a part of an organism, within the framework of the Yishuv as a whole. The Arabs were thus compelled to copy this organization to be able to deal with the Jews on equal terms, just as the integrated nations of Europe compelled less-developed societies to organize on national lines to be able to deal with them.

The efforts of leading Zionist circles, mainly in the labor movement, to interpret the conflict in sociological class-struggle terms, not in political-national ones, avoided the fact that the social problems engendered by Arab urbanization and industrialization under the impact of Zionism did not necessarily by themselves lead to a Jewish-Arab conflict. These tensions developed between the closed, conservative, patriarchal structure of Arab society and the new forces that began to arise within it among the urban bourgeoisie and intelligentsia. If there was any validity to the conception that the feudal effendi class led the opposition to Zionism, inciting the mob to divert attention from its own class oppression, it would be reasonable to expect that the popular, politically conscious elements would have seen through this maneuver and opposed the feudals, following the recurrent pattern of Third World countries. But on the contrary, these groups opposed Zionism even more vehemently than the effendis, who, more than any other group, benefited from Jewish settlement.

The Arab struggle, then, was a national struggle. It was waged against Zionism for the very reason that it was a national enterprise and not the settlement movement of an idealistic sect such as the German Templar settlers, who encountered no Arab opposition precisely because they were not a national movement. People like Berl Katzenelson, who grew up in the pogrom-laden atmosphere of Eastern Europe, viewed the Arab violence as an "anti-Jewish" outbreak, merely another version of the Russian and Polish pogroms. They never paused to ask themselves how Palestinian Muslim peasants could become anti-Semites without a Christian Jew-hating tradition and without the European sociocultural context within which anti-Semitism developed. The vast differences between the sociocultural traditions and history of Europe and those of the Middle East should have opened their eyes to the fact that although the effects, murder and pillage, seem to be the same, basically these are utterly different phenomena. In the one case it was anti-Semitism and in the other it was the traditional form of struggle of a community trying to defend itself against the penetration of a powerful, well-organized, alien national movement that endangered its own position in the country. The intelligent observer also would have noticed that the native community was discerning enough to distinguish between elements that did not imperil it (like the German Templars), and Zionism, which constituted a mortal danger. Moreover, Palestinian society as a whole united against this danger.

There were undoubtedly some elements that wished to exploit the hostility to Zionism to further their own ends. It is also true that many Arabs collaborated with the Jews to further their own interests. Both sorts are to be found everywhere and at all times. It would have been impossible, however, to exploit or foment the hostility to Zionism had not the awareness of its potential as a menace to them all, as a collectivity, been pervasive in all sectors of Palestinian society, irrespective of class, occupation, or even religion (a significant proportion of the Palestinian Arab population was and still is Christian). Indeed, the fact that Katznelson and others could not understand the difference between the anti-Jewish outbreaks in Europe and the Palestinian riots shows that mentally they remained in Eastern Europe and never realized the nature of the region in which they took their abode.

How did the various currents within the Zionist movement deal with this unforeseen problem?

The first attempt of a political nature was the Weizmann-Faisal agreement of 1919. This agreement was connected to the plans of the dynasty of Husayn ibn Ali, sharif of Mecca and leader of the "revolt in the desert" during World War I, to establish a great Arab kingdom that would encompass Syria, Transjordan, and Palestine. The agreement contained a paragraph about the encouragement of a large Jewish immigration to Palestine and its settlement on the land, while protecting the rights of the Arab farmers and tenant-cultivators and the provision of economic assistance to them. On the part of the Zionist organization the agreement contained an undertaking to send a commission of experts to assess the economic possibilities of the country, a commission that would be "placed at the disposal of the Arab state." It also agreed that "the Zionist organization [would] use its best efforts to assist the Arab state in providing the means for developing the natural resources and economic possibilities thereof."

Faisal, a son of Husayn ibn Ali, added a codicil to the agreement in his own handwriting, signed by him and Weizmann, stipulating that "provided the Arabs obtain their independence as demanded . . . I shall concur in the above two articles. But if the slightest modification or departure were to be made, I shall not then be bound by a single word of the present Agreement."[14]

This agreement, referred to repeatedly in the succeeding decades by Zionist and other polemicists as an example of a possible Jewish-Arab compromise (while the Arabs, for their part, generally ignored it and denounced Faisal as having had no authority to sign it in the first place and as a traitor to the Arab cause), contains a whole complex of assumptions and conceptions leading down to the present day. I shall try to unravel and explicate some of them.

The agreement itself very shortly lost all practical significance, for the circumstances under which it had been made had changed completely. It had been made based on the assumption that Faisal would soon be declared king of Greater Syria and that the Zionist movement would lend him political and economic assistance to achieve his ends. This was the "Arab state" mentioned in the agreement. The Sykes-Picot pact and Faisal's ouster from Damascus by the French put an end to this possibility. But the context of assumptions and intentions of the sides involved merits study.

The British, who arranged the meeting and initiated the agreement between the two sides, clearly considered themselves the sponsors of the projected Arab state. They wanted to forestall potential tensions between Arabs and Zionists in order to preserve the stability of the Pax Britannica they envisaged for the Middle East. T. E. Lawrence ("of Arabia"), who initiated the meeting, did not take the French presence into account (or did, but hoped to oust them completely from the region).

It seems that in Faisal's view, the "national home" referred to in the Balfour Declaration was not a state in its own right but one component of an Arab state. Wherever the word *state* is mentioned in the agreement, it always denotes an *Arab* state, which is really Greater Syria. Jewish settlement, according to the agreement, would take place only in Palestine and not in the other areas of the state. The "national home," in Faisal's view, was meant to extend only over the area of Palestine and constitute a district with an undefined measure of autonomy within the frame of the larger Arab state.

Ben-Gurion, in his accounts of meetings with Arab leaders, stressed that his repeated proposals for the establishment of a Jewish state, which would become integrated within a larger Arab federation, encountered a sympathetic hearing on the part of Arab nationalists such as George Antonius, who favored Greater Syria, and were rejected out of hand by leaders who conceived of the problem in a purely Palestinian framework. This may be be viewed as a continuation of Faisal's basic attitude. Throughout the mandatory period, as Porat notes in his book on the Palestinian national movement, the pendulum of Arab national thinking in Palestine swung between the Palestinians, who aimed at the establishment of Palestine as an independent Arab state, and the adherents of Palestine's inclusion in Greater Syria. It is obvious that compromise with or acceptance of Zionism by the former was impossible, since they claimed the identical territory claimed by Zionism—Palestine on both sides of the Jordan.

Weizmann's endorsement of the agreement with Faisal indicates that at the time his goal was not full sovereignty but rather the status of a unit within a federal or confederal arrangement. (It should be recalled that for many years, most Zionist statesmen and thinkers did not aspire to full sovereignty but to a status of limited sovereignty within the British Empire, on the order of a dominion. The inclusion of the national home within a federated Arab framework did not, therefore, seem to them a completely alien or repellent idea. In any case, Weizmann, with his practical wisdom, always considered it foolish to commit oneself to any final framework, since human affairs are in constant flux.) The clause in the agreement about the protection of the rights of Arab farmers and tenant cultivators is almost identical with the phrasing of the Balfour Declaration, but here it is a Zionist commitment to that end, not a reservation by the British government.

The efforts of leading Zionist circles to reach an agreement with the Arabs were from this point on based on the theoretical framework of the Weizmann-Faisal agreement, namely a settlement wherein the Arabs would give up Palestine in exchange for the participation of Jewish Palestine in a regional federal accord. The Zionists argued that compared with the immense tracts of land in the Arab world, Palestine—to the Arab national movement—constituted a marginal, easily negotiable area.

The Achdut Ha'avoda (mainstream Labor) party's attitude toward the Arabs had been set at its Ein Harod convention in 1924. A proposal for a Jewish initiative for a constitutional change in the country was turned down, and it was decided to adopt instead a motion for Jewish-Arab cooperation in the socioeconomic field in the form of a common labor organization. Anita Shapira writes:

> The resolution was based on the assumption that it is not in the interest of the Zionist movement in general, and of the Labor movement in particular, to propose any political blueprint while the country is in a process of dynamic change. Any blueprint is liable in the future to become a constraint on the development of the national home. The feeling that time is working in favor of Zionism derived among other things from the tenet, opposed by only a few, that the conflict between Arabs and Jews is not national but of a class nature. Its source is the conflict of interests between the effendis, the feudal leaders of Arab society, and the Zionist dynamic which introduces change and progress to the country. The inability, nay the reluctance, to agree to any political settlement at this stage of the development of the national home was rationalized away as the unwillingness of socialist workers to make deals with the effendis. ... Unlike Achdut Ha'avoda, which repressed the political problems by the use of class definitions, the Hapo'el Hatza'ir [another labor faction] party emphasized the political aspect of the Arab problem, and its leaders ... sought a political accommodation with the Arabs.[15]

The struggle between the two approaches, which became particularly vehement after the 1929 riots, also determined positions as to whether a national Arab Palestinian movement did or did not exist. Members of Achdut Ha'avoda, who had undertaken the task of making Zionism a reality, refused to admit the existence of such a movement, since this would be tantamount to an admission that there are limiting factors to the Zionist potential. Shapira continues:

> The argument that no long-term settlement of the Arab problem should be negotiated, because of the changes effected by Zionist dynamism, really implied an assumption that perhaps there is no need for a settlement, as the Zionist movement could achieve ascendancy without it. This hope was based on the assumption that the opponent had not yet reached a stage enabling him to interfere with the development of the national home, that no Arab national movement exists.[16]

It seems never to have occurred to the Achdut Ha'avoda adherents that the Zionist dynamic itself spurred the emergence of a Palestinian Arab nationalism and that the relations between the two national groups were functional, so that no ascendancy could ever be assured. This was well understood by Shmuel Dayan, of Hapo'el Hatza'ir, who in the debate about the 1929 riots stated in rebuttal to Achdut Ha'avoda: "This is a national movement, and it does not want to have anything to do with us. It is now gathering momentum, and this is its first revolt."

Typical of the stubborn effort to ignore the national basis of the Arab opposition to Zionism is the approach of Berl Katznelson, in many respects the acknowledged moral authority of the labor movement, particularly of Mapai. In his voluminous writings and speeches, Katznelson never faced the Arab problem squarely. All his interest focused on the Jewish people, on the Histadrut and on the party. His references to the Arabs were basically polemical, namely attempts to refute the arguments of the Arabs and their supporters in the British administration or the world socialist movement. The only time that he tried to analyze the Arab national movement was in his address to the Mapai party convention on June 13, 1936.[17] (Even in this case, he made no effort to understand it but tried polemically to prove its reactionary character—a movement not of fellahin and workmen, but of "sons of effendis" seeking employment in government.)

The underlying purpose must have been the suppression of moral compunctions in the labor movement as regards a rival national liberation movement. It is no accident that Katznelson was also one of the main opponents of the 1937 partition plan, and claimed for Zionism all of Palestine, without regard to the rights of the Arabs. But beyond the polemics, the most significant statement of his ideological strategy vis-à-vis the Arab problem appears in volume 8 of his collected works:

> In my opinion, there is no chance at present of achieving an agreement with the Arabs. Not because of any ill will on our part, nor because our people are unwilling to discuss this matter seriously, but for a simple reason: it is possible to achieve a settlement between two national movements seeking independence, but not between one which seeks independence and the other seeking dominance.... The Arab movement, as it exists today, is not a liberation movement.... It is not satisfied with independence for itself but seeks dominance over everyone within its compass....
>
> The Weizmann-Faisal agreement indicates the only way for reaching a settlement. If there existed a great Arab movement aiming at a federation of Arab lands, as Faisal did, it could have reached an agreement with us over this little province called Eretz Israel, in exchange for generous help from us. But the Arab leaders in Eretz Israel, whose ambitions are wholly focused on lording it here, over this province, and everything which the Jews do here infringes on their authority and undermines their political and social status—what can they agree with us about, except about diminishing and limiting us? If a political juncture arises in which the Arabs in the neighboring countries will feel that they need our help, then perhaps a treaty can be drafted which ensures our national aspirations for Eretz Israel.[18]

It is most instructive that Katznelson, heralded as a humanist and the conscience of the Zionist labor movement, was so blinded by his political

convictions that he was incapable of seeing that the Arab national movement's claim to the whole of Palestine was no more dominance-inclined
than the Zionist claim. His unspoken implication was that there could be
no questioning from any quarter whatever of the fact that the whole country belonged, by right, to the Jews. The Arabs' refusal to accept this claim
was merely a dominance-motivated aggressiveness. Katznelson's arguments also contain a seemingly self-evident truism, which in reality begs
the question. His statement that "the Arab leaders in Eretz Israel, whose
ambitions are wholly focused on lording it here," etc., is really an assertion
that the conflict is not with the Arab *people* but only with its "leaders," the
venal, selfish upper classes, who are the only Arabs adversely affected and
diminished by Zionism and who incite the mob for their private gain.
These, however, are not statements of fact, though they masquerade as such,
but polemical arguments. Although it is doubtful whether they convinced
many outside the Zionist camp, they undoubtedly did serve to ease the
conscience of a large part of the labor movement.

Even so, in other places Katznelson admits in a roundabout way that the
conflict is truly with the Palestinian *people*:

> We want from them only one thing: not to hamper us. This is the one thing we
> demand from them: not to prevent our growth. This the Arabs of Palestine are
> not prepared to give us. They realize that if already today our weight and
> power is great and massive, then after a period of further continuous growth
> they would be unable to resist us. It is as plain as two and two that no such
> accommodation can take place. It would have been different if there existed a
> unified Arab movement including Syria, Iraq, and other countries, for whom
> Eretz Israel would be a mere province over which a negotiated settlement is
> possible. They could have then demanded a financial price for it, like credits,
> loans, etc. If there existed such a movement which would have been ready to
> negotiate, not this xenophobia for which any Jew is anathema (we also would
> have preferred that no Eretz Israelian Arabs existed, but they are the reality
> and we have to take it into account), then we could discuss it.[19]

In addition to admitting that the conflict is not with the "status-seek-
ing" leaders of the Palestinian people but with the people itself, Katznelson
here also expresses with rare frankness the wish that the country had been
Araber-rein. (And he has the gall to accuse the Arabs of xenophobia! One is
overwhelmed by the moral blindness and one-sidedness of this renowned
moralizer.) Toward this people he shows no readiness to compromise, although he does add a reservation: "There is no doubt that a Jewish state will
grant full rights to its Arab citizens. No Arab will be dispossessed, none
shall be expelled, none shall leave the country against his will."[20] He failed
to explain, however, how this people would accept minority status, even
with equal rights, in a land which it considered to be uncompromisingly
its own.

Of all the Zionist leaders in the interbellum period, it seems that Ze'ev
Jabotinsky (and, as we shall see, Ben-Gurion, too) had the clearest vision as

regards the nature of the conflict and the nature of the enemy with whom Zionism had joined battle. Whereas Katznelson wrote about the Arab people "which believes that by means of a second and third pogrom it can get more than it is given now,"[21] thus betraying his essentially Diaspora mentality (he was unable to understand that the Yishuv was facing a war and not pogroms), Jabotinsky understood that the Arabs were fighting Zionism and defending themselves from it, not rioting against it. He wrote:

> True, there are among us deluded people who imagine that one can "win the hearts" of the Palestinian Arabs by economic benefits; . . . but such a delusion can only derive from a boundless contempt for the Arab soul. . . . It is possible to buy individual Arab traitors, but nobody can ever seduce a whole people to willingly forgo national aspirations for the sake of economic advantage.

Jabotinsky went on to argue that as a matter of fact, the Jews had nothing to offer the Arabs in the three areas of major concern to them: control of Jewish immigration, a greater Arab federation, and the expulsion of the European overlords. Control of immigration would aim at preventing the Jews from becoming a majority in the country, while support of Arab federation and liberation would entail action against the powers that undersigned the Balfour Declaration, which provided the irreplacable conditions and framework for the development of the Jewish national home under the sponsorship of the mandatory power. The Jews could not play such a double game, and would fail even if they tried. Therefore there was no sense in even trying to reach an agreement with the Arabs:

> Eventually there will be peace in Eretz Israel, but only after the Jews become a majority, or when the Arabs realize the inescapability and inevitability of such a solution; namely, when they realize that the "solution" of the problem does not depend on their consent. . . . Until that time—all the attempts to negotiate a Jewish-Arab political agreement are futile and harmful.[22]

Jabotinsky laid particular stress on the Arabs' right to live in the country as equal citizens:

> My emotional attitude toward the Arabs is the same as toward all other nations: a polite indifference. My political attitude toward them is determined by two principles. First, I consider their removal from the country as absolutely inconceivable. Eretz Israel will always be a home for two nations.

His realism also led him to cast doubt on the attempts to reach a compromise with an Arab national movement, which would presumably trade Palestine for Zionist aid in the formation of a large Arab federation. He rejected the idea both because of a correct appraisal that Zionism would be liable as a result to clash with the European powers, thanks only to whose mandate Zionism had been able to gain a foothold in the country, and because of his recognition that a Palestinian Arab national consciousness had already been formed:

Many Zionists are beguiled by the following scheme: if it is impossible to gain the acceptance of the Arabs of Eretz Israel, it may be possible to gain the acceptance of other Arabs—the Arabs of Syria, Mesopotamia [Iraq], Hijjaz [Saudi Arabia], perhaps even Egypt. Even were this possible, it would make no basic difference, for it would not change the attitude of the Arabs of Eretz Israel toward us. . . . Even if it were possible (which I greatly doubt) to persuade the Arabs of Baghdad and Mecca that for them Eretz Israel is a small, unimportant marginal area, for the Arabs of Eretz Israel the land would still remain not a marginal area but their homeland, the center and basis of their independent national existence.[23]

But this courageous recognition of the true nature of the Arab resistance to the Zionist enterprise—in contradistinction to the attempts of broad circles in the labor movement to ignore it, as exemplified by Katznelson's circumlocutions—did not lead even Jabotinsky to draw the necessary conclusions from this recognition. For if the Arabs of Palestine refused to forgo their national consciousness and aspirations, they would never be satisfied with the status of equal citizens of a Jewish state (which by its very definition, even with the best will in the world on the part of the ruling Jews, would put them at a disadvantage), just as the Jews, even as a minority in mandatory Palestine, were never resigned to this status and aspired to become the ruling majority. And if the Jews had behind them the pressure of Jewish misery in Europe, particularly after the Nazi rise to power, as a mighty goad to the achievement of sovereignty and independence, Jabotinsky should have realized that the Palestinian Arabs would always enjoy the powerful backing of the entire Arab world. His assumption that the Palestinian Arabs would resign themselves to the status of equal citizens in a Jewish state when "they realize that this is a necessary and inevitable solution, namely, when they realize that the 'solution' of the problem does not depend on their consent," clashed with the fact that the Arabs of Palestine would never have to resign themselves to an imposed solution, because historical change would sooner or later undermine the "iron wall" on which Jabotinsky based his assumption—the "wall" that would force them to accept the inevitable. If by that time no agreed arrangement or voluntary coexistence was achieved between the Jewish state and the Palestinian Arabs, the question would be reopened. Again we find here the willful blindness which the Zionist leaders, even the most realistic among them, imposed on themselves when confronting the Arab problem. Jabotinsky, who understood the nature of the Arab opponent, was incapable of developing this understanding to its logical conclusion. This contradiction between his clear-sightedness and his political maximalism finally led him, in his 1923 article, "The Morality of the Iron Wall," to the following argument:

It is estimated that the Jews of the world number fifteen or sixteen million people. Half of them lead, quite literally, the life of harried, homeless dogs. The Arabs number about thirty-eight million. They occupy Morocco, Algeria, Tunisia, Tripolitania, Cyrenaica, Egypt, Syria, Mesopotamia, and the whole of the

Arab peninsula—an area which, if we deduct the deserts, is about half the size of Europe. Each square mile of this vast area is inhabited by no more than sixteen Arabs.... Eretz Israel is only 170th part of the immense area occupied by the Arabs....

The requisitioning of a tract of land from a people of vast holdings to make a home for a wandering people—this is an act of justice. And if the owner refuses (which is quite natural), he must be forced into it.

So when we strip off Jabotinsky's moralistic arguments—which are quite spurious, for why should the Arabs, who are among the least to blame for the persecution of Jews, give up a part of their broad territories to Jews who are being persecuted in other places and not the Christians who are guilty of the persecution; why shouldn't the Russians, Canadians, Americans, or Brazilians give up a marginal part of their even vaster and even more sparsely settled lands in favor of the Jews?—we find him reverting to the compromise over a marginal territory of the great Arab state agreed upon by Weizmann and Faisal. The Palestinian Arab nation, so clearly discerned by Jabotinsky, again disappears. We have here only the unspecified "Arabs" and their "immense territories." The only difference between Jabotinsky and the more moderate groups was that he thought that the Arabs should be "forced" to "resign themselves" to this solution. But who would force them? Jabotinsky never deluded himself that the Jewish people was capable of imposing its will on the whole of the immense Arab world. The only ones capable of doing this were the original masters of the "iron wall," the British. (Jabotinsky thought of using the World War I Jewish battalion for the purpose, but the battalion existed only thanks to the British, of whose army it formed a part.) But why should the British do this contrary to their own interests, when even their limited commitment to an unspecified Jewish national home, not Eretz Israel on both sides of the Jordan, embroiled them in intolerable complications and drove them more and more to the desire to rid themselves of this commitment?

Maximalist Zionism proved to be a dead end. Subsequent attempts, during the Arab revolt of 1936–1939, to "demonstrate strength" by the anti-Arab terrorist acts of the Irgun Zvai Leumi, thus proving to the British that it was more worth their while to side completely with the Jews and form with them the hoped-for iron wall, yielded no results whatsoever. Jabotinsky failed to comprehend the broader considerations of the British Empire, which led it to adopt the anti-Zionist White Paper policy, which was indeed crowned with success. It achieved its implicit objective, the neutrality or cooperation of most of the Arab world with Britain during World War II.

It was Ben-Gurion, after the 1929 Arab riots, who drew the realistic conclusion from this seemingly hopeless quandary. Shapira writes that

Ben-Gurion, characteristically, hit the nail on the head from a pragmatic political viewpoint: "The debate whether an Arab national movement does or doesn't exist is a futile verbal exercise. The main point, as far as we are concerned, is that this movement rallies masses. We don't consider it as a [national] revival movement and its moral value is dubious, but from the political point of view it is a national movement."[24]

Ben-Gurion began to provide the response to this realistic recognition from the 1920s on. As described in the preceding chapter, his recognition of Jewish inability to compete with cheap Arab labor led him to advocate the establishment of two separate national societies. The true meaning of his scheme to create a continuous area of Jewish settlement was the partition of the country, although in his meetings with Arab leaders he continued to insist on Jewish sovereignty over the whole of Eretz Israel. He eventually arrived at the following formula: "Eretz Israel belongs to the Hebrew people and to the Arabs residing in it. The Arabs residing in the country should have full rights, both as individuals and as a national group, but they have no right to full sovereignty over the country."[25] Which is to say that he recognized that the Jewish people and the Palestinian Arab population have equal claims to the country. It was on the basis of this recognition that he advocated the formation of two separate communities, as against the binational slogans then prevalent in the labor movement, the authors of which aspired to draw the two peoples closer to each other and to establish organizations for a joint class struggle.

It was this conception that led Ben-Gurion to accept the Peel Commission's partition plan, whereas his close associate, Katzenelson, because of his denial of the authenticity of the Palestinian Arab national movement and his complete immersion in Zionist and Jewish affairs, opposed it. The plan was in reality merely a political confirmation of the geographical reality that emerged as a result of the settlement policy recommended by Ben-Gurion. Indeed, the decision to divide the land between the two rival national movements was the only logical compromise possible in that situation. Ben-Gurion held to this agreement-in-principle to a partition down to the establishment of the state, with the single deviation of the "Biltmore program" of 1942, which he indeed soon abandoned. As claimed by various historians, the War of Independence was conducted with a tacit understanding between Ben-Gurion and King Abdullah (of Jordan) to divide the country between them, with the Jordanians taking control of areas predominantly Arab and the Israelis of those predominantly Jewish. As a matter of fact, by the end of the war (after the defeat of the Egyptians and the Syrians), Israel could easily have seized the whole of the West Bank of the Jordan. The reasons for Israel's failure to do so must have been purely political. Such a large Arab population, with its separate and hostile national consciousness, would have been beyond the absorptive capacity of the new state.

The question raised at the beginning of this chapter—whether the national conflict could not be abated and whether a modus vivendi could not be found between the two rival national movements—is as problematic as any historical "what-if" question. Perhaps, if there had been more good will and consideration on the part of the Zionist leadership, or if Jewish immigration had shrunk to a scale modest enough not to threaten to turn the Palestinian Arabs into a minority, perhaps then the Palestinian leadership would have been prepared to compromise on something resembling the Brit Shalom program. But with the intensification of aggressive anti-Semitism as an international political movement, and particularly after the Nazi rise to power in Germany, Zionism would have been incapable, even if it had wanted to, of compromising on the flow of immigration without betraying its very raison d'être.

Christopher Sykes, an independent observer, seems to sum up this point best:

> Zionist leaders had often insisted that in demanding a national home the Jews were not asking for a luxury but the satisfaction of a vital need. The point was never difficult to argue, but, in the more normal years from 1917 to 1933 . . . counter-argument was never difficult either. But after 1933 the need of the Jews for a national home, their need for a state in which they could take pride, became completely and rapidly self-evident to many Jews who had doubted it before, and to their sympathisers. . . . After this year the "Palestine Problem" proved to be entirely beyond any peaceful solution, and looking back now it is clear that after 1933 it could never be so solved in Palestine but (if at all) only by strong pro-Jewish counter-measures throughout the world. . . .
>
> From the very beginning of the Nazi disaster the Zionist leadership determined to wrest political advantage from the tragedy. Where such advantage might lead none of them could tell, and it is wrong to think of their decision, as the Arabs did, as an elaborately planned conspiracy. But it is true that . . . in the forseeable future it did in fact lead them to the forcible occupation of most of Palestine. . . .
>
> The decision . . . was fatal in the sense that it removed still further from reality the possibility of a peaceful solution. It meant the discredit of Zionist gradualism and a rapid heightening of the Arab sense of injustice with which Arabs found sympathy among many British people both in Palestine and England.[26]

EIGHT

Zionism without Mercy

Chapter 5 mapped the process by which the Zionist pioneers attempted to exorcise the exilic mentality from their souls and to replace it, by dint of an act of will, with a sense of rootedness in the Eretz Israel soil. The deeper logic of the process led to other, unexpected, results as well.

Persons who undertake such a process are marked for life by an identity crisis. Their new, homeland-rooted being becomes the center of their awareness and activity, and with a vengeance. They are not, after all, soil-rooted in a simple, uncomplicated way. They acquired their new being as a result of an immense, traumatic effort. The constant energy required to repress the pretransformation self that seems always to hover at the edge of consciousness, arousing doubt in the reality of the transformation and in one's very identity, tends to generate a violent hostility toward the former self. This self, because it was rejected and repressed, appears inferior, contemptible, and hateful. If only it could be erased! And indeed, a phrase was coined to give an ideological dressing to this mental dynamic: "negation of the Diaspora."

Thus a contradiction emerges between the primary motivation of Zionism—the plight of the Jews and the need to find a cure for it—and the transformation which Jews who have realized Zionism go through. These Jews becomes different persons, and as such become estranged from the original context of the plight of the Jews. Furthermore, it is a context which they wish to erase from their awareness. From the moment they accomplish the transformation and become homeland-rooted, their new self becomes the focus of their consciousness and effort, whereas the primary "plight" is henceforth not the basis of their self but at most a means of serving it. This new self is not only more important; it is the only one of real importance. It is a positive entity, whereas the former, rejected self existed under the sign of negation. Not unlike religious converts, these Jews want others from their former, hated background to undergo the same process of transformation and join them in their great undertaking, building an actual homeland around their new homeland awareness. Furthermore, instead of viewing their undertaking as a means of solving the Jewish problem, their perception of their role is profoundly inverted: they view the Jewish problem, the plight of the Jews, as a means of furthering their own undertaking. In addition, since in their view only the plight of the Jews could spur others to undergo the same process, they have a vested interest in its persistence. The abatement of anti-Jewish pressure would militate against their purpose. Thus an objective community of interests is formed between anti-Semitism and Zionism.

Another point: A. D. Gordon, the prototype pioneer described in chapter 5, and most of his contemporary equivalents in East European Zionism—men such as Achad Ha'am, Weizmann, Katznelson and Ben-Gurion—had their origins in that sector (largely petit bourgeois) of East European Jewry that preserved an affinity to tradition and religion, though they themselves rebelled against and rejected both. It is impossible to ignore the central role of Eretz Israel, the "Holy Land," in this tradition. As a result, Zionism became for them a secular guise of this role, a return to the land of their forefathers in the secular sense of the idea. But the very viewing of Eretz Israel as the self-evident basis of the national renaissance contained an explosive duality; never has a sharp and clear line been drawn between the secular element of the solution of the Jewish problem, turning the Jews into political subjects, and the religious, Ezra and Nehemiah style of "return to Zion." On the contrary, Zionism deliberately exploited and appropriated the religious motivation for its own ends. Such a duality would never have arisen had the territorialists gained the upper hand. (Of course, large parts of the East European Zionist movement rejected Jewish tradition altogether. They were to be found on the Left, like the members of the Labor Batallion and Hashomer Hatza'ir, as well as on the Right, like certain groups connected with the revisionist movement which later became prominent in the anti-British underground movements and included personalities such as Yonatan Ratosh, founder of the Canaanite movement, and Eri Jabotinsky, son of the founder of revisionism. And as is well known, the father was himself indifferent to Jewish tradition.)

We see then that the very heart of the transformation undergone by pioneers such as Gordon contained a religiously significant element (not shared by the territorialists, the autonomists, and the Bundists), which had a definite affinity to the petit bourgeois social origins of most Zionists. This element in a way served to connect their old and new selves, and from the start implanted in them an ambivalent attitude toward religion and its adherents. On one hand, as Achad Ha'am taught, religion was seen as the outworn and hateful historical manifestation of Judaism. On the other hand, there was an element of self-abnegation before religion, for having "preserved the national substance." As a result, in times of loss of faith and doubt in Zionism, an inclination appears to hold on to religion. This affinity to tradition is most apparent in Berl Katznelson, who wished to preserve large parts of it, although he had no religious faith. The very choice of Eretz Israel as the focus of Jewish nationalism contained a concession to Jewish tradition, a reluctance on the part of Zionism to draw full conclusions from its own premisses. On the other hand, it is a moot point whether a Gordon, who according to his own testimony, was a traditionalist Jew in Russian exile, could effect an inner transformation and see any other country as his homeland except the Holy Land. It would appear that at a certain level of consciousness he felt that the transition to secular life in Eretz Israel contradicted his previous religiosity only on the surface, that in reality he was not betraying his religiosity but undertaking a far more difficult and lofty mitzvah (religious precept). But the choice of Eretz Israel, out of all other possible territories, contained an ambiguity, a potential for a retreat from secular nationalism into a communal separateness, even if it paraded as nationalism. On the other hand, the connection of the Bible and the Hebrew language to this particular territory also carried with it the potential for a revival of pre-Jewish, archaic-Israelite strata.

Thus far I have discussed the process from its psychological and conceptual aspects. I shall now explore its other implications—sociological, political, and institutional. As noted, a shift had taken place in Zionism from a solution of the Jewish problem in purely secular-political terms to "salvation," in which the plight of the Jews becomes secondary to the interest of salvation. It appears that, historically, this shift took place as a result of the Uganda controversy (in 1903–1905), when the salvationist school won the upper hand. During the course of this controversy, Zionism ceased being a territorialist movement aimed at the solution of the problems of the Jewish people, and as a matter of fact ceased being Zionist in the Herzlian sense of the word. The exclusive concentration on Eretz Israel had far-reaching consequences. David Vital describes the controversy as follows:

Herzl and his closest associates . . . had always assumed that Zionism will make peace between the Jews and other peoples, that the Jews will join the family of nations on the basis of equality and for the common good. Like his predecessor Pinsker, he saw no reason to reject the non-Jewish world for being such. . . . *Altneuland*, the new Jewish society, was presented as a *new* society, a society which had broken the bonds of tradition and in which the Jews had finally become a nation like all other nations, in all significant respects, and within which the recently acquired territorial concentration and the political autonomy serve as a basis for an inner social revolution. This is what enables the Jews to assimilate as a collective within the family of nations on equal terms, and without their individuality transcending the permissible and the comprehensible. . . . This was rejected completely by the rival party. It viewed the ancient burden—the past in itself—as a central and vital part of the national consciousness. True, past tradition should not be preserved whole. Like other Zionists, these too distanced themselves from the rigid, uncompromising orthodoxy. But they were divided and vague about what should be preserved and what should be scuttled. . . . Still, what united all the anti-Herzlians in the movement was that they all advocated continuity and a real affinity to the heritage of the past. . . . All true Zionists, argued Achad Ha'am, "are adamant about one common basis: on the faith in the historical connection between the people and the land, a connection which will arouse the spirit of our people to find itself again and fight for its true being until it succeeds in creating the conditions necessary for its free development." This then was the reason why they never showed any interest in settling Jews anywhere but in Eretz Israel.

In Achad Ha'am's view, the Yishuv should be allowed to develop gradually, organically, at its own pace, and above all—one must be resigned to the fact that the amelioration of the immediate material needs of the broad Jewish masses is possible only by non-Zionist and nonterritorial means. . . . No wonder then that on this background the East Africa (or any other territorialist scheme) plan seemed monstrous, a complete distortion of the original ideas. For that reason, the dramatic reappearance of the pogroms in 1903 failed to spur this school of opinion to renewed efforts to save the Jews of Russia and Poland. On the contrary, the pogroms aroused in them the worry lest the Herzlians would act at any cost to "force the issue of salvation." They [the Jews of Russia and Poland] believed in "quick salvation," or at least wanted to, and were attracted to Herzl because of his energetic efforts for their early succor from their desperate state, as was well understood by Achad Ha'am and most of his followers. . . . The result of the disintegration of Herzlian Zionism in the last months of his life and the first two years after his death was first and foremost the revival of Hibbat Zion. As we well know, the adherents of Hibbat Zion always had a somewhat narrow and proscribed vision. The real external world, with its tough policies and the necessity of making cruel decisions, was a world which they did not hope nor perhaps even wish to act in. They thus became used to the idea that the task of providing aid and succor is beyond their meager means and powers, which should then all be concentrated inwardly, toward Eretz Israel.[1]

Achad Ha'am, it should be cautioned, was not the sole spokesman for Russian Zionism. His brand of Zionism, namely advocacy of the establishment in Eretz Israel of a Jewish spiritual center, was rejected by many if not most Russian Zionists. He did not speak for those who wanted a decisive transformation of the character of the Jewish people (like the Zionist socialists), nor a continuity, which in reality would amount to nothing more than a Diaspora spiritual center, no different in kind from Babylon in the Talmudic period. Nowhere in his writings does Achad Ha'am deal with the political, economic, or military problems involved in a sovereign political existence; nor does he envisage the dynamics generated by them or how they create a qualitative and essential distinction between a political nation and a diaspora caste community. Clearly, such an omission did not result from lack of perspicacity, for other Zionist thinkers such as Borochov raised and discussed these problems and Achad Ha'am was surely aware of them. We must conclude that in the final analysis his thinking did not go beyond that of the religious caste community, and the spiritual center that he propounded was merely the continuation of that caste by other means, once it became clear that religion had exhausted itself.

Therefore it is difficult to accept Vital's main argument that the preservation of Jewish nationalism became more important to the "Zion Zionists" than the preservation of Jews as individuals. No Zionist wanted to preserve Judaism as it was. The counterposing of "Jews as individuals" against

"Jews as a nation" is also questionable. No sum can exist separately from its component parts, and that was obvious even to the most dogmatic Zionists. The real meaning of the breach between the "Zion Zionists" and Herzl was that the former set themselves the goal of effecting a change in the character of the Jewish people and eventually building Jewish power, and not, like the latter, solving the Jewish problem. As we shall see, the Jewish problem served them as a means to this end, which to this day they identify with the solution of the problem. But in reality it transpired that they and their successors had a vested interest in the persistence of the problem and in its exploitation for their own ends. Furthermore, the post-Herzl Zionist organization did not always permit other bodies to assume responsibility and care of persecuted Jews. Rather, when it seemed that these efforts contradicted the interests of the Eretz Israel enterprise, they often struggled against and sabotaged the efforts of these other bodies, even when they brought help and succor to Jews.

The difference between Herzl and his opponents among the East European Zionists may then be summed up in the fact that he did not think the new Jewish society should be informed by any specifically Jewish content. He thought it sufficient that the Jews divest themselves of the unsavory traits they had acquired over the centuries of exile to create an enlightened liberal state and society of the Western type. Nor did his opponents desire a continuation of the Jewish ghetto culture, which they detested. (Only religious Zionism was interested in preserving introverted traditional Judaism. One of the motivations for its Zionism was the feeling that the traditional religious community was doomed in the Diaspora and therefore a closed-in traditional Jewish society should be established in Eretz Israel.) Some of Herzl's opponents aimed at preserving selected elements of tradition. Others wanted a return to the pre-Exilic era, the age of kings, judges, and prophets of Israel, to achieve a renaissance of the mythical ancient Jews, free and proud, warriors and peasants, before they had become polluted by exile. But none of the factions consciously advocated a continuation of the East European caste-community culture in Eretz Israel, even if Achad Ha'am's thinking led in that direction.

It seems that the real bone of contention was the shift to an absolute concentration on the Zionist enterprise in Eretz Israel. As a result, as noted, the victorious Zionist faction not only became indifferent to the saving of Jews as such but even began to regard it with suspicion when it was not meant to serve the Zionist enterprise. It feared that any other aid extended to Jews would be at the expense of the resources and energy that rightfully belonged to Zionism. Diaspora Jews came to be regarded more and more as raw material for the needs of Zionism, whether as potential immigrants or as supporters of Zionism by financial or political activity. Zionism was not interested in them for their own sake. The Zionists even had a ready-made excuse for this approach: since Jews had no future in the Diaspora, and since sooner or later all of them would be forced to concentrate in Israel, the establishment of a Jewish homeland in Eretz Israel served the long-term interests of the entire Jewish people. It was therefore permissible to exploit the Jews for their own good, even when that happened to clash with the interests of a particular Jewish community.

The supporters of the Uganda scheme were those who wanted to take care of the existing Jewish problem, who wished to bring salvation to the Jews "as they are" (and in this they resembled the territorialists and autonomists), like the Mizrachi religious Zionists or the parties of the extreme Left, who shared much with the Bund, and who were the least "romantic" of the Zionists. The "Zion Zionists," on the other hand, were those who utterly rejected the Jewish people as it existed in the Diaspora and wished to transform it. They regarded anyone who had not undegone transformation as a means and a tool, not as an end, ignoring in fact the plight of the Jews except to the extent it served their purposes. Hence a further conclusion: since the Eretz Israelian enterprise was the only truly important activity, those Jews who had undergone the transformation and become "saved" were the ideal, the chosen, whereas all other Jews were inferior to them. The chosen ones, the pioneers, the idealists, were entitled to impose unlimited demands on the others, to instill in them a sense of endless guilt for their refusal to be saved, and the return given by the saved to their lowlier brethren for their inexhaustible help and devotion was the very existence of the saved, their becoming an ideal that has been realized by their establishment of a Jewish homeland. The very existence of this homeland was the reward for the aid extended to it. In short, this relationship contained the seed of an unlimited parasitic dependence of the "saved" on their "lesser" brethren, while the attitude of the "saved" toward themselves contained an element of narcissistic self-glorification coupled with condescension toward "those who walk in darkness."

The exclusivity of Eretz Israel, decided upon in the Uganda controversy, put a definite end to the territorialist aspect of Zionism. It also contained the following implications: since it had been decided that the aim of Zionism was Eretz Israel, unconditionally and above all else, and not the finding of some territory in which the Jews could solve their problem (to the extent that this problem could be solved by a territorial concentration), it followed that this aim was independent of the needs of the Jewish people. Jewish settlement in Eretz Israel thus ceased to be a function of the plight of the Jews. S. Beit Zvi writes:

> Parallel to the profound immunization [against territorialism] which the Zionist movement had undergone at this time, an essential change took place in it as regards its position within the Jewish people. Tacitly, it had now been incontrovertibly established that no longer is it sole guardian of the people. The function of "manager of affairs" for the Jewish people, propounded by Herzl in the *Judenstaat*, was taken to be the very basis of the movement that he

founded in 1897. In the Sixth Congress, many delegates still referred to this principle. Herzl and Nordau based on it the need for finding "a shelter for a night" for a people in desperate straits. Neither did the opponents of the Uganda scheme deny the assumption that the Zionist movement was the only authorized representative of the Jewish people. But, unlike their opponents, they found this assumption difficult to reconcile with their rejection of the temporary shelter in East Africa.... Simeon Rosenbaum's candid proposal, to tell the Jews simply that for the time being, until Eretz Israel was ready to receive them, they should emigrate to America or London, was met by shouts of "no!" from his fellow delegates.

But apart from this realistic proposal and apart from the alternative of adopting the shelter-for-a-night proposal, the Zionists were left with no answer to the misery of the masses.... This was no semantic change, but a real mutation, which determined the character and course of the movement for a long time to come.... On the eve of the Seventh Congress, when the Zionist Executive resolved to recommend to the congress to reject the Uganda scheme, it added a codicil to the resolution: "to ask other organizations interested in Jewish affairs whether they are prepared to undertake the East Africa Scheme." ... It was a highly significant turning point. First, from a Zionist viewpoint legitimacy was conferred on the existence and activity of the charitable organizations. Second, and more important, in this the Zionist movement gave notice to one and all that henceforth it was not an overall organization concerned with everything pertaining to the Jewish people but just another organization with a specific aim: to build a national home for the Jewish people in Eretz Israel. To that purpose it would strive with all its powers and would never permit anything to divert its attention. From now on, it would extend help to Jews only on condition and to the extent that this help meshed with the activities designed to realize its Zionist goal.[2]

In view of the extremely limited resources which the Zionist movement commanded at the time, it was truly incapable of undertaking a task as ambitious as the responsibility for the affairs of the whole Jewish people. Even the task of building and developing the Yishuv in Eretz Israel was almost beyond its powers, or so it sometimes seemed to those directly engaged in the enterprise. Limitation of the goal was a necessary precondition to success. Still, it is worth noting that the Zionist movement did not admit this and continued to present an outward show of responsibility for all Jewish affairs. It interfered with and hindered other organizations, Jewish or non-Jewish, whenever it imagined that their activity, political or humanitarian, was at variance with Zionist aims or in competition with them, even when these might be helpful to Jews, even when it was a question of life and death for Jews. (The persistence of this mental cast to this day is exemplified by the pressure applied in the 1980s by the Israeli government and the World Zionist Organization on the two large Jewish philanthropic organizations, the Joint Distribution Committee and the Hebrew Sheltering and Immigrant Aid Society [HIAS], to cease helping Soviet Jewish emigrants in Europe in order to force them to emigrate to Israel and the pressure on the German government to refuse to grant refugee status to Jews escaping from Russia, thus discriminating against them.)

Beit Zvi documents the Zionist leadership's indifference to saving Jews from the Nazi menace except in cases in which the Jews could be brought to Palestine. He points out that during World War II and the catastrophe that hit European Jewry, out of all the members of the Zionist leadership, only a second-echelon leader, Yitzhak Greenbaum, was named to conduct rescue operations in Europe. (Front-rank leaders, from Chaim Weizmann and David Ben-Gurion to Moshe Shertok [later Sharett], Eliyahu Golomb, and Shaul Avigur, were engaged in matters they deemed more important— land settlement, economic and military growth, the mobilization of political and financial support for the Yishuv, etc.) He analyzes the Evian conference, convened at the initiative of President Roosevelt on the eve of the war in order to find havens of refuge for the persecuted Jews of Europe. Zionist organs and spokesmen gloated over the failure of the conference, citing it as proof that only Eretz Israel could serve as a refuge for Jews (conveniently ignoring that even under the best of conditions, no room could have been found at the time in Palestine for more than a few hundred thousand refugees from Nazi Europe). He describes the dismay that spread through the movement lest the conference succeed and the efforts expended to sabotage it.[3] He points out that the attitude of the Latin American countries toward the Jewish refugee problem was characterized by a readiness to open their gates to the refugees. If the gates were later closed, it was because, being mostly poor, undeveloped countries, they were incapable of rapidly admitting large numbers of people and providing them with means of livelihood. The most outstanding example he cites is the readiness of the dictator of the Dominican Republic, Rafael Trujillo, to absorb one hundred thousand refugees and the sabotaging of this idea—as well as others, like proposals to settle the Jews in Alaska and the Philippines—by the Zionist movement.

Of all of these prospects one could argue that the Zionist leadership at the time was unaware of the scale and horror of the problem. Even after the outbreak of the war, it could surmise that what was happening was persecution and victimization, but not extermination (though even an attempt to interfere with the saving of people from "ordinary" persecution is inhuman and inexcusable, whatever the ideal this interference is supposed to serve). But it appears that no real change took place in the attitude of the Zionist movement even after the full scale of the Holocaust became clear, for it showed no interest in trying to save Jews outside Eretz Israel. This again proves the perspicacity of Beit Zvi's charge that the Zionist movement considered itself responsible only for the building and strengthening of Hebrew Palestine, not for the Jewish people in general.

Beit Zvi's study, which is a searing condemnation of the behavior of the Zionist movement and its leadership during the war, has been largely glossed over and ignored, except for the inevitable attacks on its "one-sidedness" and "extremism." But Dina Porat, in her comprehensive study of the subject, arrives at conclusions that are very close to those of Beit Zvi. Sometimes her very efforts to emphasize the attempts that had been undertaken by the Yishuv and Zionist leadership on behalf of European Jewry shed an even more lurid light on the basic apathy of the leadership toward the disaster and on its inability to react to it in a nonroutine manner.

Porat, like Beit Zvi, points out that only second-echelon leaders in the Zionist hierarchy were appointed to conduct the rescue operations. The first time a discussion was held by the Jewish Agency Executive on the condition of the Jews in the countries occupied by the Germans was in December 1941, more than two years after the beginning of the war. Almost a year later,

> in a highly emotional session of the agency's Executive held on November 1942 [the Nazis' "final-solution" Wannsee conference, it should be recalled, had been held in January of that year]—its first session since the outbreak of the war of which a considerable part was devoted to Europe's Jews—Dobkin gave an account of the meetings with the exchange group [a group of Jews with Palestinian passports who were exchanged for Germans and were thus saved from Europe, bringing with them detailed reports about what was taking place there]. He voiced the opinion that the truth of the reports was inescapable . . . and expressed chagrin that two principal members of the Executive—Ben-Gurion and Shertok—absented themselves from this part of the session. The minutes indicate that both received full details of the meetings with the members of the exchange group, but it is still most puzzling why they were absent from such a session.[4]

Most dumbfounding of all is Porat's dry, factual account of the discussions that lasted for many weeks in the agency's Executive about sending a mission to the United States to arouse public opinion there—a mission that never took place because no agreement could be reached as to who should participate in the mission. It seems that the main activities of the Yishuv on behalf of European Jews were declarations of days of mourning and fasting, which also "ended in failure." Porat concludes that after the November 1942 session of the Executive, "few discussions were held between the end of 1942 and the end of the war about the situation of Europe's Jews."[5] Porat believes that Ben-Gurion reached the conclusion that there was no possibility of saving the millions: "Reaching such a conclusion, and seeing with his characteristic almost ruthless clarity the limited resources which the Yishuv had for rescue operations, he no longer considered the issue of practical importance and continued to devote himself to the problems of the political future in Eretz Israel."[6]

A damning document in this connection is produced by Vital:

> On September 13, 1944, a senior, accredited representative of the Zionist movement called at the State Department in Washington to meet members of its

Near Eastern affairs staff. The official "memorandum of conversation" recorded by the department and relayed to American diplomatic and consular representatives in Cairo, Baghdad, Beirut, Damascus, Jeddah, Jerusalem, and London, was headed "Zionist Attitude to Palestine." It reported, inter alia, two references to the rescue of Jews in occupied Europe that retain some interest today. The first reference was to a proposal, then before the Congress, that temporary emergency shelters be established for Jews from Hungary in Palestine. The Zionist representative made it clear that he did not think much of it, partly because he distrusted the motives of those who had persuaded members of the Congress to put it forward, and partly because he did not think that they could succeed in escaping from Hungary anyway. But "in any case," he went on to say, "the Zionists were opposed to any scheme which would seek to place Jews in Palestine only temporarily, and on the understanding that they would be sent elsewhere after the war."

The second reference was to the argument current at the time between the Colonial Office and the Jewish Agency on the final disposition of the 15,000 immigration certificates that still remained to be allocated under the terms of the 1939 White Paper. The Jewish representative had this to say (and I quote from the State Department record of the conversation): "The Colonial Office took the line that preference in the issuing of certificates should be given to Jews, i.e., those in occupied Europe who were in imminent danger of death. [However, while] the Jewish Agency could not deny the priority to which such persons were entitled ... it had argued that some provision should also be made for potential immigrants in 'safe' areas like Italy, North Africa, and the Yemen." [The original Hebrew text adds here: "In other words, Eretz Israel and the reinforcement of the Yishuv as a collectivity stood above everything else, even above the Jews themselves."] ... The handwritten comments in the margin of the document suggest that our representative's American audience could hardly believe their ears.[7]

The obtuseness of the Zionist movement toward the fate of European Jewry did not prevent it, of course, from later hurling accusations against the whole world for its indifference toward the Jewish catastrophe or from pressing material, political, and moral demands on the world because of that indifference. The obtuseness itself, however, was not the result of any ill will. The fundamental reason for the movement's attitude, as Porat surmises, was undoubtedly the feeling of the leadership, first and foremost Weizmann and Ben-Gurion, that the means at its disposal were insufficient in any case for exerting a significant influence on the fate of European Jews and that investing efforts in that direction could undermine efforts to fortify the Yishuv in anticipation of future trials. As a further footnote to Beit Zvi's arguments, one can also point out that at that time, the Zionist movement and the Jewish people in general had very little power. Indeed, never since the beginning of the emancipation had the Jews been as helpless as they were in the Nazi era. This too could explain Zionist inactivity.

Still, in assessing the material, it is hard to overcome the suspicion that in addition to these reasons, the Zionists' aversion to Galut Jewry, from which they sought to disentangle themselves, was so deeply ingrained that they found it difficult to identify with it in its most difficult hour. I touch on this subject (which until recently was sedulously avoided, as if a conspiracy of silence surrounded it) not with the purpose of belaboring the Zionist movement but in order to shed light on its basic dynamic, logically derived from the change that took place in it—from a movement of rescue and salvation to one devoted to building a homeland and a nation—a change which was necessary for its success. For the establishment of the new Yishuv and its advancement to nationhood was an undertaking so gigantic, so demanding, that its realization called for fanatic devotion, for unbelievable singlemindedness and even for a great measure of ruthless determination, a readiness to ignore any other consideration, even that of the welfare of the Jews, in order to succeed. Its success even necessitated a measure of Jewish misery.

The decision taken by the Zionist movement in the Uganda controversy laid the ideological and psychological foundations for the exclusive concentration on Eretz Israel. Henceforth the order was reversed, although most Zionists did not realize then (nor do they even now) the significance of this reversal: instead of the Zionist organization and the Hebrew Yishuv serving as a means for the solution of Jewish problems, most organized parts of the Jewish people became a tool in the hands of the Zionist, later Israeli, leadership, subject to the needs of the Yishuv.

The full consequences of this reversal became apparent only many years after the Uganda controversy, particularly, as we have seen, during the Holocaust. But the basis for the reversal was laid not only with the triumph of the "Zion Zionists" at the Zionist Congress but also in the concrete activity in Palestine. Ben-Gurion was perhaps the most outstanding of those who demanded the centrality of Eretz Israel in the Zionist movement, as early as 1909, at the convention of the Poale Zion party in Sejerah. Contrary to Yitzhak Ben Zvi, who expressed at that convention a willingness to participate in the party's second world convention abroad, Ben-Gurion demanded that the convention take place in Eretz Israel, "and if not—we shall not take part in it." He and his supporters claimed that the Zionist organization must be reshaped to include only "people who carry out personally the mission of Labor Zionism in Eretz Israel and Turkey."[8] True, this attitude was not the result of the Uganda controversy, but it was its logical consequence and completion, fought for by Ben-Gurion and his supporters throughout the following years. It did not lead to a formal change in the structure of the Zionist organization, but in effect it achieved its goal. And once the Yishuv became a state, the Zionist organization lost most of its importance, as the responsibility for maintaining contact with Diaspora Jews and for activating them in Israel's behalf passed increasingly into the hands of the foreign relations apparatus of the state, whose prestige in the eyes of Jews abroad was in any case far greater than that of the Zionist organization.

This absolute concentration on the Eretz Israel enterprise, whose main bearer was the Zionist labor movement, resulted on one hand in the creation of the Yishuv "state within a state" under the British Mandate, and on the other, as we have seen in preceding chapters, in a measure of control by the labor movement over the Zionist organization abroad.

The reversal was forced by the very dynamics of and constraints on the settlement process, and not because Ben-Gurion or anybody else made an arbitrary decision in this matter. All that Ben-Gurion's demand shows is that he seems to have grasped the true significance of the process better than others. The settlement process could not achieve its aim—the creation of a nation—by just any kind of agricultural and urban settlement. Unspecified settlement had resulted, as we have seen, in the emergence of a class of plantation owners employing Arab labor. From the beginning it was necessary to select the right sort of settlers and develop specialized forms of settlement in order to create the basis for an autonomous national structure. Otherwise, as Weizmann noted after observing many of the immigrants of the early twenties, the immigration would not have led to the creation of a nation and a state but merely to another ghetto community.

The articles and lectures of Arthur Ruppin, the foremost planner of Zionist settlement between 1912 and 1919, provide a detailed itemization of settlement needs.[9] He analyzed the occupational structure needed to build the country, and his results largely corresponded with Borochov's ideas about the "upending" of the Jewish occupational pyramid. In the initial phase, he wrote, there would be a need for a large number of farmers, accompanied by diminishing numbers of administrators, service personnel, businessmen, and professional people. During this phase he opposed any major extension of higher education, as in such a relatively primitive socioeconomic structure there would be few occupational opportunities for university-trained personnel, forcing them to leave the country for places where they could use their training. He also emphasized the need for screening the immigrants to winnow out asocial elements and to ensure the influx of young, productive people. He dwelled on the requisite settlement forms, on the methods of financing and agricultural credits, and he objected to granting farming units to the settlers for free, insisting that they repay their debts to the settlement institutions out of their work. In short, he outlined the principles that to a considerable extent were to guide the Zionist settlement authorities during the coming years.

In other words, for Zionism to succeed, settlement policy had to be tailored not to Diaspora needs but to the needs of the Zionist enterprise in Eretz Israel. And indeed, only the development of a firm basis of settlement in its variety of forms as shaped by Zionist institutions made possible the later mass nonselective immigration from Europe and Islamic countries, which immediately created problems that have remained partly unresolved to this day. Throughout the period between the world wars, the organs of the Zionist movement and the various pioneering movements in the

Diaspora operated as screening and training centers for picking the most suitable people for Zionist settlement. Zionism's success in establishing the state of Israel would have been inconceivable without putting the interest of settlement above the interests of the Jewish people. The imperviousness (relatively speaking) of the Zionist leadership toward the lot of the Jews abroad was the reverse side of its success in achieving its aim.

It was the Holocaust that stamped this reversal with finality, putting an end to the equivalency of Zionist movement leadership in the Diaspora and Yishuv leadership. The immigration reserves of Jews with a national political outlook were mainly in Europe. That was also the field of operation of the large youth and agricultural training movements that channeled pioneers to the (mainly agricultural) settlements and provided most of the Yishuv leaders. There was a continuity between Eastern Europe, where Jewish national political awareness emerged in the modern era, and Palestine. It is difficult sometimes to determine with certainty where the center of activity of some parties and personalities lay, whether in Eretz Israel or in Eastern and Central Europe. Most parties in the country (with the possible exception of Mapai, the main labor party) were originally branches of the East European Zionist parties. Perhaps the outstanding example is the Revisionist party, whose main cohorts were in Poland, and whose leader, Ze'ev Jabotinsky, who was forbidden by the mandatory authorities to live in Palestine, lived with his entourage in France and other Western countries.

The annihilation of European Jewry liquidated both the immigration reservoirs and the leadership cadres of the Zionist movements. Henceforth, all leadership would be home grown—from Moshe Dayan and Yitzhak Rabin to Yossi Sarid and Ariel Sharon. Most of the leaders began to demonstrate their abilities within the military system, the only field the veteran leadership had at first been prepared to entrust to people born or bred in Palestine. By the time the state was established, however, Zionist leaders immigrating from abroad no longer had access to the inner sanctums of power that had once been the abode of the Zionist organization or the Jewish Agency but were now the province of the Israeli government. U.S. and British Zionist leaders were never really expected to immigrate, nor were they ever seriously considered as candidates for sharing power over the Yishuv and the state. They were needed in the U.S. and Britain, not in Palestine. (This was contrary to Ben-Gurion's oft-repeated ritual demands on them to immigrate, the true purpose of which, one surmises, was to instill in them a permanent sense of guilt, thus paralyzing any inclination on their part to criticize the actions of the Israeli government, and thereby turning them into its obedient tools.) The leadership cadres of the Yishuv, and later the state, consisted almost entirely of people of Russian, Polish, Galician, and Baltic extraction, later joined by a few conforming German Jews.

Thus, whereas until the war the Zionist leadership showed little interest in immigration from Islamic countries (though at one time immigration

from Yemen was encouraged in order to have a ready-made Jewish proletariat capable of working hard for modest wages, thus competing with
Arab workers and peasants on equal terms), after the displaced persons
camps in Europe and the illegal immigrant camps in Cyprus were pumped
dry, the Jewish communities in the Islamic countries remained the sole
source of immigration. All the efforts of the Zionist organization now became channeled in that direction.

Much was made in Zionist publications of the messianic fervor that
seized the Jews of Islamic lands. Indubitably, there were such cases, and
some Zionist cells did exist among the educated classes in Iraq and Egypt.
Social development in some of the Arab-speaking countries had reached
the stage of nationalism, with the xenophobia—sometimes embracing
Jews—often attending this stage, particularly in colonial or semicolonial
countries. There is hardly a doubt that anti-Jewish feelings existed, for example, among parts of the Iraqi public, who were influenced by the anti-Semitic propaganda of the Axis powers during World War II. This was the
background of the Rashid Ali Al Kailani revolt and the pogrom perpetrated
on Baghdad Jews in 1941.

But a study of Tom Segev's book, *The First Israelis*, arouses doubt
whether this fervor was always sincere. Segev quotes, for example, a report
from the operatives of the Jewish Agency's Immigration Department.

> They charged that "the urging to emigrate was done with much irresponsibil-
> ity. In North Africa, a hysteria to emigrate was fanned artificially, and the hu-
> man material urged to do so is of a very low quality as far as its absorption
> prospects are concerned." The absorption operative, Chermon, said a few
> months later: "I spoke with the people, with the Jewish leaders, and I know for
> sure that there was no messianic movement in Tunisia. The messianic fervor
> was [artificially] organized."

Concerning the emigration of Iraqi Jewry, Segev comments:

> According to the official version, which in time was even buttressed by a court
> verdict, the Aliya from Iraq ... was the result of "the yearning of Iraqi Jewry
> for the Holy Land and also the consequence of intolerable oppression by the
> Iraqi authorities, including persecution, arrests, hangings, etc." The Jewish
> exodus was made possible when the Iraqi parliament decided to permit the
> Jews to leave within a limited period, starting in the first half of 1950. In fact,
> it was an expulsion order: most Jews were forced to leave and their property
> confiscated. Several sources, including reports of the Aliya Institution, testify
> to the fact that the decision of the Iraqi parliament was caused, inter alia, by
> actions of the Zionist movement, with the help of agents of the Aliya organiza-
> tion, including the smuggling of Jews across the Iranian border. The organiza-
> tion's files do include innumerable cables reporting the persecution of Iraqi
> Jews, but practically all of the persecuted were involved in the activities of the
> Zionist underground or suspected of complicity with it. As a rule, there are no
> reports of victimizing Jews as Jews. But the heads of the organization wanted

to foment a noisy worldwide campaign against Iraq in order to speed up the passage of the law for the emigration of the Jews. They therefore proposed a series of actions. . . . Propaganda in the foreign press, an attempt to sabotage a request for a loan submitted by Iraq to the World Bank, pressure and the fomenting of disturbances around the Iraqi ambassador to the United Nations, . . . all designed to drive Iraq to the point of becoming disgusted with its Jews, some of whom were Zionists who wanted to emigrate to Israel but others who wanted to stay on in Iraq. Shortly before the Iraqi Parliament decided to permit its Jews to leave the country, the organization's offices in Tel Aviv received a cable from Baghdad saying: "We continue our usual activity aimed at cooking the law faster and to find out how the Iraqi government intends to carry it out."

It appears that Eastern Jews were assigned in advance a lowly position in the emerging Israeli society.

A secret protocol in English keeps on record what Berl Locker, chairman of the Jewish Agency's Executive, said to the American Jewish statesman Henry Morgenthau in October 1948: "It is our opinion that the Sephardi and Yemeni Jewries will have to take a very large share in the building of the country. We must bring them here both in order to save them, and also to get the human material needed for the building of the country."

They were assigned the most difficult and least profitable share of the country's building, being settled in the hilly parts of the Galilee and Judea. The fertile, easily cultivable soils on the coastal plain and in the south were handed over to immigrants from Europe. There were exceptions . . . but most of the "good units" were not awarded to immigrants from the Arab countries.[10]

The author also quotes Liova Eliav, a central figure of the settlement enterprise in the early years of the slate, who argues that this result was not deliberate but a natural, incidental result of the common background of the Jewish Agency's officials and the Jews of Europe. But one way or another, the results of these decisions were fateful for the social and political future of the state.

Thus the Hebrew labor movement—the dominant factor in the Yishuv and in the Zionist movement and the backbone of the state establishment—presumably socialist and egalitarian, created a stratified class society in collaboration with the bourgeois elements of the Yishuv. On the most sympathetic interpretation, these steps were taken without sufficient awareness of their significance, definitely not of the future disastrous results of this policy, and it may be asking too much to expect such prescience from harassed officials who could hardly cope with the tremendous flow of immigrants reaching the country. The very decision to admit masses of people all at once was highly problematic from the start, as it precluded any organic, orderly absorption and inflicted a traumatic shock on the immigrants and their descendants. Physically, this abortive absorption was perpetuated in hopeless development towns and decaying public housing, the inhabitants of which seem to have been doomed from the start to corrosive idleness or employment in public works. It may be conjectured that the authorities were motivated by two considerations: first, that there was a need for a rapid increase of the Jewish population; second, that as long as it was possible to bring to the country any immigrant group, that should be done immediately, overruling all other considerations, for in a few years these people might no longer be interested in immigration, and then the best-laid absorption plans would be useless. Possibly, memories of the immigration fiasco of the early Mandate years, when the meager trickle of immigrants failed to take advantage of the opportunities opened by the Balfour Declaration, were still smarting. Pangs of conscience over inactivity during the Holocaust may have contributed their share, as well as the realization that saving Jews meant renouncing any selection and screening process.

It is difficult to quarrel with the latter considerations, and they may have been right. But the the need for a rapid increase in the country's Jewish population may be viewed from several perspectives. On one hand, the national nucleus became a full-fledged nation. On the other hand, that created numerous backward pockets of population teeming with neglected, uneducated children, ready nurseries of crime and prostitution, with many people second- and third-generation welfare recipients—in short, a population which, far from being an asset, became a social and political liability. Since these people were backward to start with, they were treated as backward, a priori deserving less than others, and this redoubled their backwardness. In addition, the encouragement of large families, aimed primarily at this sector, pushed them into greater depths of poverty, ignorance, and crime. The people who initiated this policy failed to realize that many members of such a population are useless even as manual workers. Their advancement depends on smaller families, better housing, better education, and improvement of the status of women.

The picture that emerges from a collation of these observations moves one to ponder the motivations of the founders of the Yishuv and the state. Needless to say, any action can be interpreted in its context, which elucidates the immediate motives of the persons involved. Modern historians, understandably shy of the elaborate historiosophical designs erected by past historians, tend to limit themselves to immediate contexts and regard with suspicion any ascription of more far-reaching aims to the people involved. But that provokes another question: what prompted these people to view their position and the surrounding conditions as they did? Mossad agents undoubtedly were convinced that their provocations in Iraq and Morocco really meant the salvation of Jews there in the long run, for if the Jews had remained in these countries, they eventually would have suffered grievously. But self-persuasion of this kind is conditioned by an ideology that dictated such an interpetation. Similarly, Zionist leaders persuaded themselves that the building of Eretz Israel was the only lasting solution to the Jewish problem, and it was therefore permissible to sacrifice whole Jewish communities to that distant goal. But we have still not answered the question, for in the last resort these are nothing but excuses. Almost despite myself, I hazard the conjecture that one profound, fundamental motivation of the Zionist system may be defined as a will to power. I further wonder whether it is not an accident, and not merely a consequence of regional political-military circumstances, that the Israel Defense Forces became not only a vital necessity in a violent, seething, and hostile region but far more than that—a focus of values, an exemplary way of life, the central symbol and hub of activity of the state of Israel—and that the basic tendency of Israeli policy and people is to solve problems by means of force and see it as the be-all and end-all, rather than trying diplomatic and political solutions. It would seem that this tendency can only be explained by psychological factors originating in the conditions of Jewish life in Eastern Europe.

The will to power is apparent in both branches of the Jewish national movement in Eastern Europe: those who sought a framework for national existence for existing Jews—the territorialists, the autonomists, and the Bund, which aimed mainly at organized political power (though in the organization of self-defense units against pogroms the Bund created actual fighting forces)—and those who wished to liquidate Jewishness as they knew it and establish instead a different, "saved" Jewish people. As noted, the decisive difference between the two was symbolized by the choice between Hebrew and Yiddish (or any other language spoken by Jews) as a national language. For the latter, the "Zion Zionists," Jewish Diaspora existence was inherently rotten. One must read the "national" works of the great Jewish poet and storyteller Caim Nahman Bialik (who lived most of his life in prerevolutionary Russia) to realize the intensity of the aversion with which the "Zion Zionists" regarded the misery, humiliation, and degeneracy, coupled with the nouveau riche vulgarity of the better off, of Jewish existence in Eastern Europe. The works of another great Jewish writer, S. Y. Abramowitz (more famous under his pen name, Mendele Mocher Seforim, "Mendele the Bookseller"), contain descriptions of terrifying squalor and human decay in the shtetl, which in a later age became the subject of sentimental nonsense and counterfeit nostalgia.

Perhaps the gloomiest and most savage expression of this aversion is to be found the in the works of Y. H. Brenner, who was younger than Mendele and a contemporary of Bialik, and who was murdered in Jaffa in 1921. The most acidic ingredient in his portrayals is disgust with the Jewish weakness, the impotent lachrymosity, the helpless ineffectuality, and their inevitable attendant evils: self-pity, cowardice, slyness, twisted mentality, garrulity, the compensatory stale self-importance, accompanied necessarily by flinching on encounter with the firm, hard real world, the world of action and power of the *goyim*. Brenner's literary portrayals are an artistic complement to the works of Ber Borochov, who analyzed the same traits from a sociohistorical perspective. It is no accident that both Brenner and Borochov became spiritual fathers of the Zionist labor movement. The Zionist right wing, on the other hand, in its aspirations for power, fell into the trap of fatuous daydreams about power and magnificence, which for Brenner was just another manifestation of Jewish ineffectuality. Only the merciless analysis of Brenner and Borochov, their unflinching gaze at the darkest aspects of reality, their readiness to adopt the principles of Marxist criticism and praxis, could achieve the transformation of weakness into power. And a precondition for power was the power to recognize and describe weakness.

The gloom overshadowing most of Brenner's works (as in the opening of his story "Winter") is essentially the gloom of impotence, the inability even to *will* something. In this respect, Brenner's and Bialik's descriptions are not so far from Otto Weininger's half-crazed masterpiece *Geschlecht und Charakter* (Sex and Character), in which he considers the Jewish "race" as inherently feeble and "effeminate," lacking virile energy, the energy of willing, acting, artistic creativity, and fighting. A symbolic expression of a similar attitude toward Judaism is to be found in Noah, the hero of Bialik's story "Behind the Fence," who in his (partial, finally abortive) escape from the suffocating, sickening milieu of the shtetl joins the young gentile toughs, rides horses with them, and makes war against his own brethren.

This self-hatred of the greatest Zionist creators provides the key to their deepest and strongest obsession—power. This note is heard from all sides, from left to right. The horror of weakness, the determination to overcome it by dint of determination, are clearly audible in a passage from Weizmann's autobiography describing a friend of his student days, Zvi Aberson, who

> summed up in his person all the aspects of the Jewish spiritual and economic tragedy. . . . Aberson was the *Luftmensch* par excellence, gifted, rootless, aimless, untrained and well-meaning, that type of lost soul which haunted me, filled me with dread for myself, and served as a terrifying example. . . . His field was "the humanities," the kind of material—history, philosophy, literature, "things-in-general"—which one can take up, drop, take up again, vague and attractive subjects to which the bright type of "eternal student" was usually drawn.[11]

One detects here an extreme reaction, a horror of weakness and aimlessness that results in a seeming contempt toward the full range of the humanities, leading Weizmann (who was himself definitely a humanist) to study chemistry, of all things. It is the same reaction that led A .D. Gordon, Ben-Gurion, and Katzenelson to engage in farming.

At the other extreme of the Zionist movement we have the will and testament of Samson, the Judge, to his people in Jabotinsky's novel *Samson*, about the Biblical hero: the people must "procure iron," "everything should be sacrificed in exchange for iron"—iron meaning armaments, power, liberty. The second commandment in the will is that they "choose themselves a king"—namely, that they must organize themselves politically in a disciplined, goal-oriented manner, to forge the tools that will make it possible to set a national goal and the conditions for its achievement. The final commandment in the will is "to learn laughter." Laughter is the product of power, an expression of freedom, life in its full breadth, in its physical exuberance and aesthetic beauty. Samson goes to the Philistines and learns from them, like Noah in Bialik's "Behind the Fence." He wants to emulate them and turn his people into "Philistines"—strong, aesthetic, self-controlled, organized, Nietzchean *übermenschen*, everything that his own people are not.

That could be the chief reason for the Zionist leadership's amazing and horrifying apathy to the catastrophe that overwhelmed Europe's Jews. What bothered Yitzhak Greenbaum, in one of the few discussions on the subject to take place in the Jewish Agency Executive, was that the Jews of Poland were behaving "like dishrags," without "self-respect," under Nazi rule. And he himself was a Polish Jewish leader who had only recently immigrated to Eretz Israel! This is undoubtedly the reason for the obsessive need to emphasize Jewish heroism, to prove that the Jews did not go like sheep to the slaughter—as if these were not puerile, silly, and even obscene considerations in the face of such a vast calamity. As Beit Zvi rightly comments,

> The Germans could not hurt the dignity of the Jews, because the two sides had no common definition of the concept of dignity and honor. The victimization of the Jews is another crime in the long roster of Nazi inhumanity, but it did not dishonor their victims. Much torture was inflicted by the murderers on ghetto Jews, but they could not shame them, at least in the eyes of people for whom the meaning of honor and dishonor had not become completely confounded.[12]

Brenner and Bialik undoubtedly would have endorsed this judgment. It did not occur to Bialik at all that the victims of the Kishinev pogrom, about which he wrote one of his most moving poems, should have impressed the thugs who attacked them with their "bravery." As far as he was concerned, these were beasts in human form whose opinion about anything, including their victims, had no importance whatsoever. But it seems that the revulsion of the Zionist leaders toward their origins, their adoption of a new scale of values, their total rejection of Jewish *galut* existence, particularly its weakness, created a psychological barrier between them and the Jewish disaster, although it affected relatives and friends of most of them.

The claim that Zionist efforts would not have made much of a difference is merely an excuse. It is impossible to know whether any serious attempt would have succeeded, since none was attempted. And to cover up this inactivity, much was made of the dropping of a few parachutists from Eretz

Israel into occupied Europe. But as much as we admire their heroism and self-sacrifice, this did not constitute a serious effort, even considering the limited means then at the disposal of the Zionist movement.

What arouses doubt and skepticism in all this is the self-righteous posture of the Zionist movement, its readiness to accuse all and sundry of indifference toward the fate of Europe's Jews and its determination to extract all possible material advantage, in cash and political support, from the Western sense of guilt about this indifference—a guilt which the Zionists themselves largely shared. What bothers the Zionist movement even today is not its apathy and inactivity at the time but its belief that the victims should have made heroic gestures to salvage their honor. The true meaning of this preoccupation with heroism, with revolts in the ghettos (and the frantic efforts to discover such, even in places where there were none), is that to the extent that the Zionists see themselves as part of the Jews which have been destroyed, they feel that their own honor was blemished because their brethren did not put up a fight.

NINE

The Maturation of Power and the Emergence of a Nation

The Zionists' sedulous accumulation of power in Palestine began to yield fruit during World War II. The leadership in Palestine was able to gain control of the world Zionist movement and later of most of the Diaspora even beyond the Zionist organization. This expanded control came about as a result of the Hebrew Yishuv's development into the nucleus of a nation in its own right, generating autonomous energies independent of Diaspora Jewry and gradually achieving a separate national consciousness.

To a certain extent, this separatedness was also the result of the fact that the Palestinian Yishuv was what was now left of the Jewish "national nation" of Eastern Europe. Beyond this, however, it was also a consequence of self-realization. Unlike the synthetic feeling of the early pioneers, a new, mostly Palestinian-born generation had grown up with a natural feeling of a homeland. This was the Zionist movement's greatest success. Its ruthless singlemindedness had finally achieved its aim.

The process was greatly aided by the growth of the Yishuv's economic power. The kibbutz and moshav forms of agricultural settlement proved their efficacy both economically and socially, while the war-imposed isolation of the Middle East from the rest of the world forced the Allied armies stationed there to rely increasingly on the rapidly developing industrial services of the Hebrew Yishuv, which became the Allies' regional workshop. The talents and training of the industrialists, engineers, and managers who escaped to Palestine from Germany, one of the world's leading industrial powers, now found their proper scope. The emergence of a trained corps of expert industrialists, managers, engineers, and skilled workmen, with the attendant economic boom, strengthened the Yishuv's self-confidence.

Most important, there developed a Hebrew military force capable of undertaking offensive operations, starting with Charles Orde Wingate's special night squads, then the Palmach, then the Jewish Brigade formed within the British army, whose veterans supplied the Yishuv with a cadre of professional soldiers and officers (to which were later added immigrants from

Europe who brought with them the military experience of the Red Army). Thus the agricultural-industrial base of the Yishuv acquired a fighting arm with an organically developing, homegrown military doctrine that enabled it to begin to maneuver independently in the international arena. As Yigal Elam puts it,

> Post–World War II Zionism no longer resembled the Zionism of the Mandate period on the eve of the war—neither as far as the condition of the Jewish Yishuv was concerned nor as far as the Jewish people were concerned. The Jewish Yishuv increased and gained power during the war both materially and numerically. It now numbered close to 600,000 persons, with a relatively large proportion of young people (more than 150,000 men aged fifteen to forty-five, after having increased by more than 25 percent during the war. . . . The strategic role played by Palestine during the war effected a tremendous, almost revolutionary, economic development. . . . The Yishuv's participation in the war effort enhanced on one hand its sense of power and self-confidence, particularly thanks to the establishment of the Palmach and the Jewish Brigade, but, on the other hand, in view of the extermination of the Jewish people [in Europe] due to the impotence of both the Yishuv and the Jewish people and the harsh British treatment of the few refugees who succeeded in escaping from Europe and tried to reach a safe haven in Eretz Israel, frustration and bitterness boiled up and the conviction struck roots that in a violent world, Zionism will have to forge its course by forceful means.[1]

Chaim Weizmann, visiting the country toward the end of 1944, sensed this fundamental change in the Yishuv and concluded that the "national home" already existed, although it had not yet been recognized internationally. The implication was that the Hebrew Yishuv had already become a self-supporting national organism in its own right with its specific self-awareness, differing in kind from just any Jewish-national self-consciousness. The struggle it began against British rule, pioneered by the Lehi (Fighters for the Freedom of Israel, also known as the Stern Group or Stern Gang) and the Etzel (National Military Organization, also known as the Irgun), did not derive basically from the plight of the Holocaust survivors, as propagandists would have it. Had the survivors not emigrated to Eretz Israel, they either would have settled wherever they found themselves or would have emigrated to the West—as a third of them indeed did. The struggle was the result of the consciousness of inner power, the awareness of potential sovereignty, of what may be defined as the emerging Hebrew nation.

Elam rightly points out that had it not been for the Balfour Declaration and the British Mandate, the Yishuv would never have developed to this point.

> From the beginning, the British had to play an ungrateful role in Palestine. Their historical undertaking—the role assigned to them by Zionism—was to make possible the growth of the Jewish national home in Palestine, namely, to

enable a Jewish minority to develop, despite the violent opposition of the Arab majority, to a level which would win it sovereignty and independence. Without the legal and security framework provided by the mandatory regime, the Zionist project could never have been realized. In the two decisive aspects—the legal and the military—the Jews could never have achieved a breakthrough under the conditions that prevailed in Palestine until the end of World War I. In order to achieve that, the presence of a third party, representing a *force majeur*, was needed, not only as far as physical force is concerned but also as a force representing legitimate authority in the international arena. . . . Zionism did not seek at all to liberate itself from the British presence, as long as the Jews were a minority in the country and as long as the original mandatory policy was being carried out. . . . An early British withdrawal and the granting of independence to a Palestine with an Arab majority would have meant the establishment of the Arab state of Palestine. This was the meaning of the White Paper of 1939.[2]

The common notion that Israel was established as a result of the enlightened world's guilt feelings about the Holocaust, moving them to support Zionist aspirations in Palestine, is therefore only partly true. When Weizmann described the members of the Yishuv in 1944 as "capable of a vast concentrated action in behalf of the remnant of Jewry in Europe . . . capable of such action, frantically eager to undertake it, and forbidden to do so,"[3] he was portraying a great potential force striving to save the remnants of European Jewry. Essentially, though, they were aspiring to what any such force naturally aspires to. They sought to break their fetters, to become independent and sovereign. It is no accident that the Canaanite movement appeared during World War II. This movement expressed a sense of independence and power—both completely independent of and unconnected with Jewry and the disaster that overwhelmed it.

Only such considerations explain the establishment of Israel. It was established by the Hebrew Yishuv of Palestine when it became fully conscious of its inner strength. Its supreme test came during the War of Independence, and in this ordeal the Yishuv had to rely almost exclusively on its own resources. True, just as any strong fighting body in the international arena attracts interested backers, the Yishuv received much aid in armaments and a great deal of political and financial support. But had it not been for its own inherent power, it would not have attracted them. It was the emerging Hebrew people of Eretz Israel who waged the war and won it. The diplomacy of statesmen such as Weizmann and Nachum Goldmann was indeed very helpful, but only in support of the main action, of the central and real burden: the war. Outside experts and volunteers also contributed their share, but these contributions were effective only because they were given to an inherently powerful body. Of itself, this aid would have been of no avail had the Yishuv not been capable of using it properly.[4] In this context, it is again pertinent to quote Elam, who, after discussing the difficult situation of the Yishuv during the early stages of the war, writes:

At the same time, the Haganah's higher command had no doubt whatsoever that it was capable of moving over into the offensive and of overwhelming the Arabs' irregular forces. Most people knew and felt that the Haganah had not yet brought its potential power to play, and that this power would find expression the moment that the mobilization and training of the new units was completed, the heavy armaments acquired in large quantities in recent months had arrived in the country . . . , and the British presence, which could frustrate the durability of any Haganah achievement, would dwindle and fade away. From an insider's point of view, aware of the real strength of the Haganah and the revolutionary changes occurring within it . . . the difficult situation at the time should have misled nobody, for it was merely a result of the strategic conception which the Haganah imposed upon itself.[5]

Of course, one should not belittle the sense of moral obligation the enlightened Christian world felt toward the Jewish people after the Nazi horror. Even so, it is difficult to measure the weight of this obligation in the processes that led the majority of the United Nations General Assembly to support the partition plan in November 1947. Within the essentially friendly United States, there was much dithering between the pro-Arab inclinations of the Pentagon and the State Department and the pro-Zionist positions imposed on the politicians by their Jewish constituencies until President Harry Truman threw his weight in favor of the partition resolution. Even later, in the course of the war, there were hesitations and proposals to retreat from this position (reflected in the U.S. decision to accord Israel at first only de facto and not de jure recognition). One cannot deny moral considerations to Soviet policy either, although its resolute support of the Yishuv's struggle and the establishment of Israel was basically dictated by its intention to drive British imperialism from the region. Although Soviet-Israeli relations soured almost immediately after this brief honeymoon, the Soviet Union never rescinded its recognition of Israel or of Israel's right to exist in the Middle East—despite the pressures of its Arab clients.

Still, these were only peripheral factors that eased the struggle. When the Yishuv faced attack by Palestinian Arabs and, later on, invasion by Arab armies, no foreign force was on hand to provide assistance. Had it been defeated in battle, all the U. N. resolutions and all the sympathy for the plight of the persecuted Jewish people and all the diplomatic talents of the Zionist leadership and those who volunteered to help it would have been to no avail. At most, there would have been efforts to find some haven for the remnants of the Yishuv or to secure for them tolerable terms of protection under Arab rule. And it should be emphasized that the force that won the fight was composed primarily of the Eretz Israel–born younger generation, the offspring of the revolutionary national development that began in the mid-1930s and in which the Yishuv achieved self-awareness as a national community in its own right.

Another of the many paradoxes in Yishuv history was that the British

White Paper, which specified a freeze on the Yishuv's development policy, actually aided it. Issued by the British government in 1939, it had a clear political-strategic aim: to ensure peace and quiet in the Middle East during the impending struggle against Germany and Italy. This aim was largely achieved, with minor exceptions. David Niv, Irgun Zva'i Le'umi historian, notes that Irgun activities in 1938–1939 were meant to show the British that the Jews could cause more trouble than the Arabs and therefore should be accorded greater weight in British calculations.[6] The Irgun failed in its purpose; it had not grasped Britain's broader considerations. The British, while suppressing the Arab revolt by force, basically acceded in the White Paper to the demands of the Arab countries to freeze the "national home" by a drastic limitation of immigration and to prohibit the sale of land to Jews within defined zones of the country. The reasoning behind this policy decision was clear. Not only did the Arabs enjoy a vast preponderance over the Jews in the extent of their territories, population, and natural resouces (factors that are still of paramount importance in determining the great powers' policy in the Israeli-Arab conflict), but in the imminent world struggle, it was clear that the Jews had no choice but to support the British. There was no need therefore to buy their support.

But the fact that Palestine was at peace during the war enabled the Yishuv to rapidly develop its economy and to build its military forces without interference, and even with the help of the British, who thus enjoyed the best of the two worlds. Also, as the struggle against British rule gained momentum, the Arabs assumed a neutral stance. Had they initiated hostile action against the Yishuv at that time, the anti-British struggle might have failed.

The Holocaust, by creating a favorable moral climate in international public opinion, only marginally helped the Yishuv in its fight for independence. Even without this moral support, the Yishuv would have won independence, although perhaps with greater difficulty. On the other hand, the Holocaust destroyed the great reservoir of nationally conscious European Jews, hundreds of thousands or millions who might have become citizens of the new state. The Nazi extermination machine was therefore not the midwife of the state, as is commonly assumed. In actual fact, its contribution was minimal; by denying the country its natural source of immigration, it greatly weakened the state even before its establishment.

The establishment of the state, when looked at from the outside, seems like a revolution. In reality, however, the foundations of the Yishuv's self-governing institutions and its various institutional and political bodies had been developing since the twenties, and even long before that. The relationships between the old parties and power blocks cooperating within the National Committee (Va'ad Leumi) of the mandatory era were transferred to the new state structure, with the addition of the Arab population bloc that remained inside the borders of the state (a makeshift representation was arranged for them, partly through Mapai collaborators and partly through the Communist party). I have noted the forces that propelled the new Israeli government to adopt a pro-Western orientation. But it should be emphasized that the structure of the Zionist movement and all its political and economic ties have always been Western. Just as the new state structure was essentially conservative, it was to be expected that the traditional Zionist foreign relations orientation would also continue under the state. The conflict with Britain was in truth opposed to a cornerstone of political Zionism, which had always sought the support of an imperial power to back it against local forces.

The new state's pro-American orientation, which became clear immediately after its establishment, was merely a supplanting of one imperial patron by another. The aim of Zionist policy remained constant: the mobilization of an external power to counterbalance the opposing local powers seeking to rid themselves of the foreign body introduced among them. During the Mandate period, it was primarily the Palestinians who opposed the Jewish presence. After the establishment of the state, however, the scope of the hostility steadily increased and finally—until the peace treaty between Israel and Egypt—it embraced all Arabic-speaking countries. Although Israel became disproportionately powerful militarily, it is still essentially weaker—militarily, and also in terms of economic-geographical-political weight—than the combined forces opposing it.

The Zionist movement had hardly taken into account that the East European reservoir on which it had hitherto fed would be replaced by population groups from Islamic countries. The traditional "Zionist triangle" consisted of Jews in countries of hardship (the natural candidates for immigration) on one side; the state (formerly the Yishuv), which absorbs the refugees, on the second side; and Jews from prosperous Western countries, mainly the United States, who finance the absorption comprising the third side. As the sources of immigration dried up, only two sides of the triangle were left— the state and the prosperous Jews. Still, here too the pattern of the Yishuv's relationships remained largely unchanged, with Western Jews continuing to finance the state.

This structure, which in mandatory times constituted a state within a state, in a paradoxical way hampered and undermined the Yishuv's transition to full-fledged nation-statehood. The independent Hebrew nation, which had fought and won the War of Independence, was only one element of the Yishuv. The Yishuv's structure, despite the development of its self-governing institutions, was still a compromise between a traditional Jewish caste community, with its self-governing communal institutions, and genuine national institutions. That representatives of religious parties became equal members of purely national-political bodies and imposed on them their communal conceptions of group identity is one consequence of this halfway stage, which impeded the development of a truly secular national consciousness. The very idea of a new political orientation for the state, raised by certain circles on the left, both Zionist (Mapam) and non-Zionist

(Communist), as well as some ex-Lehi members, who called for a neutralist foreign policy, clashed with the fact that with the exception of political independence, almost all of the Yishuv's frames of reference—both internal and international—remained unchanged. Such a change in orientation would have called not merely for a government decision but also for a complete overhaul of all the traditional prenational Zionist conceptions. It would have called for a complete overhaul of the nation's definition of itself and its relationship with Diaspora Jewry, and this would have shown that Zionism, indeed the midwife of the newly born nation, had itself become an obstacle to the nation's definition of itself. It is no accident that most nationalist circles in the early days of the state advocated a pro-Soviet or at least a neutralist policy. This was not because they were socialist or pro-Soviet in principle but because this was the only way to crack the Yishuv's prenational mold and to advance it to the status of a full-fledged nation.

In other words, external Jewish and pro-Jewish support helped the newly formed Hebrew nation's fight for independence and the establishment of Israel. But this support, in turn, created a dependence by the new state on foreign Jewish communities and prevented the completion of the process of national individuation. Just as no revolution took place within the Yishuv, thus condemning the state to continue the semicommunal constitution of the Yishuv, neither could the state's system of foreign relations be revolutionized. Most members of the Yishuv saw themselves as European aliens in a threatening region in which they needed foreign backing. Nor did this attitude change after immigrants from Islamic countries came to account for half the Jewish population of Israel. In place of the old European feelings of alienness, these immigrants came hating and resenting the Arabs among whom they had lived and with a desire to get even with them by humiliating local Arabs.

In chapters 5 and 6, I briefly discussed the psychological dynamics which, following the collapse of religion and the religious tradition, made Israel almost the sole ingredient of Jewish identity (with the evocation of the Holocaust a close second) for broad segments of Western, particularly American, Jews. I stressed that this connection with Israel has become a substitute for and an evasion of shaping their identity as Jews. It may be added here that this evasion, and their hiding behind their support for Israel, serves to blur their Jewish identity even further and hastens their assimilation into the mainstream culture. Identity, after all, is shaped by a person's daily behavior, not by buying Israel bonds or attending an occasional banquet in honor of an Israeli dignitary. If people refrain from behaving as Jews in their daily life, accepting all the norms of their non-Jewish environment, on the comfortable assumption that an occasional identification with Israel suffices to define their Jewishness, then the net result of such an identification is the acceleration of their assimilation into non-Jewish society. Identification with Israel becomes an external, meaningless ritual that can be easily dropped for the very reason that it is not part of daily life, not part of the personality. The corollary is that not only is Zionism the mirror image of assimilationism, growing from the same root, being in fact a form of group assimilationism, but that the support of Zionism on the part of a large segment of Diaspora Jews is one form of assimilation as well as being an accelerator of the process, by quieting the supporter's Jewish consciences, and thus easing assimilation.

Furthermore, the conversion of Jewish identity into an external, quantifiable action, a tax-deductible contribution, or political pressure on Congress and the U.S. administration, externalizes the entire question of identity and makes it a ritual act lacking inner content. Another ingredient of the act is its public nature. The contributions are often pledged in formal dinners, in which the size of the contribution is also a reflection of the contributor's financial prowess, thus converting the occasion into a display of wealth and power. The phenomenon is somewhat reminiscent of the scandal of the sale of indulgences, by which the Renaissance popes financed the building of Saint Peter's in Rome. In both cases it is an expression of the ultimate decay of an idea and ideology, the conversion of values into financial and power values.

There are, undeniably, Jewish groups whose attitudes toward Israel are not burdened by complexes of the sort described here. They consider themselves American, French, British—but they still have a strong ethnic and cultural affinity to Israel. However, this is a critical, open-eyed affinity. The members of these groups are fully aware of what goes on in Israel; they reject Israel's official positions and have no intention of becoming tools in the hands of the Israeli leadership. But they still consider themselves to be true friends of the state and feel responsible for its fate and policy. The political system guided by the Israeli leadership is not interested, as a rule, in this kind of sympathy, and does its best to silence it and to create a monolithic Jewish front subservient to any whim of the Israeli establishment. As a rule it also succeeds in this, as shown by its suppression of the Brerah circle in the United States, which was affiliated with the Peace Now movement in Israel.

The relationship of Israelis to the Diaspora is also beset by complications. Some of its implications may be understood from an examination of the Zionist position toward members of the Hebrew people in Israel. From a purely Zionist ideological standpoint, the very sojourn of a Jew in Israel is considered the fulfillment of a national mission. It has moral significance, unlike the residency of, say, a French person in France, which is considered an act of neither heroism nor idealism. Aliya to Eretz Israel is not a mere act of emigration. The word is derived from the Hebrew word meaning "ascent," connoting a religious pilgrimage, but also denoting immigration to Israel (for immigration to other countries, the mundane word *hagirah*, meaning simply "migration," is used). All Jews are expected to become *olim* (immigrants) if they seek to live "a full, proud Jewish life." It is an act of moral purgation. Jews' refusal to "make Aliya" puts them in the Zionist view on an inferior moral level. And if they adopt the Zionist ideology, they become inferior in their own eyes as well.

On the other hand, this view makes many Israelis, including the native-born, feel that their life in Israel is conditional, that they are doing something for someone by the very fact of living in the country. This means that people who live in Israel are not simply living in the country of their choice but also making an act of self-sacrifice. They are idealists. The implication is, of course, that it is not easy to live in Israel, that the Jew is there in an exposed, dangerous outpost. But this stands in grave contradiction to the Zionist tenet that Israel is a safe haven from the persecution and discrimination that Jews suffer everywhere else.

There is a further implication to this claim that Israelis are doing someone a favor by living in the country: if Israel does not meet expectations, the individual will "punish" Israel and leave. And indeed, Israel has developed a whole set of moral anathemas toward any Jew who decides to emigrate, from the pejorative *yored* (a person who "descends") to instructions to Israeli missions abroad to treat *yordim* with maximum coolness and reserve (except those who have become highly successful abroad, and they are then assiduously wooed and cultivated by state dignitaries, as in the fulsome abnegation before the billionaire ex-Israeli Meshulem Riklis). This mercenary attitude also highlights Zionism's loss of moral content, its opportunistic and cynical exploitation of situations.

As against this treatment of emigrants, the state has established a parallel system of inducements to attract new immigrants, and even gives the emigrants a sort of amnesty by offering an equivalent set of inducements designed to compensate for the good life they will be relinquishing if they consent to return home.

The implication, then, of the set of Israel's attitudes toward *olim, yordim,* and penitent *yordim* (namely emigrants who decide to come back home) is that in reality the good life is not a free life in one's homeland, as the basic Zionist tenets teach us, but higher levels of income and life's comforts. This implication is also strengthened by the fact that the pecuniary standard has become the main, sometimes the only, standard in Israeli society, which has developed into a typical conspicuous-consumption society. This amounts to a tacit admission by the state of the bankruptcy of the idealistic Zionist motivation and of the fact that economics is the decisive factor in the motivation of Jews to move from country to country. And, as regards the penitent emigrants, the only nonmaterialistic factor that impresses them is not Zionism or the condition of the Jews among the *goyim* or the pathetic economic inducements offered to bring them back home, but plain Israeli patriotism, love of homeland, homesickness, the feeling of hominess which Israelis have in Israel. What obscures the fading away of Zionism as a factor with any influence on the behavior of Israelis in Israel or of Jews abroad is that the term *Zionism* in Israel has become synonymous with patriotism, whereas in the Diaspora it has become synonymous with philanthropic community activity. Both cases are clearly distinct from the original meanings of the term. Thus *Zionism* continues to exist as a political-emotional term, at the cost of losing any precision of meaning.

In short, the notion that Jewish existence in Israel is Zionistic makes Jewish Israelis feel they live in their country on condition, as performers of a mission, and that they deserve perks and preferential treatment for consenting to live there. That undermines the immediate, natural connection between these persons and their country, namely, their patriotism. Furthermore, it gives them a means to blackmail their country. They are "volunteers," "idealists," "Zionists." These terms imply that they are engaged in an effort that is above and beyond what is expected from citizens of an ordinary state. As a result, they have a self-indulgent attitude, prepared at any moment to declare that they are fed up with being idealists, that they prefer the good life in America, and that the country must strive to provide them with satisfactory conditions so that they will consent to continue to live in it. Since much time will elapse before Israel is able to provide its citizens with the standard of living of the world's wealthier countries, and since most people are not idealistic, or if they are, then only for a limited span, an Israeli of this sort may be expected to leave the country eventually. This means that Zionist motivation is self-defeating. A case in point is the wave of Zionistically motivated immigration that reached Israel in the wake of the Six-Day War, almost all of it from affluent Western countries. Hardly any of the immigrants remained in Israel. But people who came as refugees, without ideology and with nowhere else to go, like most of the immigrants from the Soviet Union, did remain.

Only Israelis' sense of home, their feeling that it is better and more pleasant for them to live in Israel than any other place, not any idealism or Jewishness or Jewish-Zionist sense of mission, can serve as a true and firm basis of the connection between them and their country. The true connection to Israel is not Zionistic but purely hedonistic, an ordinary patriotic connection. In this sense an *Israeli* nation has indeed begun to emerge in Israel, a nation whose tie to the country is not spiritual or ideological or historical or deriving from historical rights or Jewishness, but a natural one, like any other nation's.

The active discouragement of such normal national sentiments leads to the peculiar result that the Jewish Israeli citizens' threat—that if they fail to get from the state what they demand, they will emigrate—means, of course, that they will emigrate to their true, "natural" place, namely any place where they do not have to make a special effort to gain the good life denied to them in the Promised Land of spartan dedication. In the final analysis, then, the emphasis on Zionist motivation is in effect subtle propaganda for emigration, the perpetuation of exilic attitudes, and the relapse of the emigrants to the state of the "natural" Jews, namely the Diaspora Jews. Just as the assertion of Israel's centrality to the Jewish experience distorts the spiritual and cultural identity of Diaspora Jews and serves them as a means of avoiding confrontation with their problem of identity, permitting them to have an illusory, infantile existence as vicarious Israelis, the Zionist motivation creates a barrier between Jewish Israelis and their country, undermines their natural patriotism, and establishes a sort of transformation mechanism that enables them to change their identity as members of the Israeli nation into a reserve form of existence, as members of the worldwide Jewish caste.

TEN

The National Aim Blurred

The Zionist leaders, thanks to their ruthless, singleminded determination to create a new Hebrew nation in Palestine, did succeed in establishing a socioeconomic-military framework for that nation. They did this, however, without ever having clarified in their own minds what the nature of that nation would be.

Most of the founding fathers of Zionism regarded Jewish religion with varying degrees of antipathy. The nation they wished to forge was meant to be secular and even explicitly antireligious. For them, Jewish religion and "exilism" were different manifestations of the same obnoxious essence. Berl Katznelson, as usual, was of two minds. He hung on to the tattered remnants of tradition as a means to cement a continuity and identification with the past but lacked the nucleus of religious faith to hold it all together (he was one of the originators of the sentimentalization of Jewish tradition and of the pernicious blurring of the Israeli cultural identity). Achad Ha'am, in contradistinction to the clarity of his perception in other matters, was, on this central issue, as vague as Katznelson. Nowhere in his writings do we find any clarification of the spiritual content of the "spiritual center" he advocated. It is clear that this content was supposed to include many traditional, even religious, elements, and it is therefore no wonder that his definition of the nature of the Jewish people is so nebulous. On the other hand, being the only leading Zionist thinker who foresaw that most Jews would remain in the Diaspora even after the realization of Zionism, he also tried to envisage the nature of the relationship between these Jews and the future Jewish community in Eretz Israel. His writings clearly imply that in such a case this community could not become "a nation among nations," as most Zionists then predicted. By its becoming a center, spiritual or otherwise, of a larger worldwide Diaspora, it would necessarily have a different character than ordinary European nations. As far as the religious Zionists were concerned, clearly what they wanted to establish was nothing but a politically sovereign, territorial religious community.

Ben-Gurion's and Jabotinsky's hopes of establishing a "normal" nation implied either the immigration of all Jews to Eretz Israel or the dissociation of the Eretz Israelian nation from the Jewish Diaspora and its becoming a separate, distinct national group. No normal European nation is also a Vatican of a national diaspora. (The Irish Republic, for example, does not demand the loyalty and identification of the Irish in the United States). However, Ben-Gurion's repeated declarations that Israel should be "a quality nation" and "a light unto the nations" seem to contain some of Achad Ha'am's teachings, as well as an echo of the socialist vision that guided Ben-Gurion in his youth and led him (and others in labor Zionism) to believe that Hebrew, labor-led Eretz Israel could offer the world an example of a successful, free, socialist society, as against the failure of the Soviet experiment.[1]

But aside from and independent of these ideological preconceptions, the pressures of reality shaped the means, and as an unexpected result, they shaped the ends, too. The Old Yishuv, for example, was primarily non-Zionist, structured largely on the pattern of the traditional Jewish communities in Eastern Europe and the Islamic world. The self-governing institutions established in Palestine under the mandatory regime, such as Knesset Yisrael (not to be confused with the Israeli parliament, the Knesset) and the Jewish Agency, necessarily included, with the exception of the extreme Orthodox Neturei Karta, the representatives of the Old Yishuv as well. It was therefore necessary to compromise and reach agreements with them. These agreements, by the very nature of things, began to shape the ideological goals. The clearly defined secular-national vision that guided most Zionist pioneers began to blur. The vision of "a nation like all nations" began to erode as a result of the ties between the Zionist parties in Palestine and their mobilization and financing sources abroad. In addition, the coalitions and alliances with the Yishuv's bourgeois elements, many of whom had not immigrated for Zionist reasons but because of pressures in their countries of origin and who hardly differed from their Diaspora equivalents, watered down even further both the explicitly secular Zionist conceptions and the socialist ethos of the labor movement. The structure that eventually emerged resembled the one advocated by Achad Ha'am (although the "center" is not very spiritual, and its only message to the Diaspora seems to be one of military force). The radical Zionists argued that this was only a transitional stage, until all Jews were concentrated in Israel. But as this situation bears all the signs of permanence, the state developed certain domestic patterns of relations toward its citizens and external ones of relations toward the Jewish Diaspora and the non-Jewish world that contain insoluble inner contradictions. They stem basically from the problem of the relationship between nation and state.

Membership in a nation is a subjective category that defies formal definition. It is not always membership in a linguistic group, because one can find several nations speaking the same language (such as England and the United States), or one nation speaking several tongues (like the Swiss). Nor is it adherence to a common religion or a shared genetic background.

Perhaps the only possibility of an objective definition of a national group is the recognition of the subjective definition, e.g., the recognition of any persons who declare themselves voluntarily as belonging to a certain nationality as indeed belonging to it, perhaps with the added proviso that other members of that nation should also perceive those individuals as belonging to it. There is no possibility of an immediate objective recognition of membership in a nation. And any legal definition of such belongingness depends on the definitions of an extrapolitical institution or authority.

Citizenship, on the other hand, is an objective category. It is determined by law. As a state is the political framework by which a certain territory is organized, it necessarily establishes a juridical affinity toward each individual residing within that territory.

The law, in the modern parliamentary state, is general by its very nature and aspires to equality. This is a logical consequence of the fact that it is enacted by the legislature, which represents the plurality of all citizens, and it is inconceivable that some citizens would consent to a law that discriminates against them and favors other citizens. They would consider such legislation as sufficient cause for secession from the state. If the state restrains such secession by force, it ceases being representative and becomes a coercive state that contains the seeds of its own dissolution, for in times of weakness, which necessarily occur in political history, the group that feels discriminated against would seize the opportunity to realize its right to secede.

The principle of national self-determination is not, therefore, identical to the principle of the modern parliamentary state. The former is ethnic and subjective, the latter territorial and objective. Only rarely, when the political boundary is coterminous with ethnic affiliation, as in Norway or Japan, is the basic contradiction between the two principles not apparent. But the history of Central and Eastern Europe over the past 130 years teaches that there is usually no such correspondence. The movements of the various European tribes during centuries of migrations, invasions, and peaceful penetration made it impossible after World War I to draw rational boundaries that would correspond exactly with ethnic distribution.

From its inception, Israel suffered from all these problems, but with greater acuity than other nation-states.

First, as stated explicitly in Israel's declaration of independence, it is the state of the Jewish people, the vast majority of which lives outside its boundaries. But from its inception it also had within its borders a substantial number of non-Jewish residents. Moreover, most of these residents were ethnically and linguistically affiliated with nations that willed the destruction of the state and actively fought against its establishment. Even so, because the state was established as a parliamentary democracy, these residents immediately received Israeli citizenship and the right to vote and to be elected to the legislature.

By being the state of the Jewish people, Israel grants Jews the world over, even those with no interest in Israel, exterritorial rights that it denies to its non-Jewish citizens. It was a foregone conclusion that, even apart from the active discrimination they suffer, these minorities would feel like barely tolerated, unwanted second-class citizens and that the acute national consciousness of the majority population would necessarily arouse in them an equally intense nationalist reaction—even though they might also wish to become integrated into Israeli society, whose level of cultural and social development is higher than that of the Arab countries.

The minority's nationalistic bent is also intensified as a result of the basic aspiration to strengthen the Jewishness of the state by bringing in as many Jews as possible. This exerts constant pressure on the non-Jewish minority, cramping and inhibiting it in order to clear space for more Jewish immigrants. This is not a situation in which a stable majority claims precedence over a stable minority with which it has lived symbiotically for generations. The minority's condition in this case is not static, since the majority group aspires to increase its own numbers, thereby reducing the proportion of the minority within it (and some among the majority even wish to eliminate the presence of the minority altogether).

Furthermore, under the influence of Ben-Gurion and the Mapai leadership, Israel's Constituent Assembly, after the establishment of the state, refrained from drafting a constitution, with the exception of a few basic laws establishing the Knesset and the government and other elementary laws vital for the functioning of law and government. This abstention encapsulates the problematic nature of the state of Israel and poses the ultimate question of whether the state is viable at all. The claim has often been made that a state like Israel cannot formulate a constitution, that it does not need one, and that a de facto constitution, like the British one, shaped by the peculiar Israeli conditions, will gradually emerge. But certain tendencies that gained prominence in recent years tend to demote the state to a loose confederation of extraparliamentary sects opposed to the very conception of the modern state and undermining it.

The abstention from formulating a constitution was no accident. The massive expropriation of lands and other properties from those Arabs who fled the country as a result of the War of Independence and of those who remained but were declared absent, as well as the confiscation of large tracts of land from Arab villagers who did not flee, and the laws passed to legalize these acts—all this would have necessarily been declared unconstitutional, null and void, by the Supreme Court, being expressly discriminatory against one part of the citizenry, whereas a democratic constitution obliges the state to treat all of its citizens equally. It would have been easy to prove in court that such laws, despite their wording, are designed to discriminate against certain categories of citizens.[2]

A second and even graver problem is the definition of the state of Israel as Jewish, or as the state of the Jewish people. The definition of Israel as Jewish could be purely descriptive, just as Great Britain could be described as an essentially Protestant or Italy as a Catholic state. Britain could also be described as English and Italy as Italian, implying that most of their populations belong to the English or Italian people. But neither in Britain nor in Italy do the "English" or the "Italian" people have a *legal* status. Italian nationals can become citizens of another country, say the United States, and Italian law then rescinds power over them. Nor do they have any citizenship rights in Italy if they give up their Italian nationality.

Israel's definition as the state of the Jewish people, however, is not descriptive but prescriptive. It implies that the state is a tool of the Jewish people, and as such any Jew has rights in it and a say in its affairs. Thus a situation is created in which non-Israeli Jews theoretically have the right to oblige Israel to behave according to their lights, while, as Israel is supposed to serve as the future home of all Jews, it feels entitled to press them to act for its ends, in spite of their being citizens of other countries. This is tantamount to an infringement of the sovereignty of any country where Jews live and to a statement that the Jewish citizens of all countries owe political allegiance to an external sovereign body.

A constitution would have enabled non-Jewish citizens of Israel to demand, and the Supreme Court necessarily would have upheld this demand, that the state refrain from extending any preferential treatment to an ethnic group whose members are not citizens, and definitely not at the expense of citizens. They could claim, and be upheld by the court, that the status of the Jewish Agency in Israel is unconstitutional, for the agency, which serves the interests of only one group of citizens, had been delegated some of the executive functions of the state. They could also challenge a whole array of laws and regulations whose purpose is to prefer Jews to non-Jews, although this is not apparent in their wording (such as the housing grants to exservicemen, when Arabs are largely excluded from military service, or grants given to new Jewish immigrants via the Jewish Agency), and cause them to be declared unconstitutional.

But above and beyond all, the definition of Israel as the state of the Jewish people raises the question of who is a Jew. Which in turn raises the question of who is entitled to decide who is a Jew.

If Israel were to adopt a constitution that defined the Jewish nation, it would mean that the nation was being defined by secular lawmakers, who would be obliged to define it in secular terms. They could not define the Jewish people in religious terms, because they would then have to phrase the definition somewhat as follows: "A Jew is whoever has been defined as such by the authorized and appropriate religious authority." Since the Zionist view, which underpins the state, is that Jewishness is not a religious but a national category and that the state is essentially a Jewish state, such a definition would mean that the "authorized and appropriate religious authority" stands above the secular legislator, namely, above the state.

On the other hand, the legislators cannot define *Jew* in anything but religious terms, as became clear in the case of Brother Daniel, in which the Supreme Court found that allegiance to Jewish religion is the indicator of belonging to the Jewish nation. Therefore, even if persons are born Jews and consider themselves Jews, they lose their Jewish identity if they take the formal step of conversion to another religion. This matter calls for a more detailed discussion.

In the early sixties, the Catholic monk Daniel Rufeisen, also called Brother Daniel, appealed to the Israeli courts to be declared a Jew and to have it entered on his identity card. He had been born to Jewish parents and saw himself as a member of the Jewish people, although he adhered to another religion. The high court ruled that the term *Jew* should be interpreted according to secular criteria, since the law of the return, granting every Jew the right to immigrate to Israel and become a citizen, is a secular law. As Amnon Rubinstein writes,

> The Supreme Court thus assumed that there are two separate definitions of the term *Jew*. What is the secular interpretation? Justice Berenson says: the term should be interpreted "in the sense in usage among the people." The four justices who adopted this popular test found that according to it, a Jew who converts excludes himself not only from Jewish religion but also from the Jewish nation.[3]

Rubinstein notes that the paradox in this case is that according to the Halacha, or Jewish religious law, the appellant would have been considered Jewish, for the Halacha rarely admits the validity of conversion. He mentions that Guido Tedeschi, the eminent Israeli jurist, disagreed with the Supreme Court ruling in his article "Who Is a Jew?" claiming that a Jew is anyone who feels Jewish to the point of wishing to immigrate to Israel as a Jew: "Basing ourselves on secular law, it is none of our business to delve into this person's attitude to religion, whether he did or did not do what the Halacha requires him to do in order to be considered a Jew according to its criteria, too." Supreme Court Justice Chaim Cohen, in a dissenting opinion, took a similar stand, arguing that anyone who declares "honestly and in good faith" that he is a Jew should be accepted as such.

Justice Cohen's and Professor Tedeschi's opinions were not adopted by the Knesset, by the courts, or by the majority of public opinion in the country. In current usage, as Rubinstein notes, the secular and the religious viewpoints coexist. But, as we have seen in the Rufeisen case, where the high court adopted the popular usage of the term *Jew* as seemingly distinct from the Halachic one—this usage establishes that a decisive element in the definition of a person as a Jew is his or her affiliation to the Jewish religious community, or at least his or her abstention from formally seceding from it by joining another religious community. In reality, then, the secular position ultimately is derived from the Halacha, from religion, even if in this particular case an accidental "technical contradiction" appeared between the two viewpoints. In the final analysis, if the decisive (secular) test of a person's Jewishness is whether he or she did or did not retire from the Jewish religious community, then the body that determines the boundaries of the Jewish religious community also determines who is a Jew, and this body is none but the Halachic authority as embodied in the appropriate religious institutions. (It should be noted further that in this case there is no difference between orthodoxy and reform. According to reform thinking, too, joining Judaism involves a Judaizing ceremony.)

We are then back where we started. The Supreme Court, on the face of it, rejects the authority of the Halacha to determine who is a Jew and adopts the popular usage for defining the term. But when we delve into the meaning of this definition, we find that its core is again the Halacha and that, in actual practice, the court elevates the Halacha above the law of the land. The court's bowing to popular usage is, as a matter of fact, the surrender and retreat of the state from the basic national assumptions of Zionism, which are either antireligious or religiously indifferent. This court ruling, handed down in 1962, was symptomatic of the mood of the country even then. It also had far-reaching political and ideological implications, which I shall discuss presently. Suffice it to say that the abstention from drafting a constitution neither solved nor evaded the problem of the legal status of the Jewish people in the country, for it became clear here that the secular law is incapable of defining who is a Jew.

The significance of the Rufeisen ruling is its recognition that the true substance of Jewishness is Jewish religion. I have shown that the secular interpretation of the term is merely the watered-down Halachic definition, not a parallel and different definition. We may then conclude that there are many different levels of belonging to the human group named Jews. The heart of the group is extreme religious orthodoxy, keeping meticulously to the finest points of the Halacha. Around it there exists an envelope of traditionalist Jews, keeping some of the strictures at their own convenience. They in turn are surrounded by a broader envelope of those who hold to some ritual connection with the religious tradition. And around these concentric envelopes there spread ever wider, ever fainter peripheries of people who vaguely define themselves as Jews or are defined as such by their non-Jewish environment but whose Jewishness lacks any positive content. Many of them, even without such content and with no formal connection to Judaism, have a "Jewish mentality"; that is, the deep patterns of thought, values, and feeling typical of the Jewish tradition still live within them and still condition the basic forms of their world outlook. They also, in a way, are Jewish, but mainly because they haven't yet chosen another framework of affiliation. But the moment they decide to cross the line of formal religious affiliation, a decisive step has been taken. True, converts may still consider themselves Jews and react to their environment as Jews, as Benjamin Disraeli and Heinrich Heine did, or for that matter Rufeisen himself. But once they take this decisive step, they have consciously and formally entered a different social-spiritual circle of affiliation, with a different mental and attitudinal structure, and their descendants lose any contact with the Jewish world.

Only an awareness of this reality can explain the infinite forbearance with which the state of Israel treats the extreme Orthodox, anti-Zionist communities, despite all their recalcitrance and obstinacy, despite their objection to the very existence of the state, despite their violent and sustained baiting of secular citizens. Since the leadership has really lost its faith in the original national tenets of Zionism, it considers these Orthodox extremists as the "real Jews" and necessarily feels itself to be "less Jewish" than they are. For that reason, they are practically immune to the laws of the Jewish state. The law, which derives, as Zionism sees it, from Judaism, must not be turned against the "sources of Judaism." The effectual admission of the Halacha definition of Jewishness, as revealed in the ruling in the Ruffeisen case, which puts the Halacha above the state, finds expression in the effective exclusion of its authentic representatives from the domain of the law.

Cohen's and Tedeschi's arguments follow the reasoning of traditional secular Zionism, and it is well worth discussing their meaning in brief. Tedeschi connects a person's group definition with his subjective state, with his desire to become a Jew to the point that he is prepared to emigrate to Israel and join the Jewish people living there, irrespective of whether "he did or did not do what the Halacha requires him to do in order to be considered a Jew according to its criteria, too." The test is of that person's volition to join the Jewish nation in Israel, and definitely not the Jewish religion. Cohen, as related, was of the opinion that the revolution caused in Jewish history by the establishment of Israel also calls for a revolution in the definition of who is a Jew, the corollary being that anyone who declares "sincerely and in good faith" that he is a Jew should be accepted as such. That means that Justice Cohen is also of the opinion that the national definition should be determined by the desire to join a certain polity. Obviously, a Jewish Diaspora community, organized around its religious institutions, could not admit a person as Jewish unless he passed the religious criteria involved.

What do "sincerity" and "good faith" mean in this connection? Since the law cannot delve into the depths of the soul, it should be assumed that such a person would be required to pass certain objective tests of sincerity and good faith, tests that are not religious (since we have already agreed that he must not be required to pass such tests). What could such tests be but the readiness to discharge all the duties imposed on an Israeli citizen and speak the country's official language? In short, these are nothing but ordinary citizenship tests. Moreover, ethnic-national affiliation is largely involuntary. A person is born an Englishman, a German, or a Russian. This affiliation is determined by familial, cultural, to some extent even genetic factors. But a person's declaration "in good faith" signifies an act of choice. A person cannot choose his people or race (he is born either black or white), but he can choose his religion or citizenship, and the fact that he does not repudiate his religion or citizenship may be interpreted as an implicit voluntary choice to keep them. It seems then that the real meaning of

Tedeschi's and Cohen's recommendations is not joining the *Jewish people*, but the *Israeli nation*, as defined by its territory and citizenship. The Israeli nation, if we interpret correctly Justice Cohen's dissenting opinion in the Rufeisen case, could consist not only of members of the Jewish religion but also of Christians (hence also of Moslems). In short, a consistent application of the classic Zionist secular position, which Chaim Cohen represents here faithfully, leads to a complete break with the traditional conception of Judaism, and as a matter of fact, to the creation of a new nation. For obviously, Diaspora Jews could not accept the Israeli Christian or the Muslim "Jew" as one of them. And, just as obviously, the Israeli Jew would consider a Hebrew-speaking Christian (or Muslim) who studies in the same schools and fulfills the same civic duties, including military service and sharing the risks involved, as much closer to him than Diaspora Jews.

Upon independence, Israel's leadership faced a critical choice (a choice it had not had to face before independence, when its institutions were essentially voluntary and lacked the coercive powers of a state): to accept the Halachic position on the definition of Jewishness, thus in effect abandoning the Zionist national ideology, or to hold to that ideology and develop consistently all of its implications—down to a dissociation in principle from the Jewish Diaspora and to a creation of a modern nation-state whose citizenship is defined by territory, with a constitution imposing complete equality upon its citizens, thus abrogating the preferred status of the Jewish people in the state.

The leadership did not dare to make a clear-cut decision either way, preferring to leave the issues vague and ambiguous. But decisions that could be postponed in the absence of state authority could not be left dangling after organized statehood had become a fact. As long as the mandatory regime existed, those who declined for reasons of conscience to avail themselves of the services of the Jewish communal authorities could apply to the religiously neutral mandatory authorities. Once these authorities ceased to exist, however, no neutral ground was left. The state tried to create a secular national jurisdiction in matters of personal status, parallel to the religious one, but as in the Rufeisen case, this secular zone was largely nothing but a watered-down religious approach. On one hand, there was the well-organized, ideologically clear and compact religious camp, which, as a result of its conception of the Halacha as superior to any secular legislation, was hostile to the very concept of the state (in its sense as a voluntary sovereign association of the inhabitants of a territory); and on the other hand there was the secular camp, lacking any clear positive definition of its nature, save for the negative one of being nonreligious. Even here, the negation had several levels of intensity, often accompanied by feelings of guilt because of the alienation from religious tradition and the recognition of tradition as the bearer of Jewish historic continuity (considering itself "empty" in comparison to the "fullness" of the tradition). This feeling of inferiority intensified with the waning of the pioneering values that served as the unifying cement of the various Zionist movements. The secular camp also, inevitably, lacked any clear definition of fundamentals, such as who is a Jew, what is the state, what is the status within the state of a Jew who is not a citizen, what is the status of a non-Jewish citizen, etc. It is not difficult to guess who has had the edge in such a confrontation.

As a matter of fact, the readiness to be a consistent Zionist and develop to their logical conclusions all the implications of the national conceptions of Herzl, Nordau, Jabotinsky, and Borochov was not very prevalent even in the extreme left wing of the labor movement, Hashomer Hatza'ir. At the height of the movement's Marxist-atheist fervor, the rabbi was still invited to perform wedding ceremonies among kibbutz members, even when the newlyweds had been living together for months. Throughout the mandatory period, the New Yishuv's educational system taught the watered-down "traditionalist" conception of Jewish nationalism, based on the rabbinic-Orthodox interpretation of the Jewish past and the nature of Jewishness, and only the separate educational system of Hashomer Hatza'ir dared also teach the critical-scientific approach to the Bible and to Jewish tradition. It should be noted that a much greater readiness to challenge these sanctified concepts was to be found among circles that had been in contact with the revisionist movement, whose very exclusion "beyond the pale" of official Zionism encouraged the connection with it of people of independent and radical thinking on these subjects.

Zionist historiography and ideology always sided with the Halacha against any ethnic or ideological concretion that deviated from it. It condemned in retrospect any opportunity to form an ethnic-territorial nation distinct from the religious caste community, or to create a religion that exceeds the bounds of that community. It backed Ezra and Nehemiah against the people of the land, the Pharisees against the Sadduccees, the Halacha against secessionist sects like the Christians, rabbinical Judaism against the Karaites and the Frankists. It is equivocal only where the Halacha itself is equivocal, as in its attitude toward the great revolt of 69 A.D. and the Bar Kochba revolt. Had Zionism adopted a truly national way of thinking, it would have sided retrospectively with the people of the land against the arrogant exclusivity of the Babylonian returnees to Zion, headed by Ezra and Nehemiah; considered the Hellenizers and the Sadduccees an integral part of the nation, which proposed another and perhaps culturally and politically more fruitful course than the one adopted by the Pharisees, as well as condemned the rabbinical attempt to expel them from Judaism; and would have opened the portals of the people to the descendants of the Karaites and the Frankists. But instead, Zionism adopted the tautological, hypocritical argument that the Halacha preserved the people—whereas it is clear that all that the Halacha preserved was itself, by means of that group that accepted its authority unquestioningly and was the only one defined by it as "the people," while the masses of others were expelled from the framework of the Jewish community and were lost to it forever. In other words, while the Halacha preserved itself, it destroyed the existence of the people as a nation and constantly diminished its numbers. Zionism, by accepting the Halachic claims, put itself implicitly, from the beginning, under the Halachic authority, thereby contradicting itself.

The notorious status quo arrangement, set out in a letter sent by the Jewish Agency's Executive to the Agudath Israel Orthodox party on June 19, 1947 (signed by Ben-Gurion, Rabbi Y. L. Fishman, and Y. Greenbaum), contained two key paragraphs—that laws pertaining to personal status will be enacted in the future state to satisfy the needs of the Orthodox and "prevent, heaven forbid, the division of the Jewish people into two," and that "there will be no infringement on the part of the authorities on the religious feelings and conscience of any part of the Jewish people." These paragraphs are rightly cited as the source of religious coercion and the gradual spread of religious control over ever-widening spheres of Israeli life. But at the same time this arrangement, which effectively forestalled any possibility of drafting a constitution, could not have been drafted if the secular members of the Executive had true nationalist convictions. The arrangement cannot even be presented as a sort of concordat between the future state and the ruling church of the Jewish people (like the concordat signed by the Roman Catholic Church and Mussolini's Italian state). Agudath Israel is not the Catholic Church, which commands the religious loyalties of most Italians. It, along with ultra-Orthodox Judaism in general, represents only a small portion of the Jewish community in Eretz Israel and is almost nonexistent among the members of the main Diaspora left after World War II, namely the North American. Furthermore, it was an actively anti-Zionist body, whereas most conservative, and later most reform, Jews in America are pro-Zionist. These U.S. groups, whose support of the future state was considered vital, were discriminated against in advance by the obligations undertaken toward the Agudah.

In view of these facts, the pious phrases about preventing, "heaven forbid, the division of the Jewish people," and about not infringing on the "religious feelings and conscience of any part of the Jewish people" seem like cynical sophistry. The seasoned politicians who sat in the Jewish Agency's Executive must have been well aware of the full import of these paragraphs, particularly as they were quite familiar with the Agudah. It had always been intertwined in the Yishuv's politics. Moreover, these politicians must have been well aware that the imposition of the Halacha in its extreme, ultra-Orthodox version on sectors of the state's public life would definitely cause the division of the Jewish people into two and more than two and the infringement not only of the conscience of the secularists (who apparently have none, nor should anyone worry about the violation of their freedom of conscience and elementary intellectual integrity) but also of other, religious, currents in Judaism. The only conscience (religious or not) that is not violated by the arrangement is that of the extreme Orthodox.

It is well known that the Agudah applied heavy pressure at the time on the Zionist leadership, threatening to appear separately before the U.N. fact-finding commission for Palestine if its demands were not met. But political blackmail in a passing situation cannot become an excuse for a permanent policy that determines in advance the nature and course of the future state and renounces the principles and beliefs of most parts of the national movement. Any court of law would declare conditions, let alone a political agreement, wrested under blackmail invalid, as they had not been reached freely by both sides. Anybody who keeps terms wrested from him under the threat of a gun long after the gun had been put away, shows thereby not only that he does so of his own free will, but also raises the suspicion that in reality the threat was merely a clever piece of staging. There was no dearth of opportunities to declare any arrangement null and void that ties in advance the hands of the Constituent Assembly contrary to the principle of people's sovereignty. The arrangement was kept because the Israeli leadership wanted to keep it.

Furthermore, the Executive's commitment was not to the Mizrachi religious party, which was both Zionist and with a far larger electoral backing than the Agudah, but to a much smaller and weaker anti-Zionist group. There certainly was also the consideration that the Mizrachi party was well integrated within the Zionist movement and the Jewish Agency, and therefore its bargaining position was weaker than that of an external party willing and able to cause the movement much damage if its demands were not met. In any case, these considerations of convenience were transitory, whereas their results had the effects of principle: the granting of the power of decision and control over the most fundamental issues of ethnic affiliation to a group that denies ethnic definitions and insists on strict formal criteria of religious ritual and observance.

The background of the arrangement was a history of bargaining and compromise, begun even before World War I, between the Zionist movement, led by the labor movement on one hand and religious Zionism and the Agudah on the other. Each of the compromises meant another regression from the conception of the Jewish people as an ethnic-cultural-national entity to the religious conception of Jewishness. Furthermore, the arrangement, by being concluded with the Agudah, meant in practice that the anti-Zionist Agudah was recognized as the decisive authority as far as religious definitions were concerned, and in essence became a watchdog over the behavior of the Zionist Mizrachi. Nevertheless, because of its collaboration with the Zionist heretical state and sharing in the benefits of participation in governmental power, the Agudah was, in turn, vilified and intimidated as profane and sacrilegious by the ultra-Orthodox Neturei Karta, which thus became the watchdog over the Agudah. Thus the final moral authority to define who belongs to the Jewish people has been handed over to a Jewish body that denies categorically the very existence of Jewish nationality, at the same time being regarded by the Zionist establishment as immune to any infringement even when it acts incessantly against the nonreligious population, against state institutions, and even resorts to violence.

The absurdity of this situation is doubly manifest in view of Zionism's original aim to provide a solution to the Jewish problem, that is, to solve the problem of people who are persecuted or discriminated against because the external world defines them as Jews (and not because they are defined as such by the Orthodox establishment). The original Zionist ideology, particularly in its Herzlian version, considered those Jews persecuted because of their Jewishness as members of the Jewish people. Its traditional argument against those who sought assimilation was that they would never succeed at it, because the external world would always see them as Jews and would never ask for their personal opinion whether they are or not. The anti-Semites, for their part, never ask those they hate as Jews whether they are really Jews according to the Halacha. The Nazis murdered people because even one parent or grandparent was Jewish (irrespective of whether paternal or maternal). In most cases, rabbinical orthodoxy would not have recognized these individuals as Jewish. Zionist ideology, on the other hand, has always striven for the broadest possible definition of the term *Jew*. Acceptance of the Orthodox approach is, therefore, a betrayal and denial of the principles of Zionism. Irrespective of the political and opportunistic considerations that brought the Zionist-Israeli establishment to this point, whatever the constraints on it and the personal convictions of any particular Zionist leader, what counts is the actual political result. The betrayal of the definition of Jewishness and the passing of it into the hands of the orthodoxy meant the abdication and demise of the Zionist conception.

The implications of this situation appear even graver if we ponder the conjectured aims of orthodoxy, as analyzed by Moshe Amon. He points out that the deposition by the Israeli establishment of matters of personal status in the hands of orthodoxy was marked by an extremely aggravated, sharply reactionary attitude on the latter's part. On the face of it, this was in complete contradiction to what was needed now that the country's gates were finally opened to free Jewish immigration, particularly as the new state was eager for more Jewish immigrants. The religious parties' policies were in direct opposition to the the declared immigration policy of the state. What then is the aim of rabbinical Judaism? Amon writes:

The question is whether any accommodation of the law will really help secure the existence of the Jewish nation as a whole and as Jewish, and whether the majority of the people, who nowadays are secular, will abide by such a practice. Another question involved in this issue concerns the fact that if the Orthodox circles will admit the Jewishness of the secular majority, they will have to admit its right to interpret the law as it understands it. Their position therefore is that they can lose all they believe in and might gain nothing, as secular people might choose not to recognize religion in any form. Consequently, it seems that they decided to draw the line at the point which was approved by the whole nation in the days when it still formed one unit, and to wait and see what turn the events would take.[4]

Since no rabbinical document stating this position explicitly exists, Amon's conclusions cannot be confirmed. Still, the behavior of orthodoxy in Israel seems to bear out this thesis.

Amon adds:

The Halacha does not apply to the state which it does not recognize as Jewish. The question at stake is the criteria for a definition of a Jew. Administrative measures were taken, so it seems, only to prevent people from identifying themselves as Jews according to any other measures than the rabbinical ones.[5]

The author concludes that rabbinical orthodoxy has despaired of the bulk of Jews. It seems that the Jewish people is about to break up into several blocs, each with its separate identity, and that "the struggle is, which sector of the nation will carry with it the right to define a Jew and by what standards."[6] In other words, orthodoxy is engaged at this historical juncture in the process of ejecting from Judaism those elements of the Jewish people who are not prepared to submit to its exclusive jurisdiction—just as the Pharisees ejected the Hellenizers, the Sadduccees, and the Christians and as later upholders of the Halacha ejected the Karaites, the Sabbetaians, and the Frankists. Again we witness the process by which the Halacha preserves the people, namely preserves itself and ejects most Jews from Judaism.

What, then, prompted the state of Israel to adopt this narrowest, most exclusive interpretation of Judaism, which was also in direct opposition to basic Zionist ideology and practice and which contradicted the leadership's perceived vital need for a large-scale immigration? What made the Zionist leadership forfeit its right to define Jewish nationality and to deliver that right into the hands of an antinational body? Amon proposes the following explanation:

Besides sentiment there is nothing in common between the Israeli Jew and the Jew in the Diaspora. Besides citizenship and sentiment there is not too much in common among Israelis themselves. . . . The only viable answer that seemed to serve as a common denominator among all Jews and seemed to prove itself through long experience was the religious one. According to the religious outlook, the Jewish nation is dissolving through inter-marriages resulting in non-Jewish offspring. Facing the fact that the Zionist solution is rejected by most of the nation, the state chose to follow the religious one.[7]

This explanation needs elaboration. The narrowest interpretation of Judaism was not adopted after the failure of the masses to immigrate but even before the establishment of the state, in the arrangement letter. Moreover, the growing severity of religious legislation occurred at the very height of mass immigration, in the early fifties, when there was as yet no reason to assume that the majority of the Jewish people rejected the Zionist solution. It again intensified its strictures after the Six-Day War, when there was much hope for the renewal of immigration.

The destruction of Europe's Jews and the closure of the Soviet bloc to Jewish emigration after World War II (in addition to the accelerated assimilation of the Jews left within the Soviet population) put an end, more or less, to the East European Jewish nation, and to the hopes of the state to benefit from it. Since the emergent Jewish national life of Eastern Europe no longer existed, the basis for the Jewish national movement was lost. East European Jews, particularly those from the Pale of Settlement, had no problems of identity. They were Jewish nationals. The majority of the survivors of the Nazi camps were also members of the Jewish nation. But the Zionist leadership was well aware that apart from them, no further East European Jews were candidates for immigration. On the other hand, the leadership faced the problems of immigration and absorption of Jews from Muslim countries—Jews whose culture contained no national component; their Jewishness was strictly religious-communal. Any attempt to impart Jewish national content to them made it immediately clear that this content was not common to Jews as Jews but typified only one Jewish group, the East European. This was the only group that had undergone a nation-forming process in the context of modern nation-states. Other Jewish groups were still in a prepolitical stage.

It thus became clear that the various Jewish communities had no common ethnic culture except the religious one. General national content was not found, while that content which was upheld, like secular political movements, press, a secular national ideology, etc., was always that of East European Jewry, its West European and American branches, and a thin scattering from the more developed Arab countries such as Egypt and Iraq. For the Zionist leadership, this East European Jewish culture was the national Jewish culture per se, while other Jewish cultures, all religious-communal, were conceived as having a folkloristic-communal character, distinct from the dominant national culture. But as any Jewish community, according to the Zionist ideology, is a part of the Jewish nation, the national culture that developed in Eastern Europe could be nothing but another communal culture, no different from the Yemenite or Moroccan Jewish community culture. And indeed, as far as the communal customs of the Eastern European group go, like Hasidic lore, dress, and songs, this is indeed the case. But obviously, this was not what was meant. Achad Ha'am, Herzl, Borochov, Bialik, Sokolov, Jabotinsky, Weizmann, Ben-Gurion, Brenner are not the representatives of just another Jewish caste community but of the Jewish nation. Their common denominator is not their East European religious background but their rejection of it in the name of nationalism.

The Israeli Zionist leadership was indeed right to downgrade the culture of the other communities to a folkloristic level, but its ideology did not permit it to diagnose why it was the right thing to do, why it should have rejected the cultures of *all* Jewish communities, including the East European. The Eastern (or Oriental) communities in Israel have it all wrong when they imagine that the veteran Zionist leadership is merely the representative of another Jewish community. The Israeli leadership, for its part, is also incapable of answering this accusation, because of its assumption that all Jewish communities are equally national, because all the Jews in the world constitute a single nation. Thus there began the "cultivation and preservation of the heritage of Oriental communities," out of perplexity at this bundle of inescapable contradictions and out of a desire for a so-called balance, whereas in reality the Ashkenazi elite is not interested at all in the cultivation of its own communal heritage and even rejects it. The elite lacks the ideological basis that would enable it to reject the divisive communal cultures, unless they are to be preserved as museum pieces, and to declare that not only is Israeli culture not a mixture or a fusion or a melting together of all the separate communal cultures; it is the *negation* of these. And, lacking this cultural vista, it lacks an answer to the question of what can unify these heterogeneous fragments.

In the absence of another common denominator, and owing to the establishment's refusal to encourage the development of a separate Israeli culture, fearing that this could lead to a rupture with Diaspora Jewry, an energetic effort was made to emphasize state values, namely those elements of the Israeli experience that are shared by all the Jews who live in the country. First and foremost on this list was the army. Only in this connection does Ben-Gurion's oft-repeated claim that Israel's army, the Israel Defense Forces (IDF), is a value become comprehensible. At first glance, this claim might seem to be both typically militaristic and an inhuman mockery. An apparatus whose basic purpose is to kill people (even in self-defense) cannot embody a human value, and can at most be seen as a repulsive necessity. On deeper analysis, however, it becomes apparent that in the absence of other common national traditions, this claim was aimed at reinforcing one of the few elements common to the Jewish citizens of the state.

But the weaknesses of this approach are obvious. The state is defined as the state of the Jewish people, and the IDF is the army that defends this state. Which leads us back to the primal problem of Jewish identity. Once it was realized that there was no common national culture except the religious one and that if religion were bypassed the term *Jew* would become completely blurred (like the new definition of the term proposed by Justice Chaim Cohen), the leadership transferred the authority of defining Jewishness to the Orthodox rabbinate. By doing that, not only did it prevent the possibility of creating a common national-territorial Israeli consciousness that would also include non-Jews, but it also retreated from the national consciousness that developed in Eastern Europe and did not include other Jewish groups. The only alternative was to declare the scattered Jewish communities, lacking any connecting link save the religious, to be a nation, and to revert to the religious authority as the only possible definer of this nation.

A significant stage in this development was the conversation held in 1952 between Ben-Gurion and Rabbi Avraham Yeshayahu Kerlitz (also called "Chazon Ish," after the book he wrote on Halachic problems), the spiritual leader of the Agudah. Ben-Gurion and his secretary, Yitzhak Navon, visited the rabbi at his home. Navon reported the conversation to me from memory on January 29, 1981, as follows:

> Ben-Gurion: "How can religious and nonreligious Jews live together in this country? We must concentrate on what is common to all parts of the people, for there is a great danger of internal explosion."
>
> Kerlitz: "There is a Halachic ruling: when two camels encounter each other in opposite directions on a narrow path where only one can pass, the laden camel has the right of way, and the unloaded one must clear the path for him. We, the Orthodox, bear a heavy load of studying the Torah, keeping the religious strictures, keeping the Sabbath and eating kosher food. The others, therefore, should clear the way for us."
>
> Ben-Gurion: "You mean to say that the nonreligious Jews carry no loads? Isn't settling the country a heavy load? . . . Even completely nonreligious Jews, like members of the Hashomer Hatza'ir party, build the country and protect *you*."
>
> Kerlitz: "They exist thanks to the fact that we study the Torah."
>
> Ben-Gurion: "If these youths did not defend you, you would have been destroyed by the enemies."

This conversation may be interpreted as a demand by Ben-Gurion on the "Chazon Ish" to recognize the legitimacy of the Jewishness of the nonreligious. The preeminent Zionist leader, incarnating the thesis that the Jews constitute a nation and that religion is but one of the national manifestations, here came to Rabbi Kerlitz as the supreme authority in Jewish affairs. It would seem that if Ben-Gurion had had full faith in Zionist principles, it would never have occurred to him to seek such validation. According to the original tenets of Zionism, the pioneers, builders, and fighters, not the petrified, hoary, and musty citadels of the Halacha, are the true and legitimate representatives of the modern Jewish people. In this case Ben-Gurion undoubtedly acted as a result of practical political constraints, but these very constraints must have aroused in him uncertainty and inner doubts regarding his principles and his political course.

This meeting, it should be noted, came at the very height of a state effort to stem and roll back the spontaneous process of an emerging Israeli-Hebrew national consciousness, which could have served as an alternative to the fading Jewish one. It could be argued that the meeting took place within that context. The very term *Hebrew*—which was current in the prestate Yishuv to distinguish the "liberated" native from the Diaspora Jew and which within the Yishuv served as a code term for the locally born (or raised) in order to define their distinct milieu and outlook—was erased from public currency. In the mid-fifties the Ministry of Education established compulsory courses in Jewish consciousness to fight against the emerging separate Hebrew national self-awareness. These courses taught Jewish customs, festivals, prayers, etc., in short—lessons in religion. The establishment-controlled media began to disseminate information that emphasized that the Jews are one people sharing a common destiny. One of the main objects of the Adolf Eichmann trial, as Ben-Gurion stated at the time, was to inculcate into Israeli youth the sense of the common destiny of the Jewish people, even though Zionism was founded, after all, to put an end to this sharing, to become liberated from the Jewish fate. The constant financial and political dependence of the state on the support of foreign Jews, mainly in the United States, also undermined the sense of a separate nationality of the Israelis born or bred in the country.

The retreat from national to religious-communal conceptions was further aggravated after the conquest of the West Bank, the Gaza Strip, and the Sinai Desert in the Six-Day War. The impact of the stunning victory caused a wave of religious ecstasy not only among traditionalist circles. (The enthusiasm did not affect the ultra-Orthodox, who remained as hostile as ever to the state, and touched the Agudah only marginally. But it caused a revolutionary change among the circles who defined themselves as "national religious," about which more later.) It also touched many who considered themselves secular. Beneath a thin veneer of secular rationalism, mythical and religious-eschatological patterns of thinking still persisted among many. These were perhaps the unconscious motive power of their nationalistic idealism. The cracking of this veneer caused some to revert consciously to a form of religious affiliation, although subject to their own interpretation of Judaism. It often appeared that this reversion was nothing more than a search for an excuse resting on divine promise to annex the conquered territories to the state.

If a Jewish state had been established elsewhere, the conquest of large territories might possibly have been viewed as a consequence of a superior social organization or superior military technology and training, not as proof of the intervention of providence and the imminent arrival of the messiah. Still, the experience of other nations shows that major military successes are often accompanied by mystic notions of "manifest destiny," like the national mystique generated by the Prussian victory over France in 1870, and the "white man's burden" ideology developed by Kipling and others for the use of the British Empire. The impact on Israel, where wide circles are influenced by eschatological literature and liturgy, by mysticism and Kabbalism centering on "salvation," was far greater. This was compounded by the fact that the land conquered had millennia-old associations in the collective historical memory and that the conquest came so shortly after the shock of terrible weakness and passivity in the face of Nazi extermination. The ground was thus prepared for a mystic interpretation of events, which seemed to many to fit a traditional mythical pattern of purgation by suffering, followed by the war of Gog and Magog, then capped by the coming of the messiah.

Behind this wave of pseudonational mysticism stood the basic problem of the essence of the state and the nature of its people, particularly after a large Palestinian-Arab population had been added to Israeli political-military control. In "old" pre-1967 Israel, with its relatively small Arab minority, one could ignore the question to some extent. The annexation of the territories to Israel, as demanded by the extremist nationalist groups, would oblige Israel to extend citizenship to their inhabitants, thus resulting in a situation in which more than a third of the population would be non-Jewish, that third also having the highest birthrate. In a single generation, all claims that Israel was a Jewish state would clash with the fact that half the population (and in a more distant future more than half) were not Jews. In other words, the continuation of Israel's occupation of the territories (assuming that the expulsion of their inhabitants is morally and practically out of the question) posits inescapably the question: will Israel become an essentially territorially defined state, belonging to its citizens, or will it retreat from the very concept of state and instead veer toward a tribal mindset that will be accompanied by an intensified discrimination against and repression of its non-Jewish elements? The outburst of eschatological euphoria was one possible answer to this question, since it ignored the existence and aspirations of the large non-Jewish population now under Israeli rule, and therefore conflicted with the principle of the territorial state.

Another aspect of this development is the expropriatory settlement by Israeli (and non-Israeli) Jews of land in the West Bank, the Gaza Strip, and the Golan Heights, wrested from its Arab owners in a variety of ways—legal, ostensibly legal, and illegal. (A substantial number of the settlements were established on what were definded as public lands and not on land officially registered as privately owned. But not all the lands that in reality belonged to Arab individuals or communities in the West Bank and the Gaza Strip were registered as such. In any case, the public lands were originally designated as a land reserve for the use of the local inhabitants, not for settlement by the Israeli occupiers. Some of the settlements were indeed built on land purchased from Arab owners, but under the unequal conditions in which the potential seller faced the potential buyer, backed by the coercive and persuasive means of an occupying power aiming at the dispossession of the Arabs. In the course of time the methods of pressure, threats, and deceit applied in many of the sales were indeed brought to light.) The Israelis who settled in the territories were assured all the rights of Israeli citizens, whereas the Arabs there became subject to the full rigors and regulations of an occupation regime. They have had no say in the formulation of these regulations, nor any ability to challenge them. At the same time, the laws regulating daily life have remained Jordanian in the West Bank and Egyptian in the Gaza Strip. Thus the two populations live side by side according to separate sets of laws and regulations—with one of them deprived of all political rights.

The denial of political rights is natural under the conditions of an occupation intended from the start to be temporary, until a final peace settlement is achieved. But under such conditions, international law, which prohibits changes in the status of conquered territories, forbids the settlement of the conquerors' population in such territories. But when the occupation is permanent (and all signs indicated, until Labor's election victory in 1992, that the Israeli establishment meant to hold on to the territories as long as it could), such settlement leads to the formation of a privileged ethnic group lording it in perpetuity over a subject population. This necessarily undermines the concept of the territorial nation-state, because the rights of citizenship in a nation-state (in reality, not citizenship rights but the rights that inhere in the Jewish group, with or without the Jews being citizens) are here extended beyond the boundaries of the state, according to an ethnic, not political, affiliation, thus causing a further degradation of the concept of the state and a worse blurring of its territorial definition.[8]

Additional grave infringements of the concept of the state were committed by the first Likud prime minister, Menachem Begin. Begin initiated the use of terms completely dissociated from the legal principles of the territorial national state. He hardly ever referred to the "state of Israel" and used instead the nonlegal geographical term "Eretz Israel," with its implication that all the territory of Palestine has been unified de facto under Jewish rule. He apparently preferred this to a formal act of annexation, because in the latter case it would be most difficult to avoid granting Israeli citizenship to any inhabitant of the occupied territories who so wished. In addition, in his declarations and speeches Begin did not address the citizens of the country but "the people of Israel," an ambiguous term that could denote either Jewish citizens of Israel or the Jewish people, but not the non-Jewish citizens of the country, whom Begin ignored almost completely throughout his years in office. He refrained from the demands of his Labor party predecessors, particularly Ben-Gurion, that Diaspora Jews emigrate to Israel, but on the other hand, in response to what seemed like anti-Semitic baiting on the part of some German and French neofascists, he warned that "Israel's hand" would reach the baiters. The implications of such a threat are that Israel considers itself responsible for the protection of Jews everywhere and will act to protect these Jews in disregard of the sovereignty of the countries where such acts take place, and of which these Jews are citizens. This implies that Israel is also entitled to the loyalty of these Jews in preference to their countries of citizenship. Such a threat is, in reality, an implicit or explicit struggle of Israel and the Jewish people against the whole world.

Ben-Gurion offered refuge and protection to the Jews in Israel, but only on condition that they relinquish their foreign nationality and settle in Israel. His approach respects the sovereignty of other nations and enables

Israel to function among them as an equal. Begin's approach, by infringing on others' sovereignty, also conflicts with Israel's, for disregard for the sovereignty of others will necessarily cause others to disregard one's own.

The logical development of this attitude is the polar opposite of the aim of classical Zionism to normalize and to naturalize the Jewish people in the family of nations. It brings to the surface the fact that the self-absorption and hostility of the Jewish caste community toward the entire world were not only passive. The emergence of Jewish power revealed the active and aggressive aspect of this hostility, in the form of an active struggle against the entire world, and as an eternal hatred between "circumcised" and "uncircumcised," as the nationalist Hebrew poet Uri Zvi Greenberg put it. It is no accident that this aggressive stance won support particularly among religious circles in Israel (and in the Diaspora, from which religious fanatics such as Rabbi Meir Kahane began to arrive in Israel, avid to wage war against the *goyim*), who with the right-wing extremists in the secular public formed an alliance radically opposed to the aims of traditional Zionism. Thus Israel itself became but a base of the struggle against the gentile world. For that reason, the traditional Zionist demand that Jews immigrate to Israel has lost its validity, for the battle is joined wherever Jews live, and there is therefore little difference between Israel and the Diaspora. This seems to have been the deep-lying reason for Begin's failure to call for immigration. Israel, according to this interpretation, is conceived as a fortress, as a combat base, while the Jews elsewhere are outposts and vanguards, as well as support units. Needless to say, such an attitude can lead to one of two results, or perhaps even both. On one hand, there could be the creation of a disastrous conflict between Jews everywhere and their environment (which by itself would arouse little compunction among the extreme Israeli nationalists, who would see this as an advantage). On the other hand, the danger which such a development generates for Jews everywhere could alienate from Israel most of world Jewry, thus accelerating the processes of assimilation that steadily erode the Jewish people to the point of possible extinction.

ELEVEN

Canaanism

Solutions and Problems

The most systematic and audacious attempt to cut through the tangle of contradictions described in previous chapters is Canaanism (Kna'aniut), a movement that arose in the 1940s and declined, at least organizationally, in the early 1950s. It was conceived on the eve of the outbreak of World War II in a series of meetings between the poet-politician Yonatan Ratosh and Professor Adia Gurevitch (Horon). As James Diamond[1] and Ya'acov Shavit[2] describe it, Canaanism was the first attempt to give ideological expression to the territorial-specific consciousness that had been developing in Palestine. Shavit sees Canaanism primarily as a confluence of intellectual, scientific, literary, and ideological trends that prevailed in Europe during the 1930s. But beyond this, there were several other forces at play. Canaanism arose as a dialectical complement and antithesis to Zionist thought. It was an expression of the transformation of a native-born generation, with its immediate or unmediated sense of homeland, as distinct from the acquired sense of homeland of the foreign-born pioneers. It was also an expression and continuation of the "Biblical revolution," the resort to modern Biblical research and criticism as a means of attacking the establishment that had been erected on the foundation of those very writings. And paradoxically, it brought an alliance of some Orthodox Canaanites with extreme aspects of messianic Jewish activity.

Originally called the Committee for the Consolidation of Hebrew Youth (*Canaanism* was originally a pejorative term purportedly tacked on to the movement by the poet Avraham Shlonsky), it drew much of its inspiration from the spiritual upheaval that took place among a large part of European Jewry. In the sphere of ideas in which the ghetto Jew was raised, the great role models were the pious and the devout, the scholars and the kabbalists—or the wealthy. All forms of physical activity—whether the work of farmer, fisherman, hunter, or warrior, even builder, architect, or stonemason—were considered inferior (and, with regard to the warrior and hunter, even contemptible and morally repugnant, "the work of Esau") as opposed to the values of spirit and learning on one hand (not the values of spirit and learning as such, since study of the sciences and philosophy was prohibited, but only of the Torah and its traditional exegesis) and on the other hand to material values. The social elite among the Christians (and the Muslims) consisted at one time primarily of the military and landed aristocracy, which determined the fundamental rules of honor and behavior, beside the tremendous influence of values imbued by the Church. Only at a later stage, with the rise of Protestantism and especially of Calvinism, did the values of industriousness, intellectual prowess, and material achievement attained by means of work and commerce become dominant. By contrast, the Jewish social elite was produced when the wealthy businessman found a young Talmudic prodigy as a husband for his daughter (as described abundantly in the works of Sholem Aleichem, Bialik, Agnon, Gnessin, Brenner, and many others). The aristocracy of wealth, based on sharpness of mind and objective quantitative calculations, and the aristocracy of the exegetic intellect were always joined in the European Jewish tradition.

Assimilationist Jews turned away from these role models and adopted the identification options and the scale of values of the European nations in which they became integrated. Heine and Herzl were raised on the *Nibelungenlied* and on Goethe, and their heroes were not the Vilna Gaon or Maimonides (nor even the Rothschilds), but Frederick Barbarossa and Heinrich "the Lion." Jabotinsky's *Story of My Life* and his articles resound with the echoes of Russian folktales and the shades of Russian folk heroes such as Ilya Murometz and Prince Igor, or Garibaldi and the heroes of the Risorgimento in Italy, where he spent his formative years. There is nothing in these writings of the role models that had been ever-present during the lives of his forebears. Even when the Europeanized Jews became Jewish nationalists, they did not return to Maimonides and the Vilna Gaon. Their mentality had become so transformed, the Vilna Gaon could no longer mean anything to them. What they did, then, was to translate the world of the German *Nibelungs* and the Russian *bylini* into Jewish equivalents (a constant motif with the poet Tschernikhovski, for example, who translated the Greek, Norse, and Russian epics into Hebrew and, under the influence of works like Goethe's *Hermann und Dorothea*, transformed even traditional Jewish characters into epic figures, as in "Elka's Wedding" and other idylls). What they also did was to translate this world into ancient Hebrew terms. Thus Bialik wrote the tale "King David in the Cave," which relates how the hero-king and his warriors sleep deep inside a cave, waiting for the blast of the ram's horn that will arouse them from their millennia of slumber to redeem Israel. In fact, this is nothing but a Hebrew reworking of an ancient German legend about Frederick Barbarossa slumbering with his knights deep inside a Bavarian mountain until, at a time of great distress for the German people, he would awaken from his sleep and save his nation. (There is also a British version of this legend, about King Arthur.)

We see that even Bialik, who unlike Tschernikhovski, Jabotinsky, Herzl, and Heine, was still steeped in a rich Jewish culture, wrote in this manner.

The values of their forebears had become alien to these Jews, and they began to model their traditional heroes on those of the nations among whom they lived. Heroes who had been remolded to suit the image of the scholars of rabbinic Judaism in the Talmudic period—"Jacob sitting in his tent studying the Torah," "King David reciting psalms before the Lord"—were revived in their original mythical, almost pagan, form. Other heroes, the memory of whom Talmudic tradition had almost erased, or else described as criminals and heretics, like Judah the Maccabee, Eleazar Ben-Yair, Yohanan of Gush-Halav, the Sicarii and the Zealots, were extricated from under the mounds of refuse and deliberate oblivion, cleaned up, and reinstated as national heroes, equals of Leonidas, King Arthur, and Siegfried. Once again we see that the Zionist revolution, which purportedly brought about the return of the assimilationists to their origins, was in reality, to a large extent, nothing but a form of collective assimilation. Zionism and assimilationism are both, after all, a rejection of historical Judaism. Once Zionism began to realize this, it recoiled from its own fundamental essence and lost confidence in itself. From that moment on, it ceased to be a revolutionary political and national program. Canaanism, in a certain sense, is an attempt to continue on the path from the point where Zionism left off.

I have described elsewhere the process by which A. D. Gordon consciously forced himself to create for himself a territorial subconscious—to possess Eretz Israel as his mother. This process involved a simultaneous break with his religious-traditional background in Russia. He sensed that the shift to Palestine meant a break with that tradition, and, as it turned out, he never succeeded in transferring himself wholly to Palestine. It appears that he was aware of the contradiction between Zionist realization and Jewish tradition. Had Gordon succeeded fully, had he managed to tear himself completely away from his connections to Jewish tradition and to the soil of Russia, he would have identified himself wholly, "naturally," with the territory of Eretz Israel, and he would have related to it in a down-to-earth, unromantic manner. It would never have occurred to him to use the term *Holy Land*, which still clearly bears the imprint of religious tradition, for Palestine.

In other words, the completion of the Zionist process should have been the creation of Israelis who were connected solely to their land and to the people dwelling in it. And here a problem arose: since Zionism began as an answer to the plight of the Jews and from the concept that the Jews were a nation that had been excluded from its territorial base, how could it separate itself wholly from the dispersed nation that had given birth to it? The very concept of the return to the land of Israel meant an essential connection with those who had not yet returned. This meant that the essential and characteristic connection of the Zionist who settles in Eretz Israel is not with the country but with the Jewish people—and even if this entire people were concentrated in the country, the basis would still be ethnic-communal, not territorial-national. The completion of the process thus required an additional act—a denial of the existence of the ethnic connection, a revolt against the very essence of this connection.

It is worth noting here that the rebels had, after all, grown up within the framework of concepts against which they were rebelling, and their thought had been shaped by the terms of this framework. Hence their attack is the most effective and fundamental, because they exploit these terms against the very framework itself. It is illuminating that Canaanite theory, which calls for a total separation from Judaism, attained its systematic elaboration during the very period when the attack on the Jewish people had reached its peak—the outbreak of World War II and the extermination of the Jews of Europe. There was an element of defiance in the insistence that the Hebrew nation in its homeland, as a a new nation, was exempt from the historical laws determining the fate of the Jewish people in its dispersion. It was a deliberate secession from the Jewish fate at the very time that this fate was revealing itself in its full horror.

This secession was not limited to the Canaanites, who only gave extreme and ideological expression to sentiments already prevalent in the Yishuv and in the Zionist movement. The Zionist leadership, as we have seen, viewed the development and fortification of the Yishuv as its primary task. The interests of the Jewish people in the Diaspora were definitely secondary to this goal. This was true even when the Jews of Europe were being exterminated. An additional example was the attempt made by the founders of Lehi,[3] led by Avraham Stern, to contact representatives of Nazi Germany in the Middle East with a view to a possible alliance in the struggle against the British. True, this attempt was not made as part of an act of secession from the Jewish people, as the Canaanites had recommended, but it did focus its goals for national action upon the Yishuv in Palestine, which it conceived as the only sector of the Jewish people that functioned as a political subject, which made it therefore also the most important one.

The Canaanite movement, which made its first public appearance with a pamphlet published in 1943 entitled "Letter to the Fighters for the Freedom of Israel" (Lehi), was the fullest and most systematic expression of this mood of dissociation. The principles of the movement, as formulated in "The Opening Address" (Summer 1944), insist that "a Hebrew cannot be a Jew, and a Jew cannot be a Hebrew." The significance of this statement was the drawing of an indelible line between the entity of a territorial nation and the Jewish entity, which was defined as "the entity of a religious community."

What, then, was the nature of the territorial Hebrew nation proclaimed by the founders of the Committee for the Consolidation of Hebrew Youth? This nation is composed of the Hebrew-speaking residents of the land of the Hebrews, or the "Land of Kedem,"[4] which extends over the entire area once populated by peoples who spoke Hebrew in its various dialects. Included in this area are present-day Syria, Lebanon, Jordan, and Palestine.

This was where the ancient Hebrew nation, which created the Hebrew civilization, was born. The Hebrew nation, according to the Canaanite movement, was a pagan nation, like all the nations around it, until it was overwhelmed by foreign conquerors who destroyed its various kingdoms. Some traces of this nation's literary heritage have been preserved in the Biblical anthology, though much was distorted by later Jewish redaction. This nation, whose renascent nucleus was the present Yishuv in Eretz Israel, would spread once more throughout the Land of Kedem and restore its populace—which had been coerced by the Arab conquerors to accept Islamic culture and the Arabic language—to its original, authentic Hebrew culture. The Hebrew state, which in the future would extend throughout the Land of Kedem, would maintain total separation between religion and state, establish absolute equality among all its citizens, and enforce the Hebrew language and Hebrew culture as its common language and culture. This nation has no connection with the Jews in their dispersion, apart from the fact that people who had come from the Jewish dispersion were the very ones who had created the nucleus of the Hebrew nation.

Here, then, we see another step in the direction of territoriality. Whereas previous Hebrew thought, like that of Tschernikhovski and Ben-Gurion, had aspired to transform the Jew into a Hebrew, a step that contains an internal contradiction since it involves the premise that the Jew is a potential Hebrew, meaning that the basic connection was still ethnic rather than territorial, the Canaanite movement insisted on an absolute separation. There is no "common basis" for the Jew and the Hebrew. These are mutually exclusive entities that are not on the same existential level. Official Zionism sees the Jew as "raw material," as implement and means for the Hebrew. From the opposite point of view one can therefore conceive of the Hebrew as a parasite on the Jew. Whereas the Jew can definitely exist and survive without the Hebrew, the Hebrew had created a situation in which he could no longer exist without the Jew. The Canaanite position breaks this connection. The Hebrew doesn't need the Jew. He is neither a utopian continuation of the Jew nor "the realization of the messianic vision of Judaism." The Jew exists in his own right, and the Hebrew exists in his. Both entities are legitimate and self-sufficient; neither is teleological and neither should be anything but what it is.

The major problems arising from this attempt at separation are obvious. The first and principal problem is that even if we accept the claims about the existence of an ancient Hebrew civilization that extended throughout the "Land of Kedem,"[5] this civilization has come down to us primarily via Judaism, which had continued to create in the Hebrew language (in addition to secondary languages like Aramaic, Arabic, and Yiddish) for centuries after the collapse of the ancient Hebrew civilization. Thus there is no possibility of separating the isolated and distant elements of ancient Hebraicity from the rich and manifold accumulations of Jewish culture that accrues to them and had been reinterpreted by them. This is so especially since the archaic traces of the ancient Hebrew culture are too fragmentary to provide a contemporary individual with anything more than objects for antiquarian and archeological or anthropological interest—not real cultural-spiritual nourishment, as, in contrast, ancient Greek civilization can. Anyone desirous of studying Hebrew literature, for example, can do no more than begin by studying the hymns of Anath, the tablets of Ugarit, and the archaic chapters of the Bible. From then on he will need to learn the Book of Esther, the Books of Ezra and Nehemiah, the Mishnah, and Aggadah, and after that also Yehuda Halevi, Ibn Gabirol, M. H. Luzzatto, Bialik, and Agnon. It is simply impossible to skip 2,500 years of history and bury them in archives. Even if an Israeli-Hebrew nation, clearly differentiated from Judaism, does develop, Hebraic consciousness would necessarily have the deepest attachments to its Jewish levels, in the same way that it would be impossible to separate the consciousness of the peoples of modern secular Europe from the Christian world of thought and association or from the decisive role of Christianity, and especially of the Catholic Church, in the creation of modern Europe. Similarly, it would be just as impossible to separate the consciousness of the Arabic-speaking peoples from the world of Islamic ideas and associations, a fact that is true even of the Christians and Jews living among these peoples. A Hebrew national consciousness will always have affinities to Judaism. There is no possibility of creating a Hebrew nation in the land of the Hebrews with ties only to the archaic Hebrew territory and culture. Attempts to repress the Jewish heritage would only result in a distortion of the Hebrew cultural image and a compensatory overreaction of the repressed levels.

An illuminating example of this process can be found in a very significant sphere—the names adopted by novelists and poets. In the 1940s, and even before, there was hardly a creative writer who did not Hebraize his name—Ratosh, Amir, Megged, Shamir, Tammuz, Yizhar, Bartov, Guri, Shaham, Aloni, Kenan, etc. This adoption of Hebrew names was not accidental, at least not among self-aware intellectuals. It had a programmatic content, and represented a decision to break the connection with the world of the Halprins, the Steinmans, the Smilanskis, and the Levins. Twenty years later, the young creative writers were retaining their old Jewish names: Wieseltir, Mittelpunkt, Wollach, Auerbach, Horowitz. This too implies a programmatic declaration, for it is a clear reaction against the fashion of Hebraizing that preceded it. It contains a statement that the high-toned Hebrew names do not correspond to the subjective feelings of these writers, that these names involve an artificiality and a separation from their innermost consciousness, and that this consciousness is continuous with the Jewish world. One can distinguish here the reaction of repressed material. Judaism has taken its revenge on the proto-Canaanites of the 1940s.

But by the same token, just as there is no possibility for the Hebrew to completely break away from the Jewish strata of history, it is doubtful whether the Arabic-speaking peoples of the Land of Kedem could possibly be separated from their Islamic-Arabic heritage and have imposed on them a Hebrew culture that is alien to them, even if many of them are Christian and Druze. After all, the Druze and Christians feel that Arabic is their language and the language of their culture, and this does not prevent them from remaining Christians or Druze.

The Canaanite claim is that Hebrew is the ancient language of these peoples, that Arabic is the language of the conquerors and has been forced on them, and that imposing Hebrew on them would not be an imposition but a liberation of their true essence, bringing them back to their original language, the only language which came into being in the Land of Kedem and which is natural to the region.[6] This cultural claim has an obvious political aspect as well—that Hebrew is the only language that does not lead the inhabitants of the Land of Kedem to loyalties and connections outside the land (even though Hebrew, as the Jewish "language of the book," the language of prayer and intercommunity communications in past generations, clearly leads to such connections). But it would be just as reasonable to argue for the abolition of French and Spanish, both of them Latin dialects that developed in Gaul and Iberia while they were provinces of the Roman Empire, and to claim that the expression of the true spirit of the peoples of these lands required the revival of the ancient Celtic languages, their original tongues. But the fact is that France and Spain function very well as modern secular nations, with rich national cultures, even though the Latin which is the basis of their cultures not only is the language of their Roman conquerors but also has strong ecclesiastical affinities. Thus, even if the peoples of the region were willing to unite in some sort of broader political framework, it must be assumed that they would be willing to do so only if there were no attempt to impose on them foreign cultural and spiritual forms and contents. Hebrew language and culture are unsuitable for such a purpose. They involve much more than a secular culture.

Much of the criticism leveled against the Canaanites has been on the cultural level—against their drawing pictures of the past on insufficient historical evidence and inconclusive data. But such criticism largely misses the political intentions behind the cultural ideology. Through concentrating too heavily on Ratosh's poetic images—Ashtoreth, Anath, the Baal, and the Asherah—most critics failed to grasp the political vision that largely dictated the official ideology of Canaanism. Most critics saw it as a cultural movement and failed to realize that its basis and principles were distinctly political. Thus they failed to understand the real nature of the movement.

Four political premises underlie Canaanite thought. First, the subject of a state is a nation, or, put differently, a state is a political expression of a nation. In this, Canaanism does not differ from the political conception of Zionism, which sees Israel as the political expression of the Jewish nation.

The difference lies in the fact that Canaanites believe that the Jewish people is not qualified to be the subject of a state because it is not properly a nation at all.

Second, a state must be large enough and strong enough to initiate independent action. In this respect, none of the states of the Middle East—Israel, Syria, Jordan, Lebanon, perhaps even Iraq and Egypt—is capable of conducting a truly independent policy. As political units they are too small, and certainly this is the situation today, when even yesterday's superpowers, Britain, France, and Germany, are no longer capable of being truly independent. As long as these units continue their separate existence, they are forced to rely on external forces to defend them; of themselves they are too weak to maneuver independently and to defend themselves against the great powers. Conversely, the great powers exploit these regional units for their own benefit, and it is in their interest to ensure that these units will continue to be small and in conflict with each other. Otherwise they would not need the protection of the great powers against other small units, when they in their turn are backed by another great power. The fact that Israel, for example, relies on U.S. support forced Syria to rely on Soviet support in its dispute with Israel. Both the United States and the erstwhile Soviet Union were interested in the continuation of the Syrian-Israeli dispute; if it had been settled, they would not have been called on for assistance and would not have been able to intervene in the affairs of the region, which is, above all else, strategically and economically important in the world arena.

This means that the independence, stability and prosperity of the region, its transformation into a sovereign and independent force acting in its own interests in the play of world forces, is conditional upon its unification and the creation of a political framework common to all segments of its population. Indeed, the only times the region was not subject to either direct or indirect rule of foreign powers occurred when it was united under a single authority, as during the reigns of David and Solomon, the House of Omri, and the Khalifate of the House of Umayyah in Damascus. As long as the region is not united, it constitutes a transit route for the powers to its north and south. Therefore there is no middle path. There is either unity and might or disintegration and enslavement.

It is noteworthy that such thinking also guided the Lehi leadership during the climactic stage of the struggle against the British in 1946, with the publication of its pamphlet "Guidelines for a Hebrew Foreign Policy." The goal of the struggle was defined as the establishment of a federation of Middle Eastern nations that would take a neutral position between the two great power blocs. The reasoning behind this pamphlet, as I learned in conversations with the former head of the Lehi Central Committee, Natan Yellin-Mor, was as follows: Lehi's purpose in fighting the British had not been to get them to rescind the policy of the White Paper while agreeing in principle to the legitimacy of their rule in the country. Lehi saw the British as foreign imperialists that must be expelled from the country. If the British continued to control the surrounding region, the liberation of Eretz Israel would mean only partial liberation; soon enough the British would be able once again to exert their will on the country by maneuvering its neighbors. That is to say, the liberation of Eretz Israel depended on the struggle for the liberation of the entire Middle East, which could be achieved by means of cooperation among its peoples, and this, for the reasons stated, would lead inevitably to the establishment of a neutralist regional federation. There is no doubt, in this context, as to the reciprocal influence of Lehi and Canaanite thinking—and it is no accident that the first public appearance of the Canaanites was in the "Letter to the Fighters for the Freedom of Israel." One argues with those who are closest.

This basic view was not foreign to an important segment of the Zionist leadership. Both Weizmann, in his talks with King Faisal, and Ben-Gurion, in his talks with Arab leaders during the 1930s, proposed as self-evident the idea that the future Jewish state would become a full member, with equal rights, in a regional Arab federation. It seems that it was clear to them at that time that there was no long-term future for a separate and isolated Jewish state in the region.

The third premise of Canaanite thought is that for the region to be truly independent, the political processes occurring in it must originate from the needs of the region itself, and not from considerations external to it. No regional policy can succeed if it is not rooted in the political and economic needs of the region. In this respect Zionism, which is supposed to represent the interests of the Jewish people, most of whom live outside the region, and Arabism, which claims to represent an Arab nation extending from the Atlantic to the Indian Ocean, are not different from the various foreign imperialist powers. Zionism indeed is a classic example of a body that insists on preserving its distinction, its separate character, and endeavors to link itself with foreign imperialist powers as a counterweight to the local peoples with whom it is in conflict.

Even Ben-Gurion, by insisting on the transfer of the central Zionist executive to Palestine at the beginning of the century, showed signs of budding Canaanism. I have already mentioned the attempt of Avraham Stern to contact the Axis powers. Even in Zionist circles, then, it appears that the concept that the needs of the nation living in the country, not the situation of Diaspora Jewry, should determine political processes was striking ever deeper roots. And this growing attitude is a natural outcome of the fact that every group, including the Israeli leadership, is concerned first of all with its own interests.

The fourth premise is that the unity and power of the region cannot therefore be based on the Jewish people or the Arab people—not only because both are connected with much broader entities in distant and foreign lands but also because the very definitions of these two entities imply their exclusivity. In the eyes of the Canaanites, both are connected with exclusive religious cultures, both are ethnocentric and intolerant. The attempt of either to seize control of the Land of Kedem means oppression, coercion, even the expulsion or extermination of any other ethnic-communal or national body. Such an attempt would also entail an even greater aggravation of the friction in the region, as well as the subordination of the region's interests to those of people who mostly live outside it (the Jewish people or the Arab people), hence another form of foreign intervention and rule.

Furthermore, the Canaanite analysis of the nature and history of the Jewish people (an analysis I accept in part) claims that it is a nonterritorial nation, that Jewish immigration to Eretz Israel has always been, in the main, a response to distress and not a voluntary national act, and offers no hope for the mobilization of the human resources required for the consolidation of the region. It is even possible (and this is only a guess) that the development of such thinking during the Holocaust was influenced by the realization that the population reservoir of European Jewry would no longer be available for Zionism; thus an alternative population base, upon which regional unification might rest, had to be sought.

In other words, the federative conception proposed by Weizmann and Ben-Gurion was not accepted by the Canaanite thinkers. If we develop their line of reasoning further, this was probably because even if a Middle Eastern federation of this kind—a Jewish state joined with Arab states—were to arise, each of its components would still be influenced by extraregional forces and interests, and these would of necessity cause the federation to be flimsy and in constant danger of disintegration. Hence there would be a need for a much more cohesive structure, one based not on the extant regional forces but on a foundation of a new kind, which could serve as a common platform for all the populations living in the region.

In this context, the development of the Canaanite idea appears to be a deliberate creation of a single mythos for the region—a mythos aimed at neutralizing the centrifugal influences at work in the region and at creating an ideological basis for the formation of a new national unit that would encompass Jews, Moslems, Christians, Druze, and other sects and ethnic groups in the region. In this respect the idea resembles the various national mythoi that came into being during the flowering of the national movements in Europe. The recognition of the need for such a comprehensive, integrative mythos was perhaps what led to the denial of the genuine national qualities both of Zionism and of the Arab national movement (like ignoring the fact that the latter movement was not essentially identified with Islam and that its first thinkers had been Syrian Christians). Creating a regional nation required this kind of denial of competing fragmentary national consciousnesses. If one's goal is indeed the creation of a regional political unit, the Canaanite argument seems unassailable—unless we question the first of the basic premises outlined above, that the necessary subject of a state is a single ethnic group.

The founders of Canaanism claimed that the primary nucleus of the emerging Hebrew nation was the existing Yishuv. The Yishuv was the most

developed and most progressive body in the region, hence its younger generation would attain early development of a genuine national consciousness, liberated from Zionism, rooted in the soil of the Hebrew homeland. Its
task would be to carry out the regional Hebrew revolution, to conquer all of
the Land of Kedem, and to establish in it the Hebrew national culture, liberated from both Jewish Zionism and pan-Arabism. This liberation would
be achieved in alliance with the non-Arab peoples in the region, who lived
in danger of being dominated and repressed by the Sunni Muslim majority,
which the Canaanites considered to be a barbaric and destructive element.
For this reason they (and not only they) recommended the creation of an
alliance of minorities in the Middle East as a means of breaking the Sunni
dominance: an alliance between the Hebrews in Palestine; the Druze of
Jebel Druze, Galilee, and the Shouf Mountains; the Maronites in Lebanon;
the Kurds; and others.

For this reason, the founders of Canaanism sharply criticized the Israeli
government for halting the Israeli army in the 1948 war at the borders of the
areas densely populated by Arabs. The Canaanites interpreted this halt
both as a surrender to imperialist Anglo-American dictates and as a self-
imposed limitation by Israel to a solely Jewish-Zionist framework. The
creation of the Hebrew nation in the Land of Kedem, Ratosh and Horon
taught, would be achieved not by cultural influence and propaganda but by
war and conquest, in the wake of which the Hebrew nation would forcibly
impose Hebrew culture and nationhood on all the peoples of the Land of
Kedem, while simultaneously shaking itself free from both Zionism and
Arabism.

This demand for war and conquest had two main aspects: the belief that
historical action always takes place in a Bismarckian manner, by "blood
and iron." In this the fathers of Canaanism were true heirs of the Jabotinsky school that had formed them. War is the historical action par excellence, the midwife of nations; by the force of the imperial sword their various fragments are forged into a single whole.

But how could the Hebrew nation impose its culture on the inhabitants
of the region when it was still Jewish-Zionist, ghettolike and insular, and all
the other pejorative epithets with which the Canaanite founders labeled it?
Here we come to the second, hidden aspect of the demand for conquest: the
premise that the very fact of the conquest, which would bring under Israeli
rule an increasing number of non-Jewish inhabitants, would force Israel to
gradually shed its exclusively Jewish character and develop a Hebrew territorial political framework. For this reason they opposed the teaching of
Arabic to the Arab population in Israeli schools and insisted that textbooks
be in only one language for all the children in the state, with a clear distinction between the secular-national Hebrew curriculum common to all
and the different religious and ethnic programs for specific groups. In effect they recommended a policy similar to the Russification policy of the
tsars or the successive attempts of the Germans and the French to impose

their language and culture on the population of Alsace-Lorraine, in order to make the population an inseparable part of the German or French nation.

The dialectical—and grotesque—corollary of this approach is the consistent support by Ratosh and the orthodox Canaanites of the appropriation-settlement activities of Gush Emunim, even though these activities are the antithesis of Canaanism. The Canaanite assumptions in this matter have been as follows. The conquest and settlement of territories in the Land of Kedem would bring about a mixing of populations. The *mitnahalim* (appropriator-settlers), exclusivist religious Jews though they be, are unwittingly the bearers of Hebrew culture, albeit in a distorted religious form. The superiority of this culture will gradually bring about its percolation into the surrounding non-Jewish population, which will become Hebraized, as had already happened to a certain extent to the Arabs in the territories of "old" Israel. That these two peoples live side by side will, with time, bring them increasingly closer, even if initially there is hostility and conflict—the outcome of acts of expropriation and oppression—but these are familiar phenomena, known since ancient times, in the history of appropriation-settlement by conquering nations. Hadn't the Vikings and the Normans—and before them the Saxons and the Angles—settled in England, each in turn ruling the previous inhabitants, sometimes in the most savage and cruel manner, and hadn't they ultimately merged to form a single nation? The process of appropriation-settlement will create an irreversible situation and the territories will be annexed to Israel, thus creating the opportunity to struggle for equal rights and obligations for all inhabitants, for the penetration of Hebrew culture among members of all ethnic and religious groups, for the separation from religion of the expanded state, half of whose population will by then be non-Jews.

This concept assumes as self-evident that the Canaanite thinkers are attentive to and understanding of the real processes of history, that they are sharers in the Hegelian "cunning of Reason." From this perspective, there is perhaps not such a great difference between them and the leaders of Gush Emunim, who are convinced that their activities correspond to the divine plan for the messianic redemption of the Jewish people.

The orthodox Canaanites' approach to the settlement of the conquered territories lacks adequate understanding of sociological and political processes and displays a certain naivete in its assumption that mixture will lead inevitably to blending and integration. Despite the precedents of the Viking settlement in England and France, the Mongols in China, and the Franks in Gaul (in all three cases, it should be noted, the conquering peoples were more primitive than those they conquered, and it was the conquered who soon assimilated the conquerors), there are also the examples of the settlement of the Colons in Algeria, the English Protestants in Ireland, the Dutch in South Africa, the British and other white colonists in Rhodesia and Kenya and North America, none of which led to a homogeneous blending of populations but rather produced friction and wars of liberation, ending, in the case of North America, with the extermination of the native population and in other cases with the expulsion of the colonists to their mother countries. The Middle East itself has been conquered numerous times throughout history and contains many autochthonous peoples who have lived side by side for centuries but have nevertheless not merged.

A closer observation of these phenomena reveals the differences between the positive examples on which the Canaanites base their arguments and those which I have cited. The first difference is that all the examples of blending and homogenization of populations are ancient, while all the examples of the failure of such attempts are modern, taking place within the past two centuries. The appropriating (or colonizing) population in this case has a radically different culture from that of the native population. Moreover, both populations have opposed and isolationist ideologies, especially the Jewish one. It should be recalled that as long as the Jewish religion (or ideology) remained viable, Jews did not merge with their host populations, even when they lived among them for centuries. Often the Jews did not even speak the language of the people among whom they lived. A group that is imbued with an ideology including closed and crystallized structures of behavior and rituals and that also has a strong sense of mission is not liable to merge. That two populations are in mechanical-external contact is no indication that they will ever merge with one another. More often than not, this proximity is a source of friction and mutual hatred. In India, members of various castes have lived in close proximity for thousands of years, and this has not produced any blending.

These tensions and hatreds are much more extreme in the situation of Israel, where one population is imposing itself on the other by force of arms, creating a master-slave relationship which the masters have a vested interest in perpetuating. No dominant class or caste ever gives up its position without a hard, frequently bloody, struggle. And as in the examples of Algeria and the German populations in the Baltic countries after World War I, these dominant castes join hands with reactionary forces and militarist circles in the motherland, where they try to engineer military coups and create reactionary fascist regimes that will in turn support the castes in question. The outcome of the imposition of such castes on a native population may therefore be national disruption, dictatorship, or civil war and destruction in the motherland. The struggle between the oppressed population and the ruling caste heightens the separate, independent, and hostile self-awareness of the oppressed population, and the final outcome in most cases is the expulsion or departure of the ruling caste. Thus, instead of leading to blending and integration, this colonization creates an even more acute sharpening of the separate national consciousness of the oppressed, which is in contrast to the entire Canaanite conception.

In addition, it is often the case that this separate consciousness arises where no national consciousness existed before, as was the case, to a large extent, with the rise of Jewish national consciousness. It is also worth noting that in contrast to the intentions of the Canaanites, there appears to be no intention on the part of the Jewish appropriator-settlers to press for the official annexation of territories of the West Bank and the Gaza Strip to Israel. If annexation took place it would be difficult to refrain from granting civic rights to the inhabitants of the territories. It is more convenient for the appropriator-settlers that the inhabitants of the territories continue to have Jordanian citizenship, thus avoiding the constitutional tangles that would arise with the annexation of the territories to Israel. In actuality, the real goal of the appropriator-settlers is not the subjugation of the Arabs but their expulsion, so the settlers' success—if they do succeed—will not lead to any mixing of populations.

The avoidance of annexation and of granting Israeli citizenship to the Arab population thus increasingly intensifies its separate Palestinian national consciousness. Even under optimal circumstances, in conditions of equality and a uniformly applied law, the mixture of the kind that the Canaanites seek often fails in practice. The Swiss example is essentially unique, and there too there is no mixing and integration. The different language groups—French, German, Italian, and Romanche—live in separate cantons, cooperating in a federal superstructure. On the other hand, there is friction between various linguistic and ethnic groups even in stable, long-established countries such as Belgium and Canada, and these groups also maintain their linguistic-cultural identity despite the equality before the law and even though no section of the population there tries to attack or expropriate the others. In the conditions prevalent in the occupied territories, all that can be expected is a continuous exacerbation of conflict and hatred.

An additional point, and a most ironic one, with regard to the occupation of the territories is that it would not have been possible without the support of the United States, a support influenced in no small degree by the pressure of American Jewry. The execution of the Canaanite program thus requires the support of an extraregional factor, this support being extended under the auspices of Zionist ideology. Furthermore, this support activates an extraregional superpower against intraregional forces, which would otherwise not allow Israel to hold on to its loot. Thus the execution of the Canaanites' grand design requires the use of means that negate it a priori. At one time I posed this argument to Yonatan Ratosh, whose reply suggested that every political body is entitled to obtain external support, no matter from what quarter, to realize its political goals. The result in this case is that these political goals are in effect identical with those of the most extreme religious and rightist wing of Zionism, and they involve the effective surrender of political independence, because in return for this external support Israel is obliged to serve the political strategic goals of the United States in the region.

The strategic thinking of the orthodox Canaanites did not go so far as to understand that the only possible condition for the neutralization of the Middle East and the unification of the Land of Kedem is not the attainment of greater power by one of the states in the region. No regional state could, by itself, in the forseeable future muster the power to deter a superpower from interfering in the region's affairs. But the powers should be brought to an understanding that it is in their interest to withdraw from the region and to allow it to develop toward unification independently.

Furthermore, any attempt to use Israel's military might to conquer a part of the region would provoke that part to immediately ask for the support of the superpower opposed to the one that supports Israel or the superpower that now effectively controls the region, the United States, and inter-bloc pressure would be applied to stop Israel. The Lebanon War clearly showed that although Israel's theoretical military strength—i.e., the amount of firepower it can deploy against its regional enemies—is sufficient for the conquest of the entire Middle East, since there is no Arab army that can stand up to the IDF in the field, its real strength is not adequate to seize control even of Lebanon or its capital, Beirut. The balance of international and regional forces within which Israel must operate prevent it from doing this. Hence the elimination of overriding external influences from the region can come about only by means of an agreement among its local components, who could then present to the superpower or powers a proposal that safeguards the powers' legitimate interests and ensures that in the future the region will not serve as a base that can threaten any of them.

A part of the Canaanites' plan of operation to achieve the unification of the Land of Kedem under Hebrew rule is, as stated, the idea of the alliance of minorities. This idea did not originate with the Canaanites. It was proposed as early as the beginning of this century by the Gideonites,[7] later by Itamar Ben-Avi,[8] and then again by various Zionist forces that sought to be integrated within the region. It will be recalled that in 1967 Yigal Allon expressed regret that during the Six-Day War the IDF had not advanced as far as Jebel Druze, in order to "liberate" the Druze there and create a link with them which, he believed, would have undermined the structure of the Syrian state.

As long as the premise stood that compromise between the Hebrew national entity in Israel and the Sunni-Arab world was impossible and as long as the Arabic-speaking states in the region remained distinctly Sunni Muslim in character—a character that automatically discriminates against all other elements in the population—there was a certain logic in the aspiration to undermine the Sunni supremacy in the region. It is worth noting, by the way, that the people in the mainstream of the Yishuv leadership were of the opposite opinion. They believed that this would lead to a permanent conflict with the majority of the Arab Middle East, a situation antithetical to the final goal of Zionism. The very idea of an alliance of minorities thus entails the premise of a permanent conflict between the Arab world and the Hebrew nation.

But if the alliance of minorities is proposed as part of a process aimed at the establishment of a Hebrew nation in the whole of the Land of Kedem, the very fact of such an alliance would become an obstacle to the establishment of such a Hebrew nation. Ethnic groups like the Druze, the Maronites, and the Kurds, even if they ally themselves with each other and with the Israelis, will still constitute a numerical minority and will still occupy only limited territories within the Sunni-Arab space. Granting the premise of Sunni-Arab supremacy, this Sunni-Arab power will always be able to foment disputes among the other groups, to offer one of them its assistance against the others, and, above all—because the Sunni-Arab element is the largest and most enduring force in the area—the various groups will always prefer to form an alliance with it rather than with each other, because they can receive greater benefits from it than from each other. Furthermore, since these groups (except the Hebrew-Israeli nation), are tolerated minorities among the Sunni-Arab population, they have never developed any true state-political thinking. They deal in sectarian politics, not in state strategy. Like the Jewish communities in their dispersions, they are concerned not with the structure and future of the region but with their own narrow interests, and they are not capable of looking beyond these. Thus they are more backward, in terms of political development, than the Sunni-Arab group, which is the one that has established most of the states in the region and has therefore had to contend, from the outset, with real state-political problems, including the structural problems deriving from the existence of the minorities. For that reason, the Arab national movement has developed as a result of an alliance between Christians and Sunnis. As for the argument about the inevitable hostility between a Hebrew state and Sunni Arabism—the fact is that the first peace treaty between Israel and the Arabs was signed with the largest Sunni-Arab state of all, the actual leader of the Arab world. This is to say that an alliance of minorities would in fact be an alliance with the regressive elements in the region, elements that hold back the region's political development toward broader and more objective political frameworks. The very idea of the creation of a single regional nation-state cannot be based just on opposition to the Sunni-Arab majority. Any unit of the kind must include this majority as its principal component. Otherwise it cannot exist.

The original Canaanite approach stressed the development of a Hebrew cultural consciousness, and the state appeared to Ratosh and his associates as an expression of the national essence. Here, hopefully, I have raised enough points to show that there is no possible chance of creating a lingual-cultural-national unity of the region that has been defined as the Land of Kedem. Yet the formation of a neutral political framework that dictates no national, cultural, or ethnical content and is structured as a federation or a confederation is a reasonable possibility. The existing states in the region could function as components in a political union of this kind, whereas their dissolution (which is what an alliance of minorities implies) would be regressive in terms of the process of the unification of the region. We find, then, that the program for the unification of the Land of Kedem on the basis of an Israeli conquest and the imposition of Hebrew culture on the inhabitants in order to create a unified Hebrew nation throughout the whole region meets with insoluble contradictions and that only an agreement of union among the region's components, according to which each will maintain autonomy, can be a solution of these difficulties.

On some points, however, the Canaanites were right. First, Canaanite thought brought to full logical development and conclusion the basic theses of secular political Zionism, which aspired to a normalization of the Jewish people. The Hebrew nation toward which the Canaanite thinkers aspired was in fact, to a decisive extent, the nation that had been the aim of Herzl, Jabotinsky, and Borochov, and to a certain extent of Ben-Gurion, too—an open, secular nation in which religion is separated from state, and which is capable of absorbing members of other faiths and nations.

The sharp distinction between Jew and Hebrew, though the Canaanites were not quite able to explain how the one evolved from the other, is nevertheless an essential distinction for the creation of the Israeli nation. The ideological impasse reached by the Canaanites was in their failure to grasp that the solution did not lie in the creation of a Hebrew nation but in the creation of a state framework that would not impose values and content, a framework of the West European or North American type, which allows for cultural and ethnic pluralism within the framework of a shared and neutral citizenship. Such a state would exist on a completely different plane from that of the present Jewish community, so that someone might be an Israeli Jew in the same way that a British subject is an English Protestant, without these two definitions being identical even though there does exist a close dialectical-historical connection between them.

Another correct Canaanite conception, and perhaps the truest of all, is the realization that true independence and peace in the Middle East are dependent on the creation of overall political frameworks that are much broader than the existing ones. The Canaanite belief that a prerequisite for such broader frameworks is a common national ethos, without which fragmentation will occur, appears erroneous. Such an ethos might well develop in time as an outcome of the establishment of a common framework, as in the development of a European spirit in the framework of the European Community, but not as a precondition. To be precise: the European spirit does not *replace* national loyalties in Europe but transcends them. It does not contradict them but exists on a completely different plane, one which to a certain extent is a kind of reconciliation of those national loyalties. The attempt to impose an artificial Hebrew nationhood on the region conflicts with affinities so profound and broad that it has no chance of defeating them. But the creation of a framework that functions on a different plane may neutralize them and eliminate the fear that the unity may be disrupted by the centrifugal tendencies of Zionism or pan-Islamism, in the same way that the inter-Jewish or inter-Irish affinities do not subvert the federal framework of the United States.

TWELVE

The Messianic Farce

The definition of Israel as an instrument of the salvation of the Jewish people removes the state from the category of ordinary countries, whose raison d'être is the well-being and security of their citizens, and subordinates it to another aim, which the country's citizens may not question. On the face of it, the definition seems to contradict what I have argued in previous chapters—that in reality the Jewish Diaspora was manipulated by the Zionist movement and the Israeli establishment for the promotion of the power accumulation of the Yishuv and the state that succeeded it. In fact, there is no contradiction here but rather different perspectives, two magnetic foci of the same power field. This power field includes the state and the Jewish Diaspora, mainly in the West, while the rest of the world, the non-Jewish part, is excluded. This in turn leads to Israel's dependence on the power and influence of the largest and wealthiest segments of the Jewish Diaspora, which heavily shape its policy. Were it not for the power and wealth of the American Jewish community, it is doubtful that Israel would have adopted the pronounced pro-American policy that it has, a policy that has not always served it well in its foreign relations. This mutual dependence dissociates it from the natural context of international relations, thus causing distortions in its domestic and external affairs. That made it possible for some circles in Israel to delude themselves into acting as if Israel were a planet separate and apart from the world political system, and therefore capable of acting outside it.

This delusion has been fed by a traditional Jewish trait, a trait which Zionism had originally intended to put an end to: the Jews' dissociation from history, their self-conception as a people apart, disdaining other peoples and keeping away from them. This Jewish force-field, within which Israel operates, is then a regression on a new plane to the Jewish ghetto world, the world of the separate religious caste, although this regression coincides with accumulation of power, which has become the guiding ideal of the Israeli political system.

That is the background of the most significant sociopolitical phenomenon in Israel in the seventies and eighties—the rise of Gush Emunim and its seizure of control, to a large extent, of the policy of the state. The ideology and modus operandi of the Gush are a pathological magnification of the hunger for domination fused with ghetto mentality, of a typical ghetto fear of and abnegation before the threatening external *goyish* world, coupled with a desire to trample it underfoot. This ideology also unites the two elements which the prevalent conceptions within Israel view as standing above the state and which the state was supposedly established to serve: the conception of the nation as an entity superior to the state and the conception of religion as the basis of the nation, hence being doubly superior to the state. From these two aspects, the Gush is the greatest threat that has ever arisen to the state, since it is the direct outgrowth of the essential contradictions we have detected in the state's structure. In addition, it uses those ideologies, ideals, techniques, and institutions developed in order to realize Zionism and the state as a means to undermine them. In this way it unites within it the antistate energies of both Zionism and religion.

Some of the attractive power of the Gush derives from its leaders' readiness to state openly things that official Zionism pretends do not exist, or that it has consciously suppressed. Amnon Rubinstein quotes in this connection the challenge of Gush thinker Yoel Floresheim to the preamble of Israel's declaration of independence, which maintains that the Jewish people, its culture and religion, arose in Eretz Israel, where it led an independent existence and bequeathed the Bible to humanity.[1] Floresheim argues that these statements are not unique to the Jewish people and could also apply to other peoples: "You have only to replace the terms 'Eretz Israel' and 'the Jewish people' by the corresponding non-Jewish terms, and instead of 'the eternal Book of Books' put the corresponding cultural contribution. In other words, it [the declaration] expresses the Zionist craving for the normalization of the Jewish people." One by one, Floresheim demolishes all of these tenets. "The Jewish people was not founded in Eretz Israel," he writes, "but in Egypt and in the desert, with God's addresses to Jacob and Moses; its spiritual, religious, and political attributes were mainly shaped in the Diaspora—from the Babylonian Talmud down to Zionism itself." This, Floresheim argues, is the basic error of original Zionism: "It failed because it tried to turn the Jewish people into something it is not—a nation similar to all others—and thereby also to turn Eretz Israel into something it is not—namely, into what any country is for its inhabitants." In short, Floresheim points out exactly what I have argued here: that the Jewish people is not a territorial nation.

Rubinstein notes that the new religious Zionism, which forbids yielding an inch of Eretz Israel's territory under mortal religious sanction, does not share with Zionism and the moderate secularists the traditional fear of Israel's international isolation. On the contrary, the new religious nationalists and their secularist allies view such isolation and world hostility as a blessing: this, they believe, is why Jews have managed to keep their identity and uniqueness throughout history. The Jewish people has always stood alone, on one side of the barrier, while the rest of humanity has stood on the other.

According to another Gush thinker, Chaim Peles, this uniqueness has one meaning only: "To build and develop Jewish settlement in Eretz Israel as an early stage of messianic redemption. Israel could become a small, meaningless Levantine state, without any bearing on the end of days. But the state of Israel could also become the throne of the messiah."[2]

Gush thinkers denounce peace, for war is the only way to preserve the unity of the people and prevent its disintegration. Relations between Israel and other nations should be based on "that eternal hatred, cultivated mainly during the times that the Jews were a persecuted minority among the gentiles."[3] The enmity that ensues toward all non-Jews extends as far as sanctioning their killing, women and children not excluded, and is the background of the following statement by Rabbi Eliezer Waldenberg, winner of the Israel Prize for 1976: "I, for instance, am in favor of the Halachic ruling that a gentile must not be allowed to live in Jerusalem. If we were to follow the ruling properly, we should have expelled all the gentiles from Jerusalem and cleansed it completely."[4]

While pointing out that the Gush grew out of an approach that is the antithesis of traditional, secular Zionism, which aspired to normalize the Jewish people, Rubinstein fails to face several questions. If so, how could this movement, which comprises only a small segment of the Israeli public, succeed in imposing its aims on successive Israeli governments, the majority of whose members, whether of the Left or of the Right, have always considered themselves secular Zionists whose aim is normalization? How could it gain such influence among the general public? How did it channel huge sums from government and Jewish Agency sources to finance its aims? What has been its message to the secular public? How did broad circles of the nonreligious public accord legitimacy to both the ideology and the approach, which posit "Zionism" and the "supreme national interest" above the legal, institutionalized structure of the state?

A part of this success may derive from the fact that Floresheim's analysis of both the Jewish people and the role of Eretz Israel in its history corresponds with historical facts and with the popular awareness of these historical facts far more than does the official Zionist historiography and ideology, as I have tried to show. That the ideology has lost its meaning and that the public feels that it fails to explain reality, despite the lip service universally accorded to it, explains in part the attractive power of the opposite, essentially anti-Zionist, ideology. This reversal is camouflaged by the Zionist phraseology used by Gush leaders and thinkers, as well as by the traditional Zionist methods it seemingly uses ("settlement on the land," "redemption of the soil") and its manipulation of the traditional organs of the Zionist establishment to gain its ends. But the very reversal of the normalization trend shows that we are facing a post-Zionist phenomenon. This means that even when a new ideology represents itself as Zionist, it is no more than camouflage, as the Israeli public finds it difficult to free itself from the prestige of the term *Zionism*.

The stirrings of the movement preceded its formation by decades. The normalization ideology was abandoned long before the appearance of the Gush. We have seen in previous chapters the failure of Mapai, headed by Ben-Gurion, to find a common nonreligious denominator of all Jewish population elements, when the flimsiness of the purported common national basis became apparent. Jewish communities in Islamic countries, for example, had not undergone the national transformation that took place among a part of East and Central European Jewry, thus remaining religious-communal in outlook. As a result, the Labor party leadership, consciously secular and atheistic, discovered that it had no common ground whatever with these communities.

Thus the fifties witnessed a search for a common denominator of the Jews in Israel, and it was found that the only factor of this description lies not in the national but in the religious sphere. As one of the most distinguished contemporary Jewish historians, Ya'akov Katz, puts it: "The Jewish national tradition is stamped with religion. Anyone who resorts to Jewish symbols, almost involuntarily links the affinity to religion with the national identification."[5]

As a result, the secular, atheistic values of the labor movement were seen as nationally divisive, and the abolition of the separate labor educational system by a government controlled by labor parties was supposed to strengthen national unity. But whereas religious content was instilled into the general educational system, the separate religious educational systems were left intact. The corollary is that a proletarian or secular-atheistic education is "divisive," whereas a religious education "unifies." Thus nationalism is reabsorbed in religion, whereas, historically and essentially, Jewish nationalism could rise only on the ruins of the Jewish religious world.

A retreat from the national definition of Judaism, implying that the specific contents of Judaism are solely and purely religious, thus has been in progress since the fifties and sixties. In addition, the ongoing educational emphasis on the lessons of the Holocaust was designed to inculcate in the younger generation the axiom about the Jewish "community of fate" at all times and at all places, thus nullifying the traditional Zionist doctrine that the normalization of the Jews will put an end to this community of fate and turn the Jews into a normal nation and not preferred targets of hostility. The state thus becomes just another ghetto, albeit a heavily armed one. This inculcation of Holocaust lessons, to the extent that for nonreligious Jews they have become the central content of Jewish consciousness and identity, is really tantamount to a deliberate breeding of paranoia. These lessons are not accompanied by any positive humanistic message, such as participation in a worldwide struggle of all peoples against dehumanization and genocide. The meaning of the Nazi genocide is limited to the Jewish victims, as if they were the only ones, and mention of the millions of non-Jews murdered by the Nazis, first and foremost the Gypsies, who were exterminated with the same thoroughness as the Jews, is suppressed. Thus, instead of cultivating universal human values of a fight against the evil that can befall all and which should unite all against it, a ghettolike, exclusivist mentality is bred. This mentality, acquiescing in the notion of the abysmal division between "circumcised" and "uncircumcised," condones in advance any inhuman treatment of non-Jews, for the prevailing mythology is that "all peoples collaborated with the Nazis in the destruction of Jewry," hence everything is permissible to Jews in their relationship to other peoples.

The emphasis on a common fate, which received its main encouragement by means of the Eichmann trial, foreshadows the doctrine of the eternal enmity between the Jews and the rest of humanity, regardless of whether the Jews are a nation dwelling in their own country or whether they are scattered among the gentiles. If Zionism is indeed incapable of eradicating the common fate, as implied by the Israeli educational and propaganda indoctrination, then many of the Gush doctrines can be deduced from this indoctrination with an almost mathematical rigor. And if religion is indeed the true inner content of Jewishness, it is obvious that secular Zionism is merely a passing phase of Jewish history.

Furthermore, if religion is true Judaism, and if the state is an expression of the nation, an instrument for the realization of Zionism, then obviously the instrument is subordinate to the goal, and it follows that the laws of the state must make way for the realization of Zionism. But as Zionism has never been a body of doctrine held by consensus, nor have its aims ever been defined in an unambiguous manner (for they include the aims of Achad Ha'am on one hand and Jabotinsky on the other, or of Ben-Gurion and Avraham Stern), permission is thereby granted in principle to anyone who considers himself a Zionist to define according to his own lights what Zionism is and what its goals are and to see his views as superior to and overriding the laws of the state. In the final analysis, anyone who views the state as an instrument for the realization of Zionism cannot submit to the authority of the general will represented by the Knesset, as this general will does not express Zionism and the Jewish people. The Knesset, after all, includes non-Zionist and non-Jewish delegates, such as the representatives of the Arab minority and the Communist party, or any other political grouping that may define itself as non-Zionist and run for the Knesset. This general will cannot then express the pure, "authentic" reason for the existence of the state. The only legitimate general will, according to this approach, could be that of the Jewish people, as Israel was meant to be the state and homeland of the Jewish people. But again, within the Jewish people many, perhaps even the majority, are not Zionists (whatever the meaning of this term), and many hardly consider themselves Jews, and at any rate the vast majority never intended to visit Israel, let alone settle in it. The general will of the Jewish people, even if it were possible to verify it by elections and representatives, is hardly Zionist. The general will of which the Zionists spoke is not necessarily that of the Jews who actually live today; it involves a far more abstract entity, "the ageless Jewish people," a metahistorical, imaginary being, which manifests itself in history but some-how exists outside and above it. This being is supposed to have a will of its own, but, being indefinable and never having had a formal embodiment (except in the Halacha, which expresses the will of God—but the secular Zionist does not recognize the authority of the Halacha), any Zionist is entitled to interpret it in any way he pleases and still consider his interpre-tation as outweighing the law of the country. And, it should be noted, the law of the country has indeed been often violated to achieve Zionist ends, like the confiscation by the authorities of Arab lands on the flimsiest pre-texts, or as happened when the territory of some Maronite villages in Gali-lee was seized by neighboring Jewish villages, who refused to relinquish it even when ordered to do so by the Supreme Court.

Thus, as far as the secular public was concerned, the activities of the Gush had a priori legitimation. Both religion and the "Zionism of force," which consecrates faits accomplis, have always been largely beyond the reach of the law. The Zionism of force even enjoyed a certain macho pres-tige, as a way of getting things done with scant attention to legalistic nice-ties. This sort of tough-minded pragmatism has always been prevalent among the settlement movements of labor Zionism, as well as in business and administration, suiting as it does the Israeli national ethos, charac-terized by initiative and aggressiveness.

That a large proportion of the Israeli population emigrated from pre-political Islamic societies, where nationalism had yet to develop, may also have helped Israeli nationalism to become absorbed by religion, a contribu-tory factor to the appearance of the Gush. But this was a strictly subsidiary element, since the participation of the Oriental Jewish community in Gush activities is quite low. All the leaders and most of the members of the move-ment are from Ashkenazi East European backgrounds, mainly the circles that underwent the national transformation to only a limited extent, namely the religious Zionists. These have preserved the traditions and cul-ture of the exclusivist religious community and have often fallen under the influence of the most extreme elements in Judaism, far more extreme than the Oriental rabbinate.

Zvi Ra'anan maintains that religious Zionism, the cradle of the Gush, consists of two main currents.[6] The first, which has been dominant through most of the history of Zionism, was born of a partial absorption and accep-tance by religious Judaism of elements of modern civilization. This current rationalized the acceptance of Jewish political independence, with its im-plied violation of the stricture against forcing the hand of God, by citing the Halachic precept that the Holy Land must be settled. It thus retained its beliefs and traditional way of life, yet joined the Zionist movement as a junior partner. From the very outset, religious Zionism was subject to con-stant harassment and criticism from ultra-Orthodox circles for violating this stricture. They in turn defended themselves by accentuating the rescue aspect of their Zionism. They spoke of the need to save the Jewish people in

Eastern Europe from its poverty and degradation and from the physical danger it was subject to. There were messianic elements in their thinking, but these were suppressed—on one hand because such elements were anathema and sacrilege to the ultra-Orthodox and on the other because these religious Zionists were embarrassed to reveal such thinking to the rationalist secular Zionists, who might consider them unenlightened. They thus suffered from a double sense of inferiority, lacking a center of their own or a clear self-definition.

These were the people who founded the Mizrachi and Hapoel Hamizrachi movements, the religious kibbutz movement and its youth movement, Bnei Akiva, all of which were united after the establishment of the state within the National Religious party (NRP). Politically, the party always accepted the leadership of the Mapai Labor party, and its leadership constituted the dovish wing of the Zionist and Israeli establishment. Their moderation stemmed from their very position midway between Zionist secularism and orthodoxy, as well as from their traditionalist Jewish legacy of caution and anxiety in relation to the gentiles, feelings which the secular sector had largely shed in the national transformation it had undergone as a result of its revolt against Jewish tradition.

The self-image of the national religious youth, as well as its image in the eyes of the secular public at large, was then one of weakness, compromise, and to some extent, of parasitism. The secular majority had in fact always tended to regard the entire religious community as to some extent parasitical, and largely ignored the differences that split the religious community into Zionists and anti-Zionists, Neturei Karta and Agudat Yisrael, etc. They were conceived, justly or unjustly, as preferring to engage in business and trade and to avoid manual or productive (in the sense that labor Zionism defined the term) work. Also, the fact that ultra-Orthodox youth have shirked military service on the excuse that they are yeshiva students has created the impression that most religious youths, even the Zionists among them, do so. Thus from the security aspect as well they are thought of as parasites on the secular public. Beyond all else, the religious circles, even the Zionists among them, seemed to the secularists to be a continuation of the same abhorred exilic caste-community existence, which the secular public wished to erase from its memory.

This was the basic attitude of the secular public toward the religious community before and after the establishment of the state, through to the Six-Day War. But underground pressures were at work even before that. In the late fifties, traditional Zionism began to lose its meaning, and the conquest in 1967 of large territories aroused religious and mystical sentiments even among circles that until then had considered themselves secular. An eschatological mood took root, awaiting the realization of the messianic vision. In certain religious Zionist circles, mainly in Bnei Akiva, this atmosphere provided a fertile ground for the release of suppressed states of mind that originated in eschatological conceptions of Zionism.

The spiritual genealogy of this approach contains luminaries from various currents of Jewish thought, including Martin Buber, Abraham J. Heschel, Joseph B. Soloveichik, and Moshe Una. All of them have rejected the term *nation* in describing the Jewish people, claiming that the Jews are a unique phenomenon, partaking in a sanctity beyond rational definition. The same goes for the relationship between the people and its Promised Land, a relationship that differs in essence from that of normal nations.

But the most important direct influence on the thinking of these circles was that of Rabbi Avraham Yitzhak Hacohen Kook (1865–1935), also known by the acronym the Raya. His greatest innovation in evaluating the Zionist movement was a conviction that in their heart of hearts all returnees to Zion wish to return to God—even though this desire is still suppressed among some of them and they are unaware of it. Raanan writes:

> Therefore, secularism is merely a veil. The Zionist pioneer, by the root of his soul, is not a breaker of Halachic strictures but a potential, though unconscious, penitent. . . .
>
> By this reasoning, the Raya lent sanctity to the whole Zionist movement, despite its dominant secular character, and religious Zionism was thereby released, at least in this point, from its contradictory position and became elevated in the view of its adherents to a status of a leading minority elite.[7]

The Raya's conception may then be defined as a two-stage process of salvation. The first is the stage of secular Zionism, which builds the country and fights for it while being guided unconsciously by the divine plan of redemption. This prepares the ground for the second stage of conscious salvation, led by religious Zionism. This is where the younger generation of religious Zionists, mostly members of Bnei Akiva, found its raison d'être.

The Bnei Akiva youths, educated in state religious schools, found it difficult to resign themselves to the atmosphere of a religious ghetto, of a minority living under the shadow and leadership of the secular majority, according to Raanan. As children they witnessed the War of Independence and as teenagers the Sinai campaign. But being Orthodox, they had been taught that they should study Torah even when their secular contemporaries were fighting wars. The euphoria that attended Israel's victory in the Six-Day War led a group of young students from the Merkaz Ha'rav Yeshiva to meet in the autumn of that year. At that meeting they read in the victory all the signs of the approaching salvation, seeing just around the corner "the redemption of the Jewish people, chosen by God to be his own, a solitary among the nations, to which ordinary human reason and the 'natural' laws of history do not apply."[8]

But these messianic stirrings apparently needed the shock of the Yom Kippur War to ripen into fruit. These young people conceived of this war not as the contradiction but the confirmation of the messianic idea, as a purification by suffering, as the labor pains of the messianic revelation.

Israel's feelings of isolation, deepened by the war, received a compensatory theological interpretation: "The war of the gentiles is a war against God, and since they cannot fight against God directly, they fight against Israel."[9]

This circle established Gush Emunim, which has undertaken to realize God's plan for redemption in our time, and thus, by a single audacious leap, succeeded in revolutionizing its self-image. No longer is it a marginal satellite of active secular Zionism. On the contrary, secular Zionism is but the stage that prepares the ground for the appearance of messianic Zionism, the palpable realization of the age-old hope of Judaism, according to the Gush interpretation of Rabbi Kook's teachings. And, on the other front, religious Zionism is not inferior to anti-Zionist orthodoxy. On the contrary, the latter failed to understand the real meaning of the historical processes of recent generations, failed to fathom God's plan for the salvation of Jewry, comprehended only by the members of the Gush, who are realizing it by their own efforts. In this manner the Gush members placed themselves, in their own view, in the center of Jewish history. And as Judaism is the central meaning of the world and the arrival of the messiah is the key to world history, they consider themselves as entrusted with the execution of the central course of world history, the summit toward which history has striven since creation. In this manner, the inferiority complex of religious Zionism was solved. The solution, however, was typically neurotic—it converted an inferiority complex into a superiority complex, thereby sealing itself ever more hermetically in a cell completely divorced from reality. This undoubtedly has been the secret of the great influence the Gush has had on most circles of religious Zionism, and of the fact that one hardly hears any criticism of its actions from those religious Zionists who obviously disagree with Gush ideology and actions. The Gush ideology seemed to turn religious Zionism, in its own eyes, into the leader of the nation. Its traditional dovishness collapsed when countered by the self-importance and psychological compensation provided by this view of history, and doubly so since this dovishness, in many cases, was nothing but an expression of exilic caution and timidity, not of moral conviction. For, were it not for this belief, were it not for the self-importance it provides to religious Zionists by helping them to conceive themselves as fulfilling a leading role in the historical processes undergone by the Jewish people and the state, they would have reverted to their previous, true state, one of a shaky, undignified compromise between the secular political forces and antipolitical, anti-Zionist orthodoxy. The messianic ideology and the structure of the divine plan of redemption are precisely tailored to the psychological needs of religious Zionism at this historical juncture.

But what are the actual contents of the messianism and redemption that the Gush advocates? They do not represent a universal human vision. One of the Gush's main characteristics is its abhorrence of anything that is not Jewish—another legacy of the East European ghetto communities. Nor do they represent an otherworldly state. On the contrary, following Maimonides and the Talmud, the Gush insists that the only difference between the present world and the messianic era is that Jews will be freed from subjugation to other nations. The world will continue its course as before, with its rich and its poor, its strong and its weak. Even the messiah will eventually die and be succeeded on the throne by his son and grandson. "Redemption," Raanan writes, "is conceived without any universal-cosmic peace, but as a Jewish-imperial peace, under the auspices of God."[10]

The aim of the Gush, then, is a Jewish empire subject to the rule of the Halacha in which the "aliens" are subject to the Jews, and even the Jewish society will be divided by classes and human exploitation. What this amounts to, then, is a daydream—a daydream that focuses on exacting revenge on the gentiles by that sector of the Israeli public which, owing to its ghetto community origins, its hatred and fear of the world, has not even begun to internalize the national liberation and the openness to the world that such a liberation involves. But this daydream also reflects in an extremely distorted way the deification of power, which, as previously noted, had become a major motivation of the Israeli establishment and which is at the root of the contradiction that developed between Zionism and the normalization of the Jewish people. In this respect, at least, the Gush has become the most faithful exponent of a Zionism that had lost its raison d'être and had become a blind striving for power. The Gush expresses a drive for an incessant, limitless expansion, for it envisages a future of endless struggle between Israel and the surrounding world, the inevitable cost of ignoring the rights of others and expansion at their expense. In this respect, there is no distinction between Arabs and non-Arabs. That is why the Gush talks about the "illusion" of an Israeli-Arab peace and about the "eternal hatred for the Jews," which this expansion, of course, provokes, and which in its turn serves as a pretext for further war and expansion. That the Gush had never set itself an ultimate and defined territorial limit is highlighted by its bitter opposition to the evacuation of the Sinai and the settlements established there in sovereign Egyptian territory—even though the Sinai had never been included even in the Biblical "boundaries of the promise."

Such a political conception challenges the basic conventions of international life, according to which every nation has a right to self-determination and each state admitted to the family of nations must keep to the rules of international behavior and accept the limitations attendant on its international obligations. But the Gush accepts with equanimity the conflict its approach will create with the entire world. That raises questions. Whence this calm confidence? What is the meaning of this somnambulist assurance? The only explanation seems to be that this calm is the result of the protected position of the Gush within the Israeli system. It was the secularists who founded Zionism. It was they who established the physical framework of Israel's existence, fought its wars, were forced to compromise with its enemies and friends. It was they who came in contact with the real external world. Religious Zionists, many of whom have never served or fought in the army, who have always been generously subsidized by world Jewry and the Israeli establishment, live in a protected, illusive world in which the IDF is omnipotent, in which there are always funds available for expropriatory settlements in the occupied territories, in which one never feels the price that the state, the people, and the army must pay for such a messianic policy. Within this protected bubble, Gush thinkers and members can spin their eschatological schemes and speak calmly about "eternal warfare" and about the desirable aspect of the hatred of the *goyim*. Thus Gush members continue in effect their traditional parasitism on the secular Israeli establishment, the very parasitism that moved them in the first place to try to reverse their self-image, and which by this very attempt increased their parasitism by a quantum leap. Until this reversal, many of them had dodged military service, but now their settlements have become a millstone on the neck of the army, which has to protect them in their exposed positions among a hostile Arab population. Before, they had limited themselves to the handouts of the secular establishment; now the policy they forced on it is causing severe damage to the country's very economic foundations.

Essentially, the antigentile policy of the Gush is a regression to the xenophobic, nonhistorical existence of the ghetto, though now seemingly from the opposite side. The ghetto shrank into itself in fear of the external world. Messianism aims at fighting and overcoming that world. Both approaches derive from a negation of the external world. But the rules of international existence are based on the recognition that no monism can exist in international life, that a state's functioning in the international arena necessitates giving due consideration to forces, pressures, and limitations which even the mightiest cannot ignore. The world and reality are always stronger than any unit operating within it. That seems to be the reason why the Gush clings in the last resort to the mystic promise of the messiah and the divine plan, because in the real world such a program can never be realized and is bound to result in disaster. That is why the movement pokes ridicule at the rationalists and the faint at heart, who know that history never ends and its processes are inescapable. As a matter of fact, the movement's very assumption that even after the arrival of the messiah the world will take its course, that history will continue, is an advance admission of defeat. If the messianic kingdom will be subject to the laws of history, it is bound to decline and fall like all kingdoms before it, including the Jewish ones. The believers who try to keep their faith after this collapse will undoubtedly find for it any number of excuses, such as "the time was not yet ripe" and "we have been exiled from our country for our sins." It would again be the old cycle of imaginary sin incurring just divine punishment, a closed, hermetic, self-sustaining, completely impenetrable psychological mold.

But how did this mindset succeed in gaining control, to a large extent, of the policy of the state of Israel, and force the saner elements in the Israeli political system to bend to its will? To comprehend this, we must take a brief look at basic structural interests of the kibbutz and moshav movements and the political organizations connected with them, bearing in mind that the Gush has always felt that its natural allies are to be found in the labor movement, and has even imitated the labor movement's methods of rapid settlement (the "stockade and tower" settlements of the thirties and forties).

By the late fifties and early sixties, the country's agricultural deployment was fairly complete. It had achieved a high level of efficiency and mechanization, which placed it among the world's leading agricultural systems. It supplied all domestic demand or, alternatively, developed crops whose export counterbalanced equivalent agricultural imports, like the export of fruit and flowers in exchange for grain. By the early sixties, there was no longer any need for a significant increase of agriculture (taking into account the country's limited water resources, as well), and hidden unemployment began to spread in the kibbutzim and moshavim, alleviated in the kibbutzim by turning increasingly to industrial development. In brief, agricultural settlement, which from the beginning was almost synonymous with Zionism, reached the saturation point and even went beyond it. Henceforth, industrial development and research became the focal area of investment and effort. The kibbutz and moshav movements, despite their high level of development, their wealth and excellent connections with the establishment, lost their primacy and became secondary to industrialization and its attendant urbanization. That the country's future lay primarily in industry and not in agriculture was obvious to many far-sighted persons even before the establishment of the state. Now it became the conventional wisdom. Demographically, also, a paradoxical set of shears was in operation: the more efficient agriculture became, the less people it had to employ, thus diminishing its share of the population and reducing further this population's political and economic influence.

The conquest of the West Bank, Gaza Strip, Golan Heights, and Sinai Peninsula gave the land settlement movements a new lease on life. They began pressing for settlement in the conquered territories, to be carried out, of course, by them, thus making them again the spearhead of the Zionist enterprise. In the name of this supreme national goal they could again demand priority in the allocation of national resources. Thus one could set again in motion the well-oiled machinery of the Land Settlement Department of the Jewish Agency and the relevant departments of the ministries of agriculture, housing, health, etc., thoroughly versed for decades in the techniques of rural and urban settlement and regional planning. This is not meant to impute conscious opportunism to these movements, the cynical manipulation of nationalist slogans in order to regain their leading role among the national priorities. Nor is there any doubt that people like the venerable leader of Achdut Haavoda, Yitzhak Tabenkin, were completely sincere in their belief that the settlement of the territories by Jews and their annexation were of the utmost national importance. The Achdut Haavoda faction had always been activist as regards the frontiers of the Yishuv and the state. But it is impossible to ignore the structural interests that coincided with the settlement drive, nor the fact that such interests have a way of generating ideologies to suit them.

Furthermore, some sections of the kibbutz movement felt that the renewal of the settlement drive might revive the flagging pioneering spirit among their youth. The settlement of the veteran movements in areas demarcated by the government within the Allon plan, designed to create Israeli strategic control over the West Bank while avoiding as far as possible any friction with the Arab population (except in the Hebron area), preceded by a few years the Gush settlements, which began only after the Yom Kippur War. But the very fact that the Ein Vered Circle, which consisted of the annexationist elements of the labor movement, found a common language with the Gush and collaborated with it shows that there was no essential difference between the two approaches. We see here the embodiment of the paradox—messianic antipolitical energies, reflecting the apolitical and exclusivist attitudes of traditional ghetto Judaism, establish an alliance with the same pioneering secularist movements that led to the establishment of the state but rebel against its authority, whereas the state lacks sufficient self-confidence in being a state and allows itself to be coerced by the same forces that have always viewed themselves superior to it.

As Raanan comments, the attitude of the Gush to state authority is paradoxical. While religious Jews in all other countries unquestioningly accept the authority of the state, the Gush, in a Jewish state, refuses to accept its authority. In this respect, there is no difference in principle between the anti-Zionist Neturei Karta and the Gush. The former rejects the state because it tries to bring redemption by mundane means, while the latter rejects it (in the sense of being an expression of the general will) in the name of redemption. But the rejection of the democratic general will as embodied in the state contains the seeds of civil war, of the ripping of Israeli society apart.

The question remains: what is the common basis of the Gush and its secular allies in defying the state and its elected institutions? The secularists, after all, do not consider themselves subject to divine authority, and they do not consider the Halacha as superior to the laws of the state.

Two traditions are at work here: that of the dissident underground movements of the mandatory period, which refused to accept the authority of the Jewish Agency and the Zionist movement (mainly Lehi, the Stern Group), and that of the activist pioneering movements (mainly Achdut Haavoda, which during the struggle against the British was closest to Lehi). Gush messianic thinking is very close to that of Israel Scheib (who wore the nom de guerre "Eldad"), formerly a member of the leadership nucleus of Lehi and propagator of the idea of "the Kingdom of Israel," which, according to the "Principles of Revival" formulated by Lehi founder Avraham Stern, will extend as far as the "frontiers of the promise," from the Euphrates to Wadi El-Arish. Scheib is indeed one of the most influential spiritual mentors of the Gush. The argument which Lehi used in its call on Yishuv youth to defy the authority of the official Zionist institutions was that these were not truly democratic and representative because they operated with the permission of the British and therefore did not reflect the true and free will of the people. National authority is obligatory only in a free state. This argument, for what it is worth, was copied in the sovereign state of Israel to justify the defiance of established state authority. The argument this time was that there exist superior national interests, which are beyond the proper authority of any legislative body. This means that these interests are the true, unwritten constitution of the state of Israel. Scheib has argued on occasion that if the Knesset were to abrogate the Law of the Return, this abrogation would be invalid, since the state was established for the purpose of that law. But nevertheless, what are these superior laws, who formulated them, who accepted them? Scheib refers back to the "Principles of Revival." But these principles themselves are in need of a legitimizing authority, for the fact that they were formulated by Stern carries no weight as far as the state of Israel and the Jewish people go. In such straits, Scheib has been forced to fall back on religious messianism to legitimize his doctrines.

Neither is the tradition of the radical elements in the labor movement so far removed from this contempt for any state authority, whatever its source. When Ephraim Ben Chaim, who had his origins in the kibbutz movement and who became a prominent member and spokesman of the Techiya (Revival) party, which included the Gush, was asked by Raanan whether he was bothered by the fact that it was the authority of the Jewish state, not that of the mandatory government, that was being flaunted, he replied: "The Kibbutz Meuchad movement has not always behaved in the most parliamentary manner. . . . In my own opinion, the whole kibbutz movement—and definitely Kibbutz Meuchad—has always considered itself, well, not above the government, but we have always held that it is we who established the state and not the other way around, and therefore this matter [of democracy] never bothered me."[11]

Of course, the Palmach, or the IDF which followed it, or the dissident underground movements could all claim that it was they who established the state and not the other way around, and therefore also flaunt its authority. It would be interesting to hear Ben Chaim's opinion about such claims. But absurd as the argument is, it sheds a lurid light on the man's way of thinking, as well as that of those in the labor movement who share his views. For them, pioneering and settlement in "redeemed" territories are the very essence of Zionism. That, in their eyes, was the purpose for which the state was established. And if the state does not follow this existential commandment, it thereby violates the supreme unwritten law, the real constitution of the state of Israel.

Ben Chaim's statement clarifies the common denominator of the religious Gush and the secular circles connected with and supporting it. What then is the ultimate goal of these various movements? I previously noted that despite the preaching of the Gush about the "frontiers of the promise," it violently opposed the evacuation of the Sinai desert, although the Sinai was never included in these frontiers. In the early stages of the Lebanon War, there was even talk of establishing settlements in southern Lebanon and of considering it part of Eretz Israel. Scheib believes the borders promised to Abraham by God are the true and "natural" borders of the "Kingdom of Israel." Apparently the concept of "Greater Eretz Israel" is a very flexible one and could be any place conquered by the Israeli army. Borders are then nothing but a function of power relations. It is worthwhile to recall the opposition of the Achdut Haavoda founders in the twenties, based on their feelings of growing and expanding strength, to reaching any final agreement with the Arabs as regards the boundaries of the Zionist enterprise. Even then they viewed the limits as a function of the power relations between the two movements.

The truth of the matter is that deep down all of these bodies, religious and secular, in the settlement movement are united by a drive for unlimited expansion, by an untrammeled will to power. They do not view the rights and interests of other peoples as boundaries to be respected; they do not view others as people with whom one should live in peace, but rather as hostile obstructions. The Gush's rationale is "redemption." The extremists of Achdut Haavoda (to be strictly distinguished from moderate and sane elements in the party, such as Yitzhak Ben-Aharon and the late Yigal Allon) rationalize this drive by claiming that Jewish people throughout the world are faced with the the danger of another Holocaust and should be concentrated in Israel. For this reason, borders must be extended to make room for all of them. Both groups try to reinforce their positions with the claim that the hope for peace with the neighboring Arab states and the Palestinian people is an illusion, that the Arabs will never consent to make peace with Israel (and indeed, it is hardly conceivable that they would, faced with a constantly expanding state), and that their proposals for settlement of the conflict are nothing more than booby traps. Sadat's peace initiative, for instance, was nothing but a sedative whose aim was to create a false sense of calm while preparing the ground for a sudden blow. The cooling off of Israeli-Egyptian relations as a result of the Israeli invasion of Lebanon and nonimplementation of the Camp David accords as regards the Palestinians was touted by the Gush and its secular allies as flagrant evidence of Egypt's treachery and double dealing and as proof that true peace with the Arabs is impossible. The Gush does indeed speak of its desire for peace, but this peace will be achieved only when the Arabs reconcile themselves to all of Israel's conquests. In exchange for peace, they declare, Israel can offer only peace, not concessions and compromise, which are but "a surrender" and "a beginning of the end." Zionism, by their lights, is not the return of the Jewish people to history and its normalization, as orthodox Zionism saw it, but a continuous attack on the non-Jewish world, a "historical revenge" of the Jewish people on the non-Jewish world, in complete disregard of the interests of the Jewish Diaspora, which could be greatly endangered by such a policy. This is nothing but a continuation of the "ruthless Zionism" policy. But in contradistinction to the situation in the thirties, there is no organized persecution of the Jews anywhere in the world. Fear for the worsening conditions of the Jewish masses in great parts of Europe could serve as a lame excuse for the opposition to a final settlement with the Arab national movement in the twenties and thirties by Achdut Haavoda. There is no such excuse now.

These facts are rationalized away by the Gush with the argument that the eternal conflict between Jew and non-Jew will sooner or later reactivate the persecution of the Jews; and Achdut Haavoda activists argue, as noted, that the Holocaust is but a precursor to what will inevitably befall Jews everywhere. But these arguments raise the query: what is the reason for this universal condition of the Jews? why is the Jew, always and everywhere, in danger of annihilation? why, even in his own country, is he trapped in a state of endless warfare? Inevitably, this leads to metaphysical and mystical conclusions about the unique nature of the Jewish people, persecuted and discriminated against not because of palpable historical and sociological causes but owing to some metahistorical curse, because of a difference in kind between "circumcised" and "uncircumcised." Ben Chaim says that "another aspect common to us, or most of us, is this matter of a return to roots," namely theology and mysticism. Another prominent secular spokesman of the Greater Israel movement, Eliezer Livneh, wrote extensively about "the essential difference of our culture from the materialistic-permissive-nihilistic Western culture" and of the need to sever the connections with the latter. We see then that another trait common to all these factions, both secular and religious, apart from their aggressive expansionism, is their spiritual-cultural self-segregation and their turning inward, toward "roots," in short, reversion to the self-enclosed community, divorced from history, though now equipped with tanks, jet bombers, and nonconventional armaments.

If I am correct in surmising, as I have in the preceding chapters, that the profoundest psychopolitical motivation of the Zionist movement from the Uganda crisis on has been the accumulation of power, the tremendous influence these minority groups have had on the Israeli political establishment becomes comprehensible. Basically, deep down, most decision makers in the country identify with Gush aims, though most have rejected the Gush and its allies' methods because of practical considerations, not moral or ideological qualms. They have doubted that these aims could be realized or have felt their realization would incur too many risks. They have, therefore, been highly vulnerable to the Gush argument that in the past, too, there were goals that were thought to be too ambitious but that, in the course of time, were realized. The basic assumption used by the Gush in its approach to the governing establishment is roughly as follows: we all aspire to an unlimited expansion of our power and influence; you, however, are people of little faith; you don't trust the power of the Jewish people. Since this assumption about the common aspirations of the Gush and most of its opponents is correct, the opposition, despite being in the majority, is defeated in advance. Each time the Gush proved that certain goals were achievable, that steps which had aroused opposition for fear of provoking disaster were nevertheless taken and disaster did not follow, the Gush position grew stronger.

That leads to a paradoxical development. The concentration on the creation of Jewish power in Eretz Israel, irrespective of the fate of the Jews abroad, was indispensable to the establishment of the state and for the cultivation of the nucleus of a separate, sovereign Hebrew people. But the addiction to unlimited expansion and power involves a renewed ghettolike self-segregation, a return to roots and a messianic policy, that would lead to the ruin of the state of Israel and to the undermining of the condition of the Jews everywhere. The original aim of secular Zionism was not the attainment of power but of normalization, the return of the Jewish people to history as an equal. Normalization as a nation implies a change in the Israeli populace from a religious community to a national commonwealth, a separation from the Jewish Diaspora. This separation entails renouncing exploitation of and dependency on the Diaspora, refusing to serve as the focus of Diaspora daydreams, and disowning the claim to be its center. Normalization means that the Jewish people is entitled to continue living in the Diaspora without feeling inferior to the Israeli nation, while the Israeli nation will stop viewing itself as the future of the Jewish people.

Normalization, the return to the family of nations, also requires, of course, a return to the power game waged among the nations. But a power game does not necessarily mean a game of war and mutual exclusivity. Ordinary relations between nations are not conflictual but negotiatory, aiming at mutual accommodations. A study of the history of political units shows that most of the time they live at peace with each other.

Just as private individuals could not long survive if they regarded all the people around them with hatred and fear, in the real world, nations must be in mutual contact. The essential basis for the functioning of a political unit among others of its kind is the recognition of their equality as political units, for only such recognition enables it to enter mutual contacts and contract mutual obligations. Any nation that opts out of its international context is bound to collapse within short order. It would cease to send and receive mail. Its telephone and telex connections with the outside would be cut. It would receive no credit in foreign banks. It could neither export nor import. The very concept of a people unto itself is essentially antipolitical, typical of a religious sect but not of a state.

The constant state of warfare isolationism imposes could entail either of two results. If Israel conquers further territories and subjugates rather than expels the population, the Jews will rapidly become a minority and the occupied non-Jewish population the majority. An ever-growing share of Is-

rael's national energies will have to be invested in the suppression and policing of the "alien" population. Under such circumstances, the number of
Israelis leaving the country, either for reasons of conscience or because of
the never-ending tensions involved in the suppression of a mutinous population aided from across the frontiers, will steadily increase, thus reducing
even further the proportion of the ruling versus ruled populations. The
surrounding countries, fearing the expansionist tendencies of the state, will
try to damage it to the best of their ability. In short, Israel will become a
violent, fear-ridden police state—a country that is not only constantly at
war with its neighbors but is also embroiled in an ongoing battle between
the rulers and the ruled. On the other hand, if Israel expels most of the
Arab population from newly conquered territories, it will be surrounded by
an even more violent and vengeful ring of refugee camps, and the Arab
determination to reject this foreign body in its midst will grow even firmer.
The final result will be the same as in the first scenario.

A third possibility is the imperial one, following the pattern set by durable empires in the past: an expansion absorbing new populations, assimilating them and making them organic in the structure of the state. But that
is the very possibility rejected by the Gush and its secular allies. They follow the pattern of European overlordship of the natives in America and
Australia: a pattern of violent settlement accompanied by the dispossession
and enslavement of the natives. But the population which the Israeli Right
wishes to dispossess is far from being primitive. It is quite highly developed, and its rate of development may be even greater than the Israeli one.
Furthermore, with its Arab brethren beyond the borders it vastly outnum-
bers the Israeli population, as do its economic resources.

Even from the most basic *realpolitik* point of view, then, the Gush policy
runs counter to any imaginable logic. A ghettolike exclusivity is diametrically opposed to any possibility of expansion, for expansion means being
ready to open oneself to new contents. Furthermore, it is feasible only when
one is backed by considerable human reserves, which are nonexistent in
this case.

The development of the predilection for expansionism leads to the denial of the principle of popular sovereignty and the imposition of the will
of minority groups on the public as a whole, to the undermining of the
country's political (and economic) base and its standing in the family of
nations, and eventually to the undermining not only of its power base but
also of its political and moral foundations. Zionism (at least in this perverted aspect of it), the progenitor of the state, is now the main danger to
its existence.

The Gush and its periphery view themselves as self-sacrificing, frugal,
true pioneers, settling in dangerous circumstances, like the labor movement pioneers. As a matter of fact, they risk nothing. They receive ample
subsidies from the so-called hostile government. Their pioneering frugality
adds up to government grants for handsome, expensively built villas, even

though the settlements have no economic value and no reasonable chance that they will ever pay back the investment. The settlements' deployment adds nothing to security. On the contrary, the security forces are now burdened by the need to protect them.

In short, the Gush has remained what religious Zionism has always been: a parasitic hanger-on to the body of pragmatic, secular Zionism. Its expropriatory settlements are a nightmarish caricature of the raison d'être of Zionist settlement, the melting away of an ideology that has lost all meaning and functions in a vacuum. The emptiness of the settlements stage setting is but a reflection of the inner emptiness of the messianic movement and its secular adherents. It is a movement without any social or moral vision. All of its contents are Judaism, but it is a Judaism bereft of any value or content except the mechanical keeping of the Halacha (unless one defines chauvinist muscle-flexing as a value). Indeed, the whole being and activity of the Gush could be described as the power dream of the ghetto, the chance to play-act at vengeance on the *goyim* without having to pay the price of that vengeance, risking nothing, with no need to confront real enemies or to face reality in general—and thus ceasing to be a ghetto.

THIRTEEN

Conclusion

Israel and the Jewish People

Jewish impotence created the illusion that the essential attribute of independent national existence is military might. It also fostered the view of Zionism and the state of Israel as a historical revenge rather than as a means of becoming integrated as equals in both history and the family of nations.

Self-confident nations (and individuals) are not in a hurry to display force. They weigh their force and interests coolly, calculate what they wish to achieve and what they are willing to pay in order to achieve it, and behave accordingly. There is no doubt that in any accounting of the attributes of an independent nation, military-economic power is a major element. That does not mean that a nation that makes such an accounting is in a state of war with other nations. What it means is that it functions among them as an equal, in symbiotic relations that only rarely deteriorate into war. The relations between members of the European Community, for example, are those of close cooperation, in spite of elements of competition. Member nations wish the prosperity of the entire community; if any nation is unsuccessful, it could become a liability and impoverish the common organization. The United States desires the strength and wealth of Western Europe and Japan, despite their economic rivalry; their weakness would threaten the system as a whole. It has recently become clear that for the same reason the United States desires the prosperity of Eastern Europe. The assumption (typical of the age of mercantilism) that the success of one comes at the expense of another (a zero-sum game) is partially true only in war and is wholly true only under conditions of total warfare. Even so, during World War II the United States, for instance, did not seek the total destruction of Germany; in planning for the future the U.S. already considered Germany a vital component in the postwar global confrontation with the Soviet Union. In short, the system of sovereign states in the world is not anarchic; it is based on mutual balances and adjustments, with rivalries usually confined to the framework of games with recognized rules and with the requisite that all player-states have certain traits in common.

The thinking of the messianic Right in Israel fails to grasp the nature of international relations and is incapable of understanding the nature of an independent nation in the international arena. It imagines Israel's existence not in the world as it is but only in the Jewish world. The Jewish world is supposed to provide a sort of a protective envelope around the state (in an ironic reversal of the Zionist aim of providing protection for the Jewish people). But even if the Jewish world were interested in providing such a shield, it is too small and weak to permit such a flight from the facts of international life. The state must function as a state in order to exist at all. And it follows that the acceptance of the responsibilities of political existence also implies the acceptance of the rules of international behavior.

It is necessary therefore to change the basis of the Israeli national definition and found it on the conventional territorial principle—equality before the law of all citizens living within Israeli territory, irrespective of ethnic origins, race, community, religion, or sex. A national definition on the level of these differences will sooner or later lead to the fragmentation of the state. For example, the definition of the state as Jewish leads to a situation in which more than a third, and eventually a half, of the population within the Israeli political system, being non-Jewish, will not accept it and as a result will be in a state of open or suppressed revolt. This revolt will break out into the open as soon as it is felt that the dominant ethnic group is losing its grip.

Furthermore, Israel is located in an area that has been heterogeneous since the dawn of history. The ethnic homogeneity of areas such as Northern Europe, with their roughly uniform cultures and ethnic origins, cannot be duplicated in the Middle East. It cannot be duplicated even within the Jewish population of Israel. Since the region has always been a complex mosaic of ethnic and religious groups and since Israel is a mosaic itself, any attempt to impose a uniform way of life and identity on Israel or on the region as a whole is doomed to failure. In the entire Middle East there exists only one state with a unified, homogeneous national substance—Egypt. But even Egypt contains a large Copt minority. Israel, in order to survive, must not only create supraethnic and suprareligious frameworks; it also must accept in advance that it contains a broad variety of particularistic cultures and compensate for this by cultivating loyalty to the common state framework. To some extent the beginnings of such a situation already exist, with Moroccans, Yemenites, Russians, Poles, Americans, Germans, Ethiopians, and Latin Americans rubbing shoulders, vaguely unified by "Jewishness." What is needed now is to add to the mix the growing numbers of Muslim and Christian citizens, most of whom are much closer to Hebrew culture and language than the new immigrants, to say nothing of their intense connection to their ancestral land.

The shift of the national definition from ethnicity or religious allegiance to territoriality will entail a change in the nature of the connection between Israeli Jews and the Jewish world. This connection will then cease to be a state-political one and move more to the cultural and economic spheres, although it should be assumed that certain principles of political preference of the Jews will be kept, such as the readiness to grant asylum to any Jews who are persecuted for their Jewishness (just as the sister Palestinian state that one hopes will be established at Israel's side will undoubtedly extend similar refuge to any Palestinians living abroad). This asylum will not be accompanied by automatic citizenship. To gain that, the refugee would have to face ordinary tests of citizenship, which would be indifferent in respect of religion and nationality.

The elimination of the fear of Zionist expansion, which is one of the main reasons for Arab hostility toward Israel and the reluctance of a large part of the Arab world to make peace with it, will remove a major obstacle to a regional and later perhaps a federal collaboration of Israel with the Arabic-speaking countries. In this way the visions of Weizmann and Ben-Gurion in the twenties and of Lehi in the forties, of a regional federation with a Jewish state as an integral part of it, may yet become a reality. (I omit to mention the Canaanites in this connection, since they envisaged the "Hebraization" of the region by conquest—an impossible eventuality, as I showed earlier.)

I do not pretend to know or be able to prescribe how such a federal or confederal arrangement could be achieved. But it would appear that the only alternative to such integration in and becoming a fully legitimate member of the Middle Eastern system is the continuation of the current situation in which armed confrontation between Israel and its Arab neighbors erupts every few years. This alternative will, in turn, lead to the inevitable decline of Israel's military superiority vis-à-vis the Arab countries. History shows that such superiority is a transient affair. Such an evaluation is particularly apt when a small force, even a highly efficient one, confronts a large, long-winded force endowed with a great capacity for absorbing punishment. (Israel could never have withstood the attrition undergone by Iraq in its eight-year war with Iran followed by its capacity during the Gulf War to absorb frightful aerial punishment.) Under such conditions, the small force is compelled to strain all its resources and to act with maximum efficiency. But, though such an effort is a spur to continual alertness and advancement, the continual confrontation also obliges the opposing side to improve and increase its force in anticipation of the next round.

One way by which a small force can permanently overcome a large one is by becoming a large force itself, and it does this by assimilating and digesting its conquests, turning conquered populations into organic parts of its system and into full partners in its interests. Because of the exclusivist, self-segregating nature of the Jewish state of Israel, it is incapable of absorbing non-Jewish populations. Many Israeli Arabs and Druze have expressed the desire to become integrated as full patriotic partners in the state, but they have been rebuffed by the state's discriminatory policies. On the other hand, the Jews of Israel, and Jewish people throughout the world, have no demographic reserves that could even remotely match the immense Arab numerical superiority.

I believe that the gradual decline of Israel's military superiority is not only the result of the steadily growing Arab numerical superiority but also a consequence of the processes of urbanization, industrialization, and the development of all branches of technological and scientific education taking place in Arab countries. Shlomo Gazit, former president of Ben-Gurion University of the Negev, writes that in 1970, of a total Israeli population of 3.5 million Jews, 36,000 were enrolled as students in Israeli institutions of higher learning. In the same year, of a total Middle East Arab population of 100 million, 440,000 were enrolled in institutions of higher learning, a ratio of 1 to 12. Ten years later, in 1980, Israel had 55,000 students enrolled, compared to 1.5 million in the Arab countries, a ratio of 1 to 28. Moreover, in 1970, 13,000 Israeli students (35 percent of the total Israeli student population) studied in scientific and technological faculties, in comparison to only 15,000 students working in these fields in all the Arab countries put together, a ratio of almost 1 to 1. But in 1980, the ratio between Arabs and Israelis studying in such institutes had already become 1 to 7.5. Figures from later years show that this process has accelerated.[1]

In a broader historical perspective, Israel is an ideal catalyzer for the development of the region. Once the distant European empires, Britain and France, decided that the area was not worth keeping, they retired, and their invigorating influence departed with it. A mighty local empire would have such a power preponderance over the region that no local power could challenge it (which was the case for centuries with the Ottoman Empire). Israel, as has been demonstrated, mainly in the Lebanon War, is incapable of conquering the region and keeping it. Again and again it defeats Arab armies, but the damage inflicted on them and on the Arab nations is limited, and, as a result of lessons learned in the most recent round, within a surprisingly short time their armies are restored to an even higher level of professionalism and sophistication. These confrontations serve as tests, showing the Arabs that they have not yet achieved a level that will enable them to defeat Israel, and this goads them to advance, to improve, never to rest. That is to say, Israeli might is in exactly the right dosage to spur the Arab-Islamic world to enter the modern age and shake off its somnolent traditions, while, all told, paying relatively low historical tuition fees. I noted in an earlier chapter that at the beginning of this century no Palestinian nation yet existed and that the Arabic-speaking population of Palestine was one of most backward, most ignorant, and poorest in the Ottoman Empire. In the whole of Palestine there was not at the time a single Arab institution of higher learning. Today the Palestinians are a group with a fierce national identity. They are also the best-educated and most dynamic of the Arabic-speaking Middle East peoples. None of this would have taken place had it not been for the conflict with the Yishuv and the state, the opportunity to learn from Israel and the rise of a modern, sophisticated, and bitterly determined leadership of this new Palestinian nation. It may even be conjectured that in the long view, the exile of a part of this nation, the subjugation of another part, and the constant pressure applied on it by Israel are not an exaggerated historical price to pay for such an advancement. To a lesser extent, this is Israel's effect on all of the "confrontation" states, first and foremost Syria and Jordan. Orthodox Hegelians would perhaps view this as a manifestation of the "cunning of reason," which elected the Jewish national movement as the main catalyzer for the return of the Arab world and of the World of Islam to the center of the historical stage.

It is unlikely that the erosion of Israel's military advantage will make it more amenable to a settlement with the Palestinians or its other Arab neighbors. On the contrary, if this erosion reduces the willingness of the Arab countries to compromise with Israel, assuming that they are bound to win anyway, the feelings of anxiety and xenophobia already prevalent in Israel may intensify and increase the danger to its relatively democratic institutions. Those who call for peace and openness will be branded traitors, the power of the rightist-religious reaction will increase further, exclusivity and hostility to the outside world will become dominant. This is the usual reaction to decline, for only self-confidence leads to openness. The persecution of the inner opposition, if such a scenario materializes, will undoubtedly be accompanied by expulsions and worse inflicted on the country's non-Jewish population. Such atrocities will become ever more aggravated because the subjugated population, sensing the weakening of the state, will become more rebellious.

Still, the assumption of a Holocaust-like ending, in the form of conquest of Israel and annihilation or deportation of its Jewish population, is highly unlikely. If it is ever faced with such a possibility, the nonconventional arsenal in Israel's possession will always enable it to threaten the entire region with mass devastation. But no armaments can prevent a social and economic decline or political disintegration, as has been amply demonstrated in the collapse of the Soviet Union. In addition, the Arab countries, in future wars against Israel, could state limited objectives in advance. In such a case Israel would be unable to use total weapons, since similar ones could be placed in the hands of its opponents, or their opponents could already be in possession of such armaments. Such a balance of terror would necessarily limit the wars to conventional means. But a war of attrition with conventional weapons would exact a heavy toll on Israel's human and economic resources. Its efficacy is shown by the fact that even toward the end of the eighties the country had not completely recovered from the economic blow it sustained in the 1973 Yom Kippur War (although in more recent years the Israeli economy has begun to grow again at an impressive rate). That war also undermined the smug confidence Israelis had in their perpetual military ascendancy. And the Lebanon War, which began in 1982 and lasted until 1985, dealt a mortal blow to the delusion that all problems can be solved by the use of force.

Israel's weakening will undoubtedly be accompanied by a brain drain to countries where economic and professional opportunities seem more attractive. And if the country does not change its definition, character, and structure in the directions here indicated, it is reasonable to assume that it will eventually become one of the ethnoreligious minorities in the region, like the Druze or the Maronites. It will lose its conquests one by one and will be slowly pushed back, perhaps to the coastal strip from which the Hebrew Yishuv began to expand.

Only a strong Israel can join a regional federation. And only within such a federal structure will it be possible to overcome the self-segregating, communal, and protofascist tendencies gathering strength in Israeli society. In contrast to the Canaanite conception, which predicted that conquest would encourage integrative attitudes and promote the assimilation of the occupied population as an equal in the structure of the state, experience has shown that the conquest only intensified segregative, xenophobic tendencies in Israel. We face here a vicious circle: an Israeli state that preserves its power ascendancy will probably be loath to relinquish its conquests, and such a refusal will forestall any integration in a regional federal system. On the other hand, it is reasonable to assume that the Arab world will not be inclined to reach a compromise with a deteriorating country and will be avid to press it to extinction. A possible escape from such a vicious circle could be an imposition of a regional settlement by an external power or powers, but such a development depends on an array of factors, the discussion of which is beyond the scope of this book.

Just as I have written of the growth of Zionism and the state of Israel from their start in the crisis of traditional Judaism and have made conjectures (for the above are nothing but conjectures, and no other predictions could be more than conjectures) about the probable future of Israel, I cannot avoid concluding this work with some guesses about the future of the Jewish people in the Diaspora.

Apart from the future of the Jews as a community, a caste, a people or a nation, what will be the future of Judaism as a religion, as a self-justifying way of life, as a form of group reaction to the world and a view of it? What will happen to Judaism as a result of the Israeli experience, the effect, that is, of the existence of the state on Judaism, particularly if the state deteriorates as envisaged here? What does and what will the state do to Judaism?

One thing can be predicted with a considerable measure of certainty: ultraorthodoxy, which has never reconciled itself to the existence of Israel, will see the state's decline, if it occurs, as a confirmation and reinforcement of its stand about the sinful nature of forcing the "end of days." Even if the state does not decline, it will undoubtedly undergo major changes, an inescapable consequence of its unstable position in an unstable region. Most of such changes will be interpreted by Orthodox Jews as a decline and as a divine punishment. (Were the country to follow the course recommended in this book, which would sever it from its intimate relationship with the Jewish people and Zionism, this might be acceptable to the Orthodox, who would then be able to accept Israel as another gentile state and to adjust to it and accept its authority.)

Orthodoxy will continue to maintain enclaves anywhere in the world willing to accept it, as it has been doing for more than two thousand years. Israel's existence or nonexistence would be of little consequence. Orthodoxy deliberately shut itself in for good about 250 years ago, at the time of the Vilna Gaon, and ever since then it has existed spiritually and socially divorced from the outside world. There is no reason to suppose that it will not continue to do so in the foreseeable future, as long as there are Jews prepared to accept its strictures. Its inner survival and satisfaction systems and the emotional and mental peace which its adamantine ritual frame provides, creating a whole inner universe within the confines of the Halacha community, are so elaborate that the Orthodox community will undoubtedly persist in any host society. On the other hand, it may be conjectured that despite the extremely high birthrate in the ultra-Orthodox communities, the continuous process of secularization taking place among them (a process that has been at work since the beginning of the emancipation and continues to work in any society that does not force the Jews back into the ghetto, and there are none such today) will cause the Orthodox communities to revert to what they were for centuries in the West: small, enclosed groups, exotic and strange in the eyes of the outside world (including most Jews) but endowed with remarkable powers of flexibility and adjustment in their contacts with the outside. Their members will always know how to maneuver in the fields of commerce, finance, special occupations such as diamond polishing, and other traditional "Jewish occupations." To this day, nothing has influenced these Jews to change their view of the world or to think critically about the foundations of their faith, not even the destruction of their main stronghold in Eastern Europe. The very fact that the extermination of European Jewry caused no religious crisis, aroused no misgivings about the way that the world is conducted by the Almighty, is proof that the secret of the community's stability is not in any central faith but in the protective, comfortable, and eternally firm framework of daily custom and ritual.

There is no need to do much speculating about the future of non-Orthodox Jews. Their courses of development are quite familiar. Various forms of Reform Judaism—through to the ultimate blurring of religious and communal identity within the Unitarian Church, which comprises Jews and Christians without distinction—have existed since the first half of the nineteenth century in Germany, France, Britain, and the United States. There exist the various forms of assimilation, with or without religious conversion. There also exist the various forms of nationalism, from Zionism to territorialism and autonomism (although, with the destruction of their population base in Eastern Europe, the latter two versions have become almost extinct). Almost certainly this is the full range of forms which Judaism could assume within the foreseeable future. Except for orthodoxy, all of these forms are various forms of compromise with and adjustment to modern civilization, which separates church from state. They are not the development of an independent spiritual-cultural approach. This reveals the spiritual barrenness of contemporary Judaism. Orthodoxy remains petrified within its strictures and obscurantist world view, unable to offer any spiritual sustenance or answer to the problems of modern man, except "penitence" (Teshuva, the Jewish equivalent of born-again Christianity), which is nothing but intellectual suicide, a frightened sheltering behind dead ritual formulas, not a creative encounter with the human-historical situation.

The willful ossification of Judaism, then, has resulted in its having no answer to the existential problems of modern man, not even to the limited extent that we find in Christianity. Orthodox Judaism, despite its pretension to a loftier morality than that of any other religion, has never displayed a universal social consciousness. Ultra-Orthodox rabbis and other religious worthies have never campaigned for general human causes beyond the limits of the Orthodox Jewish community. One never sees them in demonstrations against racial oppression, against war, against class rule. The mores of their host societies are not of the slightest interest to them. Their only concern is that Jews be allowed to live and prosper within these societies and to conduct their internal community affairs without outside interference. To the extent that rabbis do participate in social action campaigns (such as the campaigns waged in the United States for civil rights and against the Vietnam War), they have always been non-Orthodox. In Israel itself, where there is hardly any Reform Judaism, most of the Orthodox religious establishment is associated with the worst racist and chauvinistic positions. Most of the notorious names among fascist, anti-Arab agitators are those of Orthodox rabbis such as the late Meir Kahane and Moshe Levinger, neither of whom ever was denounced by the rabbinical establishment. On the contrary, one of Israel's two chief rabbis eulogized Kahane at the latter's funeral.

In the absence of a positive spiritual significance in contemporary Judaism, it may be assumed that the assimilation and fading away of the Jews into the surrounding populations will continue, until only the small, closed Orthodox communities are left. True, there still exist Conservative and Reform congregations numbering in the millions, mainly in the United States, but in pre-Hitler Germany and in France these did not avert the complete blurring away of Jewishness. This process has been accelerated by urbanization, the growing mobility of populations, and social atomization. In villages and small towns, with their stable populations, everyone knows everyone else, and no one can escape his origins. But in huge, anonymous societies with mobile individuals lacking any stable traditions, attracting people from all parts of the world and growing ever more cosmopolitan, ethnic and religious traits and their external manifestations fade fast. Anti-Semitic tremors will certainly recur from time to time, and individuals within modern societies will occasionally try to "establish a connection with their roots," to counterbalance the general fluidity and erosion of identity. But such foibles have little influence on the general trend. Even the Nazi tempest, which drove many Jews to Zionism or to religion, hardly changed the process. It still continues among the Jews who survived in the countries occupied by the Nazis, even among the Jews living in Germany itself.

Paradoxically, what may be termed the Israeli experience is one of the accelerating factors of the process. I dwelled in a previous chapter on the exteriorized nature of the Jewish identity formed by "identification with Israel" and pointed out that an identity that is expressed not in the course of day-to-day living but on formal occasions only, is in the final analysis a means of *evading* a commitment to a definite identity. But the Israeli experience has more aspects in the life of world Jewry. I have described how the Diaspora is manipulated by the Israeli power establishment to further its own ends. This manipulation facilitates the establishment's control of Israeli society by means of the financial resources which the Diaspora puts at its disposal. To this end, the establishment has also done its best to suppress the growth of an independent national consciousness in the Israeli population, which might have led to an estrangement from the Diaspora and the establishment's power sources there. Another powerful instrument in the hands of the establishment to foster its control of both Israelis and Jews abroad has been the systematic exploitation of the greatest Jewish trauma in modern times—the Holocaust.

Before I touch on the methods used in this exploitation, I would like to describe its destructive meaning. For many Jews, the Holocaust is now the only meaning and content of Judaism and the very basis of their identity as Jews. Theirs is not a positive identity but derives from their experience of the common horror of being Jewish. This is a paranoid basis that can only breed hatred and desire for vengeance against the rest of the world. It leads to a doctrine of a difference in kind between Jews and the rest of humanity—which is basically the photographic negative of Nazi doctrines. It is the continuation of Jewish seclusion from the rest of humanity, though in a separate state, instead of the return to history that is the basis of political Zionism. And it was Ben-Gurion's socialist Zionism that led the way to this betrayal of the legacy and mission of Zionism.

The supreme example of this approach is the Eichmann trial. From the outset, Ben-Gurion viewed the trial as a substitute for a nonexistent national bond, an educational tool to instill in Israeli youth and immigrants from Islamic countries who knew little of the Holocaust a consciousness of the common Jewish fate that found in the Holocaust its supreme and awful expression, along with an awareness of the importance of Israel as the only alternative to protect the Jewish people from another Holocaust. In the absence of a positive national bond, Ben-Gurion deliberately sought to base the national consciousness on the negative foundation of terror and nightmare, with the attendant obsession with military force and an unbounded increase of this force to avert a new Holocaust, the two aspects of the Zionist will to power.

No matter how strong Israel can hope to become, it will, obviously, never be strong enough to avert a Nazi-style new Holocaust. After all, Nazi Germany was a superpower. If the United States, for example, ever decided to exterminate its Jews, Israel would not be able to prevent this any more than the Jewish Yishuv in 1939 was able to prevent Nazi Germany from doing so.

But the aim of the Israeli establishment was not to investigate the past but to use it to create an ideology and a myth that would help the establishment to control both the Diaspora and the Israeli people. The Holocaust was eminently suitable for that purpose, and the establishment used it in two unrelated contexts, though each is traumatic in itself, and fused them together to create a sense of trauma for both the Jews abroad and the Israelis. The one, as noted, is the Holocaust. The other is the Arab siege of Israel. Although it is not my purpose here to discuss the contexts and historical causes of the Holocaust, in one respect Zionism was correct in claiming that the peculiar situation of the Jews in European society in general and in the German particular was one of the main causes of the Holocaust—although the latter may not have taken place had it not been for the Nazi goal of creating a German living space (*Lebensraum*) in Eastern Europe, which involved the enslavement and gradual extermination of the Slav peoples. The conclusion which classical Zionism drew from this grim chapter of history was that if the Jews were assembled in a state of their own, their social and political conditions would change accordingly and so would the attitude of the surrounding world. This, in addition to their acquiring a military-political might of their own, would prevent another Holocaust. But such a conclusion implies an admission of the separate character and course of the emerging Israeli nation, thus undermining the thesis that all Jews constitute a single nation.

Therefore the Zionist leadership developed a parallel argument—that the Arab siege of Israel is actually traditional anti-Semitism, but in a different form. The Palestinians' desire to rid themselves of what they see as the Zionist invader, clearly a military-political struggle of two peoples fighting for the same land, and the support extended them by sister Arab nations have been conceived, whether from deliberate misrepresentation or because of the dominance of ossified patterns of thinking, as a continuation of the traditional hatred of the Jews, not as a normal manifestation of the violent struggle. This distortion of the Arab resistance to Israel—a rational enough resistance, far removed from the irrational hatred of traditional anti-Semitism—enabled the Israeli leadership and the intelligentsia that serves it to develop the notion about the Jewish fate "common to and uniting all of us." Because the aim of the Arabs is to "inflict a second Holocaust" on the Jews of Israel, the Arabs are the "pupils of the Nazis." The danger of a second Holocaust serves the Israeli leadership as a powerful instrument for mobilizing Jewish support and for silencing critical voices both in the Diaspora and among non-Jews.

The main inner contradiction of this position is that it conflicts with the basic tenets of Zionism, hence with the logic of the establishment of Israel. If the establishment of the state has not been able to solve the problems of anti-Semitism and the persecution of even those Jews living within the state, people who are now outcasts not as individuals but as a political whole, and who are now in danger of a collective (state) Holocaust; if Jew hatred is a kind of a metaphysical datum, plaguing the Jews from time immemorial like a mark of Cain (as argued by the early church and maintained until quite recent times)—then their ingathering in a state of their own does not solve the problem of Jewish survival but only puts it in a new form, and in a way even aggravates it. All of Israel's military prowess could not sustain the state against a world bent on its destruction, for the world will always be stronger. In addition, the assumption of a metaphysical anti-Semitism negates in advance any possibility that a Jewish state could ever survive among other states and function in a real world based on the essential equality of all sovereign bodies operating within it. Were such an assumption true, it would be more desirable for Jewish survival that the Jews continue to be dispersed, thus enabling any threatened Jewish community to emigrate to more inviting climes, as Jews have always done.

In such a case, the difference between Israelis and other Jews shrinks to the fact that the former have an army and the latter don't. The fathers of Zionism never thought in such terms. They sought to change the character and structure and essence of the Jewish people, to create a different human quality, not to establish an armed ghetto. Although armaments are necessary for a country's defense, they, of themselves, do not create a different human quality. If that is the sum total of the difference, only individuals suffering from constant persecution and humiliation, or whose lives are in danger, or are haunted by feelings of inferiority and seek compensation by humiliating others, would choose to live in Israel. In short, all possible motivations for Jewish emigration to Israel are of a negative nature. The Jews coming to Israel are not offered a safer, freer, more pleasant, or more civilized life. But if that is so, there would be few Jews in free countries who would want to come to Israel. As a rule, their motivation in immigrating is religious. For them, the country is the Holy Land, and in most cases, rather than becoming integrated in Israel's true national life they continue to live a separate caste existence, within the secluded religious enclaves.

I might add that the Holocaust motif as a central point of Jewish existence necessarily leads to a negative result from both the Jewish and the Zionist perspective. If it is true that the only element unifying Jews as Jews is the permanent danger of annihilation that hovers over them, it is reasonable to assume that all sane persons would try to divest themselves, through assimilation or conversion, of this identity. If they find this possible, they would undoubtedly and rightly choose this course. No healthy identity can be based on purely negative, paranoic sentiments.

Although most Jews in the world have no intention of emigrating to Israel, many of them have developed an intense affinity to it, supporting it unconditionally, whatever its policy. The organization of Jewish communities and the Israeli and Zionist influence network, mainly in the United States, have created a situation in which there is hardly anyone in the Jewish community who dares criticize Israel in public. One needs much civic courage to give public utterance abroad to even a fraction of the criticism leveled at the Israeli government and its policy even by center groups in Israel, to say nothing of the opposition. Thus has it come to pass that the very Jewish public that in the past was supposed to keep faith with a religious or a moral scale of values today is loyal to Israeli power politics, which are by definition amoral, and defends them by inventing excuses and apologies of a moral nature.

The result is similar to what happened over the years to the Moscow-leaning Communist parties, with their apologetics for such crimes as the annihilation of the kulaks, the repression of freedom of thought and expression, the great purges, the persecution of the Cosmopolitans, the labor camps where millions died, the repression of rebellions in Poland, Hungary, Czechoslovakia. The constant effort needed to invent excuses and to adapt to the party line totally corrupted the thinking of party members, sapped their idealism and turned them into cynical hacks. We have now witnessed the final result of this situation—the collapse of the system under its own weight.

The unconditional, unquestioning identification with Israel, the fabrication of excuses for Israeli action so that it corresponds with lofty moral principles (even when Israeli policy is represented by ominous figures such as Ariel Sharon), has set in motion a deethicization process of the Jewish people in the Diaspora. The contradiction between obvious, universal moral principles and Israeli *realpolitik* and the suppression of the criticism generated by this conflict—which, when it comes from non-Jews, is immediately branded as anti-Semitic, and when it comes from Jews, as self-hating—are bound in the end to cause cynicism and nihilism among the best elements of the Jewish Diaspora and a feeling that the Jews have lost any claim to a loftier morality.

The Jews themselves may then reach the conclusion that the cult of the Jewish state has seduced them to whore after strange gods, that the moral identification with power politics is tantamount to idolatry. That may cause a collapse of the moral pretension which the Jews adopted after the decline of religious faith and as a substitute for it, and subsequently have a disastrous effect on the feelings of Jewish continuity, with the collapse of that element in which the Jews considered themselves as superior to others and therefore justifying the continuation of their identity as Jews. The realization that they are no better than others but that, unlike others, who arrived at a critical, reserved attitude toward the morality of any political system, they of all people were fooled and led astray by such a system established by their own brethren—thus becoming inferior in this respect to those who have not foregone this skeptical attitude—may become the most upsetting factor imaginable for the Jewish feeling of meaning, continuity, and solidarity.

It is quite conceivable that the sobering up of masses of Jews from this civil religion of theirs will parallel results in the Diaspora after the collapse of the false messianism of Sabbetai Zvi in the seventeenth century—a mass distancing from both Israel and Judaism. Perhaps it will even lead to an explicitly anti-Israeli formulation of Jewish identity. If Judaism is to continue to exist, and if it is to remain sane, the myth of "one people" will also have to be abolished. Israel could well inflict the true death blow to Judaism—and then the Orthodox, who instinctively fear just such a disaster, will be found to be justified.

Notes

INTRODUCTION

1. Gershon Weiler, *Theocratya Yehudit* (The Jewish theocracy) (Tel Aviv: Am Oved, 1977).

PROLOGUE

1. A concise, up-to-date review of the various schools and approaches in Hebrew Biblical research (the theory of sources, the literary analysis method, the study of forms, the structuralist school, the sociological school, etc.), along with an exposition complex problems they raise, may be found in Norman K. Gottwald, *The Hebrew Bible: A Socio-Literary Introduction* (Philadelphia: Fortress Press, 1985).

2. Ze'ev Weissman, "Reshit Yisrael Ve'Zikato Le'Artzo Bitkufa Ha'Mikra" (Beginnings of the Israelites and their connection to their country in the Biblical period), in Yaacov Shavit, ed., *Ha'historya Shel Eretz Yisrael* (History of the land of Israel) (Jerusalem: Keter, 1984), vol. 2, p. 16.

3. Albrecht Alt, "The Settlement of the Israelites in Palestine," *Essays on Old Testament History and Religion* (Oxford: Basil Blackwell, 1966), pp. 168–169 and passim.

4. Moshe Kochavi, "T'kufat Ha-hitnakhalut" (The age of settlement), in Shavit, pp. 21–26.

5. There is a hint of this in 1 Kings 9:22: "But of the people of Israel Solomon made no slaves; they were the soldiers, they were his officials, his commanders, his captains, his chariot commanders and his horsemen."

6. S.v. "Mari" in the *Encyclopaedia Judaica*.

7. M. D. Cassuto, *Sifrut Mikra'it Ve'Sifrut Cena'anit* (Biblical and Canaanite literatures) (Jerusalem: Magnes Press, 1972). See also Cassuto's article "Ugarit" in the *Hebrew Encyclopedia*.

8. Ze'ev Weissman, "Tekufat Ha'Shoftim Ba'Historiographia Ha'Mikra'it" (Era of the Judges in Biblical historiography), in Shavit, vol. 2, pp. 89, 90.

9. This is the conclusion reached, for example, by Adolphe Lods in *The Prophets and the Rise of Judaism* (London: Kegan Paul, 1955), pp. 123–124. The *Biblical Encyclopedia* arrives cautiously at the same conclusion: "It seems then that passing the children [through the fire, i.e., their burning] was done in honor of the God of Israel, according to a conception of the Israelite faith opposed by the Bible" (see the entry "Moloch").

10. Roland de Vaux, *The Early History of Israel* (London: Darton, Longman & Todd, 1978).

11. According to other authorities, the names "the god of Abraham," "the god of Isaac," etc. (in Hebrew, Elohim of Abraham, etc.) really meant the *spirits* of the respective patriarchs, from which we may infer a cult of ancestral spirits that eventually were elevated to divine status. The witch of Endor sees "Elohim rising from the ground," meaning the spirit of the prophet Samuel. Cf. Benjamin Halevy, *Ve'hadvarim Atikkim* (Ancient things) (Tel Aviv: Sifriat Poalim, 1985), p. 50.

12. De Vaux, p. 274.

13. Max Weber, *Ancient Judaism* (New York: Free Press, 1967).

14. The Judean exiles in Egypt respond to Jeremiah's upbraiding of them for their sins against Yahweh: "As for the word you have spoken to us in the name of the Lord [Yahweh], we will not listen to you. But we will do everything that we have vowed, burn incense to the queen of heaven and pour out libations to her, as we did,

both we and our fathers, our kings and our princes, in the cities of Judah and in the streets of Jerusalem; for then we had plenty of food, and prospered, and saw no evil. But since we left off burning incense to the queen of heaven and pouring out libations to her, we have lacked everything and have been consumed by the sword and by famine" (Jer. 44:16–18).

15. Cf. Halevy, p. 97. Oesterley and Robinson, in *Hebrew Religion* (New York: Macmillan, 1940), also note that the Sabbath originally was not a day of rest, and dwell on its connection to the cult of the new moon (pp. 134–135).

16. Salo Baron, *A Social and Religious History of the Jews* (New York: Columbia University Press, 1952), vol. 1, pt. 1, p. 159. See also Oesterley and Robinson.

17. Hayim Tadmor, "Yemei Shivat Tsiyon" (The period of the return to Zion), in Shavit, vol. 2, p. 253.

18. Ibid., p. 255.

19. Ibid., p. 256.

20. Weber, pp. 256, 257.

21. Uriel Rappoport, "Ta'amulah Datit Shel Yehudim U'Tnuat HaHitgayrut Biyemey Habayit Hasheni" (Jewish religious propaganda and the proselytizing movement in the era of the Second Commonwealth), doctoral thesis, Hebrew University, Jerusalem, 1955.

22. Baron, vol. 2, pt. 1, p. 133.

23. Weber, p. 364.

24. Israel Levin, "Mereshit Hashilton Haromi Ad Sof T'kufat Bayit Sheni" (From the beginning of Roman rule to the end of the Second Commonwealth), in Shavit, vol. 4, p. 239.

25. A. N. Pollack, *Kazaria: Toldot Mamlakha Yehudit Be'Eyropa* [Kazaria: A history of a Jewish kingdom in Europe) (Tel Aviv: Mossad Bialik and Massada, 1951).

26. Baron, p. 238. Cf. Emil Schuerer, *A History of the Jewish People in the Time of Jesus* (New York: Schocken, 1961), particularly pt. 1, chap. 8.

27. Weber, p. 386.

28. Josephus, *The War of the Jews*, chap. 16. The speech, as presented, is undoubtedly apocryphal, but Agrippa's political position could not have been very different from the one ascribed to him by Josephus.

29. Gedaliah Allon, in his two books, *Toldot Hayehudim B'Eretz Yisrael Bitkufat Ha'Mishnah V'Hatalmud* (History of the Jews in Palestine in the time of the Mishnah and the Talmud) and *Mekhkarim B'toldot Yisrael Biymey Bayit Sheni Uvitkufat Ha'mishnah V'hatalmud* (Studies in Jewish history at the time of the Second Commonwealth and during the Mishnaic and Talmudic periods) (Tel Aviv: Hakkibutz Hameu'had, 1953 and 1967).

30. Baron, vol. 2, pt. 1, pp. 278–280.

31. Ibid.

32. Allon, *Toldot*.

33. Michael Avi-Yonah, *Biymey Roma u'Byzantion* (The Roman and Byzantine period), 4th ed. (Jerusalem: Mossad Bialik, 1970).

34. Baron, vol. 2, pt. 1, pp. 73–77.

35. Ibid., pp. 78, 84.

36. M. Cary, *A History of Rome down to the Age of Constantine* (London: Macmillan, 1960).

37. Baron, vol. 2, pt. 1, p. 147.

1. ZIONIST THEORY AND ITS PROBLEMS

1. Yehezkel Kaufmann, *Golah ve'Nekhar* (Diaspora and exile) (Tel Aviv: Dvir, 1962), pp. 194–199.

2. See Ber Borochov, *K'tavim* (Works), vol. 1 (Tel Aviv: Hakibbutz Hameuchad and Sifriat Poalim, 1955).

3. Ibid.

4. Ibid., p. 41.

5. Hannah Arendt, *The Origins of Totalitarianism* (New York: Harcourt Brace Jovanovich, 1973).

6. Ibid., p. 39 and passim. Arendt's analysis of the anti-Semitic phenomenon is the most brilliant that I have encountered.

7. David Vital, *The Origins of Zionism* (Oxford: Oxford University Press, 1975).

2. ZIONISM:
THE PRODUCT OF A UNIQUE HISTORICAL SITUATION

1. Yehezkel Kaufmann, *Gola ve'Nekhar* (Diaspora and exile) (Tel Aviv: Dvir, 1962).

2. A. B. Yehoshua, "Hagola—Ha'oness Ha'atzmi" (The Diaspora—a self-inflicted constriction), *Migvan* 24, no. 12 (February 1978).

3. Yeshayahu Leibowitz, *Yahadut, Am Yehudi Umdinat Israel* (Judaism, the Jewish people and the state of Israel) (Tel Aviv: Schocken, 1976), particularly pp. 167–169.

4. Rafael Mahler, *Divrei Yemei Israel, Dorot Akharonim* (History of the Jews in recent generations) (Tel Aviv: Sifriat Poalim, 1952).

5. Shmuel Ettinger, *Ha'antishemiut Ba'et Hakhadasha* (Anti-Semitism in modern times) (Tel Aviv: Sifriat Poalim, 1978), pp. 193–194.

6. Kaufmann, pp. 100–102.

7. David Vital, *The Origins of Zionism* (Oxford: Oxford University Press, 1975).

3. ANTI-SEMITISM: THE EUROPEAN BACKGROUND

1. Shmuel Ettinger, *Ha'antishemiut Ba'et Hahadasha* (Anti-Semitism in modern times) (Tel Aviv: Sifriat Poalim, 1978) p. xv.

2. Ibid., p. xiv.

3. The report is contained in Yosef Algazi's article in *Zmanim*, no. 8, (March 1982).

4. David Thomson, *Europe since Napoleon* (London: Penguin, 1976.)

5. See Roberto Bacchi, "Diaspora Population: Past Growth and Present Decline," *Jerusalem Quarterly* (Winter 1982).

6. Walter Grab, *Der preussisch-deutsche Weg der Judenemanzipation*, (an essay in ms.).

4. THE TRANSITION TO CONTINENTAL SYSTEMS

1. *Ha'ir*, November 19, 1982.

2. One could perhaps hedge this conclusion by noting that the establishment of Israel was a partial realization of Zionism and that the absorption of the mass immigration in the early fifties was in a way an internalization of the last waves of the shocks that preceded 1945. From this point of view, one may perhaps move the point of demise of Zionism forward to the late fifties, although the conditions for it had been completed, as noted, in 1945.

5. CREATING A NEW PEOPLE

1. A. D. Gordon, quoted in Eliezer Schweid, *Hayachid—Olamo shel A. D. Gordon* (The individual—The world of A. D. Gordon) (Tel Aviv: Am Oved, 1970), pp. 47–48.

2. Y. M. Rivlin, *Reshit Hayishuv Hayhudi Mikhutz Lakhomot* (The beginning of the Jewish settlement outside Jerusalem's walls) (Jerusalem, 1978).

3. Chaim Weizmann, *Trial and Error: The Autobiography of Chaim Weizmann* (New York: Harper, 1949), p. 131.

4. David Ben-Gurion, quoted in Shabtai Teveth, *Ben Gurion Hatza'ir* (The young Ben-Gurion) (Tel Aviv: Schocken, 1977), p. 90.

5. Schweid, p. 61.

6. Ibid., p. 66.

7. Teveth, vol. 1, p. 95.

8. Weizmann, p. 168.

9. We find a particularly trenchant literary expression of this historical-cultural process in Chaim Hazaz's short story *HaDrashah* (The sermon) (Tel Aviv: Dvir, 1952).

10. Another explanation is feasible, of course: that the Zionist leadership was forced to recognize that most of the world's Jews are not going to immigrate to Israel. That led presumably to the conclusion that a rift is developing within the Jewish people between the Israelis and most Diaspora Jews, and the "one people" claim was meant to try to paper over this growing estrangement.

11. The concept of ressentiment was used by Nietzsche to indicate a frustrated desire for revenge, fear of the reaction which the avenger may provoke, etc.

12. Weizmann, p. 338.

6. HOLY LAND VERSUS HOMELAND

1. Menahem Friedmann, *Chevrah Vedat: Haortodoxia Ha'lo-Tsionit B'Eretz Israel, 1918–1936* (Society and religion: the non-Zionist Orthodoxy in Palestine, 1918-1936) (Jerusalem: Yad Ben Zvi, 1978).

2. Ben Zvi, *Eretz Israel Veyishuvah Biyemey Hashilton Ha'Othmani* (Palestine and its population under Ottoman rule) (Jerusalem: Mosad Bialik, 1955), pp. 403–404, 411, 363. Further details about the Austrian and German consular protection extended to Palestine's Jews are to be found in Mordechai Eliav, *B'hassut Mamlechet Austria, 1849–1917* (Under Austrian protection, 1849-1917) (Jerusalem: Yad Ben Zvi, 1985).

3. Ben Zvi, p. 366.

4. Ibid., pp. 381–382.

5. Shulamit Laskov, *Habiluvim* (The Bilu movement) (Jerusalem: Zionist Library, 1979).

6. During the First and even the Second Aliya, most immigrants were Orthodox Jews who joined the Old Yishuv and were completely devoid of any national consciousness or motivation.

7. Yonathan Shapiro, *Achdut Ha'avoda Ha'historit* (The organization of power) (Tel Aviv: Am Oved, 1975). See also Dan Horowitz and Moshe Lissak, *Meyishuv Limdina* (Eretz Israel during the British Mandate as a political community) (Tel Aviv: Am Oved, 1977).

8. Anita Shapira, *Hama'avak Hanichzav* (Futile struggle) (Tel Aviv: Hakibbutz Hameuchad, 1977).

9. Ibid., p. 16–17.

10. Arthur Ruppin, *30 Shnot Binyan B'Eretz Israel* (30 years of building in Eretz Israel) (Jerusalem: Schocken, 1937), p. 17.

11. Shapira, p. 18.

12. Still, when the Jewish workers were skilled, Jewish employers preferred them to the Arabs. Ruppin, pp. 46, 47, notes that even the German colonists of the Templar Order employed Jewish workers and paid them more than Arabs for skilled work,

and that the farmers of Kastina begged to send them Jewish workers, for otherwise they were unable to cultivate their land.

13. Shapira, p. 29.

14. Shapiro, p. 63.

15. Ibid., p. 187.

16. Ibid., p. 182.

17. Dan Horowitz and Moshe Lissak, p. 46, analyzing the "dual structure" of the population of Mandatory Palestine, note that "the truth of the matter is that the attempts to overcome the national antagonism in fields of activity which had political significance succeeded to any extent only when they were done by groups which cut themselves loose from the political and ideological system based on national separation. The outstanding example is the Communist party, which held to an outspokenly anti-Zionist ideology and was therefore capable of at least partially overcoming the obstacles which interfered with the establishment of a common Jewish-Arab organization."

18. Shapira, p. 163.

19. Shalom Reichmann, *Yetzirat Hamappa Hayishuvit B'Eretz Israel 1918–1948* (The shaping of the Yishuv settlement map in Palestine 1918–1948) (Jerusalem: Yad Ben Zvi, 1979), p. 54.

7. THE HEBREW PEOPLE VERSUS THE PALESTINIAN PEOPLE

1. It should, though, be noted that the consciousness of an overall Arab nation began to be formed at a relatively late period. George Antonius, in *The Arab Awakening*, tried to discern its early manifestations in the first half of the nineteenth century. Sylvia Haim, on the other hand, claims that a comprehensive Arab national ideology began to develop only after World War I. See the introduction to her *Arab Nationalism, an Anthology* (University of California Press, 1964).

2. Yehoshua Porath, *Zmichat Hatnu'ah Ha'arvit-Ha Palestinait 1918–1929* (The growth of the Palestinian Arab national movement 1918–1929) (Tel Aviv: Am Oved, 1976), pp. 6–7.

3. Ibid., p. 7.

4. Berl Katznelson, *Ketavim* (Works), vol. 8 (Mapai, n.d.), p. 31.

5. David Ben-Gurion, *P'gishot Im Manhigim Arvi'im* (Meetings with Arab leaders) (Tel Aviv: Am Oved, 1967).

6. Y. Gorny, *Hash'elah Ha'arvit ve'Hab'ayah Hayehudit* (The Arab question and the Jewish problem) (Tel Aviv: Am Oved, 1985), p. 175.

7. Ibid., p. 145.

8. Ussishkin originally strove for a rapprochement with the Arabs, but Gorny also confirms this later change in his opinions (ibid., pp. 310–311).

9. Ben-Gurion, p. 73.

10. Anita Shapira, *Hama'avak Hanichzav* (Futile struggle) (Tel Aviv: Hakibbutz Hameuchad, 1977), p. 17.

11. Palestine Royal Commission Report, presented to the Secretary of State for the Colonies in Parliament by demand of His Majesty, July 1937, pp. 125–129, 240.

12. The dispossession of tenant farmers served regularly as an argument against Zionism, until the mandatory government appointed a commission to investigate the matter. Its conclusions are the only detailed official evaluation of the matter throughout the mandatory period. Yehoshua Porath claims in the fourth chapter of his book (see n. 2), dealing with the influence of Jewish land acquisitions, that the number of the dispossessed was larger than 664. He also mentions the quoted figures and notes that the British official Lewis French, who was appointed in 1931

in charge of development by the mandatory government, prepared a list of dispossesed Arabs for their resettlement, and by the end of 1935 (when the investigation was terminated) approved of only 664 applications. Porath notes that the problem is far graver than appears from this final figure, as the investigation was carried on in a period of prosperity, when most of the dispossessed tenants could find other employment. Nor was the mandatory government's definition of the category of the dispossessed individuals broad enough. "Nevertheless, it seems that the real figure did not exceed a few thousands (apart from members of their families), due to the sparseness of the Arab population in the areas of Jewish settlement. Anyway, when Arab tenants were evicted, as happened in the Galilee before World War I and in the Jezreel Valley after it, the Jewish buyers generally paid the dispossessed a compensation" (Porat, pp. 114–117).

13. Ben-Gurion, p. 19.

14. Christopher Sykes, *Crossroads to Israel* (London: Mentor, 1967), pp. 40–41.

15. Shapira, pp. 53–55.

16. Ibid.

17. See "The True Nature of the Arab National Movement," in the supplements to vol. 8 of Katznelson's *Works*.

18. Ibid., pp. 30–31.

19. Ibid., pp. 188–197.

20. Ibid., vol. 12, p. 244.

21. Ibid.

22. Ze'ev Jabotinsky, "A Round Table with the Arabs" (1931), *Baderech Li'mdinah* (The Road to a state) (Jerusalem: Eri Jabotinsky, 1953).

23. Jabotinsky, "The Wall of Iron" (written according to Gorny in 1923), ibid.

24. Shapira, pp. 53–55.

25. Ibid., p. 56.

26. Sykes, pp. 145–148.

8. ZIONISM WITHOUT MERCY

1. David Vital, article in *Hatzionut* (Zionism) 7 (1982), pp. 7–17.

2. S. Beit Zvi, *Hatzionut Ha'post-Ugandit Bemashber Ha'shoah* (Post-Uganda Zionism and the Holocaust) (Tel Aviv: Bronfman, 1977), pp. 126–157.

3. Here is a quotation from a letter by Georg Landauer to Stephen Wise, dated Feb. 13, 1938: "I am writing this letter at the request of Dr. Weizmann because we are extremely concerned lest the problem be presented in a way which could prejudice the activity for Eretz Israel. Even if the conference does not propose immediately after its opening other countries but Eretz Israel as venues for Jewish emigration, it will certainly arouse a public response that could put the importance of Eretz Israel in the shade. . . . We are particularly worried that it would move Jewish organizations to collect large sums of money for aid to Jewish refugees, and these collections could interfere with our collection efforts." Ibid., p. 178. There is also a statement by Menachem Ussishkin in the meeting of the Jewish Agency's Executive on June 26, 1938: "He is highly concerned at the Evian conference. . . . Mr. Greenbaum is right in stating that there is a danger that the Jewish people also will take Eretz Israel off its agenda, and this should be viewed by us as a terrible danger. He hoped to hear in Evian that Eretz Israel remains the main venue for Jewish emigration. All other emigration countries do not interest him. . . . The greatest danger is that attempts will be made to find other territories for Jewish emigration." And the account of Ben-Gurion's statement at the same meeting: "No rationalizations can turn the conference from a harmful to a useful one. What can and should be done is to limit the damage as far as possible. He 'doesn't know whether the Evian con-

ference will open the gates of other countries to Jewish immigration, but like Green-baum and Ussishkin he fears that at this time the conference is liable to cause im-mense harm to Eretz Israel and Zionism.' It was summed up in the meeting that the Zionist thing to do is 'to belittle the Conference as far as possible and to cause it to decide nothing.' " Ibid., pp. 181, 182.

4. Dina Porat, *Hanhaga Be'milkud* (An Entangled Leadership) (Tel Aviv: Am Oved, 1986), p. 63.

5. Ibid., pp. 78–90, 472.

6. Ibid., pp. 469–470.

7. According to Vital (see n. 1), the quotation is from Department of State, Near Eastern Affairs, Memorandum of Conversation, September 13, 1944.

8. S. Teveth, *Kin'at David* (Life of Ben-Gurion) (Jerusalem and Tel Aviv: Schocken, 1977), vol. 1, p. 171.

9. A. Ruppin, *Shloshim Shnot Binyan Be'Eretz Israel* (Thirty years of building Eretz Israel) (Jerusalem: Schocken, 1937).

10. Tom Segev, *Ha'Isre'elim Ha'rishonim* (The first Israelis) (Jerusalem: Domino, 1984), pp. 163–169.

11. Weizmann, p. 70.

12. Beit Zvi, p. 385.

9. THE MATURATION OF POWER

1. Yigal Elam, *Hahagana—haderech Hatzionit el hakoach* (Hagana—The Zionist way to power) (Tel Aviv: Zmora, 1979), pp. 199–200.

2. Ibid., note, p. 117.

3. Chaim Weizmann, *Trial and Error* (New York: Harper, 1949), p. 438.

4. An outstanding example to the contrary was the behavior of the Lebanese Maronites during the Lebanon war from 1982 on: all the massive aid they received in arms, diplomacy, and direct military assistance from both Israel and the United States was of no avail in the absence of a real willingness to fight on their part. Once this became clear, their outside supporters washed their hands of them.

5. Elam, p. 281.

6. David Niv, *Bema'archot Ha'irgun Hatzva'i Hale'umi* (History of the Irgun) (Tel Aviv: Klausner Institute, 1965).

10. THE NATIONAL AIM BLURRED

1. This point is highly significant in the context of the great debate waged for many years between the Third International and socialist Zionism. The hidden in-tention of the Mapai leaders may have been to show not only that Zionism provides a solution to the national problem of the Jews that internationalist communism is incapable of providing—but more: that it will provide a more socialistic and hu-mane solution to the social problem than the one offered by international Marxist communism. They may have intended that the Zionist society in Palestine would serve as a model to be emulated by the entire world, the grand alternative to the Soviet experiment, thus deciding the great ideological debate between the two movements that had riven the revolutionary Jewish youth of Eastern Europe.

2. The legal and constitutional presentation in this chapter is based largely on Amnon Rubinstein, *Hamishpat Hakonstitutzioni shel M'dinat Israel* (Constitutional law of the state of Israel) (Tel Aviv: Schocken, 1969).

3. Ibid., p. 69.

4. Moshe Amon, "Israel and the Jewish Identity Crisis," Ph.D. dissertation, Uni-versity of Michigan, 1972, pp. 106–107.

5. Ibid., pp. 121–122.
6. Ibid., p. 53.
7. Ibid., pp. 23, 27.
8. At the time of printing of the Hebrew version of this book, in the spring of 1988, no official Israeli map was available marking the boundaries of the state before June 1967. The border exists, as far as the Israeli authorities are concerned, only for the purpose of denying the political rights of non-Jews living beyond it.

11. CANAANISM: SOLUTIONS AND PROBLEMS

1. James Diamond, *Homeland or Holy Land? The "Canaanite" Critique of Israel* (Bloomington: Indiana University Press, 1986).
2. Ya'acov Shavit, *Me'Ivri Ad Cena'ani* (From Hebrew to Canaanite) (Jerusalem: Domino, 1984).
3. Lehi is the Hebrew acronym for Fighters for the Freedom of Israel, the organization the British called the Stern Gang.
4. A word of many definitions and rich associations. *Kedem* means the east, the ancient time, and the front, that which is before one.
5. On this matter there is no agreement among scholars. Is the fact that there is a linguistic affinity among the dialects used in the region, and even similarities between religious beliefs and rituals that prevailed in it, evidence of a common culture? Were the peoples in the region possessors of a common culture like the Greeks, despite the latters' political divisions? Also, a common language is not proof of a common national consciousness, just as the fact that the English and the Irish both speak English does not attest to their being one nation. But on the other hand, that the nations of Europe speak many languages, whose distant origins are Latin, Germanic, Celtic, and ancient Slavonic, is not proof that they do not share a common civilization.
6. It is worth noting that the Canaanite movement was not the only one in the region that championed the idea of liberation from late layers of religious civilization. There was also a Phoenician movement in Lebanon that aspired to return to the Tyrean-Sidonic Canaanite origins of Lebanese culture, and in Egypt there was a Pharaonic movement that aspired to a similar goal for Egypt. Both of these were in revolt against the dominant Islamic culture. All three are without doubt expressions of the process of crystallization of modern national consciousnesses, which generate as usual myths of a glorious distant national past that must be revived—like Zionism itself.
7. A group of young Jewish farmers in Palestine at the beginning of the century.
8. A journalist and newspaper editor in the first part of the century, the son of Eliezer Ben-Yehuda, the "revivifier of the Hebrew language."

12. THE MESSIANIC FARCE

1. Amnon Rubinstein, *Me'Herzl ve'ad Gush Emunim uvechazara* (From Herzl to Gush Emunim and back) (Tel Aviv: Schocken, 1980).
2. Ibid., p. 120.
3. Ibid., p. 122.
4. Ibid., p. 123.
5. Quoted in Zvi Raanan, *Gush Emunim* (Tel Aviv: Sifriat Poalim, 1980).
6. Ibid., pp. 28, 29.
7. Ibid., p. 44.
8. Ibid., p. 41.
9. Ibid., p. 127.

10. Ibid., pp. 212, 216.
11. Ibid., pp. 213–214.

13. CONCLUSION

1. "Higher Education Is the Number One Lever," *New Outlook Magazine*, May–June issue, Tel Aviv, 1985.

Index

BOAS EVRON is Founder and Director of the Israeli Arts Council's Project of Translations of Classics into Hebrew. A former columnist and critic, he has also served as Acting Principal of Israel's National School of Drama and as Chairman of the Israeli Drama Critics' Association. His previous publications include *The Quality of Freedom* and the Hebrew edition of this volume, and he has contributed articles and essays to *Granta*, *Le Monde*, and *L'Esprit*.